The Star Trek Compendium

By Allan Asherman

A **WALLABY** Book

Published by Simon & Schuster, New York

Contents

This book is dedicated to Anne and Robert Asherman, without whose initiative, guidance, and patience the author could not have been produced.

Acknowledgments

The author wishes to thank the following people, without whose aid and encouragement this book would not have been possible: Peggy Barilla, Ron Barlow, Ruth Berman, Germaine Best, Cindy Casby, Wah Chang, Dave Cockrum, Cecilia Cosentini, Paula Crist, Madeleine Dale, Genny Dazzo, Linda Deneroff, Doug Drexler, Harlan Ellison, Jenny Ferris, Kelly Freas, Polly Freas, Adrian Fuentes, Carl Gafford, Gary Gerani, Joan Geruntho, Tom Geruntho, Mindy Glazer, David Gottlieb, Karen Gottlieb, Linda Harriman, Robert Harris, Sondra Harris, Lynn Holland, Winston Howlett, Janet Ingber, Joyce Klanit, Andrea Kline, Ivan Kline, Devra Langsam, Elan Litt, Shirley Maiewski, Michelle Malkin, Jody McGhee, Ed Miarecki, Teresa Minambres, Margie Nelson, Nichelle Nichols, P. S. Nim, Shannon O'Brien, Fred B. Phillips, Elyse Rosenstein, Steve Rosenstein, Jane Schmidt, Sally Steg, Leonard Suligowski, George Takei, William Theiss, Adrienne Tollin, Anthony Tollin, Bjo Trimble, Michael Uslan, Erwin Vertlieb, Steve Vertlieb, Howard Weinstsin, Chuck Weiss, Barbara Wenk, Allison Whitfield, Joan Winston, Joyce Yasner; and special thanks to Sharon Jarvis and Lea Braff, my agents; Eugene Brissie, my editor; David Hartwell, John Douglas, and Ellen Kushner of Pocket Books; Howard Levine of Paramount; and "Star Trek's" Gene Roddenberry and Susan Sackett. Warmest thanks to Mary Piero.

The following organizations also provided assistance: The Star Trek Welcommittee, P.O. Box 12, Saranac, MI 48881; The Leonard Nimoy Association of Fans, 4612 Denver Ct., Englewood, OH 45322, Miss Louise Stange, President; James Doohan International Fan Club, 1519 N.W. 204th St., Seattle, WA 98177, George Takei International Fan Club, 430 S. Berendo St., Apt. 30, Los Angeles, CA 90020, Ms. Mae Sanchez, President; Grace Lee Whitney Fan Club, P. O. Box 7796, Van Nuys, CA 91409; The Mark Lenard International Fan Club, P. O. Box 1018, Tallahassee, FL 32302, Gail Saville and Barbara Metzke, Co-Presidents.

Introduction

When I was growing up in Brooklyn, New York, my parents' television set was a wondrous device. At the flick of a switch, and after a minute's warm-up time, the old set brought my favorite pals and heroes into my living room. As far back as I can remember, "Howdy Doody," "The Adventures of Superman," "Captain Video and His Video Rangers," "Captain Midnight," "Rocky Jones: Space Ranger," "Ramar of the Jungle," "Hopalong Cassidy," and "The Lone Ranger" were there to extend my horizons beyond reality.

One day, I noticed that the programs I liked best were those that featured spacemen and women and rocketships. I began to read books such as *By Spaceship to the Moon* and *Rockets, Jets, Guided Missiles and Spaceships.* I learned that people could not breathe in space without space suits, and that in space there is no "up" or "down." On one especially magical day, my mother took me to Brooklyn's Abraham and Straus department store to meet Willy Ley, a pioneer rocket scientist who had written some of the books on space I had read. I talked about nothing but rockets and space travel for days afterward.

I asked my school librarian if she had any books about spacemen and rockets and rayguns, whereupon I was led to a small bookcase marked "science fiction." I devoured the books, stories, and pictures from that bookcase, and I started to look elsewhere for more such wondrous things.

At about this time, I began to frequent the center section of my neighborhood movie theater, the Marboro, attracted by colorful posters that announced such films as *From the Earth to the Moon, The Mysterians, Rodan, Earth Vs. the Flying Saucers,* and *This Island Earth.*

I saw *Forbidden Planet* on television and I loved it, and in 1960, *The Day the Earth Stood Still* was televised and I first saw this beautiful film. This was followed soon afterward by my first exposure to another classic science fiction movie, *Things to Come.*

After being exposed to more science fiction books and films, I began to attend science fiction conventions. When I heard about the annual *world* conventions, I determined that I would attend the next one. During the Labor Day weekend in 1966, I traveled by bus to Cleveland, Ohio, to attend "Tricon," that year's World Science Fiction Convention. During the bus ride I studied the convention's progress reports, which mentioned three special film events on the program. A new film, *Fantastic Voyage,* had been provided by 20th Century-Fox. The same studio's television division, with producer Irwin Allen, had also arranged to show the pilot episode of Allen's new series, "The Time Tunnel."

The third convention debut was to be another television pilot episode, the work of a producer with an unfamiliar name; Gene Roddenberry. I had difficulty remembering the title of Roddenberry's new series. It was "Star," something. "Star . . ." "Star *Ship?*" "Star *Trip?*" No, it was . . . *Star Trek!*

Today it seems difficult to conceive of a time before "Star Trek" was familiar to me. The series has given so much to so many of my friends, and to myself. "Star Trek" somehow manages to inspire its regular viewers to look for the creative talents within themselves and to look forward to the future. "Star Trek" itself, and the many wonderful people I've met through my interest in the series, have led me to write this book, which I hope will provide entertainment and knowledge to those who are involved with the series or wish to learn about it. (All opinions stated in this book are solely those of the author, unless otherwise attributed.)

1 A Capsule History of "Star Trek"

Enter "Star Trek"

After checking into the hotel in Cleveland, I was able to think only of getting a good night's sleep. Some fans were milling around the hotel lobby, and they all had convention booklets and badges; I decided to register for Tricon before conking out for the night. After putting my luggage in my room I signed in and received the convention progress reports. Flipping through the pages of the report I saw photos from "Star Trek," and all thoughts of sleep vanished for the moment.

Near the registration area was a long table, behind which stood an attractive young woman wearing an intriguing costume. I heard her tell someone that the costume was from a "Star Trek" episode that had already been filmed ("What Are Little Girls Made of?"). I realized as I walked to the table that this was definitely not something designed for a television show aimed at children.

Poised on a small stand in the middle of the table was a plaster model of what appeared to be a flying saucer with projecting tubes. The scale model bore the legend "NCC-1701." Clearly, this vehicle was not designed for travel within the Earth's atmosphere.

One of the photos surrounding the ship showed a man with weird, pointed ears. He was holding the same model that was in front of me (not the woman; the ship), and he peered at me with a menacing expression that encouraged me to find something else to stare at.

I was surprised to see stills of William Shatner, whom I remembered from his 'Twilight Zone" and "Outer Limits" appearances, wearing the same type uniform as the unfamiliar fellow with the pointed ears.

Then I noticed the two little black objects on top of the photos.

One looked like a small electric shaver. It had a grid, a metal wheel, and a small, numbered gauge. It couldn't have been too important, I thought, because everyone was picking it up and examining it. I examined the object too, not knowing that I was holding one of the original hand phasers designed for "Star Trek."

Next to the "shaver" was another little black box that was covered with a gold grillework. I did not try to open it, and in fact I did not suspect that it could be opened at all, never having seen a communicator before.

I signed a form that asked the studio to send me some of the photos on the table. I gave the form to the woman in the android suit and she thanked me for showing interest in "Star Trek." By this time I was extremely sleepy, and I soon collapsed on my bed and spent the night dreaming of my favorite science fiction films.

The next day, September 4, 1966, I awoke in the afternoon. After making myself presentable (I later discovered that most fans at conventions don't worry about such formalities) I hurried downstairs and spent the day meeting fans, writers, and peddlers of exotic merchandise such as fanzines. I attended panels, costume exhibitions, and the art show, and found time for an occasional inexpensive snack with newfound friends from all parts of the world.

I stopped over to the Star Trek table again, and was told that if I wanted to see anything else on the show I'd better hurry; the films were about to start down the hall.

The first item on the program was the pilot film for Irwin Allen's new TV series, "The Time Tunnel." Allen was not yet the king of the disaster films; *Towering Inferno* and *Poseidon Adventure* were still years away. I knew of Allen through his television series "Voyage to the Bottom of the Sea" and "Lost in Space" (which are regarded by many fans as disaster films in their own right).

Allen's TV series had started with good pilot episodes and promising plot lines. The succeeding episodes had a certain warmth to them, but they were certainly doing nothing to improve the public's understanding of science fiction's serious potentials.

An assistant of Allen's materialized with the "Time Tunnel" print (a seventy-five-minute version that was never televised), and apologized that Mr. Allen could not be at the convention himself as a result of production deadlines. The lights went out and the film was shown. It was well received.

A few minutes after that screening, a tall man appeared at the front of the room. Although he looked formidable, his voice was contrastingly gentle. He sounded almost timid when he introduced himself as Gene Roddenberry, a lifelong science fiction fan. He told the audience that he had produced a new television pilot which had already been accepted by NBC for a series called "Star Trek." The series would debut the following week with a "sneak preview" episode, but our opinion was still extremely important to him.

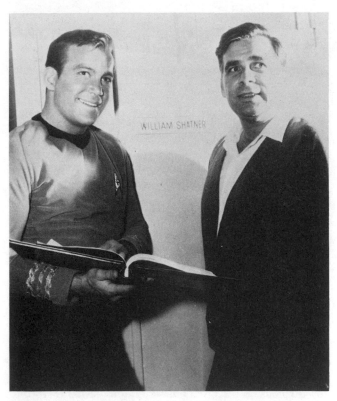

William Shatner and Gene Roddenberry in mid-1966, during early "Star Trek" series production.

Having sold his series Mr. Roddenberry was undoubtedly busy, and yet there he was; he had brought his film to us himself, just to ask our opinion.

Roddenberry left the stage. The audience quieted down and hoped for the best as the lights went out so we could see "Where No Man Has Gone Before."

There was that funny spaceship again, with William Shatner's voiceover explaining the mission of the *Enterprise*. The weird guy with the pointed ears was even stranger on motion picture film, with his slightly yellow complexion. I tried to spot the makeup seam on his ears, and couldn't find any. "Maybe he's for real," I thought.

There was nothing childish about the show; we waited for a kid or a wisecracking robot, but they never arrived. Even the music was somber and serious.

There must have been 500 people in that audience. When the *Enterprise* hit the galactic barrier, 1,000 eyes opened wide. Five hundred respiratory rates accelerated with that wonderful pleasure that comes over all lovers of all things when they see their favorite subject being treated as it should be.

Then the whispers started. "He did say this was for television, didn't he?" Maybe we'd misunderstood. I recall thinking about how Roddenberry could afford to do things like this on a television budget. If he could have read our minds at that moment, he would have been the happiest producer in the world.

We continued to watch the film with an occasional low-key dialogue to discuss the script, the visuals, and the general elation of the moment.

We watched the decor, the props, and listened to the dialogue. The only humor present consisted of comments to break the tension of the moment, and a very human captain was attempting to avoid killing a close friend. A satanic-looking first officer was pressuring the captain to liquidate the mutating individual. Someone noticed that Gary Mitchell's hair was gradually turning gray in one of many subtle touches.

We noticed people of varied races, genders, and planetary origins working together. Here was a future it did not hurt to imagine. Here was a constructive tomorrow for mankind, emphasizing exploration and expansion. This was the science fiction television series we all wanted to see. We were all extremely impressed.

There was also something strangely compelling about Mr. Spock. The females in the audience were immediately drawn to him. Giggles were intermittently heard as a new cult was born.

Captain Kirk was a commander with guts, compassion, and a delivery that was easy to understand. We liked him; we also liked Spock. We enjoyed the sparkling opticals and the sight of that interesting starship. We liked everything about that episode more than it is possible to put into words.

After the film was over, we were unable to leave our seats. We just nodded at each other and smiled, and began to whisper. As the murmuring grew louder, Roddenberry returned to the stage. People quieted down again, waiting for him to say something. But *he* was waiting for *us* to say something. Roddenberry seemed to have no idea of the effect his episode was having upon us.

Finally, Roddenberry broke the silence. He asked

Young Mr. Spock, as he appeared in "The Cage" (Leonard Nimoy).

for our opinion; we gave him a standing ovation. He smiled, and we returned the smile before we converged on him. We came close to lifting Gene Roddenberry upon our shoulders and carrying him out of the room.

From that moment on, the convention was "divided" into two factions. Those of us who had seen "Where No Man Has Gone Before" were hooked. The unenlightened convention goers were convinced we were acting strangely to lavish so much attention on one TV episode.

Later, a group of us asked Roddenberry if he had brought any other Trek film to the convention. Gene did have something else with him; the first Trek pilot that NBC had previously rejected. It wasn't in color, he explained; never mind, we assured him, we wanted to see it. Shortly afterward, "The Cage" was screened.

"The Cage" *was* different than "Where No Man Has Gone Before," but it showed the same attention to serious and imaginative detail. "The Cage" reminded us of "The Outer Limits," a series we had learned to respect.

Too Good to Be True?

Before I left the convention, I joined every discussion group that mentioned "Star Trek," and I tried vainly to track down the lucky person who had bought some of the original "Trek" set sketches in an auction held before the "Trek" pilots were shown.

I returned to Brooklyn, with my head in the clouds; I had discovered the wonders of a science fiction convention, had met some amazing people, and at 8:30 P.M. on Thursday, September 8, I watched NBC's special "sneak preview" of a new, hour-long series, "Star Trek." The episode chosen for this debut was "Man Trap." I noticed some differences between this and the pilots; there were some additional crew members and the doctor was different. The new medical officer seemed likable with some mysterious overtones. I wasn't sure how Mr. Sulu had made the transition from ship's physicist to helmsman. The episode was definitely not a humorous effort, and I was relieved to see that the serious scope of the pilots was carrying over into the series.

On September 14 I bought *Variety* to see what it thought of the show. The review was so negative I could not imagine how it had arrived at such conclusions; it was as if the reviewer had seen something completely different than what I had watched.

Variety's review began by saying that "Star Trek" ". . . won't work." The reviewer called it incredible, dreary, and confusing.

The *Variety* reviewer conceded that the leading performers were apparently trying very hard to appear credible, but concluded that Trek would be ". . . better suited to the Saturday morning kidvid bloc." The *Va-*

In a rare moment, Kirk forgets the loneliness of command with the aid of Yeoman Rand (Grace Lee Whitney, William Shatner).

riety writer wasn't sure whether Prof. Crater and his "wife" were archeologists. "That's only a guess," he said, and added that he was stumped as to how "Star Trek" had made it to television.

The *New York World Journal-Tribune* called Trek "Dubious science fiction," adding that it had ". . . a weird, comic strip appeal and no doubt will earn a high rating." The paper's reviewer mentioned the *Enterprise*'s "integrated crew," and referred to Spock as being ". . . half Earthling, half Vulcan and all spook." [1]

TV Guide, in its 1966 "fall preview issue," observed "The sky's not the limit on this TREK," [2] but in a later issue, reviewer Cleveland Amory apparently did not share the magazine's enthusiasm. [3]

The Trek episode that Amory reviewed was "Shore Leave." Although it is one of the most popular and enjoyable episodes of "Star Trek," "Shore Leave" is definitely not typical of the series. The events of this episode suggest fantasy rather than science fiction, until the story reaches its climax.

Amory began his review by reminding audiences that the phrase ". . . to boldly go . . ." splits an infinitive; an observation hardly indicative of the series' merit. Amory cited the crew of the *Enterprise* as definitely "fun" people. He listed the hallucinations, and explained that the illusions actually had reasonable explanations. But Amory's review ended with a para-

An experimental transporter shot, in which the figure is surrounded with a solid red line in "The Cage."

phrase of Kirk's dialogue; he said that "Star Trek" is best watched by adults who ". . . don't talk, don't think, don't breathe." Children, though, will love "Star Trek," said Amory, and they should therefore be permitted to breathe while watching the show.

McCoy's tragic (and fortunately temporary) sacrifice, Kirk's "painful reality" of his former love, and the near destruction of the starship with its crew of 400 people were interpreted by Amory as casual points in "Shore Leave," and therefore in "Star Trek." Whether the result of prejudice or self-imposed ignorance, Amory's review of this episode suggests a strong urge to write a humorous piece, and a far weaker wish to understand the subject of his review.

Unfortunately, others followed Amory's approach, and most advertisers greeted "Star Trek" in the same manner, probably considering it a "bad risk" because it dealt realistically with a subject they considered nonrealistic.

This probable opinion was backed up by the Nielsen Ratings Service, which supplied data by equipping random households with "Nielsen boxes" that fit into TV sets and automatically record what show the owners of the television are watching at any given time. These boxes are periodically checked, and the results are utilized to form mathematical studies of how many people all over the country are watching TV shows.

It seemed that wherever the Nielsen ratings were present with their checking systems, people would rather watch enjoyable and simpler-to-understand series such as the CBS show with the robot, the kids, and the funny doctor. The more these findings came in, the more the sponsors were convinced that advertising on "Star Trek" would be a bad investment.

These and other factors probably became the source of concern in the network about "Star Trek's" future.

Somewhere within the vast NBC offices in New York City, someone checked which series were coming up for "consideration" and they wrote out the required diabolical piece of paper that alerted the people who would decide whether "Star Trek" was to be renewed beyond its original commitment or be canceled.

Fortunately, the news leaked out that "Star Trek" might soon be in danger.

Mr. Spock was permitted to show slight emotional reactions to events in the earliest "Star Trek" episodes (Leonard Nimoy).

Mr. Spock fights to regain control of himself, as his emotions surface in "The Naked Time" (Leonard Nimoy).

The First Letter-Writing Campaign

Gene Roddenberry had been providing rewarding work for established, self-respecting science fiction writers. From the beginning, the finest minds in the field had supplied Roddenberry with encouragement, story outlines, and finished scripts. They were working on ideas for "Star Trek," and they knew that their material would not be rewritten into unimaginative, degrading scripts. They had become fans of the show, and when the series needed help, some of these writers banded together to protect "Star Trek."

Three months before Cleveland Amory's review appeared in *TV Guide,* I was not aware of "Star Trek's" problems. I belonged to the science fiction club at my university where each week's "Star Trek" episode was *the* topic of discussion. I loved the series, and had come to know the crew of the *Enterprise* as good people living through interesting adventures. I looked forward to coming home once a week and enjoying another exposure to life in the far future. Then, on December 10, 1966, I received a letter.

It was postmarked Los Angeles, California, and had no return address on the outside of the envelope. Inside was a letter from an impressive array of names who called themselves "The Committee," no relation to the group of fans who would later form the first "Star Trek" conventions. The members of this organization were Poul Anderson, Robert Bloch, Lester del Rey, Harlan Ellison, Philip Jose Farmer, Frank Herbert, Richard Matheson, Theodore Sturgeon, and A. E. Van Vogt.

Before I read the letter, I wondered why these talented people would be writing *me*. Van Vogt had written the book *The Voyage of the Space Beagle,* which was probably a source of inspiration for "Star Trek." Robert Bloch had written "What Are Little Girls Made of?" (he would later write "Catspaw" and "Wolf in the Fold"). I also knew Bloch's work from episodes of "Thriller," and the horrifying feature film *Psycho.* Richard Matheson had written "The Enemy Within," as well as many episodes of "The Twilight Zone," and the classic book and motion picture *The Incredible Shrinking Man.* Theodore Sturgeon had done "Shore Leave" (and would later do "Amok Time"), as well as scores of stories I had been advised to read. I knew of Harlan Ellison from the 1966 Cleveland convention ("City on the Edge of Forever" had not yet been produced), and I had recognized his two "Outer Limits" episodes ("The Soldier" and "Demon with a Glass Hand") as superior science fiction. I knew the others on the committee by reputation; they unfortunately never did any "Star Trek" episodes.

"The Committee," who had probably obtained my address from the mailing list of the Cleveland convention, needed the help of "Star Trek's" fans. They needed *my* help. The letter was written by Ellison, and it spoke of the inferior treatment science fiction usually received on TV before "Star Trek," which, the letter stated, had made television viewers understand that science fiction was more than monsters and robots and comedy relief. Ellison mentioned the Cleveland convention, and the interest "Star Trek" had attracted there (including the special citation it had been awarded by the convention personnel). A brief passage followed that discussed the television ratings system, and how it was unfair to judge Trek against "the competition" ("Lost in Space"), which had been given a year's head start at attracting an audience.

Worse than the thought of "Star Trek" being cancelled, the letter stated the possibility of the series' format being converted into something closer to a kiddie show. I did not want to believe that this could happen, but these very special writers were telling me that it *was* possible.

What could I do? The letter told me . . . *write letters.* Complain to TV stations, sponsors of "Star Trek," television columnists, and magazines like *TV Guide.* Let the world know that "Star Trek" had an audience; that its fate mattered to many, many individuals.

The letter ended on an especially ominous note, with its mention that whatever could be done to save "Star Trek" had to be accomplished *now,* before it was too late. Could they count on my help?

Sure they could count on my help! I became determined to help keep the series on the air and in production. I began to write letters and postcards. I called NBC and Desilu Productions and told them how I felt about the series.

The enthusiasm I felt personally was duplicated by most other fans who had received that letter. This first campaign showed NBC that even if the ratings on "Star Trek" were not incredibly high, the series had a following of many thousands of dedicated fans, and that maybe the network had something of value after all.

The Second Season

On March 14, 1967, the NBC network held its annual affiliates' convention to inform all its TV stations what the network's official schedule would be for the coming season. NBC had kept seventeen of its old series and accepted eight new ones. "Star Trek" was on the list of series that would be continued, but its old time slot of Thursdays at 8:30 P.M. (Eastern Standard Time) was now occupied by another new NBC entry, "Ironside." "Star Trek" had been moved to Friday evenings, 8:30–9:30 P.M.

This was not the most logical time slot for "Star Trek." NBC knew from the fan mail written about the series that most Trek viewers were teenagers, ranging from junior high school to university students. As it had been " . . . from the time of the beginning," Friday was a special night for students. There was no homework to do and no tests the next day (such things could be worried about on Sunday evenings).

Given the choice between staying home to see a TV program or go out on a date, most teenagers would choose to go out. Which raises the question that since this was plain, ordinary common sense that did not need the expertise of a sociologist or a network analyst, why did NBC pick this time slot for "Star Trek?" It was not that NBC was disenchanted with Trek (at least not in print). If anything, NBC seemed proud of the series as shown by the network's promotional brochure for "Star Trek's" 1967–68 season.

The NBC brochure indicated that "Star Trek" had been nominated for five Emmy Awards during its first season on television. These were in the categories of (1) best dramatic series; (2) outstanding supporting performance by a dramatic actor (Leonard Nimoy); (3) special photographic effects ("Star Trek" lost to "The Time Tunnel"); (4) special mechanical effects, and (5) film and sound editing.

Nimoy, NBC stated, had also been honored with a tour of the Goddard Space Flight Center in Washington, D.C., by the National Space Club and a dinner at which Vice President Hubert Humphrey was the main speaker.

Dr. Isaac Asimov was cited in the booklet as having called "Star Trek" " . . . the first good television science fiction." The brochure also acknowledged that "Star Trek" was very popular in college dormitories and lounges.

Most importantly, the "Star Trek" fan mail re-

Mr. Sulu and Lieutenant Uhura are dynamic and vital crewmen of the *Enterprise* (George Takei, Nichelle Nichols).

ceived by the network was discussed in what was possibly the first official NBC recognition of this "voluminous mail." These letters indicated that most "Star Trek" watchers watched the show regularly, and had their own favorite performer(s). NBC was careful to stress that every cast member would be returning for the second season (Yeoman Rand was completely ignored; Mr. Chekov was not mentioned).

The brochure also assured network affiliates that Dr. McCoy, Mr. Sulu, Mr. Scott, and Lieutenant Uhura were each going to appear in episodes in which they would be the central character. This promise was partially kept; Mr. Scott became the central figure of "Wolf in the Fold." Dr. McCoy had to wait until the third season for his episode, "For the World Is Hollow and I Have Touched the Sky."

At the start of the second season, Mr. Sulu was scheduled to appear prominently in the first script version of "The Gamesters of Triskelion." When the shooting started on this episode, George Takei, who played Mr. Sulu, was doing some shooting of his own, on location in Alabama appearing in the feature film *The Green Berets*. Because of last-minute lags in the shooting schedule, Takei could not get back to the studio in time to appear in the episode. In the finished version, Ensign Chekov (through the extremely effective efforts of Walter Koenig) got the laughs. Mr. Sulu never did get his solo break. Neither did Lieutenant Uhura, who because of her capability and beauty was the most likely candidate of the whole crew for a starring role.

With all the promises and praises mentioned in this NBC brochure, one would have thought that "Star Trek" had no future problems. But there were still the bad time slot and the low ratings; two problems that would compound each other despite the large volume of fan mail the series continued to attract.

One of the most surprising network booklets devoted to "Star Trek" was prepared in August, 1967 by the TV Network Sales Planning department of NBC. The booklet, called "Star Trek Mail Call," is exclusively concerned with the large amount of fan mail that had been sent on behalf of the show. The network, according to the brochure, was proud of the number of letters, their quality, and the cross section of people who were sending them.

The cover of the booklet was blank except for two facsimile "postage stamps" of Captain Kirk and Mr. Spock. The "postmark" read "NBC Television Network, August, 1967, N.Y., Star Trek Mail Call." The first page acknowledged that the network had received 29,000 pieces of mail from Trek fans during the series' first year. The letters, said the network, had come from viewers who were deeply involved in "Star Trek." NBC was so impressed with this fan following that it honored Trek by comparing it to the only series of that time to draw more fan response: "The Monkees."

The booklet said that sponsors would be interested in knowing that most of the fan mail for Trek was written by people who were associated in some way or another with the space program. The letters also came from students from grade school to college level, housewives, and others. While praising the series, the brochure also stated that most of the fan letters came from people with scientific or intellectual backgrounds. Television series and feature films aimed at intellectual audiences had usually failed in the past. In the next paragraph, however, the booklet described "Star Trek" as ". . . one of America's best liked television programs . . ." The Trek audience was specifically described as decision-making people who would be attractive to prospective sponsors.

In addition to the categories of viewers mentioned earlier, the booklet also carried some miscellaneous letters from people who said some highly positive things about "Star Trek." Frequently used words included "logical and adult," "good adult escape," "believable conflict," "fascinating" (probably a Vulcan fan letter), and "thought-provoking." In addition, letters had poured in citing Shatner, Nimoy, and the series' other principals as very convincing and skilled performers. The praise came from all parts of the country. Along with the letters seven petitions were selected and printed in the booklet.

One petition explained how the entire city of Las Vegas came to a standstill whenever "Star Trek" was televised. School courses were changed to let people see Trek. A local station had preempted "Star Trek" on a holiday to show a feature film instead; because of numerous phone calls the station was forced to change its schedule and show "Star Trek" later in the evening. People bought theater tickets only if they did not conflict with "Star Trek." It was almost a direct parallel to the days of radio, when theaters closed so that everyone could listen to the popular "Amos N' Andy" series. (The contrast between "Amos N' Andy" and "Star Trek" is a tribute to how much Americans had evolved culturally from the 1930s to the 1960s.)

The Great Letter-Writing Drive

There I was, sitting home again in Brooklyn, New York, enjoying another year of "Star Trek" thinking that its future was perfectly safe after the initial letter-writing campaign. Since then, I had witnessed the development of a sociological phenomenon; the "Star Trek" "fanzine." Fanzines are publications put together and distributed by fans who wish to meet friends by discussing and adding to the constructive effects and spirit of science fiction. (These are not money-making enterprises; they are expensive in terms of material and time, and rarely come close to paying for themselves.) Because of these fanzines, I had become more involved with "Star Trek" than I'd ever been before. And then . . . *it happened again!*

In December 1967, I received another letter from California. John and Bjo Trimble, from whom this letter had originated, were names that were well known to me because of their involvement in "Star Trek" fandom. Bjo's book, *The Star Trek Concordance,* is a wonderfully conceived labor of love that is prized by Trek fans everywhere as a reference work and as a means of projecting one's self into the "Star Trek" universe when desired.

The letter, dated December 11, warned that "Star Trek" was once again facing disaster. The help of fans everywhere was needed again. The Trimbles' letter announced that surveys taken in magazines indicated that Trek was extremely popular with the public even while the Nielsen ratings were saying otherwise. The network, of course, was going by the Nielsens and would continue to do so unless faced with another avalanche of fan mail pleading "Star Trek's" case.

Making sure that Trek remained on the air, the letter said, was a constant job that had to be accomplished by the fans. The old threats of outright cancellation, or a conversion of the series into a "kiddie" format were apparently spectres that haunted TV series that were sufficiently complex so as not to fall into one single category and market. "Formula" TV shows were desirable to the networks and sponsors, the letter continued; "Star Trek's" fans, myself proudly included, had come to love the show as an eloquent experiment at creating a future that was worth waiting for.

The Trimble letter was more ominous than the letter from the "Committee," confirming that the second season ratings were not as high as they were expected to be. The letter provided two suggestions for improving this situation.

First the letter suggested that Gene Roddenberry should have a more direct hand in "Trek." If he could be encouraged to devote his complete attention to the series once more, as he had done for the first half of the first season, Trek would have its original mentor calling the shots again.

The main problem was cited as being "Star Trek's" Friday night time slot. The young people who are attracted to the series are young either physically or emotionally, or both, and youthful behavior patterns do not dictate sitting home on Friday nights watching television. The puzzling thing about this was that the letter postdated NBC's "Star Trek Mail Call" pamphlet. The data discussed in that booklet indicated the same thing the Trimble letter was saying; that young, dynamic personalities tended to watch "Star Trek." The Trimble letter was not concerned with finding a reason for this; its concern was to inform Trek fans that the condition was an unpleasant reality.

Once again, time was short. TV series are generally renewed during January or February, the letter revealed. The individual craftsmen who work in the television industry are likely to find other work if their series appears to be in danger of cancellation. Even if these individuals can be replaced, the letter states, their loss to the production creates morale problems for the remaining staffers.

The letter was a thorough and ambitious undertaking, resembling the urgency and dedication that were inherent in "The Midnight Ride of Paul Revere." We fans had to rouse the populace and warn them that only *they* could help. To aid in this task, the Trimbles' letter was mailed along with a supplementary page entitled "How to Write Effective Letters to Save Star Trek," which outlined the fundamentals of what network and publicity people looked for in fan mail. On the other side of this sheet were further bits of advice. Above all, the letter repeated, procrastination could kill "Star Trek" as easily as the networks could.

Five addresses were recommended as main "targets" for the letters: (1) the president of NBC; (2) RCA (NBC's parent corporation); (3) RCA's ad agency; and (4, and 5) two high ranking people within NBC. In addition, fans were encouraged to appeal to local NBC affiliate stations, TV columnists, and *TV Guide* magazine.

It was a well-conceived program that hurriedly educated the fans in what had to be done and how they should go about doing it.[4]

The strategy apparently worked better than expected. Rumors began to leak out from New York and California about how many thousands of letters, cards, and phone calls people had received and about how many hours had been "wasted" by NBC in reading the letters, classifying and tabulating them, and writing memos concerning the large numbers of communications.[5] Then came the definite news that "Star Trek" had been renewed for its third production season.

Blueprint for Cancellation

With "Star Trek" once again on the NBC schedule, the network stopped counting the letters and again began to publicize the response of "Star Trek's" fans. NBC reissued the "Star Trek Mail Call" pamphlet, along with a statement glued to the cover of the original edition. It reminded its affiliates that last season's letters had been so numerous that NBC had decided to issue the booklet. The current crop of Trek fans, it added, had set a new NBC high of 115,893 letters, of which 52,358 were received during the month of February 1968. Star Trek fans were referred to as ". . . loyal and articulate . . . ." The NBC supplement closed by speaking of the Trek fans as being ". . . in ever increasing numbers."

With all the enthusiasm the network was still exhibiting for "Trek," it appeared that the series was slated for a better time slot.

According to an article in a New York City newspaper,[6] Gene Roddenberry had been assured by NBC that "Star Trek," during this season, would be telecast on Monday evenings at 7:30 P.M., New York Time. Rowan and Martin's "Laugh-in" was to be moved from the Monday slot to Fridays at 10:00 P.M. (NYT) to make room for "Star Trek." Roddenberry, in his capacity of executive producer of the series, set about making plans for the coming year. Then came the bad news.

On March 15, 1968, the network changed its mind. "Laugh-in," it announced to the press, would be televised on Monday evenings from 7:30–8:30 (EST). "Star Trek" was pushed into the Friday slot from 10:00–11:00 P.M. (EST). Roddenberry protested. If the series had not done well at an earlier hour on Friday, how could the network think it would do any better later that same evening? NBC was cutting "Star Trek's" audience still further. Roddenberry and the "Star Trek" staff must have been stunned by the decision; the fans definitely were. It seemed as though the network were praising the show with one hand, and trying to destroy it with the other.

Roddenberry immediately began talks with network representatives, but it was no use. Minds had been made up, apparently by logical means that were not known to outsiders then or now.

Roddenberry's reaction was to remain relatively quiet about the issue. When questioned by the press, he said only that "Star Trek" had been promised one time slot and then given another he did not feel was in the series' best interests. Considering the frustrating nature of what he was experiencing, Roddenberry accepted the unpleasant reality in a manner that would have met with the approval of his creation, Mr. Spock.

A Change of Personalities

Gene Roddenberry had originally functioned as producer in "Star Trek's" first season. Billed as "Creator and Producer" in the earliest episodes, Roddenberry oversaw every phase of the series' production while the episodes were being planned, during their production and afterward in their post-production stages. It was a full-time job. Then the low ratings came in, and there was some doubt about whether Trek would be renewed (this was shortly before the letter from "the Committee" went out). Roddenberry now had to think about "Star Trek" not as his creation but as a project that was (1) probably about to be cancelled, and (2) taking up all of his time. Whatever the reasons, after approximately a dozen episodes of Trek had been completed, Roddenberry stepped down as "line producer." The position was given to his dedicated co-worker, Gene L. Coon.

Coon was the most qualified person for the job, having worked with Roddenberry since the beginnings of Trek, and before that (on "Have Gun Will Travel"). An extremely talented man, Coon (who had also functioned as producer of "The Virginian" before his association with "Star Trek") did a fine job of maintaining "Star Trek's" continuity.

Roddenberry had moved up to the position of executive producer, and was probably divorced from most of the tasks necessary to complete each episode. Coon and Roddenberry presumably held frequent meetings to discuss Trek production. This arrangement continued until the second production season when Coon stepped down as line producer.

John Meredyth Lucas became "Star Trek's" producer after Coon left. Lucas was another multi-talented individual. He had written for "Star Trek" (including "The Changeling"), and would write more scripts for Trek during the third season. He had also directed a couple of episodes and would later direct others. Lucas produced the series until the start of the third season.

Rumors spread that NBC was trying to convince Roddenberry to return as the line producer of "Star Trek." If this were true, the network's reneging on its time slot promises was certainly not the best way to go about it. Roddenberry agreed to stay on as executive producer, and a new line producer was chosen: Fred Freiberger.

For a man who had never been exposed to the subculture of "Star Trek," Freiberger produced some worthwhile episodes including "The Paradise Syndrome," "Is There in Truth No Beauty," "The Tholian Web," "For the World Is Hollow and I Have Touched the Sky," and "Day of the Dove."

Freiberger had previously worked in the field of science fiction; he co-wrote the screenplays of *The Beast from 20,000 Fathoms* (Warner Brothers–1953) and *The Beginning of the End* (Republic–1957). He had also been associated with "The Wild, Wild West" during its last season. His selection as producer of "Star Trek" seems to have been more logical than the decision to put "Star Trek" on at 10:00 P.M. on Friday nights.

What happened to the quality of episodes during "Star Trek's" last season? The answer can be summed up by three words; "lack of continuity."

The Last Season

"Continuity" is the raw material of anything, whether it be planet or universe, real or fictional. "Star Trek," during its first fifty-five episodes, had developed a detailed continuity. The interactions of people and their specific mannerisms and reactions to various situations could be completely understood, and this made the "Star Trek" crew very real individuals who could be accepted as "friends." There was a subtle balance between science and fantasy, a set but flexible pattern, a scheme of things for Kirk and company.

But during the third year of the series Gene Roddenberry was separated from the intricacies of production, and Gene Coon was gone as his direct liaison. There was now a new producer, probably with a new way of doing things. The series was mutating, and its changes were not favorable; its positive traits were diluted or evaporated.

The first episode produced during the third season was "Spectre of the Gun." An interesting exercise in mental power, it was an atypical "Star Trek" episode and was essentially a surrealistic western. No matter how unusual it was from a favorable standpoint, the risk would be too great for the network to use that episode as the season's opener.[7]

A choice had to be made as to which Trek episode would be the season's opener. "The Enterprise Incident" and "The Paradise Syndrome" would each have made a sensitive and promising introduction for the season, but on Friday, September 20, 1968, at 10:00 P.M. (EST), the last season of "Star Trek" made its debut with "Spock's Brain." If NBC thought "Spock's Brain" was a typical "Star Trek" episode, its opinion would be a significant network "editorial opinion," because "Spock's Brain" is thought by some fans to be completely lacking in the departments of rationality, sincerity, and effectiveness. It is a hollow shell of the Trek format, just as Spock is a hollow shell clicking along throughout the episode.

In its September 25, 1968, issue, *Variety* reported that "Star Trek" "retains its vigor and spatial spookiness, although its chief characters are largely caricatures and the dialogue tends to turgidity." The male crew members, it added, are kept occupied looking at "women in tight space suits," and *Variety*'s conclusion was that the best thing about "Star Trek" was its special effects.

Another episode of that season, "The Way to Eden," had Mr. Spock partaking in a "jam session" with space hippies. Elsewhere in the third season, Spock sang a ballad and was forced to laugh and recite poetry ("Plato's Stepchildren"), reacted emotionally toward an illusion ("The Savage Curtain"), and conspired to mutiny ("Turnabout Intruder"). Although all of these actions were the result of occurrences in the scripts involved, the Vulcan's acts themselves are disturbing. In the exploitation of Spock's behavior and motivations can be seen the general decline in "Star Trek's" third season.

In addition, NBC was frequently preempting "Star Trek." There were no Trek episodes telecast on December 13 and 27, 1968, February 7, 1969, and no first-run episodes were telecast from March 21 to June 3, 1969. On June 3, the last network first-run episode, "Turnabout Intruder," was televised.[8]

One of the stages in the "matte" process, which optically combines separate pieces of film to produce the final transporter effect in "The Cage."

The Last Voyage

"Turnabout Intruder," the last "Star Trek" episode produced, began filming on December 31, 1968. Using some mental magic, let us transport ourselves back through time and space to Hollywood, California, on the last day of 1968. We are now on Stage 9 in Paramount Studios.

Our first stop is "sick bay," where DeForest Kelley delivers a line and stops in the middle. William Shatner assures him his delivery was okay. After "cut" is yelled by director Herb Wallerstein, someone says ". . . use the cut." The next few takes are uneventful.

A single scene is being shot and reshot for each individual's close-up picture and sound. "Okay, that's a print," shouts Wallerstein. "Save it, please," the soundman announces into the console microphone. Actress Sandra Smith (Dr. Janice Lester) has Shatner's speech pattern down perfectly as she realizes she's losing command of the *Enterprise*. ". . . Bad dream . . . ," she sighs. "Cut it . . . okay, good," says the director.

In the next take we see the doors to the sick bay open and close as Majel Barrett enters. The doors open in their usual manner, but instead of the expected sound we hear only two heavy, wooden doors being dragged apart by a man hidden behind them. The sound effects will be dubbed in later.

DeForest Kelley, commenting on a tongue twister of a line, exclaims ". . . Son of a gun!" In the next take he delivers the difficult line with perfection. One of the other cast members, however, is having difficulty with the word "supervision"; it keeps coming out "superstition." The scene goes through several takes. A difficult scene is completed, followed by shouts of "Beautiful," "All right, boy," and "Great!"

After the next scene, hysterical laughter breaks out on the set. In getting out of a sick bay bed, actress Sandra Smith has torn the bed's cover, just as the director has yelled "Cut it!" Amid the laughter, the set empties out for the New Year's holiday.

On January 2, 1969, the crew returns to the sick bay set. Shooting begins with a stand-in for Shatner delivering the captain's lines to provide cues for the other performers. One actor momentarily forgets who the stand-in is supposed to be; he signals to the director to "keep filming." Afterward, the actor announces that it is probably the result of New Year's Eve.

In scene number 76, "Dr. Lester" is supposed to request a visit from Mr. Spock. During the first take, actress Sandra Smith asks to see Doctor Spock. Ms. Smith and Majel burst into laughter.

The following day, scenes are shot in the corridor near the sick bay set. William Shatner announces that Mr. Spock is to be court-martialed for mutiny. The take goes smoothly, with Leonard Nimoy presenting his best deadpan delivery as the Vulcan. After the take has ended, he turns to Shatner and adds "I want a transfer." Shatner breaks up.

Captain Kirk resumes command of his ship after his experiences in "The Enemy Within" (William Shatner).

Waiting for the next take, Shatner promises to tell Nimoy about something funny that once happened to him. The director says "Ready, and . . ." as the clapboard signals the beginning of the "roll." "Action . . . ," says the director, and the scene begins. A beautiful take. "Heavy, heavy," someone remarks.

"Red light," calls a crewman, and the next scene begins immediately. Discussing their "mutiny" in the corridor, Jimmy Doohan and DeForest Kelley deliver their lines flawlessly. A closing door makes noise as it slides shut, and Jimmy pauses for an instant before he recalls that the door's sound effect will be dubbed in over the noise. He resumes the take, and Majel Barrett comes into the scene to deliver her lines. Majel's work for the day is done, and as she starts for her dressing room to change into civilian clothes, a crewmember hollers "Say goodnight to Majel." Voices from the floor and the catwalks all join in to shout "Goodnight, Majel!"

On January 5, miscellaneous corridor and set footage is completed. The transporter room and its vicinity are shot the following day, and the bridge scenes are covered on January 7.

The following day the court-martial scenes are filmed, along with part of the episode's teaser (the mind transfer on the alien machine).

On January 9, 1969, Sandra Smith and William Shatner are photographed against the alien machine's sculpted panels, and in front of black backdrops. This footage will be used to create the photographic effect of the actual mind transfer. Close-ups of Shatner's face express the captain's horror, whereas Sandra Smith's expressions relish the moment. The takes go smoothly and quickly, and the teaser is completed on time.

Suddenly, people who had worked together since 1966 realize that it is finally all over. The familiar trips to the studio, the tight deadlines, and the rushed memorization of dialogue are at an end. Some of the people will stay in touch with each other, but the day-to-day routine of "Star Trek" is over. What had developed into a smooth operation with a powerful underlying desire to "get it right" is finished. The lights are turned off.

The darkened stage nine was occupied by the *Enterprise* standing set. The last technicians leaving the familiar ship looked back with the performers who had strolled through these rooms and corridors, projecting themselves forward in time.

There was a cast and crew party later that day. People drank and joked, talking about what they would do with their time and where they would work next. Good-byes were said, small talk was exchanged, and appointments were made to "come to my place for dinner in a week or so." People left the studio that day smiling, because they had been a part of something very special. They had assisted in the production of a magic that had brought people closer together. They had helped to make "Star Trek," and though the series was over the ideas behind the series were not and there were good times to be remembered. Undoubtedly, some in the cast and crew thought that maybe someday they would all be back together doing "Star Trek" again

Syndication: A Cure for Withdrawal Symptoms

On the night of June 3, 1969, "Star Trek" fans shared these sensations. "Star Trek" wasn't really finished; the fans would not let it be finished. As Captain Kirk had so emotionally said in "This Side of Paradise"; "No . . . I Won't Leave!" And nobody really did.[9] As the last Trek reruns began on NBC, the fans anticipated what they could do to lessen the blow of "Star Trek's" cancellation.

More fanzines were introduced, in which the Trek fans devised their own imaginative "Star Trek" adventures, artwork, poetry, and trivia lists. "Star Trek" memorabilia was at a premium. Gene Roddenberry and Majel Barrett had started a mail order company called Star Trek Enterprises (also known as Lincoln Enterprises), through which they sold such treasures as original Trek scripts, photos, and artwork; even the original "Star Trek" 35mm motion picture footage, cut into individual frames for mounting as slides. They continued (and still do) to sell their line of merchandise, and were in fact so deluged with orders that for a time fans had to wait for months to receive their treasures in their mailboxes. Gene and Majel were probably pleasantly surprised when they continued to sell large quantities of film clips suitable for mounting, picture postcards of the Enterprise crew, studio biographies of the "Star Trek" cast, and other materials that they soon added to their inventory. (Their catalogue has been expanded several times, and is still available by mail from Lincoln Enterprises, Box 38429, Hollywood, California 90038.)

The phenomenon of "syndication" now entered the picture. The "Star Trek" episodes were formerly marketed only to NBC's affiliate stations all over the United States. There were now countless other markets to be considered by Paramount Television. Paramount prepared a "syndication kit," listing all the episodes in their original production order. The other necessary print and publicity materials were prepared. The trade papers were called, and press releases were sent to the newspapers. Paramount was ready to distribute "Star Trek" all around the world.

In its syndication brochure, Paramount mentioned the honors that had been accorded to "Star Trek." Of particular interest were two statements, one that credited "Star Trek" as being "the recipient of over one million letters of support and encouragement from a worldwide space oriented populace," and another that called Trek "one of the NBC Television network's highest audience response shows."

By 1978 "Star Trek" had made syndication history. The series was being seen over 300 times per week worldwide, in 134 markets in the United States and 131 international markets located in 51 countries. "Star Trek" was being seen translated into forty-two languages. At the start of 1978, there were 371 "Star Trek" fan clubs and 431 fanzines were being produced, and approximately thirty Trek conventions were being held each year.

Conventions

In June 1971, a group of East Coast science fiction fans held a modest gathering in a New Jersey public library to honor "Star Trek." Art was displayed on the walls and a comedy skit was performed. Panel discussions and individual lectures were given concerning not only "Star Trek" but other well-loved science fiction film projects as well. I was very nervous as I stood in front of the gathering and spoke about the history of filmed science fiction. I also appeared as "Mr. Sulu" in the comedy skit. By definition, this gathering would have to be called one of the first "Star Trek" conventions; perhaps *the* first. But nobody thought of it as such back then.

Two "Star Trek" fans were instrumental in planning the New Jersey gathering. Elyse Pines (now Elyse Rosenstein) was a member of one of the first Trek fan groups. Devra Langsam (co-publisher of "Spockanalia," one of the first "Star Trek" fanzines) was a children's librarian in a Brooklyn library. After the New Jersey gathering they began discussing what were at first casual plans to stage a small get-together for some of the Trek fans who had tried to keep the series from being cancelled. It was a waste of time, they were told by some other fans. Nobody would come; it was all over. But they kept talking about it, and eventually other fans (including Joan Winston, currently an executive at ABC Television and a successful author) joined the discussions. Before long, the discussions were taking place at regular intervals in the participants' homes.

These fans became known as "The Committee." Their convention, as they envisioned it, would be of modest size. If they were lucky, they might get a decent number of people. Maybe.

At that time, Elyse was attending Brooklyn College. Many of the college's mass-media students were "Star Trek" fans; and an evening was planned to honor both science fiction and "Trek." I was contacted to appear and give a short talk on the "Star Trek" fan movement, talk trivia, and discuss the upcoming convention.

I arrived at the college's Gershwin Auditorium where the program was to take place. The place could easily hold approximately 200 people, I was told. I had no trouble entering; it was still early. As I waited with some friends for the events to begin, I noticed that people were pouring into the room steadily and very quickly. Soon all the seats were taken, and people began to seek out comfortable positions in the aisles.

Photographing the full-size component of the Starbase Six exterior for "The Menagerie."

In the completed effect, the bush and a portion of the wall are gone, but an entire starbase has appeared in "The Menagerie."

Before long, people were standing against the walls, between the rows of seats.

As I started to give my short lecture, I saw that people were also sitting on top of other people. It was early in December, and piles of heavy coats placed by the doors finally stopped the entrance of additional courageous fans. I recall thinking about what would happen if we were forced to leave the room in a rush, or if I wanted to run screaming from the room before my lecture was finished. It was almost impossible to enter or leave the auditorium.

Elyse, meanwhile, had finished her last class for the day and was approaching the building. She saw many people barring her entrance into the auditorium. Fortunately, Elyse knew of another entrance into the place, and she eventually joined me in the room. Many of the crowd asked questions about the convention, which I referred to Elyse. Then someone asked how many people were expected to come to the convention. Elyse and I looked around this crowded room, and a silent realization caused us to look at each other. "Oh my Ghod," we thought. We had to get to a telephone as soon as possible to tell Joan Winston and the other Committee members that if the whole of New York City was anything like Brooklyn, we were going to have our hands full keeping people from overcrowding the hotel. After that evening, there was no doubt in my mind that the first "Star Trek" Committee convention of 1972 was going to be successful in terms of attendance.

By the time of the 1972 convention, "Star Trek" merchandise was available everywhere. There were shirts with pictures of the "Star Trek" characters and vehicles, and buttons, bumper stickers, decorative posters, and home-made duplicates of props were being sold through fan organizations, by individual fans, or by dealers most of whom were interested only in the proverbial "quick buck." The beginnings of the trend had been set.

Meanwhile, the "Star Trek" cast found itself in a new, collective role; that of "convention guests." Each succeeding convention attempted to hire more cast members than had ever appeared anywhere before under one roof. The earliest conventions were especially great because fans saw the genuine happiness that resulted when these old friends found themselves back together.

The conventions grew rapidly, and with them expanded the entire "Star Trek" fan movement. The Committee continued to hold its annual gatherings, and others staged responsible conventions that entertained their paying customers. But there were also the professional showmen. Every convention promoter with financial backing became a self-proclaimed lover of "Star Trek." Each promoter usually claimed that the others were "fake fans," interested only in making money. The exploitation of the fans reached its peak when a Chicago-based promoter's convention jammed the swank New York Hilton hotel in what can only be described as a reenactment of the overcrowding in "The Mark of Gideon." Current "Star Trek" conventions have stabilized into pleasurable gatherings where fans can ignore the commercialism in favor of seeing their favorite stars or meeting new friends.

Today there is *Star Trek—The Motion Picture*, which set box-office records during its first week in release. "Star Trek" is definitely a special sort of phenomenon to inspire such amazing interest a full ten years after its cancellation. Perhaps we can determine some of the reasons for "Trek's" lasting following by examining the series from its beginnings. This, quite logically, is the cue for the next chapter.

NOTES

1. *New York World Journal-Tribune,* 16 September, 1966.

2. *TV Guide* "fall preview issue," 10–16 September, 1966, p. 47.

3. *TV Guide,* 25–31 March, 1967.

4. *Newsday,* 27 January, 1968, p. 8, "Star Trek To Learn Its Fate Soon: Exec." Reported picketing at NBC's Burbank, California, and New York installations. Gene Roddenberry stated Trek was receiving 6,000 letters per week, including fan letters received from New York Governor Nelson Rockefeller, and Dr. Isaac Asimov. Roddenberry said of Asimov: " 'Star Trek' is the only show he watches."

NBC confirmed receiving 16,000 letters of protest.

5. Ibid. Roddenberry stated: "The network once said to me, 'Come on, Rodd—, you're behind all this.' Well, if I could get demonstrations going whenever I wanted, I'd go into politics."

6. "Squawk About Series' Spot," *New York Daily News,* 26 March, 1968.

7. Patrick McGoohan's British TV series "The Prisoner," distributed by ITC and still enjoying a large "cult" following, was originally televised in the U.S. on the CBS network. All of the episodes were run on CBS except one. The lone exception, "Living in Harmony," was a surrealistic western adventure that was reportedly omitted from CBS' schedule because its opening did not conform to the other episodes of that series.

8. WNBC interrupted this telecast for ten minutes to relay the first reports on the New Jersey primary elections, only fifteen minutes after the polls had closed. WNBC telephone switchboard operators reported a flood of calls following the interruption.

"Annoyance at Election Returns Interruption," *The New York Times,* 4 June, 1969.

9. "End of the Trek?" *Newsweek* magazine, 29 December, 1968. 500 Cal Tech students protested at NBC in Burbank when possible cancellation was announced.

Canadian fans in British Columbia took out a newspaper ad reading "Unite and Save the Show."

1,764 signatures appeared on a petition started by students at the Andrews School for Girls in Willoughby, Ohio, possibly to protest that 20 percent of the NBC affiliates in the South and Midwest elected to carry "Grand Ole Opry" instead of "Star Trek."

2 The Beginnings

"Star Trek's" Ancestors

The "Star Trek" universe exists because of the initial inspiration and efforts of Gene Roddenberry. "Star Trek," though, like all other works of art, did not evolve spontaneously from the head of its creator. Roddenberry, an avid follower of science fiction, drew upon his own memories of stories written by other authors. Various science fiction motion pictures probably also contributed to Trek's conception and evolution.

"Star Trek's" framework was originally very different than the series with which we are familiar. "The Cage," "Where No Man Has Gone Before," "The Corbomite Maneuver," and other early episodes shaped the *Enterprise* and its crew, with assists from other inspired creations.

> Rest enough for the individual man. Too much of it and too soon, and we call it death. But for Man no rest and no ending. He must go on, conquest beyond conquest. First this little planet and its winds and ways, and all the laws of mind and matter that restrain him. Then the planets about him, and at last out across immensity to the stars. And when he has conquered all the deeps of space and all the mysteries of time, still he will be beginning.

This could certainly be one of Captain Kirk's innumerable pep talks, but it's not; the speech is from the final scene of the film *Things to Come* (released by United Artists in 1936). The author of the screenplay and the original book on which the film was based was H. G. Wells.[1] In the midst of threats of World War II, Wells had these optimistic thoughts about the future of the human race, united and dedicated to scientific exploration.

In *Things to Come* we find two men of opposing views interacting in scientific matters. The technologically fearful character Passworthy wonders what exploration is all about, and whether it can really lead to human happiness. He is assured by Cabal, the future president of Earth, that exploration is not only good for humanity; it is mankind's only hope. Their exchange of views sounds almost like a rehearsal between Kirk (or Spock) and McCoy.

The Invisible Ray (Universal–1936) featured an invention that overtook light rays that had left our world centuries before. These rays could then be reflected back to Earth, and the resulting images could be watched on a large viewing screen. Animation was used in conjunction with other optical effects to depict multiple layers of stars, planets, and meteorites rushing toward the screen. The effect was very similar to the space panoramas seen on the U.S.S. *Enterprise* bridge.

The ray in this film was powered by an unearthly element, just as dilithium crystals focus the matter-antimatter power of the *Enterprise*. Properly focused, the device could dissolve cataracts in the eyes of blind people, or cause boulders and statues to melt. It was an expansion on the principle of the laser, which is particularly weird since the laser had not yet been invented. The optical effect of the ray was also an animated overlay that was identical in principle to the phaser beams produced for "Star Trek" by various optical effects experts.

Buck Rogers (Universal serial–1939) featured a small, glass-walled room called an "atom chamber." By entering and working the controls, a person could be bombarded with energies that would convert him into energy and then reconstitute him into matter once more in a different place. This serial version of the transporter required a duplicate receiver unit at the other end of the transmission. The optical effects devised for these scenes seemed to be "erasing" the subject in a swirling pattern of light, rather than the glittery particles of "Star Trek's" device.

The hand weapons in *Buck Rogers* were ray guns; when fired, they emitted beams of multipatterned light. There was also a ray cannon with which a spaceship was rendered invisible. Like the Romulan cloaking device, the ray cannon used large amounts of power and was not completely dependable.

The Day the Earth Stood Still (20th Century-Fox–1951) featured a stoic, logical alien visitor to Earth who advised our planet to join his organization of civilized planets and practice peace, so that we would ". . . be free to pursue more profitable enterprises." Klaatu, the film's ambassador, might very well have been a major inspiration when Mr. Spock's characteristics were being developed.

Klaatu did not smoke or drink; his people did not gamble and apparently held their emotions in check. He had superior strength and a great quantity of curiosity when it came to dealing with our alien culture. When Klaatu wanted to impress the Earth with his people's power, he staged a demonstration similar to that used by Scotty in "Bread and Circuses"; he cut off all power on Earth (while permitting the operation of hospital machines, planes in flight, and other emergency procedures). His robot, Gort, fired a destructive phaser-type beam. The bridge of Klaatu's circular spaceship looked something like a miniature version of the *Enterprise* bridge.

"Rocky Jones: Space Ranger" is a little-remembered television series that was produced between 1952 and 1956 by Roland Reed Productions in Hollywood. Although the series was filmed with younger viewers in mind, there were some startling similarities to "Star Trek."

Rocky Jones worked for an organization called the United Worlds, instead of the United Federation of Planets. He flew his rocketships *(The Orbit Jet* and *The Silver Moon)* to interplanetary trouble spots and provided whatever understanding aid was needed. He was answerable directly to Secretary Drake, who usually let Rocky have his own way. Rocky handled all types of emergencies, including the evacuation of doomed planets and the uncovering of villainous plots against the United Worlds. Rocky also came up against a race of space pirates who specialized in attacking Earth's defensive space stations and looked just as hostile as the Klingons.

The larger United Worlds ships were equipped with "cold light," an invention that bombarded the molecular structure of the vessels with incredible cold, causing them to become invisible (their explanation was as incredible as the cold they supposedly generated).

One friendly planetary ruler, Juliandra, the Suzeraine of Herculon (played by actress Ann Robinson who also appeared in Paramount's 1953 classic *The War of the Worlds),* sent her most loyal subject to Earth to be trained as a United Worlds spaceship pilot. For a time, Rocky's first officer was this humanoid, a friendly fellow named Biffen Cardoza.

"Rocky Jones" also came equipped with the usual space suits, ray guns, budget problems, and a blonde, miniskirted crewwoman named Vina. (Where have I heard that name before?). Many unusual looking buildings in the Los Angeles area were used as outdoor locations. Preexisting furniture was frequently used; exactly the same type of "freebies" sought by "Star Trek's" production people.

Whereas everyone in "Star Trek" wears black T-shirts, Rocky and his crew wore white ones that bore the United Worlds emblem (a ringed planet). There were also cute little hats with the same symbol. For special duty, the men wore outer jackets that bore a slight resemblance to Admiral Kirk's garment.

Besides being aimed at children, "Rocky Jones" also differed from "Star Trek" because its episodes were serialized. Three half-hour segments made up a complete adventure (although half-hour, self-contained episodes were also produced). "Rocky's" producers

were conscious of interesting background music, and the series boasted electronic melodies created especially for a TV series (composed by Alexander Laszlo) years before Alexander Courage used electronic-type music in "The Cage" and "The Man Trap" on "Star Trek."

This Island Earth (Universal–1955) was a special-effects movie milestone photographed in Technicolor. Imaginative views of the planet Earth seen from outer space were similar to those seen in various "Star Trek" episodes. An interplanetary flying saucer designed for the film bore a resemblance to the saucer section of the U.S.S. *Enterprise.* Its interior viewscreen exhibited fields of stars like those from Trek episodes.

This Island Earth also featured "thermal barriers" and other effects produced using specially photographed, tinted smoke; the same techniques that appear in "The Galileo Seven" and "Obsession" episodes on "Star Trek." The optical paintings created for the alien city on "Metaluna" are the same in principle as those created for "The Cage," "Where No Man Has Gone Before," and other Trek installments. The one-piece suits worn within the saucer ship were very similar to those worn in "The Devil in the Dark," "By Any Other Name," and "The Trouble with Tribbles," and oversized head appliances created for the aliens are similar in concept to those seen in "The Empath."

Whereas *This Island Earth* combined science fiction devices with the fantasy-oriented action of the old serials, *Forbidden Planet* was decidedly more aligned with the future. Produced by Metro-Goldwyn-Mayer in 1956, *Forbidden Planet* has a great deal in common with "Star Trek."

The saucer-shaped starship of *Forbidden Planet* was dispatched to the planet Altair Four by the United Planets. Captain J. J. Adams of the starship took calculated personal risks together with his friends "Doc" Ostrow and romantically inclined first officer Jerry Farman (the opposite of Mr. Spock). The crew included an efficient security detail, and an engineer who could fix anything (and he did not stop for breakfast). The military attitude in the crew seemed relaxed among the ship's officers.

"Doc" was not only his captain's friend but his psychiatric "watchdog" as well; the same relationship that exists between Kirk and McCoy.

Forbidden Planet's spaceship was capable of accelerating from "space normal" speed to "hyperdrive." When the ship decelerated, the crew mounted a circular platform. They stood on slightly elevated pedestals and were temporarily transformed into their energy components; beams of greenish light suspended between two points, above and below the individual.

The command bridge of the cruiser named the "C-57D" was circular. At the communications console sat the ship's engineer (played by Richard Anderson, Oscar Goldman of Universal Pictures' bionic TV series), who wore a miniature earphone-speaker device not unlike that worn by Lieutenant Uhura. His station was operated with sliding controls, like those seen in the *Enterprise* transporter room. The control panels scattered across the bridge of the C-57D were "butterfly"-shaped, like those aboard the *Enterprise*. They featured clear plastic circular indicators.

The *Forbidden Planet* crew never left their spaceship without weapons belts, which also included communications devices. Their defensive sidearms were called "blasters," and also existed as larger rifles and ship's cannon. Like the first phasers of "Star Trek," the props in the *Forbidden Planet* were built to emit light beams intended to cue the animation-effects artists.

Props and decorations in *Forbidden Planet* are like those in "Star Trek," from the modernistic furniture in Morbius' home to the archway leading to the Krel laboratories. Commander Adams used a voice-amplifying device similar in shape to the universal translator featured in "Metamorphosis."

Forbidden Planet was produced at one of Hollywood's finest studios, by a staff of practiced motion picture artists who had never before worked on a science fiction film. Like Gene Roddenberry's hand-picked production staff, the *Forbidden Planet* staff used their imaginations to the fullest while avoiding most unfavorable clichés identified with science fiction efforts produced up to that time. Devices and terminologies were carefully assembled to convey credibility rather than fantasy.

The Father of "Star Trek"

In the decade that gave birth to *Forbidden Planet,* the people who created motion pictures were usually overlooked in favor of the more obvious personalities; "the stars." Only occasionally did a writer, director, or producer achieve personal fame as a result of Academy Awards or gossip-column scandals. Only rarely did a movie maker emerge whose real life exploits could match the fictional dynamism of the movies.

When "Star Trek" made its debut, many of the series' fans were unacquainted with creator/producer/writer Gene Roddenberry's background. To some, it seemed as if he came out of nowhere to bring "Star Trek" to life. But just as "Star Trek" did not spring into existence overnight, neither did Gene Roddenberry. He had previously undergone true life experiences that enabled him to devise "Star Trek" with all its excitement and realism.

Roddenberry was born in El Paso, Texas, on August 19, 1921. His father was a cavalry officer, stationed at Fort Bliss, Texas (which was suitably the site of early U.S. rocket experiments). Roddenberry grew up in Los Angeles, and while he was in junior high school he had his first exposure to science fiction. After graduating from high school, Roddenberry majored in prelaw at Los Angeles City College, and three years later he switched to engineering at U.C.L.A.

Gene was fascinated with flying and after earning his pilot's license he left college and became a cadet in the U.S. Army Air Corps. The United States had just entered World War II, and after his Air Corps training Roddenberry was sent to Guadalcanal, out of which he flew eighty-nine combat and reconnaissance missions. While experiencing this excitement, he began to write stories that he sold to flying magazines.

After the war, Gene investigated airplane crashes for the Air Staff, while living in Washington, D.C. (where *Star Trek—The Motion Picture* was premiered). He then went to work for Pan American Airlines and piloted flights to some of the most exotic areas of the world.

While handling the Calcutta route, he lived in New York City and attended Columbia University studying literature. At this point, Gene Roddenberry's life almost ended.

On a flight out of Calcutta, his plane crashed in flames in the Syrian desert. Roddenberry, the senior officer on the flight, directed two uninjured passengers to search for help while Gene stayed and talked with natives who had come to loot the plane. The two passengers reached a Syrian Army outpost, which sent a plane to pick up Roddenberry. Reaching the outpost, Roddenberry broadcast a radio message that was relayed to Pan American. A rescue airliner was dispatched to the scene. Roddenberry and seven others were the only survivors of the India to Istanbul flight. Gene was later awarded a Civil Aeronautics commendation for his heroic behavior during and after the crash.

In 1949, having experienced sufficient drama in the air, Roddenberry moved to Los Angeles with the intention of creating drama for television. In Los Angeles, he was advised to find employment either as a newspaperman or a policeman because both of these jobs provided sufficient free time in which to write. Gene joined the Los Angeles Police Department.

Patrolman Gene Roddenberry was still an adventurer. In addition to the relatively mundane traffic detail, Roddenberry worked the jail wards and assisted in conducting investigations. He was then assigned the exotic (and dangerous) "skid row" beat. Like all other patrolmen on this detail, Roddenberry looked for trouble while hoping he wouldn't find any, or that *it* wouldn't find *him*. He came in contact with police informants, narcotics users, drug dealers, prostitutes, and other sociological innovators. He had his share of close calls, lonely moments walking through dark alleys, and rain-soaked patrols that resembled scenes from old Warner Brothers' gangster movies.

While Roddenberry was experiencing this firsthand research into city life, he was also developing an interest in the enormous narcotics problem that was plaguing American communities. He began to correlate his findings based upon his on-the-job experiences, and supplemented these with research into police records and library sources. Promoted to the head of research in the office of Los Angeles' Chief of Police William Parker, Gene was easily able to prepare realistic and constructive studies on narcotics addiction.

By now, most of Gene's time was spent in writing his studies and speeches for Chief Parker. At this time, he began to "moonlight" as a TV writer, producing his first TV treatments and scripts under pseudonyms. In 1951, Roddenberry sold his first TV script, and in 1952 he made his first science-fiction script sale, "The Secret Defense of 117," televised on "Chevron Theatre" (starring Ricardo Montalban).

Roddenberry's script ideas were attractive to such series as "Dragnet," because of his familiarity with police procedure and terminology. He was probably the most qualified script writer to write about ". . . The city, Los Angeles, California . . . ," as the original "Dragnet" introductions stated. It is not known how many times Officers Joe Friday (Jack Webb) dramatized Officer Gene Roddenberry's experiences.

In 1954, Roddenberry left the Los Angeles police force and went to work as a full-time writer. His other television sales include episodes for "Dr. Christian," "Dr. Kildare," "Four Star Theatre," "Have Gun Will Travel" (Roddenberry became head writer for this series), "Highway Patrol," "The Jane Wyman Show," "The Kaiser Aluminum Hour," "Naked City," "Robert Taylor's Detectives," and "West Point" (for which he worked as a staff writer). One police drama, To Wear a Badge, was written for "Target the Corruptors" in 1961 by Roddenberry and Harry Essex. (Essex' short story, "The Electrical Man," was adapted into the motion picture *Man-Made Monster* by Universal in 1941. It was Lon Chaney, Jr.'s, first starring role at Universal. In 1953, for the same studio, Essex wrote the screenplay for *It Came from Outer Space,* based upon a story by Ray Bradbury.)

In 1963, while producing his series "The Lieutenant" for MGM Television, Roddenberry was also thinking very seriously about "Star Trek."

"The Lieutenant," an hour-long series about the U.S. Marine Corps in peacetime, starred Gary Lockwood (Lieutenant Bill Rice) and Robert Vaughn (Captain Ray Rambridge). It did not last long, and MGM had asked Roddenberry to come up with another series idea just in case "The Lieutenant" failed to catch on. At this time Gene went to work and prepared the first draft of his "Star Trek" format. Dated March 11, 1964, this sixteen-page outline of Trek is the first printed record of the series' evolution. A revised version of the format is printed in *The Making of Star Trek.* This earlier draft is longer than the published version.[2] There are also some differences in the contents of both formats.

The first draft refers to Navigator Jose Ortega (later changed to Tyler) and omits all mention of his diversified parental backgrounds. Without the inclusion of these later elaborations, Mr. Spock would probably never have evolved to include *his* divided background. The ship's doctor, Phillip "Bones" Boyce, is aged fifty-one in the earlier treatment, and "well into his fifties" in the later draft. The revised version also specifies his continuous disagreements with Tyler; another sign that Tyler's characteristics were later transferred into the character of Mr. Spock. The starship in the earlier draft is the "S.S. *Yorktown*" rather than the U.S.S. *Enterprise.* Its maximum speed is stated to be .73 light year per hour.

Roddenberry's first draft promises possibilities of "shockingly exciting differences"; an observation that suggests the origin of the IDIC concept (Infinite Diversity in Infinite Combinations). The first draft format also features twenty-five possible episode titles accompanied by short synopses. These titles are:

1. "The Next Cage"
2. "The Day Charlie Became God"
3. "President Capone"
4. "To Skin a Tyrannosaurus"
5. "The Women"
6. "The Coming"
7. "The Perfect World"
8. "Mr. Socrates"
9. "The Stranger"
10. "The Man Trap"
11. "Camelot Revisited"
12. "100 A. B."
13. "Kentucky, Kentucky"
14. "Reason"
15. "Reason II"
16. "A Matter of Choice"
17. "The Radiant One"
18. "The Trader"
19. "A Question of Cannibalism"
20. "The Mirror"
21. "Torx"
22. "The Pet Shop"
23. "Kongo"
24. "The Venus Planet"
25. "Infection"

Some of these concepts are extremely familiar, having been adapted for actual "Star Trek" episodes. "The Next Cage" and "A Matter of Choice" were combined in "The Cage." "The Day Charlie Became God" developed into "Charlie X," "President Capone" became "A Piece of the Action," and "The Women" became "Mudd's Women." Elements of "The Coming" and "Mr. Socrates" were incorporated into "Bread and Circuses," "The Man Trap" contains features found in "Shore Leave," and "100 A.B. (After the Bomb)" became "The Omega Glory." "The Mirror" developed into "Mirror, Mirror."

Several of these ideas are suggestive of non-Trek

productions. "To Skin a Tyrannosaurus," pitting modern men against prehistoric perils fought with slings and clubs, is reminiscent of a "Space: 1999" episode, "Full Circle," in which Moonbase Alpha personnel reverted (for a temporary period) to cavemen. "The Stranger" involves an alien intelligence that has smuggled itself aboard the *Enterprise*. "Infection" has a female crew member discovered to be pregnant with the larvae of an alien. These concepts, combined, suggest other science fiction tales, including the motion picture *Alien*. "The Pet Shop," in which women are the masters of men, treats men as though they were "pets," a situation similar to that seen in Gene Roddenberry's 1974 TV pilot, "Planet Earth."

Outline for "The Cage"

Metro-Goldwyn-Mayer seemed enthusiastic about "Star Trek" at first, but they did not buy Roddenberry's format. Looking for definite interest in his project, Gene approached Desilu Studios. In April 1964, Desilu signed Roddenberry to a three-year contract, during which he would develop and produce television pilots for them. Desilu, which derived its name from its founders DESI Arnaz and LUcille Ball, had an imaginative vice president named Oscar Katz. After an unsuccessful attempt to interest CBS in the "Star Trek" format, Katz interested NBC in the series idea. Mort Werner, NBC's vice president in charge of programming, persuaded NBC to provide Roddenberry with $20,000 to be used for writing three story ideas based upon Gene's "Star Trek" format. One of those three stories, "The Cage," was chosen as the series' pilot script.

The full story outline for "The Cage," dated June 29, 1964, is printed in *The Making of Star Trek*.[3] The title of "Star Trek's" first pilot was changed to "The Menagerie" before it was completed. To avoid confusion between this original pilot, and the later, aired two-part episode "The Menagerie," this pilot is referred to as "The Cage" throughout this book.

The aliens in this story are described as six-limbed crablike creatures, which are difficult things to portray on a television budget. Puppets or costumed actors would have proven unconvincing, and stop-motion miniatures would have been too expensive.

Additional dream sequences were originally planned. April and Vina were shown as a married couple in Renaissance Italy. Earlier in the story, April had betrayed a fascination for "simpler times." In the final draft, Captain Pike wishes to retire to a horse ranch; here, it's a Renaissance household.

Instead of a picnic near the Captain's hometown, April and Vina were shown living high above a Terran city in the year 2049 A.D. "Star Trek's" original conception was taking place only ninety-six years in the future. The year was later moved ahead; in "Space Seed," Kirk reveals that his era is two centuries in the future. *Star Trek—The Motion Picture* takes place in the twenty-third century.

In one scene, April used a smuggled tool to escape from his cell and confront the Keeper, killing him. Although this entire sequence was later revealed as an illusion in the treatment, it would have showed that April hated the Keeper enough to kill him without hesitation. This would not have spoken too well for mankind's attitudes in the *Enterprise*'s era.

As April and Vina escaped, continuing this illusion, they encountered some weird characters. First came a six-legged Rigelian spider ape, another expensive and difficult costume to create. In the final draft, this character was changed to an Earth-type furry creature with four limbs. (It appears in "The Cage," but is missing in "The Menagerie.") Next came an odd fellow described as a cross between a snake and an angel. A serpentlike structure formed its body, another unnecessarily complex challenge to create. An intelligent lemur-type creature from Arcturus was next. This entity could have been portrayed inexpensively, using an animal with optically inserted human eyes. Unearthly, semiunderstandable speech could have been dubbed in to add to this effect. Roddenberry was careful to suggest that April's cage was to be positioned so that it did not point directly toward any other cage to avoid showing too many expensive views of these aliens.

Surprisingly, the aliens in the outline mentioned that their ethics would not permit them to be responsible for the deaths of intelligent entities. It may have been this strong belief in the sacred nature of all life forms that led Roddenberry to institute the "Prime Directive."

The completed story outline was submitted to the network in June, 1964. Had the project been rejected at this stage, "Star Trek" would have been like the Talosians' hope for a future; an illusion, a dream that might have been. But thus far, "Star Trek" was in luck. The network gave the go-ahead to develop the outline into a completed script. The synopsis of this script follows.

"The Cage": A Synopsis

The U.S.S. *Enterprise*, under the command of Captain Christopher Pike, is en route to the nearest Federation starbase for rest, recreation, repairs, and replacement of personnel. The damage has been suffered during the exploration of Rigel VII, resulting in the deaths of three *Enterprise* crewmen and seven injuries, including chief science officer Lieutenant Spock.

Despite the status of his ship, Captain Pike decides to investigate signs that a spaceship may have crashed

The final version of the Rigel Fortress matte painting is extremely realistic in "The Cage."

on planet Talos IV, one of eleven worlds in the Talos group. A landing party is selected consisting of Pike, Lieutenant Spock, Dr. Phillip Boyce, Navigator Jose Tyler, and others. Number One, the ship's female first officer, is left in command of the *Enterprise.*

Beaming down, the landing party is startled to find an encampment created from makeshift tents and old spaceship parts. A band of ragged survivors comes forward and the leader introduces himself as Dr. Theodore Haskins of the American Continent Institute and states that the aged men are all surviving scientists marooned on the planet when their ship, the S.S. *Columbia,* crashed almost a decade ago.

A beautiful young woman comes forward and is introduced as Vina, who was just a child when the ship had crashed. Captain Pike is attracted to Vina. Watching his evident attraction to her are several aliens concealed underground who view the scene on a strange television-type screen, while also "hearing" the thoughts of the captain.

When Vina lures Pike to a rock formation to show him the secret of how the old scientists have survived, the small, large-headed aliens emerge from a concealed elevator. Rendering Pike unconscious, they drag him into the elevator, which closes within the rock. Spock and Tyler have witnessed what has happened, but run to the scene too late to help their captain. Their laser pistols fail to gain them access to the concealed elevator shaft. Meanwhile, the survivors' encampment has vanished. Mr. Spock calls the *Enterprise* and informs the crew that the entire en-

campment was an illusion, and that Captain Pike has been kidnapped.

Captain Pike awakens in a small enclosure, fronted by a superstrong, transparent material. The little aliens, led by the Keeper, approach his cage and converse telepathically, angering Pike by their references to him as a specimen of an inferior species. After the Talosians leave, Pike is startled to see Vina materialize in his cage. Vina tells Pike that she is the only real portion of the illusion, having actually been the lone survivor of the S.S. *Columbia* crash. The Talosians have lured the *Enterprise* to their planet so that Pike can serve as a mate for Vina, enabling the Talosians to breed a race of humanoids.

When Captain Pike refuses to perform as the Talosians wish, the aliens try to get him interested in Vina by presenting her to him within various illusions designed to spark his masculine instincts. Vina, dressed in medieval garb, is defended by Pike against a giant Rigellian warrior. Pike also perceives Vina as a green-skinned Orion slave girl, and as his "wife," accompanying him on a picnic near his home town on Earth. When Pike fails to respond to the Talosians' satisfaction, he is reminded that they can give him both pleasure and pain. For an instant, Pike finds himself in a hellish environment, surrounded by fire and brimstone.

Failing to blast through the rock face of the concealed entrance to the Talosians' underground civilization, an *Enterprise* landing party prepares to have itself transported underground. Immediately before the transporter is activated, however, the two females in the party vanish and the machine fails to function.

Number One, together with Yeoman Colt, materialize within Captain Pike's cage. The Talosians reason that if the captain is not sufficiently attracted to Vina, perhaps he will be more attracted to either, or both of, his crewwomen. Examining Number One's laser pistol, Pike finds it completely drained of energy, but he has his suspicions about this. He has determined that the Talosians cannot probe into hostile emotional moods, and he talks himself into an apparent attitude of mindless anger. Throwing the lasers to the floor near the wall of his cage, Pike sits and waits. As he anticipated, the Keeper's arms enter the cell through a concealed doorway in the wall to remove the pistols. Acting quickly, Pike grabs the alien and, as Number One holds onto the tricky Talosian, Pike tries to shoot a hole in the transparent portion of the cage. He threatens to shoot directly at the Keeper, and a hole instantly materializes in the window. The weapon had actually worked, just as the *Enterprise* laser cannon had functioned, but the Talosians have prevented the *Enterprise* people from seeing the destruction their weapons had actually caused.

Using the Keeper as a shield, Pike and the others ascend in the elevator to the surface of Talos IV and learn the truth. Centuries ago, the Talosians had wrecked the surface of the planet with a nuclear war and were forced to move their civilization underground, resulting in their increased mental abilities and their inability to produce children. After Pike threatens to commit suicide with the laser pistols, the Talosians confide to him that they never wanted slaves; they simply wished to perpetuate their heritage in the offspring of Pike and Vina.

Number One and Yeoman Colt are returned to the *Enterprise,* and the Talosians reveal the truth about Vina. She had actually survived the spaceship crash, but was horribly injured and disfigured. Without the aid of the Talosians' illusions, Vina is really a deformed, middle-aged woman. To avoid making Vina unhappy, Pike instructs the Talosians to create the illusion that he is staying behind with the Terran woman. Standing side by side with the Keeper, Pike watches Vina walking happily away with an illusion of himself. Beamed back up to the *Enterprise,* Captain Pike refuses to discuss what occurred after Number One and Yeoman Colt were returned to the ship, and the U.S.S. *Enterprise* leaves Talos IV.

The People Who Made "The Cage"

A motion picture, whether produced for television or theatrical release, is only as good as the people who contribute their talents to the production. It is no

The laser canon from "The Cage" was never used in another episode.

accident when a film is a successful project; "Star Trek's" success owes a lot to Gene Roddenberry's unceasing efforts to employ the best available artists, both in front of and behind the cameras. Here is the most complete list of credits on "The Cage" that has ever been published.

THE CAGE

Episode #1

Pilot story outline   6/29/64

First draft script   9/8/64

Some opticals began filming in middle
September 1964

Revised script   11/20/64

Final title   "The Menagerie"

Filmed in late November, early and middle
December, 1964

Production Credits

PRODUCER   Gene Roddenberry

WRITER   Gene Roddenberry

DIRECTOR   Robert Butler

ASSOCIATE PRODUCER   Byron Haskin

DIRECTOR OF PHOTOGRAPHY   William E. Snyder

CAMERA OPERATOR   Jerry Finnerman

ART DIRECTORS   Franz Bachelin, Pato Guzman

ASSISTANT ART DIRECTOR   Walter M. Jefferies

USS ENTERPRISE DESIGNED BY   Gene Roddenberry,
Walter M. Jefferies

MUSIC COMPOSED AND CONDUCTED BY   Alexander
Courage

COSTUMES CREATED BY   William Ware Theiss
FILM EDITOR   Leo Shreve
ASSISTANT TO THE PRODUCER   Morris Chapnick
FIRST ASSISTANT DIRECTOR   Robert H. Justman
SET DECORATOR   Ed M. Parbers
SOUND MIXER   Stanford G. Houghton
PHOTOGRAPHIC EFFECTS   Howard A. Anderson Co.
SPECIAL EFFECTS   Joe Lombardi
PROPERTY MASTER   Jack Briggs
GAFFER   Bob Campbell
PRODUCTION SUPERVISOR   James A. Paisley
MAKEUP ARTIST   Fred B. Phillips
HAIRSTYLES   Gertrude Reade
RESEARCH   Kellam De Forest
SPECIAL SCIENTIFIC CONSULTANT   Harvey P. Lynn, Jr.

Cast

CAPTAIN CHRISTOPHER PIKE   Jeffrey Hunter
MR. SPOCK   Leonard Nimoy
NAVIGATOR JOSE "JOE" TYLER   Peter Duryea
NUMBER ONE   Majel Barrett (M. Leigh Hudec)
CHIEF PETTY OFFICER GARRISON   Adam Roarke
DR. PHILLIP "BONES" BOYCE   John Hoyt
YEOMAN J. M. COLT   Laurel Goodwin
GEOLOGIST   Ed Madden
TRANSPORTER CHIEF PITCAIRN   Clegg Hoyt
DR. THEODORE HASKINS (1ST SURVIVOR)   Jon Lormer
2ND SURVIVOR   Leonard Mudie
3RD SURVIVOR   Anthony Jochim
VINA   Susan Oliver
THE KEEPER   Meg Wyllie
1ST TALOSIAN   Georgia Schmidt
2ND TALOSIAN   Serena Sand
ORION SPACE OFFICER   Robert Phillips
ORION TRADER   Joseph Mell
Jeffrey Hunter's Stunt Double   Bob Herron

Byron Haskin, the associate producer, is a Hollywood veteran who entered the motion picture industry as an assistant cameraman in 1920. He became an expert in motion picture sound techniques, and in 1932 he began a career as a special effects cameraman. His effects work is seen extensively in *A Midsummer Night's Dream* (Warner Brothers–1935) and *Dawn Patrol* (Warner Brothers–1938). In 1947, Haskin returned to directing. He directed some of producer George Pal's most successful motion pictures, including the classic *War of the Worlds* (Paramount–1953), *The Naked Jungle* (Paramount–1954), and *The Conquest of Space* (Paramount–1955). Haskin also directed the science fiction films *From the Earth to the Moon* (Warner Brothers–1959) and immediately before his work on "The Cage," *Robinson Crusoe on Mars* (Paramount–1964). In 1967, he co-directed the MGM science fiction thriller *The Power* with George Pal. On television, Haskin directed some of the best episodes of "The Outer Limits," including "Demon

with a Glass Hand," written by Harlan Ellison (and co-starring Arlene Martel and Abraham Sofaer). His co-workers on "Outer Limits" included Fred Phillips and Robert H. Justman.

Robert H. Justman, the first assistant director, was also no stranger to science fiction He began his television career as assistant director on the 1953 production season of "The Adventures of Superman," over a decade before he worked on "The Outer Limits." Justman later served as associate producer and co-producer for "Star Trek." After Trek, he produced Gene Roddenberry's TV pilot film *Planet Earth* (1974), and worked on the TV movie *The Man From Atlantis* (1977).

Franz Bachelin, one of the two art directors on "The Cage," worked at Paramount Pictures as early as 1938. Jerry Finnerman, the camera operator, was later promoted to "Star Trek's" director of photography, a position he ably filled throughout most of the series. Much of what we think of as the "Star Trek" "style" is actually the result of Finnerman's techniques in creative lighting and photography. Fred Phillips, the makeup artist, is probably the only man besides Gene Roddenberry who was associated with "Star Trek" in a behind-the-scenes capacity throughout the series' entire run, *plus* working on *Star Trek—the Motion Picture*.

The First Enterprise Crewmen

Jeffrey Hunter, who played Captain Christopher Pike, was a contract player for 20th Century-Fox Studios during the 1950s, where he appeared in many diversified roles. He was equally able to portray likable professors, daring soldiers, Arabs, Indians, and detectives.

Hunter is most remembered for his very fine performance as Christ in the 1961 MGM version of *King of Kings*. He was supposedly first considered for the role because of his intensely "magnetic" blue eyes. In 1966, Hunter starred in *Dimension Five* (with France Nuyen), portraying a secret agent who wore a "time travel belt." By going back and forth in time, he was able to stop a plot to destroy Los Angeles. In a bit of offbeat casting, Hunter once played the illegitimate son of a British naval officer (Michael Rennie, who played Klaatu in *The Day the Earth Stood Still*) in the Fox film *Sailor of the King*. On television, Hunter is best remembered as the star of the series "Temple Houston."

Jeffrey Hunter's role as the first captain of the starship *Enterprise* endeared him to many people. For the actor's fans, here is a listing of his feature film and television credits.

Jeffrey Hunter's Credits

Motion Pictures

Belles on Their Toes (20th Century-Fox–1952)
Boy, a Girl and Dog, A (Film Classics–1946)
Brainstorm (Universal–1965)
Call Me Mister (20th Century-Fox–1951)
Christmas Kid, The (1968)
Count Five and Die (20th Century-Fox–1958)
Custer of the West (1969)
Date with Judy, A (Metro-Goldwyn-Mayer–1948)
Dimension Five (1966)
Dreamboat (20th Century-Fox–1952)
Fourteen Hours (20th Century-Fox–1951)
Frogmen, The (20th Century-Fox–1951)
Great Locomotive Chase, The (Buena Vista–1956)
Gold for the Caesars (1964)
Guide for the Married Man, A (20th Century-Fox–1967)
Gun for a Coward (Universal–1952)
Hell to Eternity (Allied Artists–1960)
Hostess Also Has a Count, The (1969)
In Love and War (20th Century-Fox–1958)
Joe, Find a Place to Die (1968)
Key Witness (Columbia–1960)
King of Kings (Metro-Goldwyn-Mayer–1961)
Kiss Before Dying, A (20th Century-Fox–1956)
Last Hurrah, The (Columbia–1958)
Longest Day, The (20th Century-Fox–1962)
Lure of the Wilderness (20th Century-Fox–1952)
Man from Galveston, The (1964)
Man Trap (Paramount–1961)
Mardi Gras (20th Century-Fox–1958)
No Down Payment (20th Century-Fox–1957)
No Man Is an Island (Universal–1962)
Princess of the Nile (20th Century-Fox–1954)
Private Navy of Sgt. O'Farrell, The (United Artists–1968)
Proud Ones, The (20th Century-Fox–1956)
Red Skies of Montana (20th Century-Fox–1952)
Sailor of the King (20th Century-Fox–1953)
Searchers, The (Warner Brothers–1956)
Sergeant Rutledge (Warner Brothers–1960)
Seven Angry Men (Allied Artists–1955)
Seven Cities of Gold (20th Century-Fox–1955)
Sexy Susan at the King's Court (1968)
Smoke Jumpers (1952)
Take Care of My Little Girl (20th Century-Fox–1951)
Three Young Texans (20th Century-Fox–1954)
True Story of Jesse James, The (20th Century-Fox–1957)
Vendetta (1965) (also released as *Murietta)*
Way to the Gold, The (20th Century-Fox–1957)
White Feather (20th Century-Fox–1955)
Witch Without a Broom, A (1967)
Woman Who Wouldn't Die, The (1965)

Television

Alfred Hitchcock Theatre ("Don't Look Behind You"–1962)
Bob Hope Chrysler Theater ("Parties to the Crime"–1964
    ("Seven Miles of Bad Road"–1963)
Checkmate ("Waiting for Jock"–1961)
Climax ("Hurricane Diane"–1957)
    ("South of the Sun"–1955)
Combat ("Lost Sheep, Lost Shepherd"–1962)
Daniel Boone (title unknown–1966)
Death Valley Days ("Suzie"–1964)
FBI, The ("The Enemies"–1968)
    ("The Monster"–1965)
Jessie James ("Field of the Wild Flowers"–1966)
Kraft Suspense Theatre ("The Trains for Silence"–1965)
Monroes, The (title unknown–1967)
Our American Heritage ("Tiny West"–1960)
Pursuit ("Kiss Me Again Stranger"–1958)
Temple Houston (TV Series–title role–NBC–Sept. 1963 to Sept. 1964)
Twentieth Century-Fox Hour, The ("South of the Sun"–1955)
Wonderful World of Disney, The ("The Secret Mission"–1961) (Footage from the motion picture *The Great Locomotive Chase*)

Leonard Nimoy (Spock) was born in Boston on March 26, 1931. His first exposures to the performing arts were at the Elizabeth Peabody Settlement Playhouse in Boston, where he obtained his first stage experiences between 1939 and 1949. He graduated from Boston College, which he attended on a drama scholarship, and traveled to California, where he trained at the Pasadena Playhouse. After his entry into motion pictures, Nimoy married actress Sandi Zober in 1954. Shortly after their marriage, Leonard began a tour of Army duty at Fort McPherson, Georgia, where he did extensive work putting together G.I. shows. His daughter Julie was born in Atlanta, Georgia, in 1955, and a son Adam was born a year later, after the family had relocated to Los Angeles.

Besides being an actor, Leonard Nimoy is also a noted photographer and poet. He has also made several recordings, including *Mr. Spock's Music from Outer Space, The Two Sides of Leonard Nimoy, The Way I Feel, The Touch of Leonard Nimoy,* and *The New World of Leonard Nimoy.*

Nimoy's first book was *You and I,* ironically a beautifully presented study of the emotion of love in both photographic and poetic terms. *Will I Think of You,* his second book, is also a combination of Nimoy's own poetry and photography. The most misunderstood of Nimoy's books is *I Am Not Spock.* The title is probably meant to state that Leonard Nimoy is his own

A study of Mr. Spock, as he appeared in "The Cage" (Leonard Nimoy).

person and, even if his characterization of Mr. Spock is very near and dear to him, Nimoy and Spock are still two separate entities.

I Am Not Spock is a unique and very welcome work. Other characterizations have inspired fan followings approximately as great as that enjoyed by Mr. Nimoy (as well as Mr. Spock). But Basil Rathbone never wrote of his feelings for Sherlock Holmes, just as James Arness never wrote about what it was like to portray Matt Dillon, and George Reeves never wrote about what it meant to him to portray Superman. In this book, we get into the mind of Nimoy the actor and, in so doing, we see that a good deal of Mr. Spock seems so alive to us because it is actually a direct extension of the skills and sensitivities existing in his extremely capable interpreter, Leonard Nimoy.

"Star Trek" was not Leonard Nimoy's first exposure to science fiction in films. In 1952, Nimoy wore strange makeup including upswept eyebrows when he appeared as Narab, an alien who visited Earth in *Zombies of the Stratosphere*. At the serial's climax, it is Nimoy's character who reveals the existence of a superbomb and saves the Earth. In *Them* (Warner Brothers–1954), Nimoy appears as a soldier who disbelieves reports of giant ants posing a threat to civilization.

On television, Nimoy appeared as a sympathetic newspaper reporter covering the murder trial of robot Adam Link on the "Outer Limits" segment "I Robot."

For the many fans of actor Leonard Nimoy, there follows a list of his credits on stage, in motion pictures, and on television.

Leonard Nimoy's Credits

Stage

And Then There Were None (Atlanta Theatre Guild; Atlanta, Ga.–1955)

Caligula (St. Edward's Univ.; Austin, Tex.–1975)

Camelot (North Shore Music Theatre; Beverly, Mass.–1973
Cape Cod Melody Tent; Hyannis, Mass–1973)

Cat on a Hot Tin Roof (Town & Gown Repertory Co.; Birmingham, Ala.–1959)

Deathwatch (Cosmo Alley Gallery Theatre; Los Angeles, Cal.–1960)

Dr. Faustus (Orchard Gables Repertory Theatre; Los Angeles, Cal.–1950)

Equus (Helen Hayes Theatre; Broadway–1977)

Fiddler on the Roof (Tour–1971,
the Opera House; Atlanta, Ga.–1974)

Fourposter, The (Drury Lane No. Theatre; Lincolnshire, Ill.–1975)

Full Circle (Kennedy Center; Washington, D.C.–1973
Anta Theatre; Broadway–1973)

Irma La Douce (Valley Music Theatre; Woodland Hills, Cal.–1965)

King and I The (Melody Top Theatre; Milwaukee, Wis.–1974)

Man in the Glass Booth, The (Old Globe Theatre; San Diego, Cal.–1971)

Monserrat (various locations; Los Angeles, Cal.–1963)

My Fair Lady (Melody Top Theatre; Milwaukee, Wis.–1976)

Oliver (tour-1972; tour-1973)

One Flew Over the Cuckoo's Nest (Little Theat. on the Sq.; Sullivan; Ill.-1974)

Sherlock Holmes (national touring company-1976)

Six Rms Riv Vu (tour-1973
Cherry County Playhouse; Traverse City, Miss.-1974)

Stalag 17 (Pasadena Playhouse; Pasadena, Cal.-1951)

Streetcar Named Desire, A (Atlanta Theatre Guild; Atlanta, Ga.-1955)

Three Musketeers, The (Coronet Theatre; Los Angeles, Cal.-1950)

Twelfth Night (Pittsburgh Public Theatre; Pittsburgh, Pa.-1975)

Vincent (Petunia Productions presentation tour-1978)

Visit to a Small Planet (Pheasant Run Playhouse; Chicago, Ill.-1968)

Amateur Theatre (Eliz. Peabody Settlement Playhouse, Boston, Mass.-1939-49)
Hansel and Gretel (1939)
Awake and Sing
Good News
Of Thee I Sing
U.S. Army Special Services G.I. shows (Nimoy wrote, narrated, emceed; Ft. McPhearson, Ga.)

Motion Pictures

Balcony, The (Continental-1963)

Catlow (Metro-Goldwyn-Mayer-1971)

Deathwatch (Beverly Pictures-1966) (co-produced with Vic Morrow)

Francis Goes to West Point (Universal-1952)

Invasion of the Body Snatchers, The (United Artists-1978)

Kid Monk Baroni (Realart-1952)

Old Overland Trail, The (Republic-1953)

Queen for a Day (United Artists-1951)

Rhubarb (Paramount-1951)

Satan's Satellites (Republic-1958) (Feature version of *Zombies of the Stratosphere* serial)

Seconds (Paramount-1966)

Seizure (Jozak Production-1979)

Seven Days in May (Paramount-1964)

Them (Warner Brothers-1954)

Valley of Mystery (Universal-1967)

Zombies of the Stratosphere (Republic serial-1952)

Television

ABC Movie of the Week, The
Assault on the Wayne (1971) (w/Lloyd Haynes)
Contaminated
The Missing Are Deadly (20th Century-Fox-1975)

ABC Suspense Movie (The Alpha Caper) (Universal-1973)

Bicentennial Minute

Bonanza ("The Ape"-1960)

Cain's Hundred (title unknown)

Colt .45 (title unknown)

Combat ("The Raider"-1963)
("The Wounded Don't Cry"-1963)

Coral Jungle, The (Host-2 years in syndication)

Daniel Boone ("Seminole Territory"-1966)

Death Valley Days ("The Journey"-1965)

Dr. Kildare (title unknown)

Dragnet ("The Big Boys"-1954)

Eighty-Seventh Precinct ("The Very Hard Sell"-1961)

Eleventh Hour, The ("The Color of Sunset"-1964)
("The Hunted"-1960)
("La Belle Indifference"-1963)

Get Smart (title unknown-1966)

Gunsmoke (title unknown-1961)
(title unknown-1966)

Highway Patrol (title unknown)

In Search of (Host, narrator during entire series)

Kraft Suspense Theatre ("Kill No More"-1965)
("The World I Want to Know"-1964)

Laramie ("The Runt"-1962)

Lieutenant, The ("In the Highest Tradition"-1964) (w/ Gary Lockwood)

M Squad ("Badge for a Coward"-1960)
("The Firemakers"-1959)

Man from U.N.C.L.E., The ("The Project Strigas Affair"-1964) (w/William Shatner)

Matinee Theatre (title unknown)

Mission: Impossible (Series regular—"Paris the Great"-9/69-3/71)

NBC Mystery Movie: Columbo ("A Stitch in Crime"-1973)

NBC World Premiere ("Baffled"-1973) (An Arena/ITC Production)

Night Gallery ("She'll Be Company for You"-1972)

Outer Limits, The ("I Robot"-1964)
("Production & Decay of Strange Particles"-1964)

Perry Mason ("The Case of the Shoplifter's Shoe-1963)

Profiles in Courage ("Richard T. Ely"-1964)

Rawhide ("Annko")

Rebel, The ("The Hunted"-1960)

Roughriders, The ("Gunpoint Persuasion"-1959)

Sam Benedict ("Twenty Aching Years"-1963)

Sea Hunt (title unknown-1959)
(title unknown-1960)
(title unknown-1963)
(title unknown)
(title unknown)

Shenandoah ("Run Killer Run"-1966) (w/Sally Kellerman)

Short Stories of Love ("Kiss Me Again, Stranger"-1974)

Tales of Wells Fargo ("Something Pretty"-1961)

Tall Man, The ("A Bounty for Billy"-1960)

Tate ("Commanche Scalps"-1960) (w/Frank Overton)

Twenty-Six Men ("The Long Trail Home"-1959)

Twilight Zone, The ("A Quality of Mercy")

Two Faces West ("Doctor's Orders")

Untouchables, The ("Takeover")

Virginian, The ("Man of Violence"–1963) (w/DeForest
   Kelley) (By John D. F. Black)
   ("Show Me a Hero"–1965) (w/Sherry Jackson)
   ("The Showdown"–1965) (w/Michael Ansara)
Wagon Train ("The Baylor Crofoot Story"–1962)
   ("The Tiburcio Mendez Story"–1961)
West Point ("Cold Peril"–1957)
   ("His Brother's Fist"–1958)

Majel Barrett (Number One) was born Majel Lee Hudec, the name under which she is billed in "The Cage." She grew up in Cleveland, Ohio, where she majored in Theatre Arts at Flora Stone Mather College for Women of Western Reserve University. After attending law school for a year, she moved to New York City to pursue an acting career. Her first opportunities in this field include eleven weeks of summer stock in Bermuda, and a play staged in Boston that almost made it to Broadway.

After a nine-month tour in the play *The Solid Gold Cadillac,* Majel journeyed to California where she appeared in a play with Edward Everett Horton at the Pasadena Playhouse (where Leonard Nimoy also appeared). She then studied drama with Anthony Quinn who, impressed with her talent, obtained work for her at Paramount Pictures; there she appeared in three films, including the DeMille/Quinn spectacle, *The Buccaneer* (1959).

Majel entered the "Star Trek" cast after appearing regularly in "Leave It to Beaver," a TV comedy classic. Fortunately, when Number One's number came up, Majel (in the person of Nurse Christine Chapel) stayed on the *Enterprise.*

Majel married Gene Roddenberry on August 6, 1969, in a Buddhist-Shinto ceremony conducted in Tokyo, Japan. She has aided her husband in the maintenance of Lincoln Enterprises, their mail-order business. Her interests in comparative religion and occultism had much to do with the incentives and authenticity behind *Spectre,* Roddenberry's 1977 TV movie (released as a feature film in Great Britain). Majel also appeared in the production as a mysterious, attractive practitioner of the White Arts.

Today, Christine Chapel is a medical doctor in *Star Trek—the Motion Picture,* and Majel Barrett is still pursuing her career, just as Dr. Chapel is still pursuing Mr. Spock. For all of Majel Barrett's fans, here is a list of her stage, feature film, and television appearances.

Majel Barrett's Credits

Stage

All for Mary (Pasadena Playhouse)
Solid Gold Cadillac, The (Tour)

Summer stock (in Bermuda)

Motion Pictures

As Young As We Were (Paramount–1958)
Black Orchids (Paramount–1959)
Buccaneer, The (Paramount–1959)
Domino Principle, The (Avco-Embassy—1977)
Guide for the Married Man (20th Century-Fox–1966)
Love in a Goldfish Bowl (Paramount–1961)
Quick and the Dead, The
Sylvia (Paramount–1965)
Track of Thunder (1968)
Westworld (Metro-Goldwyn-Mayer–1973)

Television

Bonanza (title unknown)
Divorce Court (title unknown)
Dr. Kildare ("Love Is a Sad Song"–1965)
Eleventh Hour, The (title unknown)
General Hospital (Recurring role)
Here Come the Brides ("Lovers and Wanderers"–1968)
I Love Lucy (title unknown)
Leave It to Beaver (Recurring role; Gwenn Rutherford,
   Lumpy's mother) (1958–63)
Lieutenant, The ("In the Highest Tradition"–1964)
Love on a Rooftop ("117 Ways to Cook Hamburgers")
Many Happy Returns (title unknown–1964)
Pete and Gladys (title unknown)
Planet Earth (TV Movie: unsold pilot) (Produced by
   Gene Roddenberry)
Please Don't Eat the Daisies (title unknown–1967)
Questor Tapes, The (TV Movie; unsold pilot) Produced
   by Gene Roddenberry)
Second Hundred Years, The (title unknown–1968)
77 Sunset Strip (title unknown)
Spectre (TV Movie; unsold pilot–1977) (Produced by
   Gene Roddenberry)
Untouchables, The (title unknown)
Wackiest Ship in the Army, The (title unknown)
Westinghouse Playhouse (title unknown)

Susan Oliver (Vina) appeared in many Metro-Goldwyn-Mayer films of the 1950s. On television, she can be seen in episodes of many series, including "Route Sixty-Six," "Longstreet," and "The Man from U.N.C.L.E."

One of her roles was astoundingly close to her part in "The Cage." On "The Twilight Zone," she starred in "People Are Alike All Over," in which a space traveler from Earth arrives on Mars via a crash landing; he is the sole survivor and he finds himself welcomed by the Martians and romanced by young Teenya (Susan Oliver). Unknown to the spaceman, the Martians consider him an evolutionary inferior. Teenya encourages him to be happy in a mock-up of the astronaut's own home on Earth, which the Martians have provided. The astronaut finally discovers that he can't get out of his "house," which is in reality a cage designed to permit Martian families to visit the zoo and see an Earth creature in its natural habitat.

Ms. Oliver is an accomplished airplane pilot who once planned a record-breaking flight that had to be cancelled when a foreign government refused to permit her to go through with the trip. She is also active in film industry programs that have helped open the field to women filmmakers. Susan Oliver attended her first "Star Trek" convention in 1976, when she mentioned that she was caught up in the creativity, artistic dedication, and intelligence the "Star Trek" fans extended to her.

Some of the other stars of "The Cage" are faces we have seen in many other movies (including other "Trek" episodes, in one case). These individuals and others who have starred in other "Trek" segments, are usually categorized as "character actors," performers who do not specialize in any one type of role, but seem equally at home whether they're playing rich men, poor men, heroes, or villains. The majority of these performers are more deserving of notice than are some of the "stars" in the film industry today.

John Hoyt (Dr. Phillip "Bones" Boyce) created a character in "The Cage" who was very similar to Dr. McCoy. His acid observations and the scene in which he functions as Captain Pike's analyst ("Sometimes a man will tell his bartender things he'd never tell his doctor") indicate that Hoyt (and Boyce) would have fit into the permanent *Enterprise* family.

In George Pal's science fiction film *When Worlds Collide* (Paramount–1951) Hoyt portrayed the stodgy millionaire who financed the construction of the film's giant rocketship. In *The Attack of the Puppet People* (AIP–1957) he was a lonely toymaker who shrank people so they could keep him company. He also appeared with Boris Karloff in *The Black Castle,* and as Professor Gordon in *Flesh Gordon.* On television, he was regularly seen as a doctor in "90 Bristol Court" (1964–65), and was the physician who told series hero Paul Brian that he was dying in the pilot episode of "Run for Your Life" (1965). Hoyt was also Martin Peyton in "Return to Peyton Place" (1972–74). His science fiction and fantasy TV roles include appearances in "Voyage to the Bottom of the Sea" ("Hail to the Chief") and "The Man from U.N.C.L.E." ("The Deadly Toys Affair"). On "Twilight Zone," he is seen in "Will the Real Martian Please Stand Up," and "The Lateness of the Hour" (in which, as an elderly scientist wanting a child, he "built" robot daughter Inger Stevens; the plot suggests that he may have been friends with Flint of "Requiem for Methuselah").

Jon Lormer (Dr. Theodore Haskins) also appears in two other "Star Trek" episodes, "The Return of the Archons" and "For the World Is Hollow and I Have Touched the Sky." Seen in many TV series episodes as priest, shopkeeper, and reluctant eyewitness, Lormer was regularly seen in "Miss Susan" (1951) and as the town judge in "Peyton Place" (1964–69). In "Twilight Zone" he is seen in "Execution," "Jess-Belle," and "The Last Rights of Jeff Myrtlebank," and he appears in "One Step Beyond's" "The Captain's Guests."

Leonard Mudie (2nd Survivor) has been seen in many feature film roles dating back to *The Mummy* (1932). (He had the best line in the film, explaining about the unfortunate scientist who saw the Mummy walking away: "He was laughing when your father found him; he died laughing ten years later.") His other films include *Captain Blood* and *Cardinal Richelieu* (1935), *The Adventures of Robin Hood* (1938), and *Dark Victory* (1939). On television, he was seen in four episodes of "The Adventures of Superman" ("Drums of Death," "A Ghost for Scotland Yard," "The Jolly Roger," and "The Magic Necklace").

Anthony Joachim (3rd Survivor) appears in a "Twilight Zone" episode "The Incredible World of Horace Ford."

Clegg Hoyt (Transporter Chief Pitcairn) also appears in a "Twilight Zone" episode, the hour-long comedy "The Bard."

Joseph Mell (Orion Trader) is in the "Superman" episode "Crime Wave," and in a "Twilight Zone" episode "Dead Man's Shoes."

The most offbeat bit of casting for "The Cage" was Roddenberry's decision to hire actresses to portray the Talosians. The women exhibit those subtle mannerisms that distinguish men from women and, because male voices had been dubbed in for the Talosians, a conflict is created in the mind of the viewers. The Talosians are therefore accepted as truly alien creatures, which adds to the credibility of the entire tale.

The original voice of the Keeper was actor Malachi Throne. Because Throne appears as Commodore Mendez in the reedited footage for "The Menagerie," the Keeper's voice was later rerecorded by another vocal artist (probably Vic Perrin).

Meg Wyllie (the Keeper) was seen regularly in "The Travels of Jamie McPheeters," from 1963–1964. She also appears in a "Batman" segment, "The Black Widow Strikes Again," and in the "Twilight Zone" "Night of the Meek."

The stunt double for Jeffrey Hunter was Bob Herron, who also did many "fights" and other stunts during later "Star Trek" episodes. He also appears as Kahless the Klingon in "The Savage Curtain."

Various tests were filmed before the actual production got underway. *The Making of Star Trek* mentions that before Susan Oliver was cast as Vina, another young woman served as the stand-in for this role.[4]

Majel Barrett appeared in an unused makeup for Number One. She had an extremely dark complexion, upswept eyebrows, and a facial expression that was devoid of emotion. Just as characteristics were traded back and forth between Spock and Number One, apparently at one time their facial features were split between them as well. In the tests, her hair covers her

A rejected makeup makes Number One (Majel Barret) appear almost Vulcan.

ears. It is therefore impossible to guess if the resemblance between this experimental Number One and Mr. Spock is complete.

The Making of Star Trek mentions that several pairs of ears were prepared for Mr. Spock before a single design was finally agreed upon. These ears were in various shapes, and none of the shapes seemed right at first.[5] *The World of Star Trek* elaborates upon the Spock ears.[6]

Leonard Nimoy, quoted in David Gerrold's book, recalls that a special effects house that also specialized in creating makeups was originally assigned to produce the Spock ears.

The final ears, which were accepted to all concerned, arrived just before principal photography was to start on "The Cage." The artificial aural augmentations bear a strong resemblance to the set of ears created for actor Rex Ingram, the genie in *The Thief of Bagdad* (United Artists–1940).

Setting the Style

"The Cage" was the nucleus of what later developed into the "Star Trek" universe. The differences between the prototypes seen in this episode, and their later refinement into the concepts we are familiar with, can be seen in both the "production" (sets, decorations, backgrounds, and costumes) and "postproduction" phases (special effects, photographic effects, sound effects, and music). The men's shirts have round, ribbed necks and the women's collars are decoratively raised into V shapes that come to a point shortly below the neck. Both male and female collars are the same colors as their garments.

The insignia are much plainer than the later versions. They are borderless, with no black outlines, and the interior shapes are crudely sewn. The backgrounds of the insignia are off-white, with interwoven gold threads.

All crew personnel wear trousers, a style that survives partially until "Charlie X." [7] None of the trousers worn in "The Cage" have the interwoven "glitter" effect seen in the series' regular uniform trousers, but they *are* bell-bottomed like their later versions. Jackets are worn in the "outdoor" scenes on Talos IV.

Dr. Boyce wears a specialized medical tunic of the same color as Dr. McCoy's medical jacket. It is similar in design to the tunic worn by Nurse Chapel during operations in other episodes, and by occasional sick bay patients. This tunic shows up in "Where No Man Has Gone Before," in which Dr. Piper wears it over his regular shirt; patient Gary Mitchell wears a sleeveless version of the tunic.

Captain Pike's wardrobe *also* includes some special items, including his little-known *hat*. Although Pike never wore it in the final cut of "The Cage," the hat is seen resting atop his "TV set," near his laser pistol.

Two other outfits were made for Captain Pike's "dream" sequences. During the picnic scene he wears a denim lounging outfit complete with jacket and turtleneck. On Orion, during Vina's seductive dance, Pike wears a jumpsuit of iridescent blue trimmed in gold, with a gold sash.

The scenes in "The Cage" that take place on the surface of Talos IV were all shot indoors. The scenic backgrounds painted for the "exterior" planet scenes are extremely detailed, life-sized dioramas. Multiple layers of rocks and clouds were painted onto the artwork and some of these rocks appear to recede off into the distance. The empty, tinted backgrounds that were used in later "Star Trek" episodes could have used some of these additional touches; more time and money were available to create the "drops" for the pilot episode.

The city seen in the background of the "picnic" illusion is also a full-sized painted backdrop. It works well here because of the surrealistic effect of the illusions, but it does not look so convincing when seen outside Dr. Leighton's window in "Conscience of the King."

The settings on the *Enterprise* are very different from their later versions; even the bridge is filled with minor variations. The turbo lifts and wooden railings are black, instead of red. The illuminated panels are differently shaped and situated farther apart, with less "butterfly-shaped" control panels around the bridge. Every bridge station and the Captain's chair have small monitor screens at the ends of short, flexible necks. These are also present in "Where No Man Has Gone Before," and one later turns up as part of the communications equipment aboard the Romulan vessel of "The Enterprise Incident."

The viewscreen is the same as that used in "Where

No Man Has Gone Before," but here it has a different paint job. The screen was later transferred to the briefing room set.

Captain Pike's quarters would make even a claustrophobic person feel unconfined. The single room is huge and round, with a high, circular roof. Pike's cabin includes a soft bed, topped by a recessed bookcase cut into the wall. In the middle of the room is a large chair, next to which is a device that resembles a television camera; a small rectangular arrangement at the end of an extension.

Most surprising is a large, wooden console containing a recognizable television screen.

Props contribute much to the image of "Star Trek." As visible references to the Federation's technological level, these devices are revealing in their size and shape. Great care was undoubtedly taken in designing these earliest weapons and communicators. Wah Chang, a highly gifted Hollywood special effects artist, recalls building some of the hand props for "The Cage."

Chang, Danforth, Gene Warren, Tim Barr, and others comprised "Project Unlimited," which created an impressive array of special makeups and effects for films including *The Time Machine* (Metro-Goldwyn-Mayer–1960), *Jack the Giant Killer* (United Artists–1961), *The Wonderful World of the Brothers Grimm* (Metro-Goldwyn-Mayer–1962), and *The Seven Faces of Dr. Lao* (Metro-Goldwyn-Mayer–1964). From 1963 through 1965 Project Unlimited created imaginative and budget-minded visual effects for producer Joseph Stefano's United Artists television series, "The Outer Limits." Their challenges included stop motion ("The Zanti Misfits" and "Counterweight"), monstrosities ("Architects of Fear"), and an assortment of ray guns, force-field projectors, and other marvels.

This earliest model of the communicator is larger than its later counterpart. Its casing is transparent, allowing the viewer to see intricate interior circuitry. The metal grid is flat, attached by means of a wire framework to the top of the transparent casing. The outside case is wider at the top than at the bottom.

Wah Chang designed stop-motion model armatures and exteriors, other miniatures, and special makeups for "The Outer Limits," while he was a member of Project Unlimited. After Project Unlimited disbanded, Chang and fellow artist Gene Warren formed the Excelsior Company, which specialized in visual effects. Mostly through his associations with these two organizations, Chang remembers designing and constructing various items for "Star Trek," including (1) the phasers, communicators, and tricorders used throughout the series; (2) the puppet head of Balok for "The Corbomite Maneuver"; (3) the Salt Vampire in "The Man Trap"; (4) Mr. Spock's Vulcan harp; (5) the Romulan ship seen in "Balance of Terror" and "The Deadly Years"; (6) the Romulan helmets; (7) the Neanderthal-type creatures of "The Galileo Seven";

(8) the Gorn of "Arena"; and (9) the initial pattern for the tribbles of "The Trouble with Tribbles." Now retired from the field of motion picture special effects, Chang is a noted sculptor whose works of art are in great demand.

The laser pistols are not only seen in "The Cage" but in "Where No Man Has Gone Before," "The Man Trap," and "What Are Little Girls Made Of" as well. They feature a ridged hand grip, adjustable barrel (for regulating the blast's intensity), and a "sight" that can be raised or lowered.[8]

Geologist Madden carries a bulky instrument that resembles a present-day portable hair dryer attached to a battery pack.

The Talosians looked especially convincing with their specialized makeups. Their oversized craniums are actually finely crafted rubber "caps," which fit over the performer's own head and ears. The edges of these appliances were extremely thin so that they could be "blended" into the performer's own face. The caps were also equipped with expandable "veins," which were inflated by an off-camera assistant holding a "squeeze bulb" attached to the caps. The pulsations are timed to coincide with the dubbed-in dialogue, to give the impression that we are "hearing" the aliens think.

Launching the *Enterprise*

Work on "Star Trek's" special effects had begun a full year before "The Cage" was filmed, according to Howard Anderson, ASC, president of the effects company that bears his name.[9] The most important item designed during this time is the U.S.S. *Enterprise,* which is the central point of identification in Gene Roddenberry's "Star Trek" format. If people refused to believe in the reality of the *Enterprise,* Roddenberry realized, they would be unable to accept his overall concept. Great care was, therefore, taken in designing the starship.[10]

Walter M. Jefferies, assistant art director on "The Cage," recalls that the final design of the *Enterprise* was arrived at after many design concepts had been reviewed by Gene Roddenberry. In each of the many drawings, which were executed by Jefferies and Pato Guzman (one of the two art directors on the production), Roddenberry saw favorable features. Each of those chosen features was in turn included in new concept drawings, and after three such sessions of distillation Jefferies constructed the first rough, wooden model of the U.S.S. *Enterprise.*[11]

Roddenberry had been conferring with representatives of the Howard A. Anderson Company and, with a final design chosen, work began on the construction of the *Enterprise* miniatures for "The Cage." A team of twenty technicians was assigned to the project, with

An extremely early shot of the largest *Enterprise* model, photographed on September 15, 1964 for "The Cage."

Darrell Anderson directing the operations.[12] During these early procedures, the Anderson people probably met with Roddenberry and Jefferies to iron out any inconsistencies or impracticalities in the starship's design.

Anderson's company constructed three miniatures, according to Howard Anderson's recollections.[13] A wooden scale model four inches long was the first, and a more detailed wooden model, three feet long, was produced next. Then came the most difficult part of the work; constructing and assembling the biggest *Enterprise* model of them all.

The largest *Enterprise* miniature, which now hangs in the Air and Space Museum of the Smithsonian Institution, is fourteen feet long according to the Anderson figures. Constructed mostly from sheet plastic, the model took shape after hundreds of hours of work. The saucer section of this model measures ten feet in diameter. The nacelles are tooled from hardwood.

This large model originally looked a little different than the one we're accustomed to seeing. For the opening shot in "The Cage," in which the camera zooms in on the *Enterprise* and penetrates into the dome's top to the bridge, the uppermost dome of the model was designed differently. When the model was modified, the dome was diminished in size and in roundness. Two metallic strips, one on each side of the saucer section, were also removed during the modifications. As further modifications, the engineering section was backed with segmented doors for the hangar deck, and interior lights were added along the cigar-shaped portion of the model.

The nacelles were changed more than any other section. The rear grids were removed and replaced with half-spheres. The metal spires were removed

from the nacelle caps and the caps themselves were replaced with translucent plastic caps so that the newly installed lighting effects could be seen. The complex electrical system that enabled the engineering lights to be installed also make the nacelle effects possible. In each nacelle, a revolving disc covered with small pieces of reflective glass was installed. The reflections from these discs are mirrored onto the nacelle caps, where they are seen from the outside as rotating lines of darkness and light, representing the matter/antimatter energies of the ship's engines.

When these modifications were added, the resulting power cables made it impossible to photograph the miniature from the left side. Any effects showing the model from the left side were photographed with the unlit model (easily detected by looking at the nacelles to spot the absence of lighting effects).

The big miniature was photographed supported from beneath. A hole was bored through the bottom of the engineering section, and a pipe mount was inserted into the aperture. The pipe was connected to a pedestal, under which was anchored a tripod mount, to enable the miniature to turn when needed. Everything beneath the miniature was painted blue to match the special screens that were behind the model. (Today, the model hangs on wires, from hooks atop the nacelles.)

During most of the "flyby" sequences involving the *Enterprise,* both the model and the camera were in motion. All these moves were controlled with motors; to enable the camera to move closer to or farther from the *Enterprise,* tracks were installed in front of the miniature. From the camera end, in addition to the dolly movements along the track, the camera boom also moved up and down. From the ship's vantage point, the tripod head that supported the model could also pan and tilt. These motions were remotely controlled, according to effects artist Linwood Dunn, ASC, president of Film Effects of Hollywood. An 18mm zoom lens was used to achieve a greater depth of field (which makes the model appear larger).

The *Enterprise* miniatures may have been altered in size; Linwood Dunn reports that the two largest models are two feet and twelve feet long. Models of different sizes were probably constructed at different times during the series. Surviving photos include views of an *Enterprise* model on Gene Roddenberry's office desk (this might be the same little ship that was exhibited at the Cleveland convention in 1966). In early publicity photos, Mr. Spock held another miniature of the *Enterprise*. However many *Enterprise*s there are, and whatever their size, the range of shots obtained by the Howard A. Anderson Company, Film Effects of Hollywood, and other optical houses are extremely diversified. By photographing the largest model and dissolving into shots of the smaller ones at matching angles, the *Enterprise* was made to appear huge and could still be depicted as sailing off into the starscape.

The outer space backgrounds for "The Cage" were produced by the Anderson Company using a two- by three-foot white background, with black stars painted on it.[14] By printing footage of this backdrop in *negative,* the desired intensity of utter blackness was obtained. Used in conjunction with an optical printer, the *Enterprise*'s brightly lit surface contrasted sharply with the black space background, making the ship appear as vibrant as possible.

The ship was "matted" into the star background using the blue screen traveling matte process. The miniature *Enterprise* was always photographed against a special blue screen. By taking the developed footage of the ship, sailing against this solid blue background, and printing it through special "separation filters," the result was the *Enterprise* floating through *nothingness.* Printed through a different set of filters that *only* register *blue,* the opposite effect was obtained; the background was now solid *black* and the *Enterprise* showed only as a blank shape. This blank shape is the "matte" (a French word meaning "mask"). Properly combined all these pieces of film are like an optical jigsaw puzzle, producing the "flybys" with which we are familiar. Each optical house that produced these effects used slightly different techniques, but the end products were essentially the same.

Even the planets seen in "Star Trek" episodes were produced with varying methods. The Westheimer Company used a black-and-white planet miniature, mounted and geared to rotate slowly. Westheimer filmed its planet footage at twenty-four frames per second. Using a triple-headed optical printer with which to complete the optical "jigsaw puzzles," planets of various textures were produced using the same miniature. With the use of colored filters, the planets could be brown, green, orange, purple, or whatever color was needed for the episode. The "planet" was approximately two feet in diameter.[15]

Some of the most popular photographic effects in "Star Trek" were produced using "optical paintings." The first of these is the Rigel Fortress in "The Cage." A section of the fortress set, which included the gate, a portion of the walls, and the pathway that led up to the gate was constructed outdoors. Jeffrey Hunter and Susan Oliver were photographed running up the path to the gate. It did not matter what was in the background beyond the set, because that area would not be seen in the finished footage.

A frame of this film was enlarged and given to an artist at the Anderson Company. The enlargement was projected onto a piece of masonite or Special Glass, on which the artist traced the area of the existing set. Then he expanded the set until the full landscape was outlined. Using the highly specialized techniques of matte painters, the artist completed the landscape, being careful to match his colors with the studio set. The area of the painting corresponding to the space comprising the actual gate, wall, and road were painted black. In the darkroom, an optical printer was used to print the footage of the actors and their set. The surrounding terrain was completely blacked out so that the actors and ground appeared surrounded by nothingness. When the painting was photographed it exactly covered the blacked-out area. The "hole" left in the painting was, in turn, exactly covered by the actors and the real set. Another type of "optical jigsaw puzzle" was thus completed, which provided a realistic view of a Rigel landscape. Other optical paintings that appeared in "Star Trek" are featured in "Where No Man Has Gone Before," "Court-Martial," "The Menagerie," "A Taste of Armageddon," and "The Devil in the Dark." Other episodes featured variations of those same painted landscapes.

Detailed view of the unlit, spired nacelle cap, before the lighting modifications were added.

The Transporter Effect

The Howard A. Anderson Company, working in close cooperation with Gene Roddenberry and other "Star Trek" production personnel, was also responsible for "The Cage's" transporter effects. This effect could have been accomplished cheaply, by having the *Enterprise* people "pop" into and out of existence with no added frills. From the beginning, Roddenberry wanted this effect to be something both spectacular and affordable from week to week. After much experimentation, the final transporting sequences in "The Cage" were accomplished using the following procedure:

(1) The subject is photographed on the transporter platform. (2) The camera stops rolling and "freezes," remaining in the same position while (3) the subject steps out of the picture. (4) The camera is started again, still in the same position, and the empty set is filmed. (5) Using a duplicated negative print of the footage including the subject, a matte of the subject is made so that (6) the subject can be "dissolved" (gradually vanished) out of the picture. By assembling this footage, we now have an image of someone climbing onto the transporting platform and gradually fading away completely. (7) The glitter effect came next. At Anderson's Fairfax Avenue installation, aluminum dust was photographed falling through a high-intensity light beam. (8) Combined with the matte of the subject's figure, the glitter produces a shower of sparkles *occupying only the area in which the subject was standing.* (9) The matted glitter effect, printed over the subject himself as he faded away, produced the final effect as the glitter effect was slowly dissolved away at the same rate as the subject.[16]

For return trips, the process was reversed, and for beamdowns the subjects were photographed on the desired set instead of on the transporter platform. The transporter effect went through some interesting experiments before this method was agreed upon.

At first, the powdered aluminum formed a "column" of glitter, not an effect that assumed the exact shape of the subject. The resulting footage was similar to the *Forbidden Planet* effect, in which the crewmen were reduced to pillars of energy.

After it was decided to use the prefilmed glitter effect together with mattes of the subject, the intensity of the glitter had to be determined. A memo that Roddenberry wrote at this time refers to the "Peter Pan" type of sparkle, and asks that it be toned down.[17] Experiments were also conducted with the color of the effect. Originally, plans called for each person to have an individual color,[18] possibly an attempt at showing each person's different "ionic matrix." In "The Cage," everyone was finally tinted a faint blue during transporting effects.

For a short while, test shots were done in which the subject was surrounded by a thick red line as he or she faded away.[19] On the transporter platform, strong lights were shined up onto the subject being transported. This lit the subject from a generally unflattering angle; the technique is used throughout the two pilots but was dropped before series production started.

To illustrate that the energized subject was being transported to the planet's surface, an animated beam of light was planned to extend from the *Enterprise* to the ground.[20] This recalls memories of the "rainbow bridge" that extended between Asgaard and Earth in Norse mythology, and the "light bridge" that transported a Martian to Earth in *Flash Gordon's Trip to Mars* (Universal serial–1938). This concept does not, however, appear in the final print of "The Cage."

The Music of "The Cage"

Music that tells a story, or accompanies a story told in another form, is called "program music." Some of the most famous music in the world is program music; this includes music written for motion pictures. Until recently, there were tremendous prejudices directed against film music. All this is changing now, partially because moviegoers *and* television viewers are more aware of good background music. "Star Trek" is definitely one of the television productions responsible for this awareness.

Roddenberry could have acquired an inexpensive library of prerecorded "stock" music and edited it into the individual episodes, or he could have retained a small band to create improvisational melodies for the show. Fortunately, Gene Roddenberry realized that well-conceived background music could add to the "Star Trek" format. Throughout "Star Trek," the best available composers were called upon to enrich various episodes, each according to his individual style. The first composer to write music for "Star Trek" was Alexander Courage, whom Gene Roddenberry retained to write the score for "The Cage."

Alexander Courage, born in New Jersey, graduated from the Eastman School of Music in 1941. After his graduation he scored radio series, including "The Adventures of Sam Spade" and "Broadway Is My Beat." In 1948 he arrived in California, where he went to work for Metro-Goldwyn-Mayer, working under the noted composer André Previn. While at MGM Courage contributed his talents to many films, including *Porgy and Bess* and *Les Girls,* and received more than one nomination for the Academy Award.

Most of Courage's work has been for television series. Among the television shows he has scored are "The Felony Squad," "Peyton Place," "Daniel Boone," "Judd for the Defense," "The Waltons," "Voyage to the Bottom of the Sea," and "Lost in Space." His contributions for "Star Trek" include the scores for "Where No Man Has Gone Before," "The

Man Trap," "Court-Martial," "Arena," "Space Seed," "This Side of Paradise," "The City on the Edge of Forever," "Tomorrow Is Yesterday," "The Naked Time," and "The Cage."

"The Cage" is not a happy story, and Courage's music conforms to the tragic and desperate conditions in the episode. Pike is discontented with the life he has chosen for himself, Vina is not free to choose her own life, and the Talosians know that the life span of their race is limited.

The music Courage wrote for "The Cage" is more electronic-sounding than Courage's later scores (the one notable exception to this is his music for "The Man Trap"). Just as Roddenberry used everyday props in unorthodox ways to suggest an alien or future type of civilization, Courage took the orchestra's instruments and encouraged them to produce unearthly sounds. In "The Cage," even the guitars sound strange. The music that Vina dances to is unearthly and mechanical, and yet beautiful. The combination of strings and percussion that announces the Rigel illusion is gentle and weird at the same time (it is also present when Spock experiences the spores in "This Side of Paradise").

Whatever Courage's reasons and methods, the end effect is the same; a strange, effective style of music that sounds both a million miles away and emotionally close to home. Courage also used electronic-type sounds in the earliest orchestration of the series' opening theme. Paced quicker than the subsequent version, with very effective echoing sounds, this early rendition was withdrawn before the first ten episodes had been scored.

Second Chance

"The Cage" was delivered to NBC in February 1965. After due consideration, the network's answer was No. "The Cage" was rejected by the network, but "Star Trek" was not dead. After spending approximately $630,000 on one pilot film, the network felt that there was enough quality present in the episode for the series to deserve a second chance. For the first time in the television industry, a second pilot was commissioned, but some changes were to be made. Most of the original cast had been rejected; Number One, Navigator Tyler, and Dr. Boyce became casualties.

NBC reportedly wanted one other character dropped at this time. He was too inhuman, with no really likable trait; besides, he had those satanic, pointed ears. Would anyone really miss Mr. Spock if he was removed from the *Enterprise* roster? Apparently so, because instead of acting indifferently to the fate of this strange, pointy-eared gentleman (or "gentle *humanoid*"), Gene Roddenberry insisted that Spock stay in the "Trek" format.

Roddenberry was given the go-ahead to produce three new script treatments. One of these would be accepted and would become the second "Star Trek" pilot.

"Where No Man Has Gone Before"

Gene Roddenberry wrote the first story outline for the second pilot "The Omega Glory." Because of the "parallel evolution" principle included in this script, extensive use could be made of existing studio "period" sets and stock wardrobes. Only one major guest star would be needed. From the standpoint of economics, "The Omega Glory" seemed extremely practical for a second pilot.

Roddenberry also wrote a story treatment called "Mudd's Women," centering around the adventures of a likable rogue with a tendency to be menacing at times. "Villain" Harry Mudd would not really hurt anyone in the story, although his antics would cause the *Enterprise* to escape destruction by the narrowest of margins. He would help in the final crisis, and be taken away to meet his just desserts in an interplanetary court of law. The tale would have humor, drama, and a moral. And it could be almost completely filmed using the existing *Enterprise* sets.

The third outline was a quality science fiction tale with all the elements of a Greek tragedy, and all the opportunities for action-packed scenes and colorful opticals for which a network could ask. Talented writer Samuel Peeples was called in to write this story, called "Where No Man Has Gone Before."

Samuel Peeples had written novels and television scripts, and produced NBC's western series "The Tall Man" for two years. He had also written scripts for westerns. Roddenberry has stated that writing science fiction is like writing any other "period" piece. Anyone

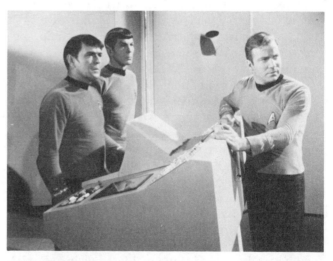

Captain Kirk, Mr. Spock and Mr. Scott (William Shatner, Leonard Nimoy, James Doohan).

who has written good westerns (period pieces set in the past) could write good science fiction (period pieces set in the future). Peeples had the required experience many times over.

By early June 1965, all three treatments had been expanded into first draft scripts and forwarded to NBC. The network decided to go with the most challenging and potentially expensive of the three scripts, "Where No Man Has Gone Before."

Science fiction is full of precedents of human beings gaining incredible physical and mental powers. Many films have been based on such premises and many comic book superheroes gained their powers as a result of some contact with (as they say in the old horror movies) ". . . things that man should leave alone." Even Superman is the result of a scientific accident. In fact, Superman's description from the old TV series can fit the central figure's metamorphosis in "Where No Man Has Gone Before"; ". . . Strange powers and abilities far beyond those of mortal men."

Pilot Number Two: A Synopsis

The U.S.S. *Enterprise*, while patroling the area near the outer boundary of our galaxy, beams aboard the flight recorder of the *Valiant*, a galactic survey vessel that had visited this area almost two centuries before the *Enterprise*.

The survey vessel, upon attempting to leave our galaxy, had come in contact with an energy barrier that disabled the ship and killed some of the crew. One of the crew, however, survived serious injury from the barrier. From this point, the tapes' information is garbled; the *Valiant*'s captain requested data on extrasensory perception (ESP), and eventually self-destructed his own ship.

Captain Kirk decides to move forward, and the *Enterprise* contacts the same glowing purple barrier that had disabled the *Valiant*. Kirk orders the ship to back out of the energy field. While the starship escapes the barrier, unknown radiations penetrate the ship, causing short circuits in key equipment. Several crewmen are killed, and two are knocked unconscious.

Lieutenant Commander Gary Mitchell, a friend of Kirk's from his Academy days, seems uninjured although his eyes now glow a bright silver. Dr. Elizabeth Dehner, a psychiatrist, is also knocked out for a moment, but seems completely normal afterward.

Kirk and Mr. Spock determine that the ESP quotient of Gary Mitchell is extremely high; Dr. Dehner's quotient is almost as high.

In sick bay, Kirk learns that Mitchell is feeling completely well; he is also reading material he has never understood before; his comprehension seems complete and his reading speed is incredible. Showing off to Dr. Dehner, Mitchell "plays dead" by stopping all his bodily functions for almost a full minute. Kirk calls a meeting of the *Enterprise* department heads. Physicist Sulu predicts that Mitchell's powers will develop at an astounding rate. Spock suggests that Kirk kill Mitchell; he cautions him not to wait too long, like the captain of the *Valiant*.

Kirk decides to change course for Delta Vega, an uninhabited planet with an automated lithium cracking station that can aid in repairing their warp drive engines that were damaged within the barrier. Mitchell is sedated and transported to the planet where he's confined within a hastily constructed brig. Gary escapes, killing crewman Kelso and taking along Dr. Dehner, who has also begun to mutate. Armed with a phaser rifle, Kirk goes after Gary, who paves the road to him with landslides and other perils.

Kirk urges Dr. Dehner to use her psychological skills to determine whether Gary Mitchell is compassionate and sane enough to survive with these awesome powers. As Mitchell is preparing to kill Kirk, Elizabeth fires huge charges of her own new energies into Gary, momentarily causing him to revert to his old, human self. But Kirk cannot bring himself to kill his old friend and Gary recovers his powers.

Gary produces an empty grave, and tops it with a stone reading "James R. Kirk." But before Mitchell can kill the captain, Kirk aims the phaser rifle at an overhead outcropping of rock. Mitchell is crushed in the grave meant for Kirk and Dr. Dehner dies from the strain of battling Mitchell.

Aboard the *Enterprise*, Kirk records that crewmen Kelso, Mitchell, and Dehner all died in the performance of their duties. Mr. Spock indicates human emotions, expressing grief for Gary Mitchell.

We had seen the glowing eyes before, accompanied by mental powers in a group of children called *The Midwich Cuckoos*, in John Wyndham's suspenseful science fiction novel. The book was filmed as *Village of the Damned* (Metro-Goldwyn-Mayer–1960).[21] The basic plot of "Where No Man Has Gone Before" shares similarities with two "Outer Limits" episodes. In "The Mutant,"[22] a scientist in a space-traveling expedition was bombarded by radioactive rain and emerged with altered eyes and mysterious mental powers. He, too, was telepathic and terrorized the others in the story until he was killed. In "The Sixth Finger,"[23] a Welsh coal miner was artificially mutated in a scientist's "evolution accelerator." The mutant's eyes remained the same, but his head expanded to accommodate his larger, futuristic brain. He, too, embarked upon a reign of terror, but was fortunately stopped when he evolved beyond his hostile emotions. (This episode was directed by James Goldstone, who also directed "Where No Man Has Gone Before.")

In "Burning Bright," a 1974 episode of "The Six Million Dollar Man," William Shatner played an astronaut who, after flying through a radioactive cloud, returned to Earth transformed into a mental mutant.

Casting "Star Trek"

Shooting began on "Where No Man Has Gone Before" on July 19, 1965.[24] Jeffrey Hunter was unavailable for this pilot. The captain's chair was momentarily vacant, but Gene Roddenberry was already considering a talented actor who could capably fill it.

Canadian born actor William Shatner had traveled to the United States in the 1950s and attracted immediate attention because of his stage performances including *Tamburlaine, L'Idiote, The World of Suzie Wong,* and *A Shot in the Dark.* Appearances on television and in films soon followed. In 1964, Shatner was cast as young Assistant District Attorney David Koster, the leading character in "For the People," a short-lived but critically acclaimed television series. The series was applauded for its relevance and courage, but unfortunately CBS had programmed it opposite the ratings' leader at that time ("Bonanza"). William Shatner was therefore available to accept an invitation from Gene Roddenberry to attend a screening of "The Cage."

Shatner was no stranger to quality television science fiction, fantasy, and horror. He had appeared twice in Universal's classic teleseries "Thriller," hosted by Boris Karloff. In "The Hungry Glass"[25] and "The Grim Reaper"[26] Shatner led one reviewer to dub him "the male Fay Wray," because of his talents for screaming in terror. On two memorable occasions, Shatner had also ". . . unlocked this door with the key of imagination" and entered "The Twilight Zone," starring in "Nick of Time" and "Nightmare at 20,000 Feet."[27] In one of those coincidences that sometimes happens in television, Shatner found himself cast as a spaceman on "The Outer Limits" episode "Cold Hands, Warm Heart."[28] A twentieth-century Earth astronaut, Shatner's character had visited the planet Venus as part of a space program called Project Vulcan.

In another television coincidence, Shatner and Nimoy had appeared together in an episode of "The Man from U.N.C.L.E.," "The Project Strigas Affair." This tale featured Shatner as a bumbling double agent, working with Napoleon Solo and Ilya Kuriakin (who have been called the closest team on TV to Kirk and Spock). Nimoy appeared as an enemy operative. In one hilarious sequence, a supposedly drunk Shatner was helped down a flight of stairs by a menacing looking Nimoy.

Following is a detailed list of William Shatner's credits.

William Shatner's Credits

Stage

Cymbeline (Stratford, Ontario Shakespeare Company–1956)

Evening with William Shatner, An (Misc. readings, one man show; 43 city tour–1976)

Henry V (Stratford–1956)

Hyphen, The (Premiered at University of Utah, Salt Lake City–1966)

Julius Caesar (Stratford–1955)

Measure for Measure (Stratford–1954)

Merchant of Venice, The (Stratford–1955)

Merry Wives of Windsor, The (Stratford–1956)

Oedipus Rex (Stratford–1954 and 1955)

Otherwise Engaged (Los Angeles–1978)

Remote Asylum (Los Angeles–1971)

Shot in the Dark, A (Broadway–1961–62)

Symphony of the Stars ("Music From the Galaxies and Beyond"–dramatic science fiction readings w/ Chicago Philharmonic Orchestra conducted by Fred Lewis–1978) (Following a similar production with the Los Angeles Philharmonic Orchestra)

Tamburlaine the Great (Stratford and Broadway–1955–56)

Taming of the Shrew, The (Stratford–1945)

Tender Trap, The (Papermill Playhouse, New Jersey–1970)

There's a Girl in My Soup (Pennsylvania–1969)

Tricks of the Trade (1977)

World of Suzie Wong, The (Broadway–1958–59) (w/ France Nuyen, Sarah Marshall)

Mountain Playhouse Summer Stock Company, Montreal, Canada; 1952–53 debut.

Canadian National Repertory Theatre of Ottawa (1952–54)

Produced McGill University variety show *(Red, Light and Blue*–1954)

Stratford, Ontario, Canada Shakespeare Festival (1954–56)

Motion Pictures

Big Bad Mama (New World–1974)

Brothers Karamazov, The (Metro-Goldwyn-Mayer–1957)

Dead of Night (Europix–1974)

Devil's Rain, The (Bryanston–1975)

Explosive Generation, The (United Artists–1961)

Impulse ((Camelot International–1975)

Incubus (independent–1975) (Filmed in the Esperanto language)

Intruder, The (independent–1961) (also released as *The Stranger*)

Judgment at Nuremberg (United Artists–1961)

Kingdom of the Spiders (Dimension–1977)

Mysteries of the Gods (Hemisphere–1977)

Outrage, The (Metro-Goldwyn-Mayer–1964)

Whale of a Tale, A (Luckers–1977)

White Comanche (independent)

Television

Alcoa Premiere ("Million Dollar Hospital"–1963)

Alcoa Presents (syndication title–*One Step Beyond*)("The Promise"–1960)

Alexander the Great (unsold MGM TV pilot–1963) (Shown in 1968)

Alfred Hitchcock Presents ("The Glass Eye"–1957) ("Mother May I Go Out to Swim"–1960)

Amy Prentiss ("Baptism of Fire"–1974)

Arrest and Trial ("Onward and Upward"–1964)

Barbary Coast (TV series–Star–ABC–1975–76)

Barnaby Jones ("To Catch a Dead Man"–1973)

Bastard, The (Universal TV Movie–1978)

Benjamin Franklin: The Statesman (TV Special–1975)

Big Valley, The ("A Time to Kill"–1966)

Bob Hope Chrysler Theatre ("The Shattered Glass"–1964)
("Wind Fever"–1966) (w/George Takei)

Bold Ones, The ("A Tightrope to Tomorrow"–1973)

Burke's Law ("Who Killed Carrie Cornell"–1964) (w/Michael Ansara)

CBS Playhouse ("Shadow Game"–1969)

Cade's County ("The Armageddon Contract"–1971)

Channing ("Dragon in the Den"–1963)

Checkmate ("The Button-Down Break") (Scriptwriter)

Circle Theater (originally telecast as "Armstrong Circle Theatre"–title unknown)

Climax ("Time of the Hanging"–1958)

Defenders, The ("The Cruel Hook"–1963)
("The Invisible Badge"–1962)
("Killer Instinct"–1961)
("The Uncivil War"–1964)
("Whipping Boy"–1965) (w/Madlyn Rhue)

Dick Powell Theatre ("Colossus"–1963) (unsold TV pilot) (w/Robert Brown, Frank Overton)

Dr. Kildare ("Admitting Service"–1961)
("The Encroachment"–1966) (w/Diana Muldaur)
("Out of a Concrete Tower")
("The Taste of Crow")
("Whatever Happened to All the Sunshine & Roses")

Doctors & the Nurses, The ("Act of Violence"–1965) (2 pts.; concluded on "For the People")

Dreams (CBS; Toronto, Canada–1956) (Shatner wrote it and starred)

FBI, The ("Antennae of Death"–1970)

Family Classics ("The Scarlet Pimpernel"–1960)

For the People (TV series–Starred as Ass't. DA David Koster–thirteen episodes–Produced by Herb Brodkin of The Defenders–started 1/31/65–CBS)

Ford Theatre Playhouse ("Mr. Finchley Vs. the Bomb")

Fugitive, The ("Stranger in the Mirror"–1965)

Go Ask Alice (TV Movie–1973)

Goodyear Playhouse ("All Summer Long"–1956)

Guardians, The (TV Movie–1972)

Gunsmoke ("Quaker Girl"–1966)

Hallmark Hall of Fame ("The Christmas Tree"; vignette: "Light One Candle")

Hawaii Five-O ("You Don't Have to Kill to Get Rich but It Helps"–1972)

Hollywood TV Theatre ("The Andersonville Trials"–1970) (PBS TV)

Horror at 37,000 Feet, The (TV Movie–1973)

Hound of the Baskervilles, The (TV Movie–1972)

Incident on a Dark Street (TV Movie–1973)

Indict and Convict (TV Movie–1974)

Insight ("Locusts Have No Kings"–1965)

Ironside ("The Chief" pilotfilm for "Amy Prentiss"–1974)
("Little Jerry Jessup"–1970)
("The Walls Are Waiting"–1971) (w/Roger C. Carmel)

John Wayne Special ("A Salute to America"–1970)

Kaiser Aluminum Hour ("The Deadly Silence"–1957)
("Gwyneth"–1956)

Kodiak (title unknown–1974)

Kraft Theatre ("The Velvet Trap"–1958)

Kung Fu ("A Small Beheading"–1974)

Lamp Unto My Feet ("The Cape"–1965)

Magician (title unknown–1974)

Man from U.N.C.L.E., The ("The Project Strigas Affair"–1964) (w/Leonard Nimoy)

Mannix (title unknown–1973)

Marcus Welby, MD ("Heartbeat for Yesterday"–1972)

Medical Center ("The Combatants"–1970)

Men at Law ("One American"–1971)

Mission: Impossible ("Cocain"–1972) ("Encore"–1971)

NBC Mystery Movie ("Columbo"–title unknown–1976)

Naked City ("Portrait of a Painter"–1962)
("Without Stick or Sword"–1962)

Name of the Game, The ("The Glory Shouter"–1970)
("Tarot"–1970)

Nurses, The ("A Difference of Years"–1963) (w/Sarah Marshall)
("A Question of Mercy"–1963) (w/Madlyn Rhue)

Omnibus ("Oedipus Rex"–1957)
("School for Wives"–1956)

Outer Limits, The ("Cold Hands, Warm Heart"–1964)
(astronaut on "Project Vulcan")

Outlaws, The ("Starfall"–1960)

Owen Marshall (Pilotfilm–1971) ("Owen Marshall, Counselor at Law")
("Five Will Get You Six"–1972)

Paris 7000 ("The Shattered Idol"–1970)

The People (TV Movie–1972) (w/Kim Darby)

Perilous Voyage (TV Movie–1976)

Petrocelli (title unknown)

Philco Playhouse (title unknown)

Pioneer Woman (TV Movie–1973)

Play of the Week, The ("Night of the Auk"–1960) (PBS TV)

Playhouse 90 ("A Town Has Turned to Dust"–1958) (By Rod Serling)

Police Story (title unknown–1974)

Police Surgeon ("50 Kilos to Nowhere"–1973)

Police Woman (title unknown–1974)

Pray for the Wildcats (TV Movie–1974)

Prudential on Stage ("The Skirts of Happy Chance")

Reporter, The ("He Stuck in His Thumb"–1964)

Robert Herridge Theatre ("A Story of a Gunfighter"–1960)

Rookies, The (title unknown–1975)

Route 66 ("We Build Our Houses with Our Backs to the Sea"–1963)

77 Sunset Strip ("Five"–1963)

Six Million Dollar Man, The ("Burning Bright"–1974)

Sixth Sense, The ("Can a Dead Man Strike from the Grave?"–1972)

Skirts of Happy Chance, The (TV Special–1969)

Sole Survivor (TV Movie–1970)

Song of the Ages (Sermonette) ("The Search")

Studio One ("The Deaf Heart"–1957) ("The Defenders"–1957) ("The Defenders" Pilotfilm; "Kenneth Preston") ("No Deadly Medicine"–1957)

Sunday Showcase ("The Indestructible Mr. Gore"–1959)

Suspicion ("Protégé"–1958)

Tactic (No information available)

Tenth Level, The (TV Special–1976)

Theatre One ("Legman")

Thriller ("The Grim Reaper"–1961) ("The Hungry Glass"–1961)

Twelve O'Clock High ("I Am the Enemy"–1965)

Twilight Zone, The ("Nick of Time"–1960) (By Richard Matheson) ("Nightmare at 20,000 Feet"–1963) (By Richard Matheson)

U.S. Steel Hour ("A Man in Hiding"–1958) ("Old Marshalls Never Die"–1958) ("Walk with a Stranger"–1958)

Vanished (TV Movie–1971)

Virginian, The ("Black Jade"–1969) ("The Claim"–1965)

James Doohan, who first played Scotty in this episode, has at least one thing in common with Gene Roddenberry, Susan Oliver, Leonard Nimoy, and William Shatner; he is a skilled pilot. He joined the Royal Canadian Air Force during World War II. The Canadian actor's career began on radio; he appeared in over 3,500 radio shows. Doohan has taught acting at New York's prestigious Neighborhood Playhouse, and has appeared in numerous stage productions, TV roles, and feature films.

Jimmy's specialty is dialects; he can recreate any accent, including those he originates himself. It was apparently this dialect specialty that landed him the role of "Scotty."

At first, Roddenberry reportedly had no ideas about the ethnic origin of the *Enterprise* engineer. Doohan has reminisced at conventions about his first audition for "Star Trek." He recalls delivering his lines in a variety of accents before Roddenberry finally heard his Scottish brogue. There was no further doubt; our friend Montgomery Scott was born at that moment (in *this* time continuum).

James Doohan's Credits

Stage

Teddy

Trial of James McNeil Whistler, The (Also staged as *The Gentle Art of Making Enemies)*

Motion Pictures

Bus Riley's Back in Town (Universal–1965)

Fellowship (Canadian)

Jigsaw (1968)

Man in the Wilderness (1971)

Pretty Maids All in a Row (Metro-Goldwyn-Mayer–1972)

Satan Bug, The (United Artists–1964)

Wheeler Dealers, The (1963)

Several films for the National Film Board of Canada

Television

Ben Casey ("A Disease of the Heart Called Love"–1965)

Bewitched ("A Strange Little Visitor"–1965)

Blue Light (title unknown)

Bonanza (title unknown)

CBS Television Theater ("Shadow of Suspicion"–1956)

Convoy ("Lady on the Rock"–1965)

Daniel Boone ("The Cache"–1969) ("Perilous Passage"–1970)

Empire ("A House in Order"–1963) (Series syndicated as "Redigo")

F.B.I., The (title unknown)

First Night ("Here Lies Mrs. Moriarty"–1962) ("Rehearsal for Invasion"–1963)

Fugitive, The ("Middle of a Heat Wave"–1965) (w/Sarah Marshall)

Gallant Men, The ("The Warrior"–1963)

Gunsmoke (title unknown)

Hazel ("Hazel's Highland Fling"–1963)

Indict and Convict (An ABC Television Movie)

Iron Horse, The (title unknown)

Jason of Star Command (Recurring role; 1978–79)

Jericho ("Eric the Red-Head"–1966) (w/Barry Atwater)

Laredo ("I See By Your Outfit"–1965)

Man from U.N.C.L.E., The ("Bridge of Lions"–1966) ("The Shark Affair"–1964)

Marcus Welby, MD ("Let Ernest Come Over"–1969)

New Breed, The ("The Deadlier Sex"–1960)

Outer Limits, The ("Expanding Human"–1964) (w/Skip Homeier, Keith Andes)

Peyton Place (Recurring role)

Return to Peyton Place (Recurring role)

Shenandoah ("Care of General Delivery"–1966)

Space Command (Regular starring role) (Canadian TV series)

Then Came Bronson ("Amid Splinters of the Thunderbolt"–1969)

Twilight Zone, The ("Valley of the Shadow") (an hour episode)
Virginian, The ("The Man Who Wouldn't Die"–1963)
Voyage to the Bottom of the Sea ("Hail to the Chief")

Jimmy's real-life exploits approximate those of Mr. Scott. Wounded on D-Day, he was later known in the Canadian Air Force for his daringly skillful performances as the pilot of an artillery observation plane.

Today, Jimmy Doohan is a welcome guest at "Star Trek" conventions; his many stories and songs and his congenial nature have endeared him to many, many fans. During his first appearance in "Star Trek," in "Where No Man Has Gone Before," Mr. Scott had a minimum of dialogue; as was the case with most of the regulars' first appearances, there was no indication in this episode that the dour "Mr. Scott" would soon metamorphose into the warmly human "Scotty."

If Scotty's debut is hardly noticeable in "Where No Man Has Gone Before," the first appearance of Lt. Sulu must be described as both miniscule and atypical. "Physicist" Sulu had two significant lines of dialogue in this adventure, and neither pointed to the adventuresome, vital individual into which he would develop.

Actor George Takei was born in Los Angeles. In the opening days of the U.S. entry into World War II, George and his family were relocated to Arkansas along with other Japanese-American families. This culturally and politically traumatic experience affected George in positive ways. It made him more determined than the average man to make himself known to the world as an individual who cares about other human beings.

George began to study architecture at the University of Southern California in Berkeley, but soon transferred to the Los Angeles campus. There he was exposed to a facet of life that apparently captivated him; he changed his major to theater arts.

While still a student, George appeared on "Playhouse 90," and joined the Desilu Actors' Workshop. After obtaining his Master's Degree in Theater, he began appearing in TV series episodes and feature films. In his first film, *Ice Palace* (Warner Brothers–1959) he aged together with star Richard Burton in makeup that was reminiscent of that later worn by other *Enterprise* crewmen in "The Deadly Years."

Today, George continues his acting career in addition to handling other "roles" as well. He has hosted an informative television series called "Expression East/West," which discussed important issues pertaining to human relationships. Active on the Los Angeles transportation board, George has a deep interest in quick and efficient rapid transit systems. After an attempt at entering political office, George is still actively involved in urban issues other than transportation. He has recently also embarked upon a new career, having co-written his first novel; science fiction, of course.

George Takei's Credits

Stage
Choice of Wars, A
Departure
Fly Blackbirds
Good Woman of Setzuan
Macbeth (Inner City Cultural Center; Los Angeles, California)
Monkey's Paw, The (Inner City Cultural Center; Los Angeles, Ca.)
Year of the Dragon, The
Zoo Story (Alaska tour)

Motion Pictures
American Dream, An (Warner Brothers–1966) (directed by Robert Gist)
Green Berets, The (Batjac–1968)
Hell to Eternity (Allied Artists–1960) (w/Jeffrey Hunter)
Ice Palace (Warner Brothers–1960)
Josie's Castle
Loudmouth, The
Majority of One, A (Warner Brothers–1960)
P.T. 109 (Warner Brothers–1963)
Red Line 7000 (Paramount–1966)
Walk Don't Run (Columbia–1966)
Which Way to the Front (Warner Brothers–1970)
Young Divorcees, The (Monarch–1975)

Television
Alcoa Premiere (title unknown)
Assignment: Underwater ("A Matter of Honor"–1961)
Baa Baa Black Sheep ("Up for Grabs")
Bob Hope Chrysler Theatre ("Wind Fever"–1966) (w/William Shatner)
Bracken's World (title unknown)
Californian, The (title unknown)
Checkmate (title unknown)
Chico and the Man (title unknown)
Courtship of Eddie's Father, The (title unknown)
Eleventh Hour, The (title unknown)
Espionage ("A Free Agent"–1964)
Expression East/West (KNBC talk show—producer, Host)
Felony Squad, The (title unknown)
Follow the Sun (title unknown)
Gallant Men, The (title unknown)
Hallmark Hall of Fame, The (title unknown)
Hawaii Five-O (title unknown)
Hawaiian Eye ("Jade Song"–1960)
    ("The Manchu Formula"–1961)
    ("Sword of the Samurai"–1960)
    ("Thomas Jefferson Chu"–1961)
Hennessey (title unknown)
House on K Street, The
I Spy ("The Barter")
    ("Tiger of Heaven")

Ironside (title unknown)

Islanders, The (title unknown)

It Takes a Thief (title unknown)

John Forsythe Show, The ("Doctor Soo"-1966)
("It Takes a Heap of Sergeants")

Khan (title unknown)

Kung Fu (title unknown)

Marcus Welby, MD (title unknown)

Mission: Impossible (title unknown)

Mr. Novack (title unknown)

Mr. Roberts ("Getting There Is Half the Fun"-1965)
("Which Way Did the War Go?"-1965)

Mr. T and Tina (Unaired pilot version)

My Three Sons ("Hong Kong Story")
("My Fair Chinese Lady"-1964)
("Lady in the Air")

O'Hara, Treasury Agent (title unknown)

Perry Mason ("The Case of the Blushing Pearls"-1959)

Playhouse 90 (Professional debut)

Six Million Dollar Man, The ("The Coward")

Steve Allen Show, The (Segment unknown)

Theatre in America ("Year of the Dragon"-1975)

This Is the Life ("Mission of Mercy")
("The Password Is Faith")

Twilight Zone, The ("The Encounter")

U.S. Steel Hour, The (title unknown)

Voyage to the Bottom of the Sea ("The Silent
Saboteurs"-1965)

Wackiest Ship in the Army, The ("The Goldbrickers"-
1965) (w/Michael Ansara)
("My Father's Keeper"-1966)

Veteran actor Paul Fix was cast as ship's Doctor
Mark Piper. Originally a stage actor, Fix's film career
dates back to *The Bar 20 Rides Again* (a Hopalong
Cassidy feature filmed at Paramount in 1935) and
After the Thin Man (Metro-Goldwyn-Mayer-1936).
His first screen exposure to science fiction was short;
he was the doomed assistant to *Dr. Cyclops* (Para-
mount-1940) in that film's opening sequence.[29] On TV
he is best remembered for his regular role of Marshall
Micah Torrance in "The Rifleman" from 1958 to 1963.
In other TV work he can be seen in "The Adventures
of Superman" ("Tsar of the Underworld" and "Semi-
Private Eye"), "The Twilight Zone" ("I Am the Night,
Color Me Black"), and "Voyage to the Bottom of the
Sea" ("The Terrible Toys"). He appeared with De-
Forest Kelley, the *Enterprise*'s regular doctor, in the
feature film *The Night of the Lepus* (Metro-Goldwyn-
Mayer-1972).

Andrea Dromm (Yeoman Smith) debuted as the
first "National Airlines Girl" on television. This was
followed by guest spots on television and roles in feature films such as *The Russians Are Coming, The
Russians Are Coming* and *Come Spy with Me.*

Lloyd Haines (Communications Officer Alden),
later attained TV stardom thanks to his recurring role
of teacher Pete Dixon in "Room 222" (1969-1974).

For Paul Fix, Andrea Dromm, and Lloyd Haines,

"Where No Man Has Gone Before" could have led to
permanent places within the "Star Trek" cast once
the series was accepted by NBC. Unfortunately, there
were more changes in personnel after the series was
committed, and for these three "Where No Man Has
Gone Before" was both their first and last appearance
on Trek. Three other performers signed on for this
voyage *knowing* it would be their only one; they all
portrayed characters who died in the episode.

Gary Lockwood (Lieutenant Commander Gary
Mitchell) had previously worked for Gene Roddenberry as the star of his 1962-63 Metro-Goldwyn-
Mayer teleseries, "The Lieutenant." He has appeared
in feature films, including *Wild in the Country* and
Splendor in the Grass. Lockwood's science fiction experience began with his role in "Star Trek"; he went
on to portray astronaut Frank Poole in *2001: A Space
Odyssey* (Metro-Goldwyn-Mayer-1968), and also
starred in the MGM TV movie *Earth Two*. In the
enjoyable fantasy film *The Magic Sword* (United Art-
ists-1962) Lockwood portrayed George, a knight in
shining armor. He appeared regularly as Eric Jason in
the TV series "Follow the Sun" (1961-62), and worked
with actress Sally Kellerman on another occasion; in
the "Kraft Suspense Theatre" segment, "Connery's
Hands," produced a few months before "Where No
Man Has Gone Before."

Sally Kellerman (Dr. Elizabeth Dehner) made her
TV debut on "The Outer Limits" ("The Bellero
Shield," in which she played the wife of Martin
Landau, an actor once considered for the role of
Mr. Spock).[30] She appeared in Rod Serling's teleplay
"A Slow Fade to Black" on "The Bob Hope Chrysler
Theater," before she achieved stardom as the orig-
inal Major "Hotlips" Hoolihan in the feature film
M.A.S.H. Ms. Kellerman appeared in "Labyrinth," a
segment of "The Invaders" TV series.

Paul Carr (Lieutenant Lee Kelso) has been active
on TV for far longer than his youthful appearance
would indicate. He can be seen in "Voyage to the Bottom of the Sea" segments "Doomsday," "Terror on
Dinosaur Island," and "Cradle of the Deep," and on
the "One Step Beyond" episode "Reunion."

Meanwhile, on the other side of the camera, additional production personnel were being recruited for
the second pilot. Robert H. Justman was now the
associate producer and assistant director, Walter M.
Jefferies moved up to production designer, Alexander
Courage was rehired as the composer, and the Howard
A. Anderson Company again did the photographic effects.

James Goldstone was hired to direct. Goldstone had
directed two episodes of "The Outer Limits": "The
Sixth Finger" and "The Inheritors." He would later
return to "Star Trek" to direct "What Are Little Girls
Made of?"

Ernest Haller was signed as director of photography. Haller's work in the film industry dates back

to 1914, when he became an actor at Biograph studios before switching to cinematography. He photographed *International House* at Paramount in 1933, and many other films including *Captain Blood* (Warner Brothers–1935) and *The Roaring Twenties* (Warner Brothers–1939). He won an Academy Award for his photography of *Gone With the Wind* (Metro-Goldwyn-Mayer–1939).[31]

Tremendous pressures were experienced by all personnel concerned with the production of "Where No Man Has Gone Before." This was "Star Trek's" final chance of getting on the air, and there were also specific problems, such as the invasion of insects, which transformed stars William Shatner and Sally Kellerman into temporary casualties.[32]

Despite the pressure and distractions, "Where No Man Has Gone Before" took only eight days to photograph. It is a tribute to everyone involved that shooting did not drag on long beyond the planned schedule.

There had been other changes in production personnel since "The Cage" had been completed. The following is a detailed list of personnel who worked on this second pilot, and some of the important dates connected with this important "Star Trek" adventure.

WHERE NO MAN HAS GONE BEFORE

Episode # 2
First draft script 5/27/65
Second draft script 6/16/65
Final draft script 6/28/65
Revised final draft 7/8/65
Filming began 7/19/65
Filmed in middle and late July, 1965

Production Credits

PRODUCER Gene Roddenberry
WRITER Samuel A. Peeples
DIRECTOR James Goldstone
ASSOCIATE PRODUCER Robert H. Justman
MUSIC COMPOSED & CONDUCTED BY Alexander Courage
DIRECTOR OF PHOTOGRAPHY Ernest Haller, ASC
PRODUCTION DESIGNER Walter M. Jefferies
ART DIRECTOR Roland M. Brooks
FILM EDITOR John Foley
ASSISTANT DIRECTOR Robert H. Justman
SET DECORATOR Ross Dowd
COSTUMES CREATED BY William Ware Theiss
SOUND MIXER Cameron McCulloch
POST PRODUCTION EXECUTIVE Bill Heath
MUSIC EDITOR Jack Hunsaker
SOUND EDITOR Joseph G. Sorokin
PRODUCTION SUPERVISOR James Paisley
WARDROBE Paul McCardle
SPECIAL EFFECTS Bob Overbeck
MUSIC CONSULTANT Wilbur Hatch

MUSIC COORDINATOR Julian Davidson
MAKEUP Robert Dawn
HAIRSTYLES Hazel Keats
SOUND Glen Glenn Sound Co.
PHOTOGRAPHIC EFFECTS Howard A. Anderson Co.
EXECUTIVE IN CHARGE OF PRODUCTION Herbert F. Solow
A Desilu Production in association with Norway Corp.

Cast

CAPTAIN JAMES R. KIRK William Shatner
SCIENCE OFFICER SPOCK Leonard Nimoy
LIEUTENANT LEE KELSO Paul Carr
LIEUTENANT COMMANDER GARY MITCHELL Gary Lockwood
ENGINEERING OFFICER SCOTT James Doohan
PHYSICIST SULU George Takei
COMMUNICATIONS OFFICER ALDEN Lloyd Haynes
YEOMAN SMITH Andrea Dromm
DR. MARK PIPER Paul Fix
DR. ELIZABETH DEHNER Sally Kellerman
SECURITY GUARD Eddie Paskey
William Shatner's Stunt Double Dick Crockett
Gary Lockwood's Stunt Double Hal Needham

A New Look for "Star Trek"

In the wardrobe department, the jackets were discarded and the captain's hat was forgotten for the remainder of the series. The costumes were altered. Dr. Dehner wore a blue uniform. Mr. Spock's shirt was changed from blue to gold. The insignia had acquired their familiar gold background, black border, and finished appearance; they were still slightly smaller than those used in the regular episodes. Continuity had also started in reference to the insignia. Kirk, Spock, and Mr. Alden wore stars. Gary and Scotty wore what would later become the "sciences" emblem. Dr. Piper, Mr. Sulu, Dr. Dehner, and Yeoman Smith wore the "ship's services" spiral.

The shirts still had their shoulder zippers; all except Mr. Spock's. To assist actor Leonard Nimoy, the collar was two separate halves that snapped together. This saved wear and tear on Spock's complex makeup.

The women still wore trousers.

Fred Phillips was temporarily replaced by another Desilu staffer, Robert Dawn, the son of MGM makeup great Jack Dawn, who created the makeups for hundreds of that studio's classic films, including *The Wizard of Oz* (1939).

Robert Dawn's "Mr. Spock" was more severe than Phillips' Spock of "The Cage." His eyebrows swept sharply upward, and his shorter "bangs" made his head seem longer. His complexion was yellowish-gold. Dawn's application of the ear tips was flawless. After

Phillips returned to the "Star Trek" staff, Dawn was kept busy designing the many incredible makeup transformations featured in "Mission: Impossible."[33]

Dawn did some very subtle things with the appearance of Gary Mitchell. To show the tremendous physical stresses that Mitchell's body was experiencing, Dawn gradually added gray to actor Gary Lockwood's hair. By the last scenes of the episode, Mitchell's sideburns were completely gray.

On the bridge, the turbo doors and railings were now red. The regular chairs were used here, but without their custom-made black backs and cushions. The navigation console was still not finished, and appears to be the same as it was in "The Cage." Likewise for the captain's chair, which still included the small goosenecked monitor screen from the first pilot. The captain's chair also still lacked an intercom speaker; but it did have a numbered plate, reading "3C-42," later used to designate someone's quarters. (No, it wasn't Janice Rand's; hers are "3C-46.")

The turbo lifts had "up" and "down" lighted signals near their doors.

In the corridors, one door was marked "Astro-Medicine, Ward 4," supplemented with the room number "3F-127." This later became the numbered designation of Dr. McCoy's quarters (in "Man Trap").

The transporter platform was topped with a large, round ceiling fixture. This was removed after shooting on "Where No Man Has Gone Before" was completed, and was never restored to the set.

The first "sick bay" set featured diagnostic beds with twentieth-century-type bedding, complete with conventional mattress, sheet, pillow, and pillowcase plus a brown bedspread. The entire room was smaller than the regular version and contained only two beds, a wooden chair, a bookshelf, and an opposite shelf with a faucet. The monitoring panels had to be activated by hand.

Outdoors on planet Delta Vega, all the planetside locations are indoor sets with painted backdrops. Most of the "rocks" are actually hastily constructed platforms built of wood, mesh, fabric, and paint. If you watch carefully, you can see Kirk "bounce" as he climbs to get to Mitchell's location.

The only hand prop built for "Where No Man Has Gone Before" was the phaser rifle. Although it was mentioned in the writers' guide, the phaser rifle never appeared in any future Trek episodes.[34]

Special Effects

After the live-action footage had been completed, part of the episode still remained to be done; the "post-production" phase, including the complex special photographic effects.

The same *Enterprise* model constructed for "The

The Mr. Spock of "Where No Man Has Gone Before" is more severe-looking than the later version (Leonard Nimoy).

Cage" was used in "Where No Man Has Gone Before"; it still lacked its later interior nacelle lights and various other surface details. Stock shots of the miniature, left over from the first pilot, were combined with new backgrounds such as the galactic barrier (colored lights reflected off special materials).

Animation was used in this episode. Aside from the phaser blasts and the flashes of light that occasionally emanated from Gary's hands in times of stress, there were also the short views of Gary and Elizabeth being "zapped" by the barrier, and the shower of energy the two threw at each other during the story's climax.

Another effect that was used depended upon a combination of animation and live action. Gary Mitchell's eyes were not always made to glow with contact lenses. The finished effect of Gary's eyes reverting to normal (and then back again) was helped along with a technique known as "freeze frame." One clear frame of actor Gary Lockwood with *normal* eyes was selected and blown up so that a studio artist was able to trace the glowing effect. The traced artwork was executed on cartoon "cels," transparent pieces of celluloid. Optically combined onto Gary Mitchell's eyes, this specialized "cartoon" caused the pulsating effect. In one effective scene, the live action footage was faded out, but the glowing eyes were left on screen for a few seconds, floating in darkness immediately before a commercial break.

The lithium cracking station was a matte painting. The only parts of the "set" that were actually constructed were a small part of the building's wall and the doorway. The doorway resembles one of the portals that led into the Krel labs in *Forbidden Planet*.

The optical painting of the lithium cracking station with the life-size doorway matted in, in "Where No Man Has Gone Before."

With some alterations, and a painted doorway of its own, the "Where No Man Has Gone Before" landscape became the Tantalus Colony exterior in "Dagger of the Mind."

A Variation of the Second Pilot

There are actually *two* different versions of "Where No Man Has Gone Before." The print that Gene Roddenberry first submitted to NBC was a variation that has never been televised.

This other version began with a view of our galaxy, accompanied by William Shatner's voiceover explaining that the *Enterprise* was an exploration vessel and that its mission was to journey "... where no man has gone before."

The first interior scene was the chess game between Kirk and Spock. But when Kirk remarked how terrible it was that Spock had "bad blood" *(human* blood) in his veins, the captain added: "... But you may learn to enjoy it someday."

When the disaster recorder materialized and began to flash off and on in the transporter room, the scene "froze," and over the picture the words "STAR TREK" appeared in plain blue letters trimmed with silver. In the same block-lettering style, the words "tonight's episode: WHERE NO MAN HAS GONE BEFORE" materialized as the opening theme was heard. This original theme was heard in later episodes, and is not at all similar to the series' regular theme. The original opening credits were very short and were followed by a commercial break.

We first saw Gary Mitchell in a short scene cut from the aired version. Walking through the corridors toward the turbo lift where he encountered Kirk and Spock, Gary spotted an attractive crewwoman and turned to admire the aft view. Returning his gaze forward, Gary spotted Yeoman Smith; as his eyes followed her down the corridor he made a gesture that revealed that he was an admirer of her physical attributes. The scene humanized Mitchell, and made his later changes more horrifying to the audience. We also understand more about Kirk's relationship to Mitchell. While Gary recalls Kirk as "a stack of books with legs," it is apparent that Mitchell was a bundle of laughs in the old days.

While Mitchell was walking through the corridors in the untelevised version, Ernest Haller's camerawork followed his walk from angles we never saw again in the series. The camera looked straight up while it was positioned under the floor level, and looked straight down onto the floor shooting down from above the ceiling grids.

This version of "Where No Man Has Gone Before" was divided into four acts, in the same style as producer Quinn Martin's series (including "The Invaders" and "The Fugitive"). The last scene was presented as a short epilogue.

The end credits were backed by music that was never heard again in "Star Trek." A fast-moving, almost cheerful electronic tune, it accompanied the end credits that listed just the main performers. The credits were very generalized ("Paul Fix as Ship's Doctor"; "George Takei as Chief Physicist"). It was probably this print that Gene Roddenberry later presented to the Smithsonian Institution at the Institution's request.[35]

"Star Trek" the Series Is Born

By October 1965, Roddenberry had overseen production on two other Desilu TV pilots, "Police Story" (a contemporary crime series),[36] and "The Long Hunt of April Savage" (a period western featuring a tragic, vengeance-seeking hero whose humanity vanished when his family was killed).[37] After these two projects had been taken care of, Roddenberry was free to finish "Where No Man Has Gone Before."

The second "Star Trek" pilot was reworked until it was delivered to NBC headquarters in New York City in January 1966.[38] In mid-February 1966, Gene Roddenberry was notified of the network's acceptance of "Star Trek," the television series.[39]

There were more changes in *Enterprise* personnel. Yeoman Smith (Andrea Dromm), Dr. Piper (Paul Fix), and Communications Officer Alden (Lloyd Haynes) were dropped from the format. Physicist Sulu became Helmsman Sulu, and George Takei signed on for his five-year mission, along with William Shatner and James Doohan.

The processes of refining "Star Trek" did not stop after these alterations in the *Enterprise* duty roster. Dr. McCoy (DeForest Kelley), Lieutenant Uhura (Nichelle Nichols), and Yeoman Janice Rand (Grace Lee Whitney) were yet to join the crew. They would become part of "Star Trek's" first regular production season, later to be joined by Ensign Pavel Chekov (Walter Koenig) at the start of the second season.

While these and other crucial format changes were taking shape, Gene Roddenberry experienced elation and nervousness. His preliminary work to sell "Star Trek" was over, but his real labors were just beginning, along with the beginning of the *Enterprise*'s five-year mission.

NOTES

1. H. G. Wells, *The Shape of Things to Come* (New York: The MacMillan Company, 1933);
   H. G. Wells, *Things to Come* (London, England: Cresset Press, 1935).

2. Stephen E. Whitfield and Gene Roddenberry, *The Making Of Star Trek* (New York: Ballantine Books, 1968), pp. 22–30.

3. Ibid., pp. 47–65.

4. Ibid., pp. 77–78.

5. Ibid., p. 113.

6. David Gerrold, *The World of Star Trek* (New York: Ballantine Books, 1973), pp. 58–59.

7. "In Charlie X," although most female personnel wear the miniskirted tunics usually seen in the series, at least two female personnel wear trousers.

8. In a memo dated 10/14/64, Roddenberry requested that a sighting device and a secondary hand grip be included in the pistol design to permit precision aiming and firing of the weapon. Only the laser pistol has a "sight"; the later phasers have neither of these features.

9. Howard A. Anderson, ASC; Linwood Dunn, ASC; Joseph Westheimer, ASC, "Out of This World Special Effects for Star Trek," *American Cinematographer* (Oct., 1967): 715–717.
   In this extremely informative article, Anderson (president of Howard A. Anderson Co.), Dunn (president of Film Effects of Hollywood, Inc.), and Westheimer (president of the Westheimer Company) discuss their respective photographic effects contributions to "Star Trek."

10. Whitfield and Roddenberry, *The Making of Star Trek*, pp. 81–83.
    Some of the earliest *Enterprise* design concepts are illustrated.

11. Ibid., pp. 79, 80, 84.

12. "Out of This World Special Effects for Star Trek," *American Cinematographer* p. 715.

13. Ibid.

14. Ibid.

15. Ibid.

16. Ibid.

17. Whitfield and Roddenberry, *The Making of Star Trek,* pp. 117–118.

18. Ibid.

19. Ibid.

20. Ibid., p. 89.

21. For some scenes in "Where No Man Has Gone Before," the glowing eyes were achieved in approximately the same way they were in "Village of the Damned," with animation effects ("cartoons") double-exposed onto the eyes.

22. "The Mutant" was written by Allan Balter and Robert Mintz, based on a story by Jerome B. Tunnis.

23. "The Sixth Finger" was written by Ellis St. Joseph.

24. Whitfield and Roddenberry, *The Making of Star Trek,* pp. 146, 147.

25. In "The Hungry Glass," Shatner was a photographer who moved into a mysterious house and was ultimately "absorbed" into the mansion's mirrors.

26. In "The Grim Reaper," written by Robert Bloch and directed by Herschel Daugherty (both of whom worked on "Star Trek" episodes), his character was killed by a strange painted portrait of death.

27. Both of these episodes were written by Richard Matheson. "Nightmare at 20,000 Feet" co-starred actor Ed Kemmer, who from 1950 to 1956 portrayed Commander Buzz Corey on the classic TV series space-opera, "Space Patrol."

28. Astronaut Shatner's boss in this episode was portrayed by Malachi Throne, who also appeared as Commodore Mendez in "The Menagerie."

29. The scene, in which mad scientist Dr. Thorkel (Albert Dekker) murders him by pushing him under a deadly radioactive ray, is sometimes missing from televised prints of the film.

30. Ms. Kellerman also appeared in "Outer Limits" episode "The Human Factor," with co-star Barry Atwater, directed by Gerd Oswald.

31. In *Gone with the Wind,* he photographed the brilliant designs of William Cameron Menzies, who had directed *Things to Come* three years earlier.

32. Whitfield and Roddenberry, *The Making of Star Trek,* pp. 156–157.

33. In "Mission: Impossible," Dawn created the disguises worn by Martin Landau (as Rollin Hand), an actor once reputed to have been considered as an alternate choice to portray Mr. Spock. Later in the series, the resident disguise expert became Paris the Great, portrayed by Leonard Nimoy after "Star Trek" had ceased production.

34. The revised edition of the *Writers' Guide* (dated 8/30/66) mentions nothing about a phaser rifle, but the third revision of 4/17/67 does. This was to have been a different device than its prototype, including an opening into which the pistol grip phaser could be inserted and amplified.

35. The Smithsonian Institution requested publicity photos and information on Trek as well, to be added (along with the print) to the archives of the National Air and Space Museum. The Museum was later presented with the *Enterprise* miniature, the Klingon ship model, the Tholian ship, and the miniature *Enterprise* silver pendant (created for "Catspaw"). Following the Washington, D.C., premiere of *Star Trek—The Motion Picture,* a reception was held in the Museum.

36. "Police Story," written by Gene Roddenberry, had a cast that included DeForest Kelley and Grace Lee Whitney. It was televised in September 1967, on NBC, but never made it into series status. It was a Desilu production.

37. The pilot segment of this unsold series was titled "Home Is an Open Grave." The episode, written by Sam Rolfe (in August and September 1965), was also a Desilu production.

38. Whitfield and Roddenberry, *The Making of Star Trek,* p. 158.

39. Ibid., p. 159.

3 The Series Takes Shape

"Star Trek" experienced many changes between the completion of its pilot episodes and the start of the regular series' production. There were replacements and modifications of principal characters. The technical details of the *Enterprise* were also redesigned as old sets were changed and others were added. Some of the earliest publicity materials and scripts provide insights that reveal how differently "Star Trek" might have evolved.

Only a few lucky "Star Trek" fans have seen one of the rarest Trek collector's items in existence, a twelve-page booklet prepared by the network sales planning division of NBC in New York, entitled "Advanced Information on 1966–67 Programming: *STAR TREK*." The booklet, which carries no date of origin, indicates that "Star Trek" was at this point expected to be produced using the same performers and characters who appeared in "Where No Man Has Gone Before."

The series' regular crew members are identified as Captain Kirk (William Shatner), Mr. Spock (Leonard Nimoy), Mr. Scott (James Doohan), Mr. Alden (Lloyd Haynes), Mr. Sulu (George Takei), Dr. Piper (Paul Fix), and Yeoman Smith (Andrea Dromm).

The description of Mr. Spock mentions his logical way of thinking and attributes this to his father, a native of the planet *Vulcanis*. People from Vulcanis are called *Vulcanians,* rather than Vulcans.[1]

Vulcanians, the booklet continues, do not lack emotion; they just don't believe in revealing their emotions in public. This description seems to be the earliest acknowledgment that Spock is a "split personality," exhibiting his Vulcan stoicism, denying his human emotions, and functioning within an environment in which his emotions *should* be expressed.

We now come to the booklet's most important feature. Two pictures of Spock are included here. In each picture, his features have been altered to appear as normal, Terran features. In both, his eyebrows have been restored to their human contours. One of the photos has Spock's ears shortened so that their pointed tips are barely noticeable. The other picture shows the Vulcan with completely human ears. The responsibility for these altered photos was supposedly traced back to a minor official in the network's art department.[2]

Was there a time when NBC was considering doing away with Spock's alien attributes, including his facial

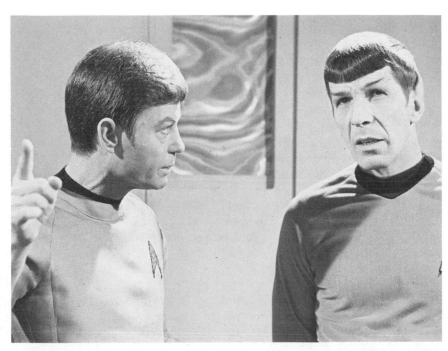

Despite their constant attempts to disguise their respect for each other, Dr. McCoy and Mr. Spock are really the best of friends (DeForest Kelley, Leonard Nimoy).

James Doohan, as Scotty, is the human extension of the *Enterprise*'s technology in "The Naked Time."

features? At approximately this time, Roddenberry had been asked to drop Spock from the "Star Trek" format completely.[3]

Chief Officer of Medicine Dr. Mark Piper is established as the oldest person aboard the *Enterprise*. Dr. Piper's duties, as mentioned in the booklet, include all those later assumed by Dr. McCoy, including physician and psychological "watchdog" to the *Enterprise* crew. Evidently it had been decided the ship's doctor should have more of a role than the few lines uttered by Dr. Piper in "Where No Man Has Gone Before." The trend here seems to be returning to the initial relationship between Dr. Boyce and Captain Pike in "The Cage."

In addition, the booklet reveals that planet explorations would largely depend upon Dr. Piper's evaluations of alien plants and animals. This duty would later be assigned to Science Officer Spock.

Communications Officer Alden is described as an efficient, respected, and young technician whose duties are vital to the ship's welfare and require constant computations and speculations. These characteristics and abilities are also attributes of Lieutenant Uhura, who replaced Mr. Alden in the final format of the series.

Sulu's title in this booklet is chief of the Astro Science Department. Like Dr. Piper, he was required to aid in determining whether or not newly discovered planets should be explored.

After Spock was finally accepted as a member of the *Enterprise* family, *he* became the precise scientific figure. Sulu was left free to develop into the capable helmsman with tendencies to reveal his fascinations for swashbuckling and other pastimes.

Yeoman Smith, on her first assignment into outer space, is described as "popular." Her qualifications are specifically identified as (1) secretarial capabilities, (2) a talent for making coffee, and (3) providing an attractive target for the eyes of drooling spacemen.

The Yeoman was apparently destined to be "window dressing" on the *Enterprise*. Fortunately, it was probably decided that since starships have few windows, they do not *need* window dressing. Yeoman Jan-

Yeoman Rand readies a new shirt for Captain Kirk in this scene cut from the aired print of "The Corbomite Maneuver" (Grace Lee Whitney).

ice Rand, who took the place of Yeoman Smith, possesses all the qualities of her predecessor. In Janice's case, however, these physical and domestic attractions serve as supplements to her main qualities of courage, resourcefulness, and loyalty.

Grace Lee Whitney was born in Detroit, Michigan. While still a teenager she auditioned successfully for radio station WJR's choral group, run by famed bandleader Fred Waring. Following her graduation from high school, she moved to Chicago and placed second in the Miss Chicago contest before becoming a lead vocalist with various Chicago bands.

On a vacation in New York City, Grace auditioned for a role in the Broadway musical, *Top Banana*. She won the role and understudied the star, even though she had no previous experience in musical comedy. She accompanied the play's cast to Hollywood and appeared in the film version of the play. Returning to New York, she repeated her success by appearing in *Pajama Game* in both its stage and film versions. After appearing in other films she acted in television series episodes. Her appearance in Gene Roddenberry's unsold TV pilot "Police Story" (as Policewoman Libby Monroe) probably led to her being considered by Roddenberry for the role of Yeoman Rand.

Yeoman Rand appeared in Trek episodes #3 ("The Corbomite Maneuver") through #13 ("The Conscience of the King"), and was then written out of the series' format for unknown reasons. For *Star Trek—the Motion Picture,* Grace returned to the "Star Trek" family as Transporter Chief Janice Rand, which greatly pleased the many fans Grace has entranced at "Star Trek" conventions. With her husband (composer Jack Dale) and her singing group "Star," Grace regularly entertains in nightclubs and at conventions.

Following is a list of Grace's stage, feature, and television appearances.

Grace Lee Whitney's Credits

Stage
Gentlemen Prefer Blondes (Broadway)
Pajama Game, The (Broadway)
Three Penny Opera (Broadway)
Top Banana (Broadway)

Motion Pictures
Irma La Douce
Naked and the Dead, The
Pajama Game, The
Some Like It Hot
Top Banana

Television
Acapulco (title unknown)
Arrest and Trial (title unknown)
Barney Miller (title unknown)
Bat Masterson ("The Good and the Bad"–1961)
Batman ("King Tut's Coup, Batman's Waterloo"–1967)
Bewitched (title unknown)
Big Valley, The ("Run of the Savage"–1968)
Bob Hope Chrysler Theatre ("White Snow, Red Ice"–1964
Bold Ones, The (segment of "The Lawyers"–title unknown)
Bonanza (title unknown)
Cannon (title unknown)
Cimmaron Strip ("Knife in the Darkness"–1968) (by Harlan Ellison)
Death Valley Days ("Angel of Tombstone")
       ("Last Shot"–1962)
       (title unknown–1964)
       (title unknown)
Eleventh Hour, The ("Make Me a Place")
Gunsmoke (title unknown)
Hennessey (title unknown–1961)
Mannix (title unknown)
Michael Shayne ("Four Lethal Ladies"–1961)
Mickey Spillane (title unknown)
Mod Squad (title unknown)
Mona McCluskey (title unknown–1965)
Name of the Game, The (title unknown)
Next Step Beyond, The (title unknown)
Outer Limits, The ("Controlled Experiment"–1964)
Outsider, The ("The Secret of Maring Bay"–1969)
Police Story (unsold pilot–1966) (Not to be confused with the later series of this name.)
Rango (title unknown–1967)
Real McCoys, The (title unknown)
Rifleman, The ("Rose"–1966)
       ("The Tin Horn"–1962)
Roaring Twenties, The ("Another Time, Another War"–1961)
Robert Taylor's Detectives ("Hit and Miss"–1961)
Run for Your Life ("The List of Alice McKenna"–1968)
77 Sunset Strip ("Falling Stars"–1962)
       ("The Missing Daddy Caper"–1961)
Surfside Six ("Neutral Corner"–1962)
Temple Houston ("Do Unto Others Then Gallop"–1964)
       (w/Jeffrey Hunter)
Twilight Zone, The (title unknown)
Untouchables, The ("Line of Fire"–1963)
Virginian, The ("The Mustangers")
Walt Disney's Wonderful World of Color ("Way Down Cellar"–1964)

In "Police Story," Grace's role was that of a policewoman judo instructor. Appearing in the cast with her was DeForest Kelly, whom Roddenberry wanted for the role of the *Enterprise*'s chief medical officer.[4]

The earliest known set of photos taken for the "Star Trek" *series,* however, features only William Shatner, Leonard Nimoy, and Grace Lee Whitney.

These earliest series photos featured Shatner and Nimoy in costumes that were trial concepts for the show's wardrobe. Ms. Whitney appeared in a female's uniform similar to the one from "Where No Man Has Gone Before."

For her solo shots in this series, Grace's Yeoman Rand makeup included bright red lipstick and heavily outlined eyes. In most photos she wore a prototype of her standard Rand hairdo, which according to Ms. Whitney, was designed by herself and costume designer William Ware Theiss. Grace posed in positions and hairdos indicating various intensities of expression and posture. Some of the shots have Janice's hair hanging leisurely down her back; Lieutenant Kevin Riley would certainly have approved.

The Yeoman's costume during this shooting session had a thin, metallic-type gold stripe sewn onto the sleeves.[5] The men's outfits were almost completely different from those of the second pilot. The colors were altered, with the greenish-gold replaced by a deeper gold, and the light blue with a darker blue. The ribbed collars of the second pilot were replaced by completely rounded, solid black velour collars. Zippers were sewn into the left shoulders, hidden under short flaps of fabric. Kirk had two solid gold leatherette stripes on each sleeve. The trousers, worn by all three performers; lack the "glitter" effect of the later pants and have a satiny appearance.

Janice wore the ship's services spiral emblem, while Kirk and Spock both had command insignia. Spock's sideburns had the beginnings of pointed ends, but Kirk's did not. (In the second pilot, only Spock had the special sideburns.)

The majority of these earliest series portraits featured a painted backdrop of a planet and a star field, with the three-foot *Enterprise* miniature suspended in front of the drop on wires. (The little ship was still not modified to match the changes in its larger counterpart.) Other backgrounds included a clear, lucite wall with an engraved system of circles. Kirk posed smiling in front of this construction. Spock frowned by the panel holding the plaster *Enterprise* miniature.

The strangest background provided for these shots was a small, science fiction-type of set featuring a spaceship window, numerous gauges and knobs, and a small microphone. This set originally appeared in two low-budgeted science fiction feature films, *Planet of Blood* and *Voyage to the Prehistoric Planet.*

Kirk and Spock held blueprints, flasks, retorts, and other scientific paraphernalia. Yeoman Rand joined her two fellow crew members in brandishing large flashlights with red, blue, and green reflectors. The phaser rifle from "Where No Man Has Gone Before" was also in evidence, although it was never used in any of the series' regularly produced episodes.

An unused angle of the *Enterprise* that would have been combined with a rotating planet surface in "The Cage."

While the designs of the costumes and props were still being finalized, so was the rest of the *Enterprise* crew. Actor DeForest Kelley was the next to sign on for the five-year mission.

DeForest Kelley was born in Atlanta, Georgia, where he obtained his first performing experience singing in his church choir. His singing progressed to solo work, and he was soon performing on a program broadcast over radio station WSB. After completing a singing engagement at the Atlanta Paramount Theatre, working with the Lew Forbes orchestra, DeForrest visited a relative in Long Beach, California. He stayed much longer than he had planned to; he had fallen in love with California and soon returned to live on the West Coast.

Kelley joined the Long Beach Theatre Group, where he met actress Carolyn Dowling; they were married in September 1945.

DeForest and a writer friend, Barney Girard, later started a radio group. With other members they wrote and staged plays at a local radio station. This led to other radio work for Kelley, who also earned additional money working as an elevator operator.

During World War II, a Paramount talent scout saw Kelley in a U.S. Navy training film. He was given a screen test and a contract with Paramount that lasted two and a half years. During this time he starred in feature films such as *Fear in the Night* (his screen debut) and *Variety Girl* (in which celebrity guest stars such as Cecil B. DeMille and Alan Ladd attracted most of the attention).

In 1948, the Kelleys went to New York, where De-Forest worked on stage and in television. After De-Forest and Carolyn returned to Hollywood, he found more television work, thanks to his friend Barney Girard who was then writing for "You Are There." Alternating between feature films and television assignments, Kelley built up an impressive list of credits that led to his role in Gene Roddenberry's pilot "Police Story," as lab chief Greene. "Police Story" never became a series, but it led Kelley to his role as Dr. Leonard McCoy on "Star Trek."

With his role of "Bones," DeForest's distinguished career of screen villainy came to an end as he swiftly developed McCoy into a powerful, likable, and lovable individual. In 1967 at the World Science Fiction Convention in New York City, hundreds of his fans applauded wildly as his second season opening credit was seen for the first time during a special screening of "Amok Time." At subsequent "Star Trek" conventions, DeForest Kelley has been an absolutely wonderful guest, filled with friendship, appreciation, and entertaining anecdotes about his career. For all his fans, who can now enjoy his Dr. McCoy in *Star Trek— the Motion Picture* as well as on television, here is a detailed listing of this diversified artist's appearances.

The complex relationship between Dr. McCoy and Captain Kirk provides assurance and friendship for both individuals in "The Enemy Within" (DeForest Kelley, William Shatner).

DeForest Kelley's Credits

Stage

Singing Engagement with Law Forbes and his Orchestra
    (Atlanta Paramount Theatre;
    Atlanta, Georgia)
Long Beach Theatre Group

Motion Pictures

Apache Uprising (Paramount–1966)
Black Spurs (Paramount–1965)
Canon City (1948)
Duke of Chicago, The (Republic–1949)
Fear in the Night (Paramount–1947)
Gunfight at Comanche Creek (Allied Artists–1963)
Gunfight at the O.K. Corral (Paramount–1957)
House of Bamboo (20th Century-Fox–1955)
Illegal (Warner Brothers–1955)
Johnny Reno
Law and Jake Wade, The (Metro-Goldwyn-Mayer–1958)
Marriage on the Rocks (Warner Brothers–1965)
Men, The
Night of the Lepus, The (Metro-Goldwyn-Mayer–1972)
Raintree County (Metro-Goldwyn-Mayer–1957)
Tension at Table Rock (Universal–1956)
Town Tamer
Variety Girl (Paramount–1947)

View From Pompey's Head, The (20th Century-Fox–1955)
Waco (Paramount–1966)
Warlock (20th Century-Fox–1959)
Where Love Has Gone (Paramount–1964)

U.S. Navy Training Film (Produced during World War II)

Television

ABC Matinee Today ("I Never Said Goodbye")
Assignment: Underwater ("Affair in Tokyo")
Award Theatre ("333 Montgomery"–1961)
Bat Masterson ("No Amnesty for Death"–1961)
Black Saddle ("Apache Trial")
Bonanza ("The Decision"–1962)
    ("The Honor of Cochise"–1961)
    ("Ride the Wind"–1966)
Call of the West (title unknown)
Cavalcade of Stars (title unknown)
Code Three ("Oil Well Incident")
Cowboys, The (title unknown–1974)
Dakotas, The ("Reformation at Big Nose Butte"–1963)
Death Valley Days ("Breaking Point"–1962)
    ("Lady of the Plains")
Deputy, The ("The Means and the End"–1961)
Donna Reed (title unknown)

Favorite Story ("Inside Out")
Frontier Justice ("Shadow of a Dead Man"–1959)
Gallant Men, The ("A Taste of Peace"–1963)
Gallery of Mme. Liu-Tsong, The
Gunsmoke (title unknown)
Have Gun Will Travel (title unknown)
Ironside ("Warrior's Return"–1970)
Johnny Midnight ("The Inner Eye"–1961)
Laramie ("Gun Duel"–1962)
Laredo ("Sound of Terror"–1966) (a doctor)
Lawman ("The Squatters"–1961)
Lone Ranger, The (title unknown–1949)
    (title unknown–1952) (a doctor)
M Squad ("Hideout"–1958)
Matinee Theatre ("Beyond a Reasonable Doubt") (w/an
    actor named Charlie Evans)
Mike Hammer ("Bride and Groom"–1961)
Millionaire, The ("The Story of Iris Millar") (a young
    intern)
Morton Downey Show, The (segment title unknown)
Navy Log (title unknown)
O. Henry Playhouse ("The Hiding of Black Bill"–1958)
Perry Mason ("The Case of the Unwelcome Bride"–1961)
Plainclothesman, The (title unknown)
Police Story (Unsold Pilot–1966) (lab doctor)
Playhouse 90 (title unknown)
Rawhide (title unknown)
Richard Diamond, Private Detective ("The Adjuster"–
    1959)
    (title unknown–1959)
Riverboat ("Listen to the Nightingale"–1960)
Rough Riders, The (title unknown–1961)
Route 66 ("1800 Days to Justice"–1962)
Schlitz Theatre (title unknown)
Science Fiction Theatre ("Y.O.R.D.") (a doctor)
77 Sunset Strip ("88 Bars"–1963)
Shenandoah ("The Riley Brand"–1966)
Silent Service, The ("The Archerfish Spits Straight"–
    1961)
    ("The Gar Story"–1958)
    ("The Spearfish Delivers"–1962)
Slattery's People ("Question: Which One Has the
    Privilege?"–1964)
Stagecoach West ("The Big Gun"–1961) (w/Barbara
    Luna)
    ("Image of a Man"–1961)
Studio One (title unknown–1951)
Tales of Wells Fargo ("Captain Scoville"–1961)
Two Faces West ("The Fallen Gun")
Virginian, The ("Duel at Shiloh"–1963)
    ("Man of Violence"–1963) (w/Leonard Nimoy) (by
    John D. F. Black)
Wanted Dead or Alive (title unknown)
    (title unknown)
    (title unknown)
    (title unknown)
    (title unknown)

    (title unknown)
Web, The (title unknown)
You Are There ("The Capture of John Wilkes Booth")
    ("The Fall of Fort Sumter")
    ("The Gunfight at the OK Corral")
Zane Grey Theatre ("Village of Fear"–1962)

After DeForest Kelley was cast as Dr. McCoy, the Desilu sales department issued a brochure intended for world circulation. The purpose of this brochure was to inform interested people within the television industry of the "Star Trek" format. The brochure features three photos, all from "Where No Man Has Gone Before." William Shatner is listed as the star of the series and Leonard Nimoy as the co-star. Under the "also starring" category are Grace Lee Whitney, DeForest Kelley, and George Takei.

One of the photos is of Spock, a shot that had been retouched in the NBC booklet. Here, the photo appears unretouched.

The Desilu brochure emphasizes that "Star Trek" was not based upon gadgetry but human drama resulting from the concentrated excitement that man will experience traveling through space in the future.

The Desilu brochure also mentions something that NBC did not include in its initial booklet; that "Star Trek" would be part fantasy and part fact, as a result

The addition of Dr. McCoy to the "Star Trek" format had just been made when DeForest Kelley sat for this portrait.

After a previous incarnation as Number One, actress Majel Barrett returned to the "Trek" format as Nurse Christine Chapel.

of the assistance of scientists from the Rand Corporation (described as "America's space think factory"). Because of the resulting scientific accuracy, the Desilu pamphlet theorized that "Star Trek" might be described as "science fiction," but it would certainly be more "science" than "fiction."

The Desilu publicity also translated "Star Trek's" title into various foreign languages, including Spanish ("Jornadae Estelar"), French ("Voyage Aux Etoiles"), Italian ("Viaggio Nelle Stelle"), German ("Sternen Trik"), and Portuguese ("Jornada Nas Estrelas").[6]

Although the series was sold and its initial publicity was being distributed, the changes in personnel were still progressing. The addition of Dr. McCoy was an important step to the completion of the "Star Trek" universe as we know it. The emotional Captain Kirk and the supposedly nonemotional Mr. Spock can be viewed as the two extremes of a collective personality held together by the extremely human Dr. McCoy.

The Trek pilots contain no hint of this important relationship, although Dr. Boyce of "The Cage" *does* provide confidence and understanding to Captain Pike. Dr. Piper's miniscule role in "Where No Man Has Gone Before" seems to digress from his predecessor's involvement with his captain, and there is no relationship indicated at all between Piper and Spock. In the first draft script of "Where No Man Has Gone

Before" (dated May 27, 1965), the *Enterprise*'s physician was Dr. *Johnson,* whose role was also in the background.

The first draft script of "The Omega Glory" (dated June 7, 1965), written as an alternate choice for "Star Trek's" second pilot, featured Ship's Doctor *Milton Perry,* who was killed during a fight on the planet Omega. The "Omega Glory" first draft also had other differences from the series, both in terms of style and personnel.

The episode would have opened with a narration concerning the *Enterprise*'s mission, rather than a captain's log entry. The starship, which carried a crew of 604, carried only two familiar people, Captain Kirk and Mr. Spock. Spock, who was from the planet Vulcanis, had "an illogical ancestor" who married a Terran female; the "Vulcanian" also possessed hypnotic abilities that were more potent than those he demonstrated during the series.

The other *Enterprise* crewmen who were included in the "Omega Glory" first draft script did not appear in either the filmed episode or in the rest of the series. The transporter officer was unnamed, Lieutenant Commander Piper was the youthful male navigator, and Lieutenant Phil Raintree, the helmsman, was killed during the script's climactic action.

The *Enterprise* crew's initial personnel changes for the series continued until after the first draft script for "The Corbomite Maneuver" (dated May 3, 1966). Most of the differences in this earliest variation of "The Corbomite Maneuver" script were concerned with the episode's story (as discussed in Chapter 5), but two significant posts were manned by personnel who would later be replaced. *Navigator Ken Easton* never appeared, and the *Enterprise* did not have a regular navigator until Mr. Chekov made his debut at the start of the series' second season. *Dave Bailey* was the communications officer here; Lieutenant Uhura did not appear in this draft at all.

It is difficult to imagine the U.S.S. *Enterprise* without Lieutenant Uhura, the starship's communications officer. In her role as the ship's spokesperson, Uhura is a living extension of the *Enterprise,* and the resemblance does not stop there. She is as dynamic and beautiful to us as the *Enterprise* is to Kirk, and like the starship, Uhura is so symmetrical that she makes the operation of her communications station appear as graceful a procedure as the playing of a musical instrument.

Nichelle Nichols (Lieutenant Uhura) was born in Robbins, Illinois, where her father served as the town's mayor and magistrate.

At the age of sixteen Nichelle wrote a ballet for a musical suite by Duke Ellington and toured with Ellington's band performing her own work and later singing with his band as well. She gained her experience in the performing arts in Chicago, Los Angeles, and New York. Twice nominated for the Sara Siddons

Mr. Sulu steals an admiring glance at the beautiful and capable Lieutenant Uhura in "Balance of Terror" (Nichelle Nichols, George Takei).

Award as best actress of the year (for her roles in the plays *The Blacks* and *Kicks and Company),* Nichelle understudied the lead in a Broadway play *(No Strings)* and, while in New York City she also appeared as a singer at two famous city landmarks, the Blue Angel and the Playboy Club. Continuing her singing career with Lionel Hampton's band, Nichelle toured the world before returning home to resume her acting career. Continuing to appear in plays on the West Coast, Nichelle was highly praised by the critics for her work in James Baldwin's play, *Blues for Mr. Charlie.*

Nichelle also began to appear in motion pictures and on television. It was a guest role in an episode of "The Lieutenant" that acquainted Gene Roddenberry with her work. While "Star Trek" was in preparation as a series, Nichelle was interviewed before the communications officer even had a name. Her audition consisted partially of reading Mr. Spock's dialogue for "The Corbomite Maneuver." [7] After demonstrating her acting technique and expertise, as well as her poise, Nichelle Nichols was signed to portray Lieutenant Uhura. Her role as a futuristic space traveler would also involve her in the present-day space program.

When Nichelle began attending "Star Trek" conventions, her personality made her an instant hit with the fans and, while listening to a presentation by a scientist from the National Aeronautics and Space Administration, she became deeply interested in the space program. After the convention, she toured the Ames Space Center near San Jose, California. Other space-oriented activities followed.

Nichelle has flown an eight-hour, high-altitude astronomy mission aboard the C-141 Astronomy Observatory (analyzing the atmospheres of Saturn and Mars). She was a guest at the Jet Propulsion Laboratory to witness the Viking probe's soft landing on Mars, and she later wrote an article about Viking for a publication of the National Space Institute. She has since been appointed to the Institute's Board of Directors and, at an annual meeting of the NSI, she cited the lack of women and minorities in the space program in a speech entitled "New Opportunities for the Humanization of Space." Following the speech, Nichelle was invited to join the Space Shuttle astronaut recruitment program.

Nichelle's own company, Women in Motion, continued to attract women and minorities into the space program, partially as a result of a promotional film called *"What's in It for Me?"* for which Nichelle functioned as producer and star, and provided two of her own pieces of music.

Nichelle's involvements with "Star Trek" and the present-day space program really came together when she attended the launching of the first space shuttle, named the "Enterprise," after Star Trek's starship.

In *Star Trek—the Motion Picture,* Nichelle appears as Lieutenant Commander Uhura, continuing her space-oriented work. Today, she continues her careers in the performing arts devising stage presentations, and composing and performing ballets and songs; whatever works of art that can convey the freedom, the originality, and the urge to explore and the symmetry present within herself. Nichelle Nichols has journeyed another full circle, in addition to her space-oriented activities. In striving to create works of art, she has become a work of art herself.

Nichelle Nichols' Credits

Stage

Blacks, The (Nomination for the Sara Siddons Award as best actress of the year)
Blues for Mr. Charlie (Los Angeles)
Carmen Jones (Chicago)
For My People (Los Angeles)
Kicks and Company (Nomination for the Sara Siddons Awards as best actress of the year.
No Strings (Broadway) (Standby for the leading actress)
Roar of the Greasepaint, the Smell of the Crowd, The (Los Angeles)

Motion Pictures

Doctor, You've Got to Be Kidding
Made in Paris
Mr. Buddwing
Porgy and Bess
Three for the Wedding
Truck Turner

What's in It for Me? (Promotional film which Ms. Nichols produced, starred in, and wrote music for; for the Smithsonian National Air and Space Museum)

Television

CBS Repertory Workshop ("The Ghost of Mr. Kicks")
Ironside ("The Deadly Gamesman"–1972)
Lieutenant, The ("To Set It Right"–1964) (written by
    Lee Erwin)
Tarzan ("The Deadly Silence"–1966)

After the arrival of Lieutenant Uhura, the starship *Enterprise* lacked only one of its regular family, who would join the series at the start of the second production season.

Over the Labor Day weekend in 1967, New York City played host to the World Science Fiction Convention, NYCON, at which "Star Trek's" second season made its debut with a specially arranged showing of "Amok Time." There were several surprises in this segment, of which the most significant was the addition of Ensign Pavel Chekov to the *Enterprise* crew. Rumors had been circulating for a month before the convention that another crewman would be signing on before long to attract the younger, female viewers. At

Mr. Chekov (Walter Koenig) joined the crew after the first season of episodes had already been produced.

NYCON, everyone who saw "Amok Time" enjoyed Chekov's contributions to the episode, and we accurately anticipated that many future good moments would be provided by the Ensign.

The first official announcement of Chekov's arrival is probably a press release issued by NBC on September 18, 1967. According to the network, a staff reporter for "Pravda," the Russian newspaper, had reviewed a "Star Trek" episode he had seen televised in Germany. The critic was understandably upset at seeing an internationally (and interplanetary) staffed spaceship without a Russian prominently in view. The Pravda reporter mentioned that since "Star Trek" is a show about space and space exploration, there should *certainly* be a Russian aboard considering that Russia was the first nation to successfully begin man's ventures into outer space. The news report had far-reaching effects; when Gene Roddenberry saw it, he could not help but agree.

Walter Koenig, who played Ensign Pavel Chekov, was born in Chicago, Illinois, but grew up in New York City's borough of Manhattan. His first stage experience was obtained during high school when he played the title role in the play *Peer Gynt,* and acted in another powerful play, *The Devil's Disciple.*

Working with underprivileged children in summer camps in upstate New York, Walter originated a theater program specially designed to function as therapy for emotionally disturbed and overly aggressive young people. Evolved from a technique called "psychodrama," the camp program reflected the two major interests in Walter's life, acting and psychology.

Walter enrolled in Iowa's Grinell College as a premed student, with the intention of becoming a psychiatrist, and then moved with his family to California, where he completed his education at UCLA in Los Angeles, graduating with a BA degree in psychology.

While in college, Walter had acted in summer stock productions in Vermont. After his graduation he returned to New York City, and enrolled in the Neighborhood Playhouse. During his second year at the famous school for actors, he was awarded a scholarship and worked as a hospital orderly to earn enough money for his living expenses. After working in off-Broadway productions for two years, Walter returned to Los Angeles, where he landed additional stage and television assignments.

Considering the degree of Mr. Chekov's popularity on "Star Trek," it is difficult to recall that an entire season of the series was done without him. This is especially true recalling Walter Koenig's many appearances at "Star Trek" conventions. Walter is at home during the conventions, and it seems that he goes out of his way more than other Trek performers to mingle with the series' fans. Whether during parties, in discussion groups, or exploring art displays and dealers' rooms at Trek conventions, Walter is welcomed as a friend as well as a celebrity guest. His current book, *Chekov's Enterprise: Journal of the Making of the Movie,* published by Pocket Books, reveals his understanding of the film industry and his closeness to the creative atmosphere surrounding "Star Trek" and Trek fans.

Walter Koenig's Credits

Stage

America Hurrah (Director; Los Angeles, California)
Becket (Director; Los Angeles)
Blood Wedding (Los Angeles)
Deputy, The (Los Angeles)
Girls of Summer (Los Angeles)
Hotel Paradiso (Director; Los Angeles)
La Ronde (Los Angeles)
Make a Million (Chicago)
Night Must Fall (Los Angeles)
Six Characters in Search of an Author (New York City)
Steambath (Los Angeles)

Summer Stock in Vermont

Motion Pictures

Deadly Honeymoon, The
I Wish I May (Writer, Producer)

Television

Alfred Hitchcock Presents ("Memo from Purgatory"– 1964) (By Harlan Ellison)
Ben Casey (title unknown)
Class of '65 (Scriptwriter)
Columbo (title unknown)
Combat (title unknown)
Day in Court (title unknown–TV debut)
Family (Scriptwriter)
Gidget (title unknown–1965)
Goodbye Raggedy Ann (TV Movie)
Great Adventure, The ("Six Wagons to the Sea"–1963)
I Spy ("Sparrowhawk"–1966)
Ironside ("The Summer Soldier")
Jericho (title unknown–1966) (w/Ian Wolfe, William Smithers)
Lieutenant, The ("Mother Enemy"–1964)
Mannix (title unknown)
Medical Center (title unknown)
Men from Shiloh, The ("Crooked Corner"–1970)

Mr. Novack ("A Boy Without a Country"–1963)
    ("The Firebrand"–1965)
    ("With a Hammer in His Hand, Lord, Lord"–1964)
Questor Tapes, The (TV Movie; unsold pilot) (Produced by Gene Roddenberry)
Starlost ("Oro")
    ("The Return of Oro")
Untouchables, The (title unknown)

NOTES

1. The term *Vulcanian* is heard in Trek episodes "Mudd's Women;" "Court-Martial;" and "This Side of Paradise," which probably accounts for an extremely early "Star Trek" fan group being called "Vulcanian Enterprises." After *Vulcanis* became *Vulcan* in the series, and the adjective *Vulcanian* was changed to *Vulcan,* the earlier terms continued to appear in NBC press releases, including "Mr. Spock's All Ears and Out of This World" (dated 11/30/66), and "Some Feelings About Feelings" (dated 5/4/67).

2. Author Harlan Ellison's introduction to his first draft script of "The City on the Edge of Forever," included in *Six Science Fiction Plays* (published by Pocket Books in 1976), discusses his discovery of this booklet and his researches to determine who had ordered the alterations.

3. Gene Roddenberry is quoted as saying that NBC asked him to drop Mr. Spock from the "Star Trek" format along with the other cast changes implemented before the production of "Where No Man Has Gone Before." Roddenberry also mentions showing the airbrushed photos of Spock to an NBC executive, and receiving a horrified reaction.

    Stephen E. Whitfield and Gene Roddenberry. *The Making of Star Trek,* (New York: Ballantine Books, 1973), pp. 126, 127.

4. Roddenberry's 1966 pilot, "Police Story," did not achieve series status, and was only televised in 1967. It bears no connection to a later TV series of the same name. Roddenberry's "Police Story" starred Rafer Johnson and Steve Ihnat.

5. The officers' stripes on the sleeves of costumes in "Where No Man Has Gone Before" consisted of gold elastic bands loosely sewn to the garments.

6. Most of the foreign language titles translate literally as either "Voyage Among the Stars" or "Journey to the Stars." While this literature was being prepared, filmmaker Stanley Kubrick was beginning work on an epic motion picture, released as *2001: A Space Odyssey* (Metro-Goldwyn-Mayer–1968). During its early production stages, the film had another name: "Journey Beyond the Stars."

7. David Gerrold, *The World of Star Trek* (New York: Ballantine Books, 1973), p. 111.

    When this reading took place, the character of Lieutenant Uhura had not yet been completely written. Nichelle read Spock's lines because she was asked to; she recalled the people she was reading for thought that Spock was the closest character to Uhura. Although most people visualize an attachment between Lieutenant Uhura and Captain Kirk (due largely to scenes in "The Gamesters of Triskelion," "The Tholian Web," and "Plato's Stepchildren"), there are indications the Vulcan is attracted to her on a personal level, and vice versa. Spock permitted Uhura to sing about him in "Charlie X"; in this episode (and "The Conscience of the King") she is permitted to play his Vulcan harp. She taunts Spock about his self-imposed coldness in "The Enemy Within," and he in turn praises her ability and his confidence in her in "Bread and Circuses."

4 First Season Production Credits

DIRECTORS   Various

WRITERS   Various

PRODUCERS   Gene Roddenberry, Gene L. Coon

EXECUTIVE PRODUCER   Gene Roddenberry

STAR TREK CREATED BY   Gene Roddenberry

ASSOCIATE PRODUCERS   Robert H. Justman, John D.F. Black

SCRIPT CONSULTANT   Steven W. Carabatsos

THEME MUSIC COMPOSED BY   Alexander Courage

MUSIC COMPOSED AND CONDUCTED BY   Various

DIRECTOR OF PHOTOGRAPHY   Jerry Finnerman

ART DIRECTORS   Roland M. Brooks, Walter M. Jefferies

FILM EDITORS   Robert L. Swanson, Fabian Tjordmann, Frank P. Keller, ACE, Bruce Schoengarth

ASSISTANT TO THE PRODUCER   Edward K. Milkis

ASSISTANT DIRECTORS   Gregg Peters, Michael S. Glick

SET DECORATORS   Carl F. Biddiscombe, Marvin March

COSTUMES CREATED BY   William Ware Theiss

POST PRODUCTION EXECUTIVE   Bill Heath

MUSIC EDITORS   Robert H. Raff, Jim Henrickson

SOUND EDITORS   Joseph G. Sorokin, Douglas H. Grindstaff

SOUND MIXERS   Jack F. Lilly, Cameron McCulloch

PHOTOGRAPHIC EFFECTS   Various

SCRIPT SUPERVISOR   George A. Rutter

MUSIC CONSULTANT   Wilbur Hatch

MUSIC COORDINATOR   Julian Davidson

SPECIAL EFFECTS   Jim Rugg

PROPERTY MASTER   Irving A. Feinberg

GAFFER   George H. Merhoff

HEAD GRIP   George Rader

PRODUCTION SUPERVISOR   Bernard A. Widin

MAKEUP ARTIST   Fred B. Phillips, SMA

HAIRSTYLES BY   Virginia Darcy, CHS

WARDROBE MISTRESS   Margaret Makau

CASTING   Joseph D'Agosta

SOUND   Glen Glenn Sound Co.

A Desilu Production in Association with Norway Corp.

EXECUTIVE IN CHARGE OF PRODUCTION   Herbert F. Solow

First Season Episodes

Although many "Star Trek"-oriented books have been written, none has ever explored the individual Trek episodes in any detail. Since the whole is the sum of its parts, it is logical to discuss each episode in a book on the series. It is also fun, because interwoven with the reviews of the episodes are many bits of trivia and nostalgic looks into the adventures of our favorite futuristic friends.

The episodes are covered in order of their production. As many dates as possible are included to give an accurate picture of when and how quickly some of the favorite episodes evolved. Some early draft scripts and storylines are discussed to show how some episodes evolved into the stories with which we are familiar.

The stories are discussed in terms of their strengths, weaknesses, and contributions to the "Star Trek" universe and their probable inspirations.

Individual roles are discussed, together with the performers who brought them to life. If any "Trek" guest star appeared regularly in another TV series, or as a guest in another science fiction, fantasy, or horror-oriented role, these appearances are included when possible. Performers who turned up almost regularly on Trek are mentioned, along with performers who are only heard, and not seen.

The four most important credits are listed for each episode in most cases: (1) writer, (2) director, (3) musical composer, and (4) producer of photographic effects. Comments on each of these important contributions are provided when needed. Costumes, sets, cinematography, and other facets of production are also cited, and if an object appears on more than one "Star Trek" episode its other appearances are mentioned.

For the benefit of Trekkers who cannot recall episodes by their titles, or enjoy refreshing memories regarding occurrences in their favorite episodes, each segment is also described by a plot synopsis, incorporating as many specific bits of trivia as possible.

THE CORBOMITE MANEUVER

Episode #3

First draft script   4/21/66
Final draft script   5/3/66
Second revised final script   5/20/66
Filmed in late May and early June 1900

WRITER   Jerry Sohl
DIRECTOR   Joseph Sargent
COMPOSER   Fred Steiner
PHOTOGRAPHIC EFFECTS   Howard A. Anderson Company

The U.S.S. *Enterprise* is confronted by an alien "warning buoy" while attempting to explore an uncharted area of space. The starship's phasers destroy the radioactive buoy. Soon afterward, a gigantic spherical spaceship traps the *Enterprise* and an alien voice promises destruction in ten minutes. A bluff conceived by Captain Kirk postpones the death threat of Balok, the formidable looking alien commander. When the alien separates from his ship and appears to be in distress, Kirk goes to his rescue. Finally, the frightening alien is revealed as a puppet operated by the real Balok, a childlike alien who has been testing them to determine whether Kirk and company are truly peaceful. Diplomatic relations are established and Mr. Bailey, who had lost his nerve awaiting Balok's "death threat," volunteers to remain on board the alien's ship as an "exchange student."

Portions of Jerry Sohl's first draft script are discussed in Chapter Three. There are several differences between this early draft and the finished episode.

In a more direct diplomatic exchange between Kirk and Balok, the alien encouraged Kirk to release his recorder-marker, with full data. Kirk referred to Balok's civilization as an "exception" to the generally friendly space travelers of the galaxy. Spock did not succumb to curiosity and put Balok on visual; Balok did this himself to lower morale aboard the *Enterprise*. Later, Spock suspected the logic of Balok's actions because of the alien's continued aggression. When Balok challenged the existence of "corbomite," Kirk invited him aboard the *Enterprise;* Balok, of course, declined the invitation.

To show his small vessel's power, Balok destroyed a small asteroid and the recorder-marker with destructive rays and emphasized that the Fesarius, his huge ship, could return instantly if needed. Finally, Balok admitted to Kirk that he thought that the *Enterprise* people would be good neighbors. Mr. Bailey did not board the alien ship in this script; he also was spared his emotional outburst, and this early version therefore lacked the drama that Bailey ultimately provided.

In the finished episode, all the characters are still largely experimental, but this is most evident with Dr. McCoy, who debuts here. As a result of his ironic sense of humor and his reluctance to admit sensitivity, McCoy is reminiscent of the Dr. Gillespie character from MGM's series of "Dr. Kildare" motion pictures. In "The Corbomite Maneuver" McCoy appears to be more psychologist than practicing physician. He lurks on the bridge most of the time, appearing menacing and short-tempered. There is already an attempt at creating behavior patterns for McCoy. Twice during the episode, Kirk reminds McCoy of something the doctor had once said, only to have "Bones" deny that he'd ever said it. This later gave way to "I'm a Doctor, not a ————."

Nichelle Nichols once complained about saying nothing but "Hailing frequencies opened, Sir." She must have been referring to this episode. In "The Corbomite Maneuver" she says nothing else; she is simply a leggy attraction seated sensuously on the bridge, a futuristic switchboard operator with no apparent talents, joys, or personal magnetism. In the briefing room, everyone else seated at the table looks as if he or she is participating in the discussion; Uhura just sits there looking tired, kittenish, and detached. Director of photography Jerry Finnerman made it a repeated point to catch Nichelle Nichols at her best here, but nobody else did. It is apparent that Uhura was a last-minute addition to this script.

Yeoman Janice Rand is worse off. She doesn't have any hailing frequencies to open, and therefore she makes her debut as a glorified maid, serving the captain's salad and bringing hot coffee to the bridge.

In a scene that was filmed but edited out of the print before its final assembly, Janice enters Kirk's empty quarters, gets a clean uniform from his wardrobe drawer, and lays it out on his bed.

Mr. Spock's half-human characteristics are present, but their effects on his individuality are inconsistent. Spock accuses Mr. Bailey of being too emotional when the young man shouts. Later, however, the Vulcan shouts about the superheating of the engines. Once, when Spock can supply no helpful suggestions, he starts to say "I'm sorry" to Captain Kirk.

The camera angles emphasize Spock's alien aspects. At one point the camera shoots toward the ceiling over his station as Spock suddenly rises into the frame. His hair is still jaggedly banged, his eyebrows pushed upward more than in later episodes. His shirt collar is higher than anyone else's to further set him apart from the rest of the crew.

All references to Spock's parents are in the past tense, and he compares his father to the shocking visage of the puppet Balok: a possible attempt to build morale with humor. The Vulcan also tries his hand at black comedy, advising the nervous Mr. Bailey to have his adrenal glands removed.

Mr. Sulu is still progressing in his metamorphosis from ship's physicist to helmsman. At this point, he has some of Spock's characteristics. His voice never wavers; his judgment and actions are always swift and purposeful. Sulu also voices the countdown of doom and quickly remedies Bailey's errors in navigation.

Anthony Call deserves favorable notice for his emotional rendition of Mr. Bailey. Although he was performing with a cast that was still not accustomed to playing off each other, Call produced a fine portrait of a young man on the brink of a nervous breakdown. The recovered Mr. Bailey would have made a fine addition to the *Enterprise* crew, had he not been assigned to stay aboard Balok's ship. Call was a regular performer on the CBS soap opera "The Guiding Light," and he also appeared in "The 30 Fathom Grave" on "The Twilight Zone."

The voice of the real Balok was dubbed by Vic Perrin, a noted character actor with considerable vocal talent. Perrin often supplies voices for all types of films. He was often heard on "Mission: Impossible" and "The Magician," and was the "control voice" that introduced every episode of "The Outer Limits." In "Star Trek," his talents are heard in "Arena" and "The Changeling." In "Mirror Mirror" he played Tharn, the only visual role he had in "Trek." Clint Howard (the "real" Balok) was regularly seen as Mark Wedloe, the young son in "Gentle Ben" on CBS from 1967 to 1969.

Director Joseph Sargent has directed feature films such as *The Taking of Pelham 1-2-3, The Man, MacArthur,* and the science fiction thriller *Colossus The Forbin Project.* He also directed the TV movie *The Night That Panicked America,* which told of Orson Welles' "War of the Worlds" radio broadcast. Sargent has also acted; he appeared on the hour-long "Twilight Zone" episode "In His Image" (which was directed by Perry Lafferty, William Shatner's father-in-law).

Writer Jerry Sohl has done other work on Trek (including "This Side of Paradise," under his pseudonym Nathan Butler). Born in 1931, his first story ("The Seventh Order") appeared in 1952, in *Galaxy* magazine. He has also written science fiction novels, including *The Haploids* (his first novel) in 1952, *Transcendent Man* (1953), *Costigan's Needle* (involving the popular Trek theme of a parallel world), and *The Altered Ego.* He also wrote the teleplay of the 1970 TV movie, *Night Slaves* (in which a town full of people is secretly enslaved to help rebuild a crashed flying saucer).

Composer Fred Steiner's score for "The Corbomite Maneuver" is possibly the finest dramatic music of the entire series. The musical theme for Balok's huge ship is heard in virtually every Trek episode where menace is conveyed. The orchestration of this music is extremely effective, considering that approximately twenty-five musicians comprised the orchestra.

The miniatures and composite photography supplied by Howard Anderson Company are also extremely effective, especially the one shot of the Fesarius "growing" until it dwarfs the *Enterprise*. The revolving cube with its reds, yellows, and blues is also reflected on the faces of the bridge personnel, thanks to special lights set up on the bridge. Similar effects are reflected off the sculpted Balok puppet head, the work of artist Wah Chang. The Anderson people added a wavering animation effect, also used over the Thasian in "Charlie X."

Toward the end of "The Corbomite Maneuver," we see Mr. Bailey in front of a completely blank main viewing screen. The large lucite screen, backed with pulsating light patterns, has no optical inserted at this point. We do see the lights, which were used as cues to alert the cast and crew that a matte would be inserted over this footage.

Another omission in this episode has Mr. Sulu observing that there is only a minute left to destruction. He then looks up at the viewing screen, glances back toward Kirk, and announces "I knew he would." Actor Ted Cassidy's voiceover for Balok was supposed to have been dubbed in, saying ". . . You now have one minute," but for some reason the line was never added to the composite sound track.

Some of the costumes made for "The Corbomite Maneuver" were heavy velour that shrunk after it was cleaned, giving the appearance of being too small for the actors. These shirts have higher collars than usual, with the zippers sewn in more visibly than in the later uniforms. In "The Corbomite Maneuver" and "Mudd's Women," Uhura (Nichelle Nichols) wears a gold uniform fashioned from velour.

Various sets constructed for this episode appear later in the series. The wall panel behind the Balok puppet head was later added to the engineering room of the *Enterprise*. The rear walls of Balok's quarters are part of the bar seen in *"Court-Martial."*

Composer Fred Steiner's score for this episode was heavily utilized throughout most subsequent episodes, as were Alexander Courage's scores for the two pilot films. For this reason, many "Star Trek" fans equate this (and other themes written by Steiner for other Trek segments) as the definitive musical representations of "Star Trek's" individuals and adventures.

Fred Steiner, a native of New York City, received his initial musical education at New York's Institute of Musical Art, and at Oberlin Conservatory of Music in Ohio, where he obtained his Bachelor of Music degree in 1943. Beginning his career writing music for radio series (including musical director for radio's "This Is Your FBI"), Steiner arrived in Los Angeles in 1947, where he continued his radio work and eventually became involved in writing for television and motion pictures. Steiner (not to be confused with composer *Max* Steiner who wrote the 1933 score for *King Kong,* which *Fred* Steiner recorded for Entr'Acte Records in 1976), has written several feature film scores, includ-

The *Enterprise* is matted against the impressively huge spaceship *Fesarius* in this effects sequence from "The Corbomite Maneuver."

ing *Time Limit* (United Artists–1957), and *The St. Valentine's Day Massacre* (20th Century-Fox–1967). His diversified television compositions include music for series such as "Gunsmoke," "The Bullwinkle Show," and "Have Gun Will Travel." Aside from his main title theme for "Perry Mason" and his "Star Trek" scores, Steiner's best known TV music appears in "The Twilight Zone" (most notably in the episodes "A Hundred Yards Over the Rim" and "King Nine Will Not Return" (music from which also appears in "Nightmare at 20,000 Feet," which starred William Shatner).

MUDD'S WOMEN

Episode #4
First draft script   5/23/66
Final draft script   5/26/66
Revised final draft   5/31/66
Filmed in early and middle June 1966

WRITER   Stephen Kandel (Story by Gene Roddenberry)
DIRECTOR   Harvey Hart
COMPOSER   Fred Steiner
PHOTOGRAPHIC EFFECTS   Westheimer Company

Harry Mudd, with his "cargo" of three beautiful women, is beamed aboard the *Enterprise* just as his ship is destroyed in an asteroid field. In rescuing Mudd and his women, the *Enterprise* burns out its reserve lithium crystals. The starship limps to a mining planet to replenish the crystals. Mudd, against whom Kirk has filed criminal charges, makes advance contact with the miners. He promises his women to the lonely and rich miners in exchange for his freedom. Kirk must cope with Mudd and induce the miners to furnish the needed crystals before his ship's power is exhausted. ("Mudd's Women," together with "The Omega Glory" and "Where No Man Has Gone Before," was submitted to NBC as a prospect for the series' second pilot.)

After "The Cage" was rejected by NBC, Gene Roddenberry included "Mudd's Women" as a candidate for the second pilot. Writer Stephen Kandel adapted Roddenberry's story line into a full script after preparation of "Star Trek's" first season had begun. Roddenberry and Kandel took a fast-talking con man and combined him with elements of a vintage space opera. The western plot device of "wiving settlers" rounded out this offbeat adventure.

Harry Mudd would be right at home doing television commercials promising to provide treasures at a fraction of their normal cost, or inducing viewers to purchase completely useless devices. Reed Hadley, the actor/host of the 1950s TV series "Racket Squad," summed up Mudd's attributes in his closing statement for each "Racket Squad" episode: ". . . Remember; there are people who can slap you on the back with one hand, and pick your pocket with the other . . ."

Mudd emerges as a likable lost soul because in addition to being a greedy scoundrel, he's also a bit of a child. He has difficulty in accepting the responsibility for his actions. He never really hurts anyone in any manner that causes physical or lasting mental harm. The thought of Mudd brandishing a phaser is laughable; he'd be frightened out of his wits just *looking* at a weapon.

If Mudd could have put things in their true perspective, in an adult fashion, he never would have come as close as he did to destroying the *Enterprise*. Even Kirk realizes this. We last see Kirk sharing a bit of black humor with Mudd, about inducing the authorities to "throw away the key" on the rotund rogue.

The really important thing about Harry Mudd is that when the chips are down he can be seen behaving in an almost fatherly fashion toward the women; they seem to respect him in a strange sort of way (he's a strange sort of guy). He lovingly induces Eve to take the Venus drug, but whether his concern is really for the women or for the money they will bring him is never really clarified. We must realize, however, that Harry is (whatever his motivations) functioning as a drug pusher. Would he have returned later and charged huge prices for more Venus drug doses?

It is amazing that NBC never eliminated the drug angle from this script. Perhaps NBC was happy with the ending, which proved the drug was not really that potent. It was like the "magic feather" that enabled Dumbo to fly, or the sugar pills doctors sometimes prescribe for hypochondriacs.

Mr. Spock still suffers from "growing pains" in this episode. He retains his special raised collar to segregate him from the other crew members. Mudd calls him a "Vulcanian." As Eve leaves Kirk's cabin, Spock is seen standing against the wall, arms folded across his chest. He cocks his head to one side and affects a mischievous smile worthy of any "elf with a hyperactive thyroid."

Jerry Finnerman's soft-focus photography of the women became a standard practice for most of the series' female guest stars.

Jim Goodwin created the role of Lieutenant Farrell in this episode.

Roger C. Carmel does a masterful job in bringing Harcourt Fenton Mudd to life. Carmel appeared regularly as Roger Buell in "The Mothers in Law" (1967–68). He appeared in an "Ironside" episode ("The Walls Are Waiting") with William Shatner, and can also be seen in "Voyage to the Bottom of the Sea" ("The Machines Strike Back") and *"The Man from U.N.C.L.E."* ("The Ultimate Computer Affair" and "The Quadripartite Affair"). Carmel's most offbeat characterization is probably his Batman role of Colonel Gumm in an episode entitled "A Piece of the Action" (now where have I heard that title before?) which featured the Green Hornet and Kato.

Gene Dynarski (Ben Childress) also appears as a council member in "The Mark of Gideon." In the movie *Earthquake* he is the first casualty (drowned in an elevator), and he also appears as Roy Neary's boss in *Close Encounters of the Third Kind.* In *Voyage to the Bottom of the Sea* Dynarski can be seen in "Journey with Fear."

Susan Denberg (Magda) was a beautiful but unlikely choice for the "monster" in the British film *Frankenstein Created Woman,* shortly after she appeared as a centerfold Playmate of the Month in *Playboy* magazine.

Karen Steele, a veteran of many TV roles, appears in *"Voyage to the Bottom of the Sea"* ("Leviathan").

The special effects in "Mudd's Women" are of the economy variety. Mudd's spaceship is seen only as a vaguely oval shape. It does not appear to be a miniature; just an animated overlay (cartoon) effect. (The same is true of the asteroids.) Another animated effect is seen briefly as the pulsating red glow of the Venus drug.

In a minor continuity goof, Spock's hair blows wildly around as he materializes on the planet's surface; in the close-ups, however, his hair is neatly combed down.

If anyone reading this ever comes across Harry Mudd, it's only fair that you should know everything about him. As a public service, therefore, the following is the complete transcript of Mudd's computerized police dossier:

Police Record

Harcourt Fenton Mudd

OFFENSES: smuggling, sentence suspended—transport of stolen goods—purchase of space vessel with counterfeit currency—

Future police record code: X731248

DESCRIPTION: Height: 6 feet, 1 inch—weight: 240 pounds—brown hair and eyes—complexion: fair

Any information pertaining to Mudd please notify authorities.

THE ENEMY WITHIN

Episode # 5

First draft script   6/6/66

Final draft script   6/8/66

Filmed middle & late June 1966

WRITER   Richard Matheson

DIRECTOR   Leo Penn

COMPOSER   Sol Kaplan

PHOTOGRAPHIC EFFECTS   Howard A. Anderson Company

A transporter malfunction divides Captain Kirk into two people. Each is a physically complete individual, but both are lacking in mental and emotional factors. One has the "good" characteristics of Kirk; his rational and sensitive mind. The other has the "bad" points; irrational, bestial attributes. Both halves must be reunited in time to save a stranded landing party led by Sulu. (This episode, the only "Star Trek" segment written by Richard Matheson, is a cornerstone of the Kirk-Spock-McCoy relationship. It is also the first time McCoy says "He's dead, Jim.")

Richard Matheson's first draft script has some interesting differences from the final version. Matheson originally conceived the "bad" Kirk as more bestial, baring his teeth and uttering animal growls when angered. At one point the double bit Kirk on the hand and, after defeating Kirk in sick bay, he covered his own scratches and then scratched the captain's face to confuse McCoy. The double then remained in sick bay, convinced McCoy that he was the "real" Kirk, and went to the bridge.

Captain Kirk was not the first to find himself confronted with an evil double. This predicament was also experienced by such TV series heroes as "The Lone Ranger," "The Cisco Kid," "Robin Hood," Napoleon Solo on "The Man from U.N.C.L.E.," Ben Cartwright on "Bonanza," "Zorro," and Ron Ely on "The Aquanauts." These unwelcome visitors were all revealed as imposters, not extensions of the hero's personality. There is, however, one noteworthy exception.

In 1957, Robert Leslie Bellem and Steve Post wrote "Divide and Conquer," an episode of "The Adventures of Superman" TV series. Superman, unjustly accused of a crime, had to remain in jail to protect a political figure; he also had to escape to prevent the politician's assassination. Superman enlisted the aid of his trusted friend, Professor Lucerne, who advised the Man of Steel that since his molecular structure was twice as dense as Earthmen's, all he had to do was concentrate. His molecular structure would then split in half, creating two "Supermen," each only half as powerful as the whole. Superman was lucky, even though his separate halves could not fly very well and were not completely invulnerable. Both his "halves" were good halves. Despite this, he faced his other half and announced "It's a cinch we're no good the way we are," as they merged into one entity once more, exactly the conclusion Kirk came to as he confronted the double in sick bay.

The success of "The Enemy Within" is primarily the result of Richard Matheson's significant treatment of the old Jekyll-Hyde theme. He explored the problems of being divided, rather than dwelling upon specific occurrences.

Matheson's original script lacked two important details, pertaining to McCoy and Spock. He suggested that Spock "slug" the double with a phaser handle. The direct violence would not have done Spock credit as a unique character. Leonard Nimoy suggested the answer; on the set, he demonstrated a neck pinch on William Shatner and, as Shatner rolled his eyes and sagged to the floor, the Vulcan Nerve Pinch was born. The script also had Spock announcing the death of the "space spaniel." This was changed to a job for McCoy, and the classic line "He's dead, Jim" was born.

William Shatner's acting training is extremely diversified, and in this episode he used all of his training to the maximum degree of effectiveness. Two stage devices are very evident here. In sick bay, as Kirk asks for help, Shatner wrung his hands; a stage gesture used to denote desperation and indecision. (Shatner also did this in "The Enterprise Incident.") The other technique was creatively incorporated into the episode's dramatic structure.

One of Shatner's favorite devices is to enter a scene facing away from the audience. He will suddenly pivot, then gesture and begin to say something; at that instant he gets the audience's attention riveted on him. In the episode's teaser, the double materializes with his back to the audience. He pivots rapidly, and the camera cuts to focus on his bestial expression, exaggerated makeup, and underlit face. The effect is thoroughly successful.

A fine bit of editing has the "good" Kirk entering the turbo-lift an instant before the "evil" Kirk's bloodied hand is thrust before the camera.

Leo Penn's quick direction and the sensitive score of composer Sol Kaplan combine to assure the quality of "The Enemy Within." Kaplan would score many episodes for Trek, but sadly Penn never returned to the series to direct. Prior to becoming a director, Penn acted and appeared in an episode of "The Adventures of Superman" ("The Boy Who Hated Superman").

The strangest "monster" of "Star Trek" is the doglike creature, actually a small canine in a false, furry body and head harness, with artificial tail and horns. Two "creatures" were needed for the scenes involving the duplicate on the transporter platform.

The pistol-grip phaser handles are painted white, instead of gray. The old-style phaser belts, sewn from gold leather trimmed with black, white, and gold lacing, were only used until the middle of this first production season.

When Kirk and the double confront each other on the bridge, the viewing screen can be seen in back of them. In one scene the screen is completely blank; just a large piece of plastic sheeting upon which no scene was rear-projected and no lights were reflected.

One of the most blatant continuity errors occurs in this episode. For the only time during the series, Kirk has no insignia when he materializes in the transporter; neither does the double. Later, Kirk is seen before he has had a chance to change uniforms, and the insignia is suddenly there.

The scratches on Kirk's face and the double's change sides during their climactic confrontation on the bridge. This may have been the result of the film editor printing close-ups of Shatner's face backward, to make the double look more like a "transformed man."

THE MAN TRAP

Episode # 6

First draft script   6/13/66
Final draft script   6/16/66
Filmed in middle and late June 1966

WRITER   George Clayton Johnson
DIRECTOR   Marc Daniels
COMPOSER   Alexander Courage
PHOTOGRAPHIC EFFECTS   Howard A. Anderson Company

The *Enterprise* visits planet M-113 to give archeologists Robert and Nancy Crater supplies and medical checkups. Years ago, Nancy was romantically involved with Dr. Leonard "Plum" McCoy. Now, she is literally a different woman. Each member of the landing party sees Nancy differently because the real Nancy is dead, killed by a shape-changing humanoid. The creature, the last surviving native of this planet, has been enjoying a symbiotic relationship with Professor Crater. Crater supplies the bodily salts to sustain the entity, and the creature provides Crater with

companionship. The arrival of the *Enterprise* party ruins the delicate balance of this strange alliance. Craving additional salt, the creature kills two crewmen and, disguising itself as one of them, boards the *Enterprise*. The creature assumes Dr. McCoy's identity before Kirk eventually tracks it down and destroys it with the aid of Spock and McCoy. (This was the first "Star Trek" episode aired, at 8:30 P.M., EST, on September 8, 1966.)

"The Man Trap" is a haunting tale, a study in loneliness and tragedy with elements of horror and mystery that make it an intriguing episode. Dr. McCoy once remarked that all of his old friends look like doctors; Nancy Crater was apparently the exception. Whatever unhappy marriage Leonard McCoy experienced, he clearly held very special memories of Nancy. Here, he shares something with Professor Crater. "Few women like my Nancy," Crater muses. A man of science, Crater prevented himself from harming the creature ("the last of its kind") when it killed Nancy for her body salts. Logically avoiding the solitude of being the only living creature on M-113, Crater and the creature came to an understanding.

Whatever the reasons for the symbiotic relationship, it is odd that Kirk never stops to think of the creature as an intelligent being; he knows only that it has killed several of his crew members, and that it therefore should be hunted down and killed. Perhaps things would have been resolved differently if the creature had never boarded the *Enterprise,* a territory that Kirk always defends to the limit. Faced with a similar situation later with the Horta in "The Devil in the Dark," Kirk would allow himself the luxury of communicating with the "monster" before permitting it to be killed.

The "Salt Vampire" (as it is usually called by Trek fans) was portrayed (in its various incarnations) by the greatest number of performers ever called upon to represent one entity in "Star Trek." Each successive performer was selected at least partially because of his (or her) resemblance to the actor who preceded him (or her) in this part. The facial transition between Jeanne Bal (Nancy) and Bruce Watson (Crewman Green) is especially perfect.

To maintain a continuity between all of these transformations, the creature was given the human habit of sucking a finger when trying to think or defend itself. The most effective use of this mannerism is seen when the camera pans between Jeanne Bal and DeForest Kelley as the two successively portray the creature.

Alfred Ryder (Professor Crater) deserves much of the credit for making the episode work in terms of drama and believability. Ryder, an accomplished director in addition to his performing talents, also stars in segments of "Voyage to the Bottom of the Sea" ("The Phantom Strikes" and "The Return of the Phantom"), "One Step Beyond" ("The Devil's Laughter" and "The Forests of the Night"), "Land of the Giants," and "The Man from U.N.C.L.E."

Jeanne Bal (Nancy) appeared regularly in "Love and Marriage" (1959–60) and as the teacher Miss Pagano on "Mr. Novack" (1959–60).

Vince Howard (Uhura's crewman) has a very short role but manages to do much with it. Howard was also a regular performer on "Mr. Novack" (as another teacher, Mr. Butler).

Alexander Courage's eerie score for this episode combines strings, woodwinds, and organ chords to produce extremely alien sounds. This score, of all the Trek episodes Courage composed, is the most reminiscent of his music in "The Cage."

The "Salt Monster" costume was constructed by Wah Chang. The head, body, and limbs of the suit are extremely effective in conveying a frightening image.

The creature was portrayed by Sharon Gimpel, a young Hollywood hopeful. Ms. Gimpel, who is under five feet in height, got the part and called her friends and family to watch her on "Star Trek" *before* she saw the costume. Her original weight of ninety-eight pounds was down to ninety-one pounds by the time her role had been completed.

DeForest Kelley turns in his strangest performance of the entire series in the scenes where he is "the unreal McCoy." The actor altered his facial and speech mannerisms and managed to convey a perpetually furtive attitude in contrast to the friendly connotations usually associated with McCoy.

Professor Crater uses an old-style phaser originally used in "The Cage" and "Where No Man Has Gone Before" and later in "What Are Little Girls Made of?"

When Kirk shoots Crater, the working phaser can be seen in one of the few times it is ever used operationally. The grillework is raised on the phaser-one, and a small light shines from the weapon's front.

As Crater is shot; he lurches back (probably aided by a hidden harness attached to a wire suddenly pulled backward). The accompanying sound effect is that of a ricocheting gunshot. Accompanied by a bright animated effect, the sequence is enhanced by slowing down Ryder's voice to suggest the stunning effect on his nervous system.

McCoy's medical tools and the ship's turbo-lifts have different sound effects in this episode. When Kirk activates his communicator the "flip open" sound effect is used instead of the "call" sound. On two occasions there is no sound at all when Kirk opens his communicator.

Mr. Sulu's botany hobby indicates that the Lieutenant's fields of expertise were being developed even before the next episode, "The Naked Time." His interest in botany is also apparent in "Shore Leave." The botany room is a redress of the sick bay set. Meanwhile, in sick bay, the diagnostic bed is used in this episode to perform an autopsy while the "dead man's" heartbeat sound effect is distinctly heard.

This episode is also the origin of McCoy's medical tools. Because of the creature's craving for salt, various scenes were planned to include saltshakers. Futuristic saltshakers were gathered, but at the last minute it was feared they would not be recognized as what they were, and the specially gathered shakers were customized into medical sensors instead.

THE NAKED TIME

Episode # 7
First draft script   6/23/66
Final draft script   6/28/66
Filmed in early July 1966

WRITER   John D. F. Black
DIRECTOR   Marc Daniels
COMPOSER   Alexander Courage
PHOTOGRAPHIC EFFECTS   Howard A. Anderson Company

The scientific research team on planet Psi 2000 reports that the planet is due to be destroyed. Arriving to evacuate the scientists, the U.S.S. *Enterprise* discovers that the researchers have frozen to death after someone in the camp turned off the life-support systems. To add to the mystery, the positions of the bodies indicate that the researchers went berserk before they died. The riddle is solved when Lieutenant Tormolen, who lands to investigate with Mr. Spock, spreads a strange germ he has contracted on the planet. As the *Enterprise* crew begins to become infected, strange things happen. Mr. Sulu threatens the bridge crew with a sword while Lieutenant Riley locks himself in the engineering control room. The disease must be conquered and control regained of the starship in time to prevent the *Enterprise* from being destroyed when its orbit decays around the doomed planet. A last-minute attempt succeeds in hurling the ship back in time to make an escape. (This was the first occasion the *Enterprise* journeyed through time.)

Whatever the "Star Trek" viewer is in the mood to see, "The Naked Time" has it. While presenting its diversified emotional situations, the episode's script aids immensely in developing the characteristics of "Star Trek's" most important people.

We have already seen Kirk split into two parts in "The Enemy Within"; in that same episode we hear Spock explain that he too is actually two halves sandwiched together. In "The Naked Time" we do not *hear* about this division, we *see* it. Once again, Spock's parents are mentioned in the past tense. With his sympathetic regard for his human mother, a resentment against his Vulcan father is also implied. This implication is later followed through when Sarek and

Mr. Spock and Nurse Chapel share an intimate moment in "The Naked Time" (Leonard Nimoy, Majel Barrett).

Amanda finally make their appearance in "Journey to Babel."

The U.S.S. *Enterprise,* we learn, makes Kirk just as divided as his friend Spock. Captain Kirk is simultaneously resentful of his ship because it keeps him from living a "normal" existence, and fearful because he may someday lose her. He sees the ship in much the same way as a frightened bridegroom readies himself for his wedding. He mourns his lost independence, while he also cannot conceive of an existence without the focal point of his love.

Spock is no better. Like the rest of his people, he lives a charade of respectable dignity. Beneath the surface he seethes to experience love openly, and yet he stays far away from Christine Chapel's admission that she loves him. Even in his "drunken" state in "The Naked Time," Spock's first impulse is to "lock himself away" so that no one (especially the woman who loves him) will see him with his defenses down, a confused child's mind locked within the brain of a technological genius.

Kirk and Spock are both in states of emotional conflict. In their confusion, they aid each other. Even with his *Enterprise* in danger, Kirk has great difficulty in recovering from the nightmare of reliving his conflicts because of the virus. It is only the sight of his friend Spock caught up in *his* confusion that forces Kirk's mind to recover. And it is only the realization that his friend Jim is ill that enables *Spock* to recover. The Kirk-Spock relationship is a symbiotic one.

William Shatner and Leonard Nimoy do superb jobs of bringing their characters' inadequacies to life. Several other episodes of "Trek" accorded Nimoy chances to emote; this was his first. In addition to his subtle flair for comedy, Nimoy exhibits a clear ability for serious drama. A simple smile from Spock would

later be enough to bring tears to our eyes in "This Side of Paradise." The admission of his great unhappiness does the same thing here.

Spock logically attempts to return to reality through the use of mathematics. Nimoy handles Spock's recitations by adding a hopeful tone when he counts, then returns to a hopeless quality when his stray thoughts trigger more unhappy memories.

Shatner's intense gazes directed at "his" *Enterprise* are extremely effective. Much of this success may be attributed to director Marc Daniels, but in terms of the final impact and audience identification it is Shatner who carries it across in an almost classical manner. His Kirk becomes a tragic subject, buffeted about by his opinion of something literally bigger than himself. His alternatively possessive gestures at the ship and his plaintive pleas to be released from her spell suggest that his portrayal may have been guided by a quote from Emily Bronte's *Wuthering Heights:* "I cannot live without my life, I cannot die without my soul."

Fans of George Takei have their first chance in this episode to appreciate the actor's portrayal of the erratic Lieutenant Sulu. Armed with endless energy and a bare chest smeared with oil, Takei roams through the corridors of the *Enterprise* menacing security men with a sword, parrying his way into the hearts of "Star Trek" fans forever. George was later given additional chances to go berserk (especially in "The Return of the Archons").

"The Naked Time" also marks the first of two Trek appearances of Lieutenant Kevin Thomas Riley, played to perfection by actor Bruce Hyde.

During his two Trek appearances, Kevin Riley became one of the most well-liked *Enterprise* crewmen. His zany antics in "The Naked Time" account for only a small part of his appeal; the vast majority of credit must go to actor Bruce Hyde for adding so much dimension to a character with so little to do. Hyde's carefully measured delivery, whatever the mood of his scenes, leads us to laugh at Riley in this episode, and to have very different feelings toward him in "The Conscience of the King."

At "Star Trek" conventions, Bruce Hyde is a skilled singer, sharing sensitive songs with Trek fans, and functioning more as a friend than a guest. Bruce Hyde has also appeared in other TV episodes, in a stage production of *Hair,* and in the Broadway production of *The Canterbury Tales.*

Nichelle Nichols was only just beginning to become the vibrant and efficient Uhura, with all her dynamic qualities. In this episode, when Sulu grabs her on the bridge and greets her as a "fair maiden," Uhura's reply is "Sorry, neither." If the network censors had paid attention, they would have realized that Uhura was disavowing that she is (1) fair (in complexion) and (2) a maiden.

The trip of the *Enterprise* backward through time is

wonderfully executed, thanks to several items. Originally, Roddenberry had intended the *Enterprise* to become transparent when it was in warp drive. The effect was abandoned, but in "The Naked Time" we see how it would have worked out. The Howard Anderson opticals are aided by Alexander Courage's tremendously effective music (also used in "Errand of Mercy" as the Organians abandon their human appearances), and the glimpse of Sulu's chronometer moving backward.

The environmental suits created for this episode were never seen in "Star Trek" again, although in several early episodes crewmen can be seen in corridors wearing similar outfits.

CHARLIE X

Episode #8
First draft script   6/30/66
Final draft script   7/5/66
Filmed in middle July 1966

WRITER   D. C. Fontana (Story by Gene Roddenberry)
DIRECTOR   Lawrence Dobkin
COMPOSER   Fred Steiner
PHOTOGRAPHIC EFFECTS   Howard A. Anderson Company

The cargo ship *Antares* docks with the *Enterprise* to deliver young Charlie Evans. The lone survivor of a crash on the planet Thasus fourteen years before, Charlie has apparently been alone since the age of three. The personnel of the *Antares,* Captain Ramart and Tom Nellis, seem unusually eager to leave the vicinity of the *Enterprise.* When the *Antares* is destroyed, suspicion falls on Charlie who seemed to know the ship's fate before the disaster. Aboard the *Enterprise,* Charlie begins to work "miracles." At first these are harmless pranks, but when Yeoman Rand spurns his advances she is erased from existence by the youngster. Various other ship personnel are victimized, and in his eagerness to arrive at Colony Alpha Five, Charlie assumes control of the *Enterprise.* The captain attempts to overtax Charlie's control abilities and switches on the starship's interior systems to their fullest extent. A shimmering humanoid materializes on the *Enterprise* bridge and identifies himself as a Thasian, come to take Charlie back. Despite Charlie's pleas, he vanishes along with the alien, doomed to spend the rest of his life on the bleak planet Thasus.

The first draft script for "Charlie X" is virtually the same in concept as the final draft, with some interesting differences. In the first draft, Charlie forced a young female Yeoman to her knees, disappointed because she does not resemble Janice. McCoy betrayed great glee at the prospect of Jim Kirk's trying to teach young Charlie the facts of life. Uhura, in this draft, was a talented mimic, who parodied all the crew members in the recreation room. The full version of the poem that Charlie originally forced Spock to recite reads:

> Saturn's rings upon my finger
> Vulcan's helmet on my head
> Jupiter's chariot 'neath my feet
> Down the road that's Martian red

In the final version, Charlie is definitely not to blame for what he does. He was never taught to curb his powers, and he was not disciplined to tame his destructive urges because those urges could do the insubstantial Thasians no harm. Charlie was never taught to deal with people because the Thasians were careful to avoid any people except Charlie.

Likewise, the Thasians are not really to blame either. They gave Charlie his power so that he could survive within their environment (which, considering their immaterial nature, is not exactly built for physical comforts). The moment they realized Charlie was gone, the Thasians probably consulted the psychology tapes aboard the wreckage of Charlie's ship and knew that they had to get this superpowered juvenile delinquent back to Thasus on the double.

"Charlie X" is a study in tragedy; in addition to the sufferings caused to the *Enterprise* crew, people die because of Charlie's actions. Yeoman Rand survives as does probably everyone else whom Charlie makes "go away." Charlie destroyed the *Antares,* and the men on the ship all died. And, particularly horrible, is the young lady whose facial features were obliterated as a result of Charlie's "tricks." It is difficult to breathe without a nose and mouth. Still, Charlie's pleas to stay aboard are extremely effective. He is just another alienated person, trying to be accepted.

While we are discussing alienated people, let us not forget Mr. Spock. In this episode, Spock silently endures the pain of sitting on two broken legs. In the recreation room, we see that Spock does have the ability to show his emotions. When Uhura sings about him, Spock lowers his head and exhibits the smile of a bashful child.

Charlie claims that he has learned to speak by conversing with his ship's computer. This is a science fiction variation on the method author Edgar Rice Burroughs employed to teach Tarzan how to write. (Tarzan had a disadvantage; he learned to read and write by comparing the pictures and words in his books. Never having heard the words used in their spoken form, though, the Ape Man only learned to talk years later.)

The most illogical thing about "Charlie X" is that Charlie goes too long before he is suspected of having "the power"; especially after he produces the perfume and the photos of Janice from out of nowhere.

An especially dramatic moment comes when Charlie begs to be allowed to stay with the humans aboard the *Enterprise*. His last word, a plea to "stay," is re-echoed several times, gradually decreasing in volume. This effect is also heard in "The Squire of Gothos" and "Who Mourns for Adonais."

Robert Walker, Jr. (Charlie), turns in a powerful and fascinating performance. His father was a brilliant performer, equally able to tackle comedy (as in *See Here, Private Hargrove)* or play a psychopath (in *Strangers on a Train).* The younger Walker's portrayal of Charlie Evans is every bit as effective and polished as any part his father ever played. In this episode, Charlie forces Mr. Spock to quote from Edgar Allan Poe's poem, "The Raven." Soon after appearing as "Charlie X," Walker portrayed Poe in a low-budget feature film.

Abraham Sofaer (the Thasian) is also the voice of the Melkotian in "Spectre of the Gun." He received his acting training in the Old Vic and Stratford-on-Avon companies, where he appeared in Shakespearean stage productions. He appeared as the disciple Paul in the film *Quo Vadis,* and has also appeared in a long succession of character parts; namely Indians, scientists, and clergymen. His science fiction and fantasy career includes roles in *Things to Come* (United Artists–1936) and *Captain Sinbad* (Metro-Goldwyn-Mayer–1963). On television, he can be seen in "The Twilight Zone" ("The Mighty Casey"), "I Dream of Jeannie" (in his recurring role as Hadji, 1965–70), "Lost in Space" ("The Flaming Planet"), and "The Man from U.N.C.L.E." ("The Brain Killer Affair," with Yvonne Craig and Nancy Kovack).

Lawrence Dobkin, the director of "Charlie X," began his career as an actor. In *The Day the Earth Stood Still* (20th Century-Fox–1951) he was one of the doctors who took care of the wounded Klaatu. On TV, he appeared regularly as "the director" in *Mr. Adams and Eve* (1956–58), and is visible in "The Adventures of Superman" episode "The Man Who Could Read Minds," and in the "You Are There" segment "The Capture of John Wilkes Booth" (with DeForest Kelley).

Charlie and the *Antares* crewmen both wear shirts left over from "The Cage" and "Where No Man Has Gone Before." In some scenes, Charlie wears a brown suede wraparound tunic that is much too large for him. This appears to be a rejected version of Kirk's fatigue shirt; a command insignia is visible on the belt of the garment. The color portraits of Yeoman Rand, which Charlie produces on the backs of the playing cards, are actually publicity photos of Grace Lee Whitney. Laura Wood, who appeared as the aged crewwoman in this episode, is also in "The Deadly Years."

BALANCE OF TERROR

Episode # 9
Final draft script   7/14/66
Revised final script   8/8/66
Filmed in early August 1966

WRITER   Paul Schneider
DIRECTOR   Vincent McEveety
COMPOSER   Fred Steiner
PHOTOGRAPHIC EFFECTS   Film Effects of Hollywood

The *Enterprise* is patrolling the Earth Outposts along the Romulan Neutral Zone, which cuts off planets Romulus and Remus from Federation space. The Romulans, a warlike race, had fought a war with the Federation a century before. As Captain Kirk is about to perform the wedding ceremony of crewmembers Angela Martine and Robert Tomlinson, an Earth Outpost announces that it is under attack. The starship witnesses the destruction of the outpost, but is helpless to assist. Kirk learns that the Romulans have perfected an invention that renders their spaceships invisible; they are testing out their new device. Kirk reasons that he must overtake and destroy the enemy vessel before it can return home. The Romulans are found to appear almost exactly like the Vulcans, which causes crewman Stiles to express overt prejudicial distrust of Mr. Spock. When the Romulan commander is finally cornered, he self-destructs his ship rather than surrender. Stiles, whose life has been saved by Spock, realizes that his prejudicial attitude is wrong. Crewmember Tomlinson is killed. (This is the first appearance of the Romulans.)

"Balance of Terror" is the script for a contemporary "war movie" translated into science fiction terms; a confrontation between a "surface vessel" (the *Enterprise)* and a "submarine" (the invisible Romulan ship). The important elements of the story are the questions of prejudice and fear, the commanders' perceptions of war versus peace, and the duties each commander has to honor.

The Romulans are examined in terms of the "faceless" picture the Federation has of them, and in terms of their own individual motivations. The young soldier Decius is impulsive, eager to confront the Federation vessel. The commander is tired of hostilities and questions what his true duties really are. The old centurian is aboard as an observer. Each has his own personal understanding of his empire's policies.

"Balance of Terror" is one of the few Trek episodes that deals straightforwardly with the concept of prejudice. Stiles, coming from a family who had fought the Romulans, distrusts Spock because of the Vulcan's Romulan-like features. Prejudice is not an accepted characteristic for a space traveler; we learn from

Uhura later in the series that racial prejudice in "Star Trek's" time era is indeed an obsolete relic of the past.

The comparisons between Kirk and the Romulan commander are very well done. Each is worried about his vessel and the responsibilities of command. The final conversation between the two, in which the Romulan admits that he and Kirk could have become friends in a different set of circumstances, is an editorial against the act of waging war.

Mark Lenard (The Romulan commander) is best known to "Star Trek" fans for his beautiful characterization of Sarek, Spock's father, whom we meet in "Journey to Babel." Today, Mark Lenard has the distinction of being the only performer in "Star Trek" to have portrayed a Vulcan, a Romulan, and a Klingon; he appears as a Klingon commander in *Star Trek—The Motion Picture*. Lenard has appeared at "Star Trek" conventions, where he is an extremely welcome guest. During his first convention appearance, fans were pleasantly surprised to learn that beneath his stoic exterior is a congenial man with a highly cultivated sense of humor.

Because of the popularity that Mark Lenard enjoys with Trek fans everywhere a detailed list of his acting appearances in feature films and television programs immediately follows this section.

Lawrence Montaigne (Decius) has appeared as almost every conceivable ethnic type. He, too, returned to play a Vulcan (Stonn in "Amok Time"), and also appears as an alien in episodes of "The Invaders" TV series. He can also be seen in "The Man from U.N.C.L.E." ("The Maze Affair"), "Voyage to the Bottom of the Sea" ("Man-Beast"), and "Batman" ("The Joker's Last Laugh," in which he portrays a robot).

Gary Walberg (Commander Hanson) appeared regularly as "Speed," the poker player on "The Odd Couple" (1970–75), and is Quincy's boss on the TV series of the same name.

"Balance" features only one new set, the bridge of the Romulan vessel. Its cramped quarters suggest a submarine-type of environment; there is even a periscopelike monitor device.

We never get a clear glimpse of the background in the Earth Outpost room. The *Enterprise* chapel is a redress of the transporter room set.

The Romulan ship was constructed by Wah Chang, who never received screen credit for his work. The model was photographed while it was supported from beneath or suspended from wires under an aerial brace (a mounting device to keep miniatures hanging steady in front of the camera). The miniature was never used after this episode; the "Deadly Years" views of the ship are taken from "stock" shots that were photographed during "Balance of Terror's" production.

The Romulan "energy bolts" were animated effects, double-exposed against a background of stars. (The background music heard during this sequence was originally used in "Where No Man Has Gone Before"; the sound-effect of the mutating Gary Mitchell "turning pages" while reading can still be heard in this episode.)

Although Kirk and Sulu repeatedly specify that phasers are being used (represented by continuous rays), the optical effect shown is that of photon torpedoes (separate blips).

Mark Lenard's Screen Credits

Motion Pictures
Annie Hall (United Artists–1977)
Greatest Story Ever Told, The (United Artists–1965)
Hang 'Em High (United Artists–1968)

Television
Alias Smith and Jones ("Exit from Wickenberg"–1971)
Another World (Recurring role of Dr. Ernest Gregory–1965)
Big Story, The ("Christmas in Camden"–1955)
Cimmaron Strip ("The Greeners"–1968)
Cliffhangers (Recurring role as leader of underground civilization)
Defenders, The ("The Non-Violent"–1964)
Directions '65 ("The World of Isaac Babel"–1965)
("The World of Isaac Loeb Peretz"–1965) (host)
Du Pont Show of the Month, The ("Battle of the Paper Bullets"–1961)
("I, Don Quixote"–1959)
("The Prisoner of Zenda"–1961)
Felony Squad, The (title unknown–1967)
Girl with Something Extra, The (title unknown–1973)
Good Life, The (title unknown–1971)
Greatest Heroes of the Bible (title unknown)
Gunsmoke ("Nowhere to Run"–1969)
Happy Life (title unknown)
Hawaii Five-O ("Secret Witness"–1974)
("To Hell with Babe Ruth"–1969)
("Will the Real Mr. Winkler Please Die"–1973)
("You Don't See Many Pirates These Days"–1977)
Here Come the Brides (Recurring role of Aaron Stempel, town villain–1968–70)
(w/Robert Brown, David Soul)
How the West Was Won (title unknown)
Iron Horse, The (title unknown–1967)
It Takes a Thief ("Birds of a Feather"–1968) (w/Malachi Throne)
Jericho ("Long Journey Across a Short Street"–1966)
John Brown's Raid (TV Movie–1960) (also telecast as Raid on Harpers Ferry)
Judd for the Defense ("Firebrand"–1967)

WHAT ARE LITTLE GIRLS MADE OF?

Episode #10
First draft script   6/26/66
Revised final script   7/27/66
Filmed in early August 1966

WRITER   Robert Bloch
DIRECTOR   James Goldstone
COMPOSER   Fred Steiner
PHOTOGRAPHIC EFFECTS   Westheimer Company

The *Enterprise* arrives at planet Exo III to learn the fate of Dr. Roger Korby, the "Pasteur of archeological medicine." On board is Nurse Christine Chapel, Korby's fiancée, who has given up a bio-research career on Earth to find him. Korby contacts the *Enterprise,* and confirms that he is living in underground caverns he discovered while he was suffering from severe frostbite five years before. At Korby's request, only Kirk and Christine beam down. The doctor shows them ancient machines that were left behind by the long-dead Exoites and tended by Ruk, a giant android. Korby's aides, Dr. Brown and young Andrea, are revealed as androids and Korby fashions an android duplicate of Kirk. His intention is to take the *Enterprise* and

"seed" the universe with androids. When Korby vaporizes Ruk, Kirk argues that the androids are neither peaceful nor human. Korby himself, transformed into an android, disputes this at first. When Korby realizes that he is more machine than man, he turns a phaser on himself and Andrea. Spock arrives with a landing party moments later; Nurse Chapel announces that she is staying with the *Enterprise* crew.

Nurse Chapel had been introduced in "The Naked Time", but here we learn her reason for signing on the *Enterprise.* Her love of Korby also explains why she is attracted to Spock, the epitome of a scientific researcher. Korby's confirmed death frees Chapel to dream her impossible dream of winning Mr. Spock.

In addition to the other story elements within this episode, Kirk is presented with another identity threat. In "The Enemy Within," the "other" Kirk is an extension of the captain's own physical and mental processes. Here, it is a machine armed with Kirk's memories. As his memory patterns are being copied for the android, Kirk forces anti-Spock sentiments to flow from his mind; this clever "distress signal" alerts the Vulcan and foils Korby's plans.

When "Kirk" joins Chapel at the dinner table, we are as shocked as Christine to learn that the dynamic young man is actually the android duplicate. The android's comment, "Androids don't eat, Miss Chapel," makes this one of the eeriest moments in the series.

Most of this episode's overtones of horror are the result of author Robert Bloch's affinity to the work of H. P. Lovecraft. Author Lovecraft's classic horror stories invented "The Old Ones," an ancient race of all-powerful entities that dominates the human race. Bloch has Ruk speak of his creators as the Old Ones, and even the pyramid-shaped doors in the caverns conform to Lovecraft's descriptions of these ancient beings. "Forbidden Planet's" underground complexes also featured such doors, as well as references to the Old Ones.

"What Are Little Girls Made of" shares similarities with an episode of "Voyage to the Bottom of the Sea," "The Cyborg" written in July 1965, by William Read Woodfield and Allan Balter. "The Cyborg" also features an android-crazy scientist. Although he was not an android himself, the scientist constructs an android duplicate of Admiral Nelson. Captain Crane spots the substitution and Nelson is ultimately saved by a "female" android who exhibits human emotions.

Actress Sherry Jackson (Andrea) steals the show in terms of her smooth performance and her William Theiss costume, designed to accentuate her natural resources. TV viewers first saw her as Terry Williams, Danny Thomas' daughter in "Make Room for Daddy." She also appears in "Lost in Space" ("The Space Croppers" and "Twilight Zone" ("The Last Rites of Jeff Myrtlebank").

Actor Ted Cassidy (Ruk) was one performer who did

William Shatner recites dialogue for a split-screen effect in "What Are Little Girls Made of?"

In the final effect, Captain Kirk converses with his android duplicate in "What Are Little Girls Made of?" (William Shatner).

not have to worry about stealing a show. His first exposure on television, as Lurch in "The Addams Family," brought him instant recognition. Cassidy appeared in Gene Roddenberry's TV pilot movies *Genesis II* and *Planet Earth,* and in episodes of "Lost in Space" ("The Thief of Outer Space") and "The Man from U.N.C.L.E." ("The Napoleon's Tomb Affair"). He appeared regularly as Injun Joe in "The New Adventures of Huckleberry Finn" and as Habib in "I Dream of Jeannie." Dressed as Injun Joe, Cassidy is also visible in the "Star Trek" blooper reel, carrying

off William Shatner during the production of "Bread and Circuses."

Michael Strong (Dr. Roger Korby) is also seen in several "Peyton Place" episodes as a town judge, and in episodes of "The Man from U.N.C.L.E." ("The Deadly Goddess Affair"), "The Night Stalker" ("The Energy Eater"), and "Galactica 1980."

Robert Bloch's first short story was published in 1934. During the first decade of his career he wrote over 100 short stories, and his writing activities have never slackened. Bloch was a science fiction fan as early as forty years ago, and despite his busy schedule he still finds time to attend conventions, conduct correspondences, and encourage young writers attempting to enter the science fiction market. In 1959 he won a Hugo Award (science fiction's "Oscar") for his short story "The Hellbound Train."

Makeup artist Fred Phillips accentuated the natural planes of Ted Cassidy's face with grease-pencil, and covered the performer's hair with a latex headpiece. The makeup, together with William Theiss's imaginative costume, made Cassidy appear more formidable here than anywhere else. Cassidy later portrayed the Sasquatch in "The Six Million Dollar Man" and "The Bionic Woman."

In one of "Star Trek's" best split-screen effects, Captain Kirk is shown conversing with his duplicate at a dinner table. In this technique, two separate pieces of film are sandwiched together to form one image; the same process was used to show both Kirks lying side by side on the android table.

The captain's brother, George Samuel Kirk, is spoken of here for the first time. He is said to have three sons, instead of the one featured in "Operation Annihilate."

DAGGER OF THE MIND

Episode #11
First draft script   7/6/66
Final draft script   7/30/66
Revised final script   8/5/66
Filmed in middle August 1966

WRITER   Shimon Wincelberg (S. Bar-David)
DIRECTOR   Vincent McEveety
COMPOSER   Alexander Courage
PHOTOGRAPHIC EFFECTS   Westheimer Company

The *Enterprise* is delivering supplies to Tantalus Five, a progressive penal colony directed by Dr. Tristan Adams. A Tantalus inmate escapes to the starship and demands asylum. The apparent raving madman, subdued by Spock, is taken to sick bay and identified as Dr. Simon van Gelder, Adams' assistant. Using a Vulcan Mind Meld, Spock determines that Adams has turned Tantalus into a chamber of horrors with a "neural neutralizer" device that is responsible for van Gelder's incoherent state. Captain Kirk and psychiatrist Dr. Helen Noel experience Dr. Adams' sadistic theories firsthand, until Kirk defeats the insane director and Adams perishes in his own machine. Dr. van Gelder becomes the new director of Tantalus Five, where his first act is to destroy the neural neutralizer. (This episode introduces the Vulcan Mind Meld.)

"Dagger of the Mind" suffers from an illogical premise. Given the technical and sociological level of the United Federation of Planets, how is it that Dr. Adams' sadistic nature could have gone unnoticed before he assumed command of Tantalus? Assuming that he was sane before his assignment to Tantalus, why didn't his staff there see something happening to his mind? In the company of trained observers, with the psychological testing Adams was hopefully subjected to, Adams should have been stopped before he had a chance to implement his theories of penology. His presence, position, and psychological state do not speak well for the Federation's screening techniques.

A device was needed to provide access to van Gelder's mind. Originally, the earlier drafts of the script reportedly stated that either McCoy or Spock would hypnotize the patient. Before "Star Trek's" staff writers were through with the sequence, the Vulcan Mind Meld had been born. The Meld adds to Spock's image by establishing him as a more-than-human being with hidden assets and strengths that present-day Terrans can never completely understand.

The Mind Meld provides some hint of why Spock has not gone mad with loneliness. A man who can enter the mind of another at will in this manner is probably capable of more informal mind sharing, so although he is under constant pressure he may also be experiencing continuous bonds with those around him.

If the Mind Meld lessens the pressures of Spock, the presence of Dr. Noel intensifies Kirk's need to hide *his* human drives. It is possible that McCoy had heard what happened "at the science lab Christmas party," and picked Helen for this assignment to keep Kirk on his toes.

Actor James Gregory's lovingly diabolical portrayal of Dr. Adams makes up for the defects in the story. Gregory has appeared in many motion pictures, including *The Wrong Men* (20th Century-Fox–1951). On television, he was a friend of Eliot Ness in "The Untouchables" early episodes. His TV series "The Lawless Years" (1959–61) starred him as real-life detective Barney Ruditsky, who cleaned up New York while Ness was busy in Chicago. On "The Wild, Wild West" Gregory appeared as President Grant in a semiregular role, and in "That Girl" he regularly appeared as Jonathan Adams *(that* Adams was a good guy). Gregory also appeared in the pilot for "Twilight Zone" ("Where Is Everybody?"). His most unique role cast him as a gorilla in "Beneath the Planet of the Apes."

Morgan Woodward (van Gelder) steals the show. It is probably extremely difficult to enter a state of raving lunacy at will on a sound stage. Woodward's pain and intensity is frightfully convincing. His training in opera gives him great vocal projection and control. Woodward also appears in "The Omega Glory," and is often seen in television westerns. He appeared regularly as chief deputy Shotgun Gibbs in "The Life and Legend of Wyatt Earp," and as Mark Hangman on "Pistols and Petticoats." In a "Kung Fu" episode he was a fearsome madman, and in a "Gunsmoke" episode he appeared as Matt Dillon's old teacher.

"Dagger of the Mind" features doorways, corridors, consoles, and furniture that recurred throughout "Star Trek." The chair in the neural neutralizer room would later be altered and used in "Whom Gods Destroy."

The exterior view of Tantalus V is a slightly reworked version of the lithium cracking station painting created for "Where No Man Has Gone Before."

The character names in "Star Trek" episodes are usually significant. Here, Lethe is the inmate who has forgotten her past criminal life. In mythology, the River Lethe is the "river of forgetfulness." This reference is more interesting than taking a character whose presence is linked to a Christmas party and calling her Helen "Noel."

MIRI

Episode # 12
First draft script   8/11/66
Filmed in late August 1966

WRITER Adrian Spies
DIRECTOR Vincent McEveety
COMPOSER Alexander Courage
PHOTOGRAPHIC EFFECTS Cinema Research Corp.

The *Enterprise* encounters a planet that looks amazingly like Earth. Kirk and company discover a city resembling a ruined, deserted twentieth-century Earth city. The inhabitants, who scurry about hidden from the *Enterprise* personnel, prove to be extraordinary "children," each over several hundred years old. Three hundred years earlier, life-prolongation experiments were conducted. After the entire planet had been exposed to the "discovery," the adults died horrible deaths, acquiring disfiguring scar tissue and going violently berserk. The children's metabolisms were slowed so that they aged almost imperceptibly. The children, upon reaching puberty, sicken and die exactly like the adults of three centuries before. Kirk and company are affected by the discovery, which is a communicable disease. McCoy must find an antidote before they go mad and die from the illness. Work is complicated by the children, especially by Miri, a young girl who develops a crush on Captain Kirk. She

engineers the abduction of Yeoman Rand, but aids Kirk in his final attempt to win the children over to his side.

The first draft script of "Miri" included more of a relationship between Miri and Jahn; almost a distorted Peter Pan type of environment, with Jahn as Peter, Miri as Wendy, and the onlies as the lost boys. In a ritualistic sequence, Miri's childhood was officially declared closed by the onlies as they announced that they could not play with her anymore.

The finished version of "Miri" includes one of the most chilling moments in the entire series as Kirk is hit, kicked, and otherwise pummeled by the children, while the camera focuses on a little girl's diabolical smile.

Kim Darby (Miri), who is best known for her role opposite John Wayne in *True Grit,* also starred in the beautiful 1972 TV movie, *The People* (based upon Zenna Henderson's sensitive books *Pilgrimage* and *No Different Flesh),* opposite William Shatner. She can also be seen in the "Man from U.N.C.L.E." episode, "The 5 Daughters Affair."

Michael J. Pollard (Jahn) achieved stardom in the feature film *Bonnie and Clyde.* He appeared regularly on "The Many Loves of Dobie Gillis" as Duncan Krebs, and can also be seen in the "Lost in Space" episode "The Magic Mirror."

John Megna (Little Boy) is best known for his role in the film *To Kill a Mockingbird.*

"Miri" may have caused someone to realize that Yeoman Rand's relationship with Captain Kirk was becoming too intimate and complex. Yeoman Rand's only subsequent appearance in "Star Trek" was a "walk-off" role in the next episode produced, "The Conscience of the King." There is no reference to Janice Rand in any Trek episodes produced after "Conscience of the King."

An extremely creative camera angle is used as McCoy passes out after taking the antidote. Part of the "lab" set was built on stilts, so that the camera could shoot the scene level with McCoy's prone figure. The "city" set used in "Miri" also appears in "The Return of the Archons," "The City on the Edge of Forever," "A Piece of the Action," and "Patterns of Force."

The fading blemishes on McCoy's face were photographed by steadying actor DeForest Kelley's head, exposing a few feet of film, and peeling away some of the special makeup. This time-consuming process is the same method used to turn Vina into her "true appearance" in "The Cage," and was used years before to transform Larry Talbot into The Wolfman.

Terminology is still flexible in "Miri." There is a reference to "Space Central," instead of to the standardized term "Starfleet Command."

THE CONSCIENCE OF THE KING

Episode # 13

Final draft script   8/23/66
Revised final script   9/14/66
Second Revised final   9/19/66
Filmed in late September 1966

WRITER   Barry Trivers
DIRECTOR   Gerd Oswald
COMPOSER   Joseph Mullendore
PHOTOGRAPHIC EFFECTS   Westheimer Company

Kirk receives a message summoning the *Enterprise* to the home of Dr. Thomas Leighton, a brilliant research scientist with whom Kirk had survived an ordeal on colony Tarsus IV many years before. The summons is a trick to lure the captain, so that Leighton can enable him to see and meet actor Anton Karidian. Leighton thinks that Karidian is actually Kodos, the ex-governor of Tarsus IV, who initiated the massacre that killed the doctor's entire family and part of Kirk's as well. When Leighton is killed, Kirk investigates and decides to transport the Karidian troupe on the *Enterprise,* so that he can study the enigmatic actor. During the voyage, Lieutenant Kevin Riley, another survivor of the massacre, is almost killed. A phaser explodes, almost killing Kirk and Spock as well. In an effort to discover the truth, Kirk romances Karidian's daughter, Lenore. Karidian is actually Kodos, but the insane murderer of the survivors is Lenore. (This episode contains the last appearance of Yeoman Janice Rand and shows us our only view of the shuttle-bay observation deck.)

The story elements behind "The Conscience of the King" are timeless enough to be presented as part of any historical period. Tales of vengeance and justification have formed the basis for dramas that span centuries in their origin and enactment. William Shakespeare favored themes of this type in his plays; "Conscience of the King" ably makes use of story elements present in *Hamlet* and *Macbeth,* and justifies its inspirations on two distinct levels. Writer Barry Trivers appreciates the source of his teleplay and uses Shakespearean devices as points of identification for his audience, and also for the characters within the story.

Kodos, an individual who appreciates the arts, also has an ironic sense of humor. He knows he cannot justify his actions. The secondary identity he creates for himself is a performer who must reenact his past deeds. Kodos, in becoming Karidian, has condemned himself to hell, in a sense, by forcing himself to confront his past life regularly. It is no wonder that Lenore Karidian was insane. She would have very little choice in the matter, growing up with a brooding, guilt-ridden father taking refuge in Shakespeare's human horrors.

Karidian, the actor, was never really alive at all. A private man who never permitted himself to be seen offstage, he regarded his sole purpose in life as raising his daughter in a guilt-free environment that he knew he was not providing. In a brief scene, cut from the finished production, he returned from a late-night walk around the *Enterprise* decks and addressed Lenore, stating "I am thy father's spirit, doomed for a certain term to walk the night." This quote from Act One of *Hamlet* includes the dialogue that Karidian, as the ghost of Hamlet's father, recites as Kevin Riley aims his phaser at the actor: ". . . I could a tale unfold whose lightest word would harrow up thy soul; freeze thy young blood. . . ."

"Conscience of the King" signaled the second (and unfortunately the final) appearance of Lieutenant Kevin Thomas Riley. We accept him as a likable person in "The Naked Time," and here we develop a greater liking for him as we learn about his tragic past on Tarsus IV. The final draft of the script for this episode does not include Lieutenant Riley; his dialogue was delivered by a character named Robert Daiken. Apparently, when actor Bruce Hyde was cast for this role, someone recalled that he had appeared in the series before, and wisely decided to continue his successful characterization.

The dramatic elements of this episode are effective largely because of its cast, and primarily because of the script, direction, cinematography, and music all focusing on the performances of William Shatner and Arnold Moss (Kodos/Karidian). William Shatner's career as an actor has its roots in Shakespearean theater. His every gesture, mannerism, and method of delivery are the result of this training. "Conscience of the King" was the first "Star Trek" episode to include moods and situations that are so clearly derived from the work of the Bard.

To offset the power of Shatner's performance, someone wisely recommended that a performer with a powerful delivery and a strong sense of drama portray Karidian. Casting director Joseph D'Agosta may have been responsible for this choice; so might have director Gerd Oswald. Oswald had previously directed Moss in a "Daniel Boone" episode ("Take the Southbound Stage" with Sarah Marshall and Torin Thatcher).

Arnold Moss, who taught acting and directing at New York City's Brooklyn College during the 1930s, has worked in radio, on stage, and in films. His most unusual film role was in *The 27th Day* (Columbia–1957), as a space traveler who briefly visits Earth with some extraordinary devices. On an episode of the vintage TV series "Lights Out" ("A Love Came to Professor Gilder") he played a man haunted by a ghost.

Barbara Anderson (Lenore Karidian) appeared regularly on two popular TV series. She was Officer Eve

Whitfield on "Ironside" (1967–72), and was featured in some of the last "Mission: Impossible" episodes as Agent Mimi Davis. She is also in the "Night Gallery" episode "Fright Night' (directed by Jeff Corey), and is featured in TV movies *Don't Be Afraid of the Dark* (with Kim Darby) and *The Six Million Dollar Man* (the series' pilot; she is Steve Austin's nurse).

Director Gerd Oswald, whose father founded Germany's famous UFA Film Studios, directed some of the finest episodes of "The Outer Limits" (including "The Soldier" by Harlan Ellison, "Fun and Games," "Chameleon," "The Forms of Things Unknown," and "Don't Open Until Doomsday"). His style of direction, which stresses drama over physical action, works beautifully in this episode. Oswald also directed "The Alternative Factor."

Composer Joseph Mullendore's music is also heard in the first seasons of vintage TV series such as "The Adventures of Superman," "Gunsmoke," and "Ramar of the Jungle." He wrote scores for "Honey West," and several of the Dick Powell (Four Star Productions) western series.

"Conscience of the King" features only three planetside sets: a darkened theater stage, a small living room, and a brief planet exterior. The lack of budget is shown in the view from Dr. Leighton's window. The window itself was taken from the lithium cracking station interior in "Where No Man Has Gone Before"; the outside view is the painting used for the picnic scene in "The Cage."

The observation deck consists of a narrow walkway, a porthole, and a window overlooking the hangar deck. The hangar itself is never seen in this episode. The lit windows included in the miniature hangar deck set are intended to conform to the observation deck. This set, however, does not appear in any other Trek episodes.

One of the "Outer Limits" episodes directed by Gerd Oswald was "The Duplicate Man." In that segment, a character appeared with a black covering that hid half his face, a device similar to the mask worn by Dr. Leighton. The suit jackets in "The Duplicate Man" were also like those in "Conscience of the King," featuring clean lines with no lapels.

THE GALILEO SEVEN

Episode # 14

First draft script   9/1/66

Final draft script   9/15/66

Filmed in late September and early October 1966.

WRITERS   Oliver Crawford, S. Bar-David (Shimon Wincelberg)
      (Story by Oliver Crawford)
DIRECTOR   Robert Gist
COMPOSER   Alexander Courage
PHOTOGRAPHIC EFFECTS   Film Effects of Hollywood

En route to planet Makus III, the *Enterprise* encounters a giant quasarlike formation, Murasaki 312. Although Galactic High Commissioner Ferris objects, Kirk orders the starship's shuttlecraft *Galileo* launched to investigate the phenomenon. When the *Galileo* crash lands on planet Taurus II, with Spock, McCoy, and Scotty aboard, Ferris demands that the *Enterprise* abandon the search and continue its delivery of important medical supplies. Spock fights Neanderthal-like creatures and the discontent of the

The miniature hangar deck and shuttlecraft ready for a "take" in "The Galileo Seven."

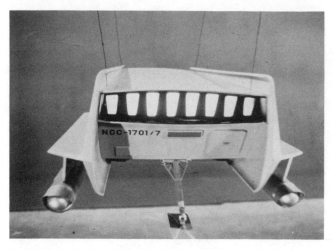

A detailed aft view of the miniature shuttlecraft, suspended from wires for an effects shot in "The Galileo Seven."

shuttle's other inhabitants. Although it appears that Spock's logical behavior has caused the deaths of two crewmen, the Vulcan makes a last-minute emotional decision that saves the *Galileo* and its remaining crew members. (This is the first appearance of the shuttlecraft, although the landing party in "The Enemy Within" could have used it a little sooner.)

This script is a very special one in terms of Mr. Spock's evolution. At first he fails miserably because he cannot accept that the ape-creatures' reactions are based upon illogical, bestial motivations. Spock behaves in a cold-blooded fashion to conceal the anxiety he feels on the occasion of assuming his first command. He is fully (and logically) prepared to leave three crewmen behind so that the rest of the Galileo's crew can return in the damaged shuttle.

In jettisoning the *Galileo*'s fuel to provide a "distress flare," Spock is acknowledging his membership in the human race. He later (stubbornly) denies that his reaction was emotionally inspired, but his denial fools no one, least of all Captain Kirk and Dr. McCoy.

The role of Yeoman Mears was created to replace Yeoman Janice Rand, who was written out of the "Star Trek" format during the preparation of this episode. In the script's first draft these lines were delivered by Yeoman Rand. A set of revised blue script pages dated September 13, 1966, contains a notice that "Rand" has been changed to "Mears" throughout the script.

The story itself, like so many other "Star Trek" episodes, is derived from a contemporary dramatic plot converted into science fiction terms. The crash, the talk of leaving people behind, and the presence of hostile conditions (or natives) are all reminiscent of the feature films *Four Frightened People* and *The Flight of the Phoenix.*

Don Marshall (Lieutenant Boma) had little to work with here, but he managed to create an individual who contrasts effectively with Mr. Spock. When the *Galileo* crashes, Mr. Boma ignores his injuries and remains scientifically formal in the performance of his duties; exactly what Spock does. Marshall later became a regularly featured performer on "Land of the Giants" (as Dan Erickson). He appeared regularly as Ted Neuman on "Julia" (1968–71).

Robert Gist directed the "Twilight Zone" episode "I Dream of Genie."

Peter Marko (Mr. Gaetano) also deserves a good review for conveying true terror as the ape-creature looms over him.

The real star of this episode is the *Galileo* shuttlecraft. The shuttle was included in the August 1966, revision of the *Star Trek Writers' Guide,* and was mentioned in "The Conscience of the King" before its debut in this episode.

Two *Galileos* had to be built; a miniature and a full-size mock-up. The miniature appears approximately three feet long, built in proportion to the miniature hangar-deck. Outside the hangar's doors, the miniature is suspended on wires with an aerial brace. For the views of the *Galileo* flying through space, depending upon the requirements of the scene, the miniature either hangs from four wires or is supported from beneath atop a special base. This base is painted blue, to match the blue screen in front of which the model is photographed. Special photographic effects expert Linwood Dunn, president of Film Effects of Hollywood, supervised these scenes (just as he later handled similar tasks for "Space Seed").

The full-sized version of the *Galileo* was built by the AMT Corporation's "speed and custom division" in Phoenix, Arizona. Fifteen workers labored over two months, supervised by automotive designer Gene Winfield. Hardboard and fiberglass were shaped over a steel skeleton to provide the craft's contours. The mockup is twenty-two feet long, thirteen feet wide, and eight feet high. Each of the craft's two power pods is fourteen feet long, constructed from eighteen-inch diameter steel tubing capped by a plastic dome.

The interior of the *Galileo* is a separate set, constructed on wooden foundations. A removable wall provides for different camera angles. There are discrepancies between this set and the big exterior mock-up. Windows are visible on the outside doors, but are omitted in the interior. The ceiling of the interior is also considerably higher than the height of the full mock-up. To convey the illusion of the craft's lift-off, the backdrop built outside the front viewing ports of the interior set was gradually lowered.

The apelike aliens appear bigger than they actually are. Actor Buck Maffei, concealed behind a mask, taloned gloves, and a heavily padded fur costume holds a shield and spear proportionate to his height. When Spock handles these objects, however, we see oversized props that make the alien seem eight feet tall in proportion.

When the Phaser Two units are fired in one scene, the "cue lights" of the working models can be seen. The performers also "freeze" while firing, to make it easier for the animators to add the beams in the darkroom.

The "Murasaki Effect" is a cloud of smoke, photographed through a red lens filter and printed in slow motion double-exposed over a star background.

The blazing trail left by the jettisoned shuttle fuel was animation, double-exposed over footage of the miniature shuttlecraft.

COURT-MARTIAL

Episode #15

First draft script   9/21/66

Final draft script   9/26/66

Revised final draft   9/29/66

Original title   "Court-martial On Starbase Eleven"

Filmed in early October 1966

WRITERS   Don M. Mankiewicz, Stephen W. Carabatsos (Story by Don M. Mankiewicz)

DIRECTOR   Marc Daniels

COMPOSER   Alexander Courage

PHOTOGRAPHIC EFFECTS   Film Effects of Hollywood

During an ion storm, the *Enterprise* takes a severe buffeting and Records Officer Ben Finney enters the starship's ion pod to take important readings. When the storm makes it necessary to jettison the pod, Kirk follows normal procedures and warns Finney to evacuate. The pod is jettisoned, with Finney apparently inside. At Starbase 12, Commodore L. T. Stone institutes a court-martial against Kirk; the records show that Kirk jettisoned the pod *before* Finney had a chance to escape. Lieutenant Areel Shaw, the prosecuting attorney and an old girlfriend of Kirk's, retains the brilliant but eccentric lawyer Samuel Cogley to defend the captain. Although all the evidence is against Kirk, Cogley (with the aid of Mr. Spock) is able to prove that Ben Finney is actually *alive*. Because of an old grudge, Finney had hoped to fake his own death, discrediting Captain Kirk.

"Court-Martial" is definitely Captain Kirk's episode. All of the action and dialogue revolve around him, and we get the impression that Starfleet Command will think twice before questioning his command abilities again.

The audience is manipulated once again into believing that Spock is a cold-blooded, emotionless alien. When we follow him to play chess with the ship's computer as the captain is fighting for his professional life, we hate Spock for his unfeeling attitude. Dr. McCoy puts the audience's reaction into loud, accusing words . . . only to be efficiently silenced by Spock's logical motive of testing the computer's memory banks.

Still, McCoy is not cured of his repeated urge to pick on Mr. Spock. In court, when Cogley denounces computers for infringing upon human dignity (anticipating "The Ultimate Computer"), McCoy shoots an acid look toward the Vulcan.

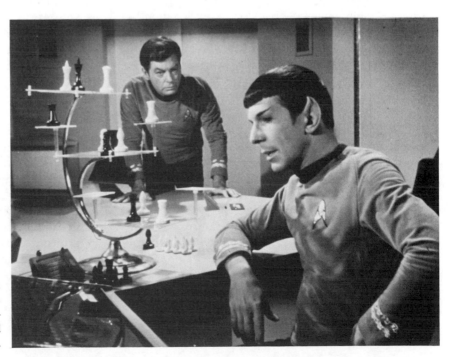

By playing a chess game, Spock determines that the computer has been tampered with, in "Court-Martial" (DeForest Kelley, Leonard Nimoy).

The beautiful landscape of Starbase Eleven; an optical painting created for "Court-Martial."

The scene between Commodore Stone and Captain Kirk at the end of Act One is beautifully charged with doubt, tension, and disbelief. The final freeze-frame on Kirk's angered face effectively completes the scene. Throughout the entire episode, the relationship between Kirk and Stone indicates a reluctant personal friction that resolves itself when Stone himself hears the single remaining heartbeat and exclaims "Finney!"

"Court-Martial" contains three well-cast secondary characters: Samuel T. Cogley, Commodore Stone, and Ben Finney.

Elisha Cook, Jr. (Cogley), is best remembered as Wilmer, the "fall guy" in the Bogart version of *The Maltese Falcon*. He has played an impressive number of murderers, crazies, and an occasional good guy. In *The House on Haunted Hill* he had the last word on Vincent Price ("The ghosts are coming for me now, and soon they'll be coming for *you*"). His television appearances date back to the 1949 pilot episode of "Dick Tracy" (he was "Coffeehead," a criminal). In the *"Thriller"* episode "The Fatal Impulse" he co-starred with Robert Lansing as a mad bomber. One of his few appearances as a lawman was in "The Adventures of Superman" episode "The Semi-Private Eye" (Lois and Jimmy hired him, as Detective Homer Garrity, to follow Clark Kent).

Percy Rodriguez (Commodore Stone) uses his imposing face and voice to great advantage. Completely at home in the command jacket of the commodore, he is better known as Dr. Miles, the resident physician of "Peyton Place." He appeared regularly as Jason Hart on "The Silent Force" (1970–71), and can be seen in the "Man from U.N.C.L.E." episode "The My Friend the Gorilla Affair."

Richard Webb (Ben Finney) is famous as TV hero "Captain Midnight," Ovaltine's classic TV series of the early 1950s in which he flew *The Silver Dart* aircraft, and worked out of a secret mountain headquarters with sidekick Ichabod Mudd (probably no relation to Harry, played by Sid Melton). In syndication, this series was known as "Jet Jackson the Flying Commando." In the 1958 syndicated TV series "U.S. Border Patrol," he was patrolman Don Jagger. His movie appearances include *I Wanted Wings* (Paramount–1941) and *Beware of the Blob*.

Writer Don M. Mankiewicz was a contributor to "One Step Beyond," having written several episodes of John Newland's classic TV series ("Epilogue," "The Navigator," "Front Runner," "The Explorer," and "House of the Dead").

"Court-Martial" boasts not one but two highly beautiful optical paintings of Starbase Twelve. A close and a distant view were prepared for the base, with one suggesting a daylight view and the other an evening landscape.

The commodore's office also appears in "The Menagerie," complete with the same building cutouts positioned outside the window. The ancestor of one of the spore plants from the later episode "This Side of Paradise" is also visible in the office. The furniture in Kirk's book-filled quarters includes a couch with a rear panel attached to the wall, not directly to the furniture. A similar piece (possibly the same one) is also evident in "Journey to Babel."

Costume designer William Theiss provided Cogley with a leatherlike outfit that appears simultaneously traditional and futuristic.

Lieutenant Shaw wears the only female dress uniform seen in the entire series. Fashioned from the same fabric as the men's jackets, McCoy's surgical jacket, and Nurse Chapel's uniform, its black neckline is topped with gold trim.

One of the least imaginative props ever designed for "Star Trek" is the "white sound device" used by McCoy to single out Finney's heartbeat. It is obviously a twentieth-century microphone.

Once again, the names of the characters are significant. "Stone" is self-explanatory as a symbol of strength. "Cogley" is a very suitable name for a man who does not want "the wheels of progress running over my client in their unbridled haste."

In the Starbase bar, a rear wall from Balok's ship in "The Corbomite Maneuver" can be seen. During this sequence, Kirk greets someone, announcing that he hasn't seen him since "the Vulcanian Expedition." This is one of the last times "Vulcanian" is mentioned in "Star Trek."

THE MENAGERIE

Episode #16

First draft script   10/3/66
Final draft script   10/7/66
Filmed in middle October 1966

WRITER   Gene Roddenberry
DIRECTOR   Marc Daniels
COMPOSER   Alexander Courage
PHOTOGRAPHIC EFFECTS   Film Effects of Hollywood

A call supposedly sent by ex-*Enterprise* Captain Christopher Pike diverts the *Enterprise* to Starbase Six. The message has actually been sent by Mr. Spock. Pike, crippled and completely paralyzed in a recent accident, is abducted and brought aboard the *Enterprise* by Spock. Starbase Commodore Mendez and Captain Kirk overtake the *Enterprise* and discover that Spock has locked the ship on course for Talos IV. To visit this planet demands the death penalty, and Kirk is forced to convene a court-martial against his Vulcan friend. The entire ceremony, however, is a charade because Mendez is not really on the *Enterprise*. His presence is an illusion, caused by the powerful telepathic natives of planet Talos IV. The reason behind all these puzzling occurrences is to get Pike to this planet, so that the Talosian's mental abilities can enable the captain to live a happy life despite his deformities and paralysis. (This episode, the only two-part "Star Trek" segment, contains footage from "Trek's" first pilot, "The Cage." During its production, the pilot's title was changed to "The Menagerie," but it is referred to throughout this book as "The Cage," to differentiate it from episode #16.)

In the first draft script of "The Menagerie," the adventure involved Commodore Don Prickett, instead of Commodore Mendez. (In real life, Air Force Colonel Donald I. Prickett is a friend of writer Roddenberry. Their acquaintance dates from World War II, and is mentioned on pages 75–76 in *The Making of Star Trek.*)

In this initial draft, the relationship between Spock and his former captain was more overtly emotional; Pike cried when he was left alone with his old friend, and Spock could not completely suppress his emotional responses to Pike.

NBC's initial commitment for "Star Trek" was for sixteen episodes. After "Court-Martial" was completed as episode #15, the series' first pilot had still not been incorporated into the aired inventory of the show. If "The Cage" *could* be counted as the sixteenth episode, "Star Trek" would meet its initial network commitment for less money than if a completely new segment were produced in its place. But the differences in format between "The Cage" and "Star Trek" were so great that pilot #1 could not be shown intact with the series. The only solution was to create a "frame" around the original footage that would preserve the series' continuity while making it possible to utilize the first pilot's footage.

"The Menagerie" is a wondrous accomplishment because it fulfilled the demands for a sixteenth episode while becoming one of the most interesting segments of "Star Trek" as well. The "frame" took shape rather quickly (less than a week between the first and final drafts of the script), but the overall story is highly imaginative and compatible with "The Cage."

We are first presented with a shocking look at Christopher Pike's ill fortune. His predicament is a disturbing reminder that starship captains are not immortal. Add to this shock the further suggestion that Spock is going insane, and Captain Kirk (along with the audience) finds his strengths and his friends falling into doubt.

Spock has somehow contacted the Talosians, and has arranged this entire elaborate charade for Captain Kirk's benefit, to keep him suitably occupied while he gets Captain Pike to Talos IV. Spock had to have the Talosians' cooperation; Spock alone could not have arranged for the illusion of "Commodore Mendez" to follow Kirk to the *Enterprise*.

Mr. Spock's behavior here is completely rational, if not a bit desperate. His loyalty and friendship compelled Spock to spare Kirk the knowledge of his plans, just as his loyalty and friendship for Pike compelled him to put his plans into effect. Spock's actions here are structured like a chess strategy, with each move completely thought out.

The "punch line" of the episode is extremely effective. Even after knowing that the Talosians are masters of illusion, it still comes as a shock that Commodore Mendez is *not* and *never has been* aboard the *Enterprise.*

"The Menagerie" is noteworthy because it marks one of the few times in "Star Trek" that Captain Kirk's fun-loving nature catches up with him. Upon his beaming down at Starbase Six, Kirk is greeted by the young and attractive Miss Piper, who informs him that she knows all about him; a mutual female acquaintance has described him. Miss Piper relays her news with an obvious, desiring smile.

Actor Malachi Throne had originally dubbed in the voice of "the Keeper" for "The Cage." Since he appears in "The Menagerie" as well, the voice was re-recorded by another performer. Because the Talosians do not move their lips when they "speak," it was unnecessary to synchronize their lip movements and dubbed-in dialogue.

Malachi Throne (Commodore Mendez) appeared regularly as Noah Bain, on "It Takes a Thief" (1968–69), as well as co-authoring scripts for the series. He is also seen in "Batman" ("True or False Face"), "Lost in Space" ("The Thief of Outer Space"), "Voyage to the Bottom of the Sea" ("The Magnus Beam," "The Enemies," and "The Return of Blackbeard"); and "The Man from U.N.C.L.E." ("The Four Steps Affair").

Julie Parrish (Miss Piper) appeared regularly as Linda in "Good Morning World" (1967–68) and as Betty Harrington in "Return to Peyton Place" (1972–74).

The matte painting of Starbase Six is executed in blues, grays, and white. Excellent use is made of perspective, showing not only the area in front of the beam-down point but the adjacent street as well. The viewer can apparently see the complex extending through many blocks, with some buildings in the complex still under construction. The muted colors give a peaceful appearance to the complex, and are similar to those used in creating the city for "A Taste of Armageddon."

A short time after this adventure took place, Mr. Spock probably returned to Talos IV and moved Captain Pike to Omicron Ceti Three to be cured by "the spores" featured in "This Side of Paradise." This would have made an intriguing story on "Star Trek," but it would not have been possible. Actor Jeffrey Hunter did not film any new footage for "The Menagerie"; all views of the healthy Captain Pike are from "The Cage." The crippled Pike was portrayed by actor Sean Kenney, whose facial structure is similar to that of Hunter's. (Kenney also appears as the navigator in "Arena," where his resemblance to actor Hunter can be clearly seen.)

From the files of Starfleet, here is the formerly top secret file on Talos IV:

TOP SECRET: For eyes of **STARFLEET** command only.

Subject: TALOS IV in third quadrant of vernal galaxy.
Known facts: Detailed information cross-referenced with 3XY phagrin level mass computer.
The only Earth ship that ever visited planet Talos IV was the U.S.S. *Enterprise* commanded by Captain Christopher Pike, with half-Vulcan science officer Spock.
Recommendations: Be it hereby noted that said following instructions be incorporated into STARFLEET. . . .

NO ONE WILL EVER VISIT TALOS IV.

The following officers have visited Talos IV and recommended that no human should ever visit it again . . .

> *Captain Christopher Pike*
> *Vulcan science officer Spock*
>
> STARFLEET Command
> By Order of
> Robert L. Comack
> Commanding Officer

SHORE LEAVE

Episode # 17
Story outline   5/10/66
Revised outline   5/23/66
First draft script   10/3/66
Final draft script   10/14/66
Filmed in late October 1966

WRITER   Theodore Sturgeon
DIRECTOR   Robert Sparr
COMPOSER   Gerald Fried
PHOTOGRAPHIC EFFECTS   Westheimer Company

Captain Kirk decides to stop at an inviting, Earth-like planet to give his men a well-deserved shore leave. The planet proves to be just what the doctor *did not* order for relaxation. Strange things happen, beginning with McCoy's sighting a giant white rabbit being chased by an Alice-like little girl. Sulu is menaced by a Samurai warrior; other crewmen are strafed by aircraft, chased by tigers, and menaced by swordsmen. Kirk meets Finnegan, an old enemy from his Academy days, followed by Ruth, an ex-lover. McCoy is "killed" by a black knight on horseback. As the perils become progressively deadlier, Spock and Kirk realize that their *thoughts* are being brought to life. A kindly old man appears, identifying himself as the Caretaker, and explains that the entire planet is an "amusement park" where advanced alien technologies synthesize the "entertainment" from the minds of the "vacationers." McCoy appears alive and well, escorted by two Rigel cabaret girls. Kirk decides that, with the proper mental precautions, this *can* be a good shore leave planet after all.

In Theodore Sturgeon's final story outline, the technical and personal aspects of the story were elaborated upon. Sulu had a folding specimen kit for his analysis of the planet's surface. For a dance held planetside, music was supplied with a hand-held high-fidelity system.

Sulu called McCoy "Sawbones" and referred to the doctor as a perennial jokester. McCoy, in turn, kidded Sulu about his many hobbies.

McCoy fought the black knight to aid another crew member. The landing party's radioman was a circus lover who materialized an entire circus. As McCoy was dying, the doctor was still unconvinced that all this was real. Kirk learned of McCoy's "death" as the circus calliope supplied incongruous background music. McCoy's body was shown being dragged into hidden doorways in the rocks by mechanical arms. The doctor was "repaired" only because the machines thought that the body was one of their synthetic creations.

The planet was programmed 1,000 years before, and had outlived its creators. It drew its power from the *Enterprise* automatically; there was no "caretaker" in this early version. Kirk determined the truth about the planet by thinking about the strange events he had experienced here. He was shown a series of mental images that explained the workings of the world.

Characterization is well handled in the finished episode. McCoy is a true Southern gentleman, and Sulu grins from ear to ear at his new toy, a "police special" pistol. Kirk is seen recollecting the most puzzling romance we have seen in his past. Whereas the mature Kirk would not fall for an older woman, the younger Kirk might have. Whatever the story behind this romance, it is both a "painful reality" and a pleasant memory for Captain Kirk. Kirk is particularly in character when he tells McCoy to follow the rabbit, while ". . . I'll backtrack the girl."

In this episode we realize how much "Star Trek" depends upon Dr. Leonard McCoy. With his apparent death, the audience suffers along with Kirk as we try to picture the five-year mission without the acid wit of "Bones."

The young woman who beams down with Mr. Rodriguez is referred to in the script as "Mary Teller," and is called Teller by Kirk in the episode. But as Rodriguez cradles her temporarily dead body, he calls her "Angela." Actress Barbara Baldavin plays this role. She also appears as Angela Martine in "Balance of Terror." Apparently, Ms. Baldavin was signed for this part and someone was reminded she had appeared as another character; the decision was made to refer to her by the same character name, but the credits and Kirk's scene were probably already filmed.

Bruce Mars (Finnegan) plays his part with great gusto. Although it is a relatively short role, some Trek fans looked forward to Kirk's meeting Finnegan in the flesh. Unfortunately this meeting never came about, but actors Shatner and Mars did face each other very briefly in "Assignment Earth," in which Mars appeared as one of the policemen accidentally beamed up to the *Enterprise*.

Elements of this story are similar to plot devices present in *Westworld* (Metro-Goldwyn-Mayer–1973), which also features an amusement park filled with robots. In *Westworld,* we saw the collection and repair of the damaged robots, something Sturgeon explained in his story line for this episode.

"Shore Leave" was largely filmed outdoors at "Africa USA." On location, the cost of set construction is saved, but environmental problems raise the risks of production. Partly as a result of its outdoor settings, "Shore Leave" is one of the most pleasant and spacious Trek episodes. "Africa USA" was a lush area frequently used by Hollywood filmmakers during the 1960s. To make its landscape seem vaguely alien, exotic plants and feathery objects were scattered around. Even this specially maintained stretch of land did not offer unlimited space for shooting. Various scenes were photographed in other locations and, during the chase between Kirk and Finnegan, we pass the same fallen tree more than once.

Gerald Fried's music adds greatly to the flavor of the story. His romantic theme for Kirk and Ruth, and his colorful theme for Finnegan are both heard in other Trek episodes.

Finnegan's Academy Cadet emblem is a smaller version of the commodore's insignia worn by Mendez in "The Menagerie" and Stone in "Court-Martial." Finnegan's shirt is also seen in the bar sequence of "The Trouble with Tribbles," worn by a background delegate in "Journey to Babel," and by a passing pedestrian outside the tavern in "Wolf in the Fold."

Author Theodore Sturgeon, who also wrote "Amok Time," sold his first science fiction story in 1939, and is regarded as one of the central writers during the years sometimes called the golden age of science fiction. Most of his magazine contributions were for *Astounding Science Fiction* and *Galaxy* magazine. His books include *More Than Human* (published in 1953), *A Touch of Strange* (1958), and *The Cosmic Rape* (1958). He novelized the film *Voyage to the Bottom of the Sea* (20th Century-Fox–1961), and has written many short stories since 1937.

THE SQUIRE OF GOTHOS

Episode #18
First draft script   10/18/66
Final draft script   10/26/66
Filmed in middle November 1966

WRITER Paul Schneider
DIRECTOR Don McDougall
COMPOSER Alexander Courage
PHOTOGRAPHIC EFFECTS Film Effects of Hollywood

In Space Quadrant 904, eight days away from Colony Beta Six, the *Enterprise* is trapped in orbit around an uncharted planet. There, Kirk and company are confronted by Trelane, an illogical but extremely powerful alien. Although he appears as an adult humanoid, Trelane is eventually revealed to be a "child" belonging to an unknown, alien race. Trelane's parents rescue Kirk and the *Enterprise* from their playful son.

"The Squire of Gothos" is an enjoyable and original episode, but it never develops into what it could have been—one of the most effective segments of "Star Trek."

We meet Trelane who, at first glance, appears to be a powerful alien hobbyist studying Earth with a super-telescope and controlling the *Enterprise* crew with sophisticated machines. He enjoys recreations such as music and dancing, and has an eye for the ladies.

Kirk treats Trelane as he would cope with Harry Mudd; he plays off the man's idiosyncracies while searching for weaknesses with which to save his ship. Kirk erroneously reasons that Trelane's power is dependent upon a machine. He destroys the mechanism . . . and promptly realizes Trelane's incredibly powerful alien nature.

Although Trelane is in reality an insubstantial creature, his parents have male and female voices (provided respectively by James Doohan and Barbara Babcock). The implications of "Squire of Gothos" are staggering to James Kirk. This "boy" has made a planet out of nothingness; he has also hurt Kirk's ego. Proud of his rank and the power he controls, the captain suffers the indignity of being called a "primitive creature" by Trelane's mother.

Paul Schneider also wrote "Balance of Terror."

William Campbell (Trelane) has appeared in many motion pictures and television episodes going back to the 1950s. His feature credits include *The High and the Mighty* (Warner Brothers-1954) and *Battle Cry* (Warner Brothers-1955). On television, Campbell and veteran character actor Paul Birch starred as truck-drivers in the series "Cannonball" (relating the adventures of Birch the veteran and Campbell the novice, a forerunner of the more modern "Movin' On").

On "Star Trek," Campbell would also appear as the popular Captain Koloth, the Klingon captain of "The Trouble with Tribbles." Koloth was supposed to have become a recurring character on Trek, but unfortunately the next time the Klingon was needed, Campbell was unavailable and Koloth was eliminated.

Barbara Babcock also appears in "Assignment Earth" (providing "meows" for Isis the cat), "A Taste of Armageddon" (Mea), and "Plato's Stepchildren" (Philana). She was also in an episode of "The Green Hornet" TV series ("The Frog Is a Deadly Weapon").

The exterior castle set was actually constructed indoors on a soundstage. It later turned up in "Catspaw" and "Bread and Circuses."

The budget of "Squire" was kept low by furnishing Trelane's home with objects of art from Paramount's large store of antiques and exotic furniture. Many of these items probably first appeared in Cecil B. De-Mille's classic epic films.

One of the "decorations" was the full body costume of the salt vampire from "The Man Trap"; it is shown briefly propped up in an alcove near the front door.

ARENA

Episode # 19
First draft script   10/18/66
Final draft script   10/28/66
Revised final draft   11/3/66
Filmed in middle November 1966

WRITER Gene L. Coon (From a story by Frederic L. Brown)
DIRECTOR Joseph Pevney
COMPOSER Alexander Courage
PHOTOGRAPHIC EFFECTS Westheimer Company

Captain Kirk receives a request to visit Cestus Three, a Starfleet base commanded by the friendly and hospitable Commodore Travers. Upon arriving, Kirk finds that the base has been completely destroyed. Suddenly Kirk and his landing party are fired upon from hidden positions by unknown attackers. Lieutenant Harold, the lone survivor of the Cestus personnel, testifies that his base was destroyed by a sudden and merciless attack; he adds that his people did *not* have time to request the *Enterprise's* presence. The call was a trap, sent by the attackers. Kirk follows the enemy spaceship. When the two vessels intrude upon the territory of the powerful Metrons, the Metrons decide to settle the conflict by having Kirk fight the alien (Gorn) captain in single combat. The Gorn is a huge, immensely strong reptile, as resourceful as Kirk in the battle. Kirk knows that the loser's ship will be destroyed, and this gives him the incentive to construct a weapon to conquer the Gorn. He refuses to kill his opponent. Perhaps one day, the Metron informs Kirk, his people and the Federation may meet as friends and equals.

"Arena," the short story written by Frederic L. Brown, was apparently too good a prospect to be turned down by both "The Outer Limits" and "Star Trek." "The Outer Limits" version was entitled "Fun and Games," starred actor Nick Adams, and was directed by Gerd Oswald.

"Arena" makes us acutely aware that the *Enterprise* is not always on time to save UFP outposts, and that the starship itself is vulnerable. Captain Kirk, too, is severely tested during the episode, and although his ship is directly threatened by the Gorn and the Metrons, he never forgets himself sufficiently to act like a predatory animal instead of an intelligent individual.

Writer Gene L. Coon's "Star Trek" scripts (especially "The Devil in the Dark" and "Metamorphosis") share a common theme; a firm conviction that prejudice is an extremely negative quality that must be ignored if mankind is ever to take its place alongside other intelligent civilizations. This realization is one of the greatest reasons for "Star Trek's" continued popularity among intelligent people. Just as Kirk refuses to kill in this episode he also refused to kill in an almost identical manner in "Spectre of the Gun," written by Coon under his pseudonym of Lee Cronin.

The fact that the *Enterprise* emerged undamaged after such a difficult experience increases our faith in "Star Trek's" principles. Kirk's victory, achieved after we have shared his fear by knowing his weaknesses (including an instinctive fear of reptiles), reminds us that Captain Kirk is a believable dramatic character.

The opening scene, detailing the destruction on Cestus III, is extremely effective. The outpost is possibly the largest set ever to appear in a "Star Trek" episode. It appears to be a redressed old fort, left over from a Paramount western film, modified by the addition of a few shattered Federation-style door frames, debris, and masked camera angles. (In the farthest view of the complex, a strategically placed girder and rock insert prevent us from seeing the studio buildings or roadways that are probably near the set.)

Carole Shelyne (the Metron) can also be seen in "The Man from U.N.C.L.E." segment, "The Cap and Gown Affair."

Two familiar but usually unsung faces are visible in "Arena." Grant Woods (Mr. Kelowitz) appears in this same role in "The Galileo Seven" and "This Side of Paradise." Sean Kenney (Mr. DePaul, the Helmsman) appears as the crippled Captain Pike in "The Menagerie." He is also aboard the *Enterprise* in "A Taste of Armageddon."

The voice of the Metrons (the warning message and the entity himself) was supplied by vocal artist Vic Perrin. His first bit of dialogue here is strongly reminiscent of his introductory speech for each episode of "The Outer Limits" (". . . we will control all that you see and hear . . .").

The grenade launcher sound effect (also used for the photon torpedoes) was first heard in *My Favorite Spy,* a Paramount film, and is best remembered from *The War of the Worlds* (Paramount–1953). The glare of the weapon's detonation was provided with a double-exposed green overlay.

The most important "prop" of this episode is the Gorn itself. Constructed by Wah Chang, the suit was fashioned from heavy rubber. An exterior "costume" hid the suit's seams. The head is a separate mask, with separately installed teeth and a provision to enable the actor within the costume to open and close the mouth. Wah Chang also constructed the costume for the "Fun and Games" "Outer Limits" creature, the head of which is seen in "The Cage."

The translator-recorder provided by the Metrons bears a striking resemblance to the Federation's own design of their universal translator (featured in "Metamorphosis"), and is also reminiscent of "Forbidden Planet's" intraship communicator.

Lazarus' small space/time vehicle gets zapped in an optical test effect from "The Alternative Factor."

The *Enterprise* phasers focus on a target thousands of miles away in an effect used only once during the series in "The Alternative Factor."

THE ALTERNATIVE FACTOR

Episode #20
First draft script   11/7/66
Final draft script   11/11/66
Filmed in late November 1966

WRITER   Don Ingalls
DIRECTOR   Gerd Oswald

Throughout the entire universe there occurs a frightening moment of "nonexistence," as though every natural law had ceased to function for an instant. Commodore Barstow advises Kirk that the *Enterprise* is orbiting the planet that is believed to be the center of the disturbance. Beaming down, Kirk discovers an alien named Lazarus, who tells an incredible story of an insane foe he has been chasing through space. At first glance it is Lazarus himself who appears to be insane, but at various moments he is also quiet and lucid. Lazarus steals the *Enterprise*'s crucial dilithium crystals, which he "needs" for the battle against his unknown foe. Kirk beams down, and learns that there are *two* Lazaruses. The madman, from our universe, is obsessed with confronting and eliminating his antimatter-universe double, even though both universes will cease to exist if both Lazaruses ever do meet face to face. Kirk aids the sane Lazarus in baiting a trap that strands both Lazaruses in an inescapable corridor between both universes.

The first draft script of "The Alternative Factor" tells the same story as the finished episode; a tale of two universes and of one man who is actually two very different individuals. The earlier version, however, has certain elements that the final version lacks. Lazarus (the *sane* one) is a dynamic personality, who becomes romantically involved with engineering Lieutenant Charlene Masters. When the *in*sane Lazarus discovers this, he proceeds to use Lieutenant Masters to steal the dilithium crystals he needs. She beams down with the crystals and finds herself in much the same predicament as Marla McGivers does in "Space Seed." The script has other plot complications, and makes it clear that Lazarus is a magnetic individual, even when compared to Captain Kirk.

The final episode is a mystery, but not the mystery that was intended. It is extremely difficult to tell the two Lazaruses apart, regardless if one has a bandage and the other does not.

Perhaps part of the problem is the result of the quick deadlines of television production. This may have been an *extremely* rushed episode. There are only four days between the writing of the first and final draft scripts. There also appears to have been a last-minute change in casting for the starring role(s) of Lazarus. Some of the publicity photos released on "The Alternative Factor" contain captions crediting actor John Drew Barrymore with this role; his name is penciled out and replaced with that of actor Robert Brown. (Brown appears in the stills.)

The romantic aspects of the plot may also have been changed at the last possible moment. For whatever reason, all references to an attraction between the sane Lazarus and Lieutenant Masters are gone, leaving a void in the story as if this element was plucked when it was too late to replace it with anything else.

Robert Brown (Lazarus and Lazarus) is a dynamic performer. He appeared together with William Shatner in the charming western pilot film *Colossus,* but Brown is best known for his starring role as Jason Bolt in "Here Come the Brides," an extremely enjoyable television series that also featured other "Star Trek" cast members (including regular roles for actors Mark Lenard and David Soul).

The transitional footage of Lazarus entering the dimensional corridor was produced by double-exposing a rapidly spinning astronomical photograph over color negative footage of the performer(s) in the corridor. The corridor itself was a small, bare room with orange and purple walls and a smoke-covered floor that hid a mattress to protect the fighting stuntmen.

If the name "Lieutenant Masters" sounds familiar, you are probably thinking of Lieutenant Rip Masters, who was featured in the vintage TV series "Rin Tin Tin."

In "The Alternative Factor" we see the area in which the dilithium crystals are recharged and tied in to the *Enterprise* engines. This procedure (and the set itself) changes throughout the series. The crystals also change. In "Mudd's Women" they appear to be rounded, quartzlike crystals. Here they are flat shapes that resemble thick sheets of mica.

TOMORROW IS YESTERDAY

Episode #21
Final draft script   11/21/66
Revised final draft   11/22/66
Filmed in late November 1966

WRITER   D. C. Fontana
DIRECTOR   Michael O'Herlihy
COMPOSER   Alexander Courage
PHOTOGRAPHIC EFFECTS   Westheimer Company

After an encounter with the gravitational forces of a "black star," the *Enterprise* is hurled backward in time to the twentieth century. Flying over Nebraska, the starship is sighted and classified as a UFO. Air Force pilot Captain John Christopher (serial number 4857932) photographs the *Enterprise* with his jet's wing cameras. When his jet is accidentally destroyed by the starship's tractor beam, he is transported aboard. This leaves Kirk and company with three large problems: (1) retrieving the film, (2) getting the pilot back where he belongs, and (3) returning to their own time without changing history. After the film is obtained, Scotty duplicates the "slingshot effect" that was responsible for their time-accident, and the *Enterprise* returns home. (The *Enterprise*'s return trip provided the springboard for other time-travel excursions such as "Assignment Earth.")

"Tomorrow Is Yesterday" is one of the most popular "Star Trek" episodes. The high opinion that most fans have for this adventure is easily understandable; it is the answer to a Trekker's daydreams. Most fanzine tales concern someone, usually a character based upon the stories' writers, who becomes involved with the U.S.S. *Enterprise* and "beams up" to share an adventure with Kirk and company. We would all like to visit that ship, but here we have the next best thing; we follow someone else from our own era as he beams aboard and discovers what life on a starship is all about.

Of course, there are complications. Captain Christopher did not ask for his visit. He wants to go home, but the question is; would sending him back after his seeing the starship make it possible for someone to transform his experience into a time paradox? "Star Trek" would later establish that time "is like a river," with the course of chronal events easily altered. The possibilities here are so fascinating that Mr. Spock commits an error because of them. Deciding that it would not alter history if Captain Christopher never returned to Earth in our era, the Vulcan then finds that Captain Sean Jeffrey Christopher (their guest's as-yet-unborn son) led (will lead?) an important expedition into space.

Christopher is certainly an extraordinary man. He weathers his first visit to a UFO (complete with strangely clad aliens who speak our language, who employ beautiful women as crew personnel, and who do not believe in little green men) and even survives his first close encounter of the Vulcan kind. The single aspect of the *Enterprise* that seems to impress him most is his first view of Lieutenant Uhura, which is perhaps the most eloquent testimony to his mental (and physical) health.

D. C. Fontana's script ties in neatly with contemporary mythology. Spock almost expresses humor at the *Enterprise*'s being dismissed as a mirage or as a mass of swamp gas.

Spock also takes definite delight in psyching out the poor Air Force security man who is beamed aboard. In another swipe at this same hapless visitor, the sergeant (Hal Lynch) is astounded to receive a plate of chicken soup from the exotically attired and accented transporter chief Kyle (John Winston).

Lieutenant Sulu finally gets to visit Earth in a relatively barbaric time period. George Takei's delighted expression while touring the Omaha installation resembles that of a child discovering a closet full of new toys.

Captured by the security people, Kirk knows that his predicament is "no laughing matter," but it is evident that he, too, regards this as a unique adventure. What wouldn't the Impossible Missions Force give for that little device that Kirk uses to open the doors at the base!

The "beaming down" of Christopher and the Air Force sergeant into their own bodies is an interesting and eerie sight. But it does make one wonder. If the *Enterprise* is traveling through time when the beamings take place, the people who leave the ship are *also* traveling through time, and are therefore insubstantial. How can the transporter function through the time barrier? And if the peoples' bodies are *already* on Earth, what is *really* being beamed down; their souls? In sending the people back "before" they ever left, the *Enterprise* is also changing their history. The travelers *did* visit the ship, but then again they *didn't*.

Captain Christopher tells Kirk that he has always wanted to become a space traveler, but flunked out of the astronaut training program. "Take a good look around," consoles Kirk. "You made it out here ahead of all of them."

Actor Roger Perry (Captain Christopher) co-starred with Pat O'Brien in "Harrigan and Son" (1960–61); a comedy/drama about a father-and-son team of lawyers. He appeared in a 1960 unsold TV series pilot called "You're Only Young Once," and starred in a segment of "The Invaders" ("The Prophet").

One would think that after 200+ years, science would have produced smaller and more powerful flashlights; not so with the one Kirk uses in this episode. Perhaps a conventional flash was used for the same reason we see contemporary saltshakers in "The Man Trap."

The only disappointing feature of this episode is an *Enterprise* flyby in which the starship is terribly matted against a globe of Earth. Parts of the ship seem to "wink out" because of technical problems (or maybe it was the stresses of time travel).

THE RETURN OF THE ARCHONS

Episode #22
First draft script   11/1/66
Final draft script   11/10/66
Filmed in early and middle December 1966

WRITER   Boris Sobelman (Story by Gene Roddenberry)
DIRECTOR   Joseph Pevney
COMPOSER   Alexander Courage
PHOTOGRAPHIC EFFECTS   Film Effects of Hollywood

The U.S.S. *Enterprise* visits planet Beta III in star system 6-11 to learn the fate of the U.S.S. *Archon,* a Federation ship that had visited the planet a century before. After beaming down to explore the planet, Mr. Sulu is hit by a rayblast and, when beamed back aboard the *Enterprise,* is found to be under the influence of a strong controlling force. Kirk, McCoy, Spock, and others beam down and see the planet's orderly populace suddenly begin an orgy that lasts for exactly one hour. They meet Reger, whose daughter Tula was a participant in "The Red Hour" orgy, and learn that monklike Lawgivers roam the planet serving the ruling mystical figure Landru. Outsiders are "absorbed" and transformed into a part "of the body." Reger and Marplon, two members of the anti-Landru underground, prevent Kirk and Spock from being absorbed. After coping with McCoy, who has been transformed, Kirk learns that Landru is a computer programmed by a scientist thousands of years ago. Kirk destroys the computer, freeing the people of Beta III to rule themselves. (This is the first "Trek" episode to spotlight Kirk's talents as a computer destroyer.)

The first draft of this script featured a very human subplot to offset the nonhuman behavior of Landru and the Lawgivers. Sociologist *Luster* (changed to *Lindstrom* in the final draft) falls in love with Reger's daughter, Tula. Although Lindstrom's protest about Tula's fate in "The Red Hour" was left in, the attraction between the two was edited out.

Captain Kirk's concerns for the rights of the individual over those of the machine may have been partially fostered by his experiences in "Court-Martial," and have fostered some debate as to whether his anti-machine acts ever constitute violations of the Prime Directive. This issue is clouded because Kirk usually induces the machines to destroy *themselves,* as in this episode. The dialogue usually sounds something like "... You have failed to fulfill your prime directive, and you must therefore destroy yourself." It's a good thing the machines never tried to reverse this tactic against Captain Kirk.

"The Return of the Archons" contains some interesting character bits. It has one of the few episode teasers to fade out on Mr. Sulu, and gives actor George Takei a chance to go berserk before the audience (although his transformation here is much quieter than that featured in "The Naked Time").

Mr. Spock is seen for a short time apparently sleeping with his eyes open. Although the Vulcan may have been in deep meditation rather than asleep, Spock's behavior in this episode is decidedly strange, partially because of the motivation to conform to "the body" to avoid the wrath of the Lawgivers. Spock has ample opportunities here to deliver his effective, brow-raising, ironic stares. He also throws a good, old-fashioned punch instead of using his customary Vulcan Nerve Pinch.

Dr. McCoy turns into an unwitting punster here, after he's "absorbed." Soon after his visit to the absorption chamber, McCoy reenters his cell and greets Kirk and Spock with the words: ". . . blessed be the body, and health to all of its parts." What better sentiments for a doctor to express?

One of the episode's most effective moments has Reger explaining that before Landru was in power, things were different. He reverently uncovers a self-contained lighting panel, while the use of heavy shadows and eerie music (lifted from "The Corbomite Maneuver") justify the awe shown to the object.

Two distinguished character actors appear in this episode.

Harry Townes (Reger) goes into convincing fits of fear whenever the plot begins to lag. Townes had an earlier opportunity to learn about fear; he appeared in the classic "Thriller" episode "The Cheaters," in which his character donned a pair of magic spectacles and saw his own corrupt soul reflected back at him.

Torin Thatcher (Marplon) also succeeds in acting terrified, which is unusual considering that he usually portrays strength symbols (as in the motion pictures *The Robe* and *The Black Shield of Falworth*). He has also created his share of screen villains, including the evil magician in *The Seventh Voyage of Sinbad* (Columbia–1958) and his counterpart in *Jack the Giant Killer* (United Artists–1961). One of his first screen portrayals was as a god-figure in *The Man Who Could Work Miracles* (H. G. Wells wrote the screenplay for this 1936 United Artists release).

Jon Lormer (Tamar) also appears in "Star Trek" as the "first survivor" (Dr. Theodore Haskins) in "The Cage," and the old man in "For the World Is Hollow and I Have Touched the Sky."

The phaser blast that vaporizes the wall of the computer room is a well-done combination of double-exposure (Landru's fading image), animated overlays (the ray blasts and heat effect), and a substituted wall (with and without holes).

The episode's first act opens with three different angles of *Enterprise* flybys dissolved into each other; a beautifully edited sequence. Most glimpses of the *Enterprise* are short or only involve one point of view.

Landru's materializations are accompanied by the sound effect that was later used for sensor and tricorder sounds.

The cell in which the *Enterprise*'s people are confined was later redressed and used in "Errand of Mercy" and "Catspaw."

A TASTE OF ARMAGEDDON

Episode #23
First draft script   11/23/66
Final draft script   11/28/66

Revised final draft   12/12/66
Filmed in late December 1966 and early
    January 1967

WRITERS   Robert Hamner, Gene L. Coon
    (Story by Robert Hamner)
DIRECTOR   Joseph Pevney
COMPOSER   Alexander Courage
PHOTOGRAPHIC EFFECTS   Film Effects of Hollywood

The *Enterprise* journeys to planet Eminiar Seven to establish diplomatic contact. Although the Eminians warn Kirk against visiting, he beams down and council head Anan 7 shows him his world's computer control center. Eminiar, Kirk is told, has been at war for centuries with its neighboring world, Vendikar. Suddenly, Kirk is informed that the *Enterprise* has been declared a "target," and all aboard her are considered dead. Through Anan and a young woman named Mea, Kirk learns that the "war" is fought with computers; "casualties" on both planets willingly enter antimatter chambers and die to prevent all-out destruction. Federation Ambassador Fox beams down and learns of the situation. Kirk, Spock, Fox, and other crew members ultimately destroy Eminiar's computers. Contact is initiated with Vendikar's council. To escape the horrors of material destruction the two worlds, with the aid of Ambassador Fox, begin to talk peace.

Steven W. Carabatsos (Trek's script consultant at the time) and Robert Hamner are credited with writing the first draft script. The *Enterprise,* damaged and in need of repair materials found on Eminiar *17,* was denied permission to orbit and make repairs. Kirk beamed down anyway, and learned that Eminiar had been at war with the planet Verikan III for over 1,000 years. The principles of the "war" were explained to Kirk by Mea as she was declared a casualty. Mea and Sar were to be married; Kirk attempted to convince them that life was preferable to death. Spock beamed down and, in the computer room, overheard a distress call from Kirk. Using his Vulcan strength, Spock swatted guards aside like flies to get to Kirk. He then destroyed the antimatter chamber (with a rewired tricorder-bomb) and fled with Kirk and Mea. Learning that a planetary defense mechanism was absorbing the *Enterprise*'s power, Kirk surrendered. When the chance presented itself, Kirk risked radiation burns and destroyed the computer. At the end of the first draft, no mention was made of the *Enterprise*'s leaving diplomats behind to help with the negotiations.

This episode is the perfect follow-up to "The Return of the Archons." Whereas a machine had rendered the followers of Landru emotionless and without progress, the people of Eminiar VII, in the final draft of this segment, have rendered themselves into mechanical monsters killing their own kind with the aid of computers.

Ambassador Robert Fox is one of the most irritating examples of Federation stubbornness (along with Galactic High Commissioner Ferris of "The Galileo Seven") ever to grace the *Enterprise*. After being exposed to the Eminiar government's policies, though, even Fox can stand things no longer. It is rewarding indeed to see Fox finally take up a sonic disruptor and follow Kirk on his rounds of computer demolition.

David Opatoshu (Anan Seven) is best remembered for his roles in such movies as *Silk Stockings, The Naked City,* and *Exodus.* He has appeared in many science fiction and fantasy tales on television, including roles in "Voyage to the Bottom of the Sea" ("The Price of Doom"), "The Man from U.N.C.L.E." ("The Alexander the Greater Affair"), "The Time Tunnel" ("Reign of Terror"), "One Step Beyond ("Ordeal on Locust Street"), "Twilight Zone" ("Valley of the Shadow"), and "The Outer Limits" ("Feasibility Study").

Barbara Babcock (Mea) also appears in "Plato's Stepchildren." Her vocal talents are heard in "The Squire of Gothos" and "Assignment Earth." She also co-stars in "The Night Gallery" segment "Brenda."

Gene Lyons (Ambassador Fox) appeared semiregularly as Raymond Burr's superior on "Ironside." He is also featured in "The Invaders" ("The Enemy") and "Twilight Zone" ("King Nine Will Not Return").

"Star Trek" familiars appear here, too. Sean Kenney is Lieutenant DePaul and David L. Ross is Galloway. Although Eddie Paskey does not appear here as "Mr. Leslie," he does play one of the citizens of Eminiar Seven.

The Eminiar beam-down is greatly enriched by the beautiful optical painting of an alien city. The style of this illustration is similar to the rendering of the starbase in "The Menagerie." In fact, the same wall built for the set in "The Menagerie" (in front of which the actors stand) is also included in this matte with the same circle (also featured as the council platform in "Mirror, Mirror"), and a different piece of sculpture. The Eminiar painting was probably wider than usual for matte illustrations; at one point we see the city from an angle beyond the matted-in wall.

The Eminiar corridors contain doorways that were originally constructed for "What Are Little Girls Made Of?" Eminian furnishings include ultramodern office furniture, stock furniture, and especially made futuristic chairs. The small monitors from the *Enterprise* bridge in the pilot episodes show up in the council room here (they're also in Mendez' office in "The Menagerie"). The computer banks from "Menagerie" are also here.

The sonic disruptor pistols were used as the basis for the Klingon sidearms; the front sections were removed and reworked.

The Eminiar costumes resemble those featured in "What Are Little Girls Made Of?" Also present in Anan's wardrobe are the ever-present black turtleneck shirts that are in evidence throughout "Star Trek's" galaxy.

SPACE SEED

Episode #24
First draft script   12/7/66
Final draft script   12/8/66
Revised final draft   12/12/66
Second Revised final draft   12/13/66
Filmed in middle and late December 1966

WRITERS   Gene L. Coon, Carey Wilbur (Story by Carey Wilbur)
DIRECTOR   Marc Daniels
COMPOSER   Alexander Courage
PHOTOGRAPHIC EFFECTS   Westheimer Company (Composites)
Film Effects of Hollywood (Miniatures photography)

The beautiful painting created to represent a city on planet Eminiar VII in "A Taste of Armageddon."

The *Enterprise* pulls alongside a "Sleeper Ship" from the late twentieth century. The surviving crew members are revived. The leader, a magnetic individual named Khan, needs additional attention in sick bay. Historian Marla McGivers has fallen for Khan. "Khan," meanwhile, is identified as Eugenics War figure Khan Noonian Singh, who is rated the most dangerous and dynamic of the 1990s artificially bred men. With Marla's aid Khan cuts off the air to the bridge, takes the ship, and almost kills Kirk. Marla rescues Kirk who unleashes anesthetic gas throughout the occupied sections of the ship and recaptures the *Enterprise*. After defeating the villain, Kirk gives Khan and his people, including Marla, the choice of facing court-martial or colonizing a virgin, hostile planet. Khan chooses to be a colonist, and Marla elects to go with him. Spock wonders what will come from these "seeds" the *Enterprise* has planted.

Carey Wilbur began his story outline for "Space Seed" by explaining how a man from Renaissance times would be out of place in today's world. The same was true, he theorized, for a man of this century transported into "Star Trek's" era. Drawing a parallel with the eighteenth-century British custom of deporting undesirables, Wilbur postulated "Seed Ships" that would take unwanted criminals from overpopulated Earth into outer space. The Botany Bay was said to have left Earth in 2096 and traveled for 500 years before being discovered by the *Enterprise*. On board the ship were 100 criminals (males and females), and a volunteer crew of a few men.

The outline's "Khan" was Harold Ericcson, a man reminiscent of the ancient Vikings. His first act was to assault Captain Kirk; he was then subdued and deposited in the *Enterprise* brig with the other survivors. The *Enterprise* people at first knew nothing about the Botany Bay, and Ericcson committed a murder to prevent them from learning the truth. Ericcson captured the *Enterprise,* intending to become a pirate using the starship. When Marla was in danger of being shot during a phaser fight, Ericcson surrendered and accepted his fate.

In the final draft, Khan is not a criminal but a fanatic. He is a challenge for Kirk and company not because of their ignorance of the criminal mentality but because of his genetic strength.

The character of Khan is one of the most magnetic ever to appear in a segment of Trek. In a startling show of chauvinism, Khan takes distinct advantage of historian Marla McGivers' attraction to him. She has been studying brawny historical types for her entire professional life. Now that she meets one in the flesh, she cannot quite cope with him. He talks her into forgetting her training, her loyalties; everything she has ever worked to achieve. He makes her an outcast and forces her to crawl to him on her hands and knees.

Khan is simply looking for someone who can aid him in taking the *Enterprise*. He would have to be an idiot not to see Marla's infatuation with him, and he encourages her feelings toward him. He does this not to create a love affair with himself as the dominant factor but to win her as a follower to his cause. Actually, Khan's choice for a follower works against him; Marla turns the tide of the entire affair.

Khan's final observation of Marla is anything but sexist. He admits there is more to her than he suspected, he states he considers her a match for him, and the two go off to face their next exile together.

Ricardo Montalban (Khan) has appeared in feature films and TV shows for over three decades. On television, he is best known as Mr. Roarke, the mysterious manager of "Fantasy Island." Montalban has appeared in two episodes of "The Man from U.N.C.L.E."; "The Dove Affair," and "The King of Diamonds Affair" (with Nancy Kovack). In the TV remake of *The Mark of Zorro,* which starred Frank Langella, Montalban portrayed Estabon Rodriguez, the enemy of El Zorro (and the same role played by Basil Rathbone in the 1940 movie version).

Madlyn Rhue (Marla McGivers) has appeared in countless episodes of Warner Brothers' TV series (including "77 Sunset Strip"), and in vintage Fox teleseries such as "Adventures in Paradise" and "Peyton Place." She co-starred in "Man from U.N.C.L.E." escapades "The Terbuf Affair" and "The Fiery Angel Affair."

Writer Carey Wilbur worked extensively on some of the earliest and most enjoyable episodes of "Lost in Space," writing the teleplays for "There Were Giants in the Earth," "The Sky Pirate," "His Majesty Smith," "A Visit to Hades," "The Questing Beast," "Treasure of the Lost Planet," and "The Astral Traveler."

Coincidentally, Blaisdell Makee (Mr. Spinelli) also appears in "The Changeling," portraying "Mr. Singh."

"Space Seed" is one of a handful of "Star Trek" episodes that includes the expensive luxury of a miniature spacecraft created especially for the occasion. Linwood Dunn, president of Film Effects of Hollywood, supervised the photography involving the miniature sleeper ship. At first glance, the sleeper appears to be a customized submarine model with an added central core and antennae. The miniature was supported from beneath, mounted on a shaft extending to a wheeled base. The shaft and base were painted blue to match the blue screen in front of which the models were photographed.

The "Botany Bay" model also appears as the freighter destroyed by "The Ultimate Computer." The pressure chamber in this episode became part of McCoy's medical lab. One of the sleeper units' door frames was salvaged from "Space Seed" and incorporated into the set for McCoy's research lab, where it became an overhead unit of unspecified function.

As Kirk bends over the sleeper unit containing

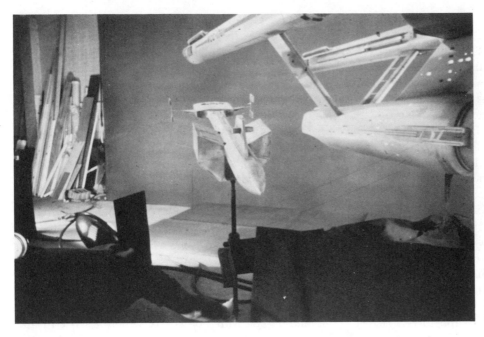

A technician adjusts the miniature Sleeper Ship beside the large *Enterprise* model for a sequence in "Space Seed."

Khan, you can see his phaser slip off his Velcro belt and fall to the ground. You can also see DeForest Kelley's eyes glance back and forth between Khan and the floor, apparently wondering whether the "take" was going to be used.

THIS SIDE OF PARADISE

Episode #25
Story outline   8/9/66
First draft script   10/11/66
Final draft script   12/15/66
Original title   "The Way of the Spores"
Filmed in early January 1967

WRITER   D. C. Fontana (Story by Nathan Butler, D. C. Fontana)
(Nathan Butler—pseudonym of Jerry Sohl)
DIRECTOR   Ralph Senensky
COMPOSER   Alexander Courage
PHOTOGRAPHIC EFFECTS   Westheimer Company

The *Enterprise* arrives at planet Omicron Ceti III and expects to find all the colonists there dead, because of a deadly concentration of Berthold rays to which they have been exposed for three years. When Kirk, Spock, McCoy, Sulu, and others beam down, the colony leader, Elias Sandoval, appears and informs them that everyone on the planet is well. Spock is reunited with Leila Kalomi, a young botanist with whom he had worked six years before. She leads him to a clump of plants that spray Spock with their spores.

The Vulcan's emotions are liberated by the spores; he is now free to express his love for Leila. The Terrans exposed to the spores become placid. Plants are beamed up to the *Enterprise* and before long everyone except Kirk is affected. Kirk, fighting the effects of the spores, discovers that violent emotional reactions are the antidote. He tricks Spock aboard, goads him into a fight, and barely avoids being killed. Spock and Kirk construct an apparatus that restores the *Enterprise* crew and the colonists to normal. Mr. Spock says farewell to Leila.

The story outline and first draft script for "This Side of Paradise" were titled "The Way of the Spores," and were extremely different from the final episode. In these early drafts Mr. Sulu was the central figure in love with the Eurasian beauty Leila. McCoy discovered an internal condition that would have necessitated Sulu's resignation from Starfleet service, had the spores not cured the condition. This illness gave Sulu the will to develop a relationship with Leila (just as similar circumstances would later affect McCoy's judgment in "For the World Is Hollow"). The spores here were a communal intelligence; when someone was possessed by them, that individual was granted telepathic abilities to link up with other possessed minds. The abilities of the spores to restore health were complete enough to enable them to return dead crew members to life. The antidotes for the spores were either the possession of a certain blood type or the introduction of alcohol into the affected person. Kirk literally leaped upon Spock and forced liquor down his throat to restore him to normal. In a surprise ending, the spores were revealed to be benevolent, conscious entities who never intended to act against anybody's will.

An emotional Mr. Spock greets his friend, Jim Kirk, in "This Side of Paradise" (Leonard Nimoy).

It is unfortunate that Mr. Sulu never enjoyed his "starring" status in the final version of this adventure, but it is not difficult to guess why Spock became the central figure instead. Fans of Mr. Spock probably wanted to see him show his emotions ever since Harry Mudd insulted him in "Mudd's Women," as he "joked" with Yeoman Rand at the close of "The Enemy Within," and after his bout with temporary insanity in "The Naked Time."

Leila Kalomi has known Spock before, and has had the misfortune to fall in love with him. It is possible that Mr. Spock had taken her aside while on Earth and explained to her why nothing could come of her attraction for him. It is not likely, however, that he admitted feeling any attraction toward her. Under the influence of the spores, Spock looks at Leila and admits "I can *love* you." The audience feels Spock's happiness because the Vulcan is the embodiment of our fear of being alienated from the rest of humanity.

In the middle of all this liberated emotion, Kirk is being deprived of his *Enterprise* by the spores. Kirk proves to be immune to the spores because they can provide only images of love and peace. Kirk's love is the *Enterprise;* he has no peace except after he sees his ship and crew through crises.

Spock is released from the spores' influence partially by guilt. The Vulcan's strength is first demonstrated in "The Naked Time," when he recovers his logical wits after striking Kirk once and sending the captain

hurtling over the briefing room table. In this episode he comes close to bashing in his captain's head. The shock frees him from the spores and imprisons him once again within himself.

The final scenes between Spock and Leila are very effective, thanks not only to the dialogue and direction but also to the rapport between performers Leonard Nimoy and Jill Ireland and the music of Alexander Courage.

Jill Ireland (Leila Kalomi) appeared in four episodes of "The Man from U.N.C.L.E." She is also in segments of "Night Gallery" ("A Feast of Blood" and "The Ghost of Sorworth Place"), and "Voyage to the Bottom of the Sea" ("The Price of Doom," with David Opatoshu and Steve Ihnat). Ms. Ireland also had a recurring role in the short-lived TV series "Shane" (as Marian Starett, from 1966–67).

Frank Overton (Elias Sandoval) treated his role with just the right amounts of subtlety and intensity, in a similar manner as he handled his role in "Walking Distance," one of the best episodes of "The Twilight Zone." He appeared on "Dick Powell Theatre's" episode "Colossus" with William Shatner in 1963, and can be seen in episodes of "One Step Beyond" ("The Justice Tree"), "Thriller" ("Child's Play"), "The Invaders" ("Genesis"), and "Twilight Zone" ("Mute"). He also appeared regularly as Major Harvey Stovall in Twelve O'Clock High (1964–67).

"This Side of Paradise" marks one of the few occasions in which DeForest Kelley functions as Southern Gentleman McCoy, sipping mint juleps, letting his full accent show, and treating the audience to his endearingly effective smile.

This is also one of the few time Eddie Paskey (Mr. Leslie) has a chance to deliver dialogue. Paskey is visible in almost every "Star Trek" episode, as Mr. Leslie or as a background character. He is one of those individuals whose recurring appearances help make us believe the *Enterprise* is a spaceship with a constant crew.

Director Ralph Senensky's work helped create many "Star Trek" episodes, as well as segments of "The Twilight Zone" ("Printer's Devil"), "Search" ("Ends of the Earth") and such popular series as "The Fugitive," "I Spy," "Mission: Impossible," and "The Wild, Wild West."

Excellent use is made of Alexander Courage's music from "The Cage" when Spock is transformed by the spores.

As the crew stands waiting to be beamed down, notice that one man is in such a hurry to leave the ship that he hasn't bothered to change from his engineering work clothes. Spock beams down in his *Enterprise* uniform, but by midway into the story he changes into a colony uniform. When and where he changes remains a mystery (except possibly to Leila Kalomi). The suit into which he changes is the same costume he wears in "Spock's Brain."

THE DEVIL IN THE DARK

Episode #26
First draft script   12/19/66
Final draft script   12/22/66
Filmed in middle and late January 1967

WRITER   Gene L. Coon
DIRECTOR   Joseph Pevney
COMPOSER   Alexander Courage
PHOTOGRAPHIC EFFECTS   Film Effects of Hollywood

The pergium miners on planet Janus VI are being hunted down and killed by an unknown creature that can secrete powerful acids and burrow through stone. Chief mining engineer Vanderberg summons the *Enterprise* to assist in locating and killing the "monster." When the creature steals a vital part of the PXK reactor, which regulates the mining colony's life support functions, Spock realizes that they are dealing with an intelligent creature. After Kirk wounds the Horta, Spock persuades Kirk to try to communicate with the creature before destroying it. Via a Vulcan Mind Meld, Spock discovers that the creature is killing only to prevent the destruction of its thousands of silicon eggs. McCoy heals the wounded Horta. When the miners learn that their "monster" is only a defensive mother, and that they have unwittingly killed many more of her children than she has of them, Vanderberg and his people form a symbiotic relationship with the Horta. The freshly hatched children dig the pergium while the miners become rich.

The last episode produced for "The Outer Limits" is called "The Probe." It concerns a gigantic alien space probe that lands on Earth and traps a small group of people. The script called for an overgrown microorganism to function as "the monster of the week," so makeup/costume expert Janos Prohaska devised a framework of metal, fabric, and rubber under which he could crawl around. He added projections of rubber to hide his limbs and head, and produced a mansized amoeba creature.

One day in 1966, Prohaska brought his creation to Desilu Studios, put it on, and crawled into the office of "Star Trek" producer-writer Gene L. Coon. Coon was impressed and decided to write an episide based upon the "creature." After some changes had been made in the concept (and the costume), the result was "The Devil in the Dark." Although the script progressed from first draft to final in three days, "The Devil in the Dark" is one of the most intriguing, tolerant, and best episodes of Trek.

"Star Trek" repeatedly explores the problem of prejudice and how mankind will deal with it in the future. "Xenophobia" (fear of different types of life forms), Trek tells us, will be a thing of the past in the *Enterprise*'s era; at least applying to entities with recognizable heads, limbs, and technologies. But suppose a definitely hostile and dangerous creature is discovered. If its chemical structure and physical shape are sufficiently different from ours, would anyone (Captain Kirk included) care whether the entity's actions are rational? Or would it be treated as a "monster," hunted down and destroyed without any attempt to communicate with it?

During the course of the story the creature kills, but it also shows that it possesses intelligence, and yet no one bothers to question its motivations. No one investigates, that is, except Mr. Spock, who has a hatred of violence and an expert's idea of how it feels to be different and unaccepted.

While the miners form a "posse" to hunt the Horta down, Spock performs a Mind Meld. Interpersed with glimpses of the hunters, Spock's mind link with the creature becomes a sensitive and emotional experience. The miners, if they traded their phasers for torches, could just as well be hunting the Frankenstein monster. Kirk and Spock look to the future while the others evoke the violence of the past.

Although Leonard Nimoy's performance during the Mind Meld sequence is noteworthy, William Shatner's performance during the last half of this episode is the most amazing piece of acting seen in all of "Star Trek." While the scenes involving the hunt for the Horta were being shot, Shatner received a phone call informing him that his father had just passed away. Despite suggestions that production be halted, Shatner insisted upon finishing his scenes for the day. His decision was probably based upon several factors: the need to emote under these terrible circumstances, the urge to be with friends while he coped with his grief, and the realization that no matter how he felt the production deadline was still the same. William Shatner's performance under these circumstances indicates that Shatner the actor is as dedicated and dynamic an individual as Kirk the captain.

In the procession of security men we see two familiar faces. In addition to the ever-present Eddie Paskey, there is the red-shirted Lieutenant Commander Giotto (actor Barry Russo). Russo later returned to portray Commodore Robert Welsey in "The Ultimate Computer."

Ken Lynch (Venderberg) was regularly seen as a police lieutenant in the TV series "The Plainclothesman" (1950–54). He appeared in several episodes of the imaginative "Men into Space" TV series (as the Air Force boss of astronaut Colonel Edward MacCauley) and can also be seen in "Twilight Zone's" "Mr. Denton on Doomsday."

Janos Prohaska reworked his "probe creature" into the Horta by omitting "limbs" in favor of a rounded shape. The exterior was composed of rubber colored different shades of brown and red. Within this shell

While engaged in a Vulcan Mind Meld with the wounded Horta, Spock shares the creature's pain in "The Devil in the Dark" (Leonard Nimoy).

ERRAND OF MERCY

Episode #27
First draft script   1/3/67
Final draft script   1/6/67
Revised final draft   1/23/67
Filmed in late January 1967

WRITER   Gene L. Coon
DIRECTOR   John Newland
COMPOSER   Alexander Courage

As hostilities between the United Federation of Planets and the Klingon Empire reach their peak, the *Enterprise* is dispatched to the strategically located planet Organia. The Organian council, a trio of smiling, elderly men, seem strangely unconcerned about the prospect of war centering about their planet. Klingon Commander Kor, with an occupation force, invades Organia. Kirk and Spock go undercover, disguised as two traders, but are recognized by Kor, and condemned to death. The Organians rescue them very easily. As the moment of all-out war approaches, the Organians reveal themselves as omnipotent creatures of pure energy. Using their mental abilities, they neutralize all weapons. Kirk realizes with horror that a part of him had been anticipating the hostilities; he is also relieved to know that from now on the Organians will be watching to see that things do not get out of hand.

"Errand of Mercy" introduces two important extremes of the "Star Trek" universe; the Organians and the Klingons. In creating each group to oppose the other, writer Gene L. Coon fulfilled the need for continuing villains in "Trek," and provided a control to keep the good guys and villains from each other's throats.

There's an old saying that "absolute power corrupts absolutely." This is apparently true only on a human level (as both Gary Mitchell and Charlie Evans could testify). The Organians, being more than human, elect to use their power to stop humans from corrupting the galaxy with war.

These mysterious beings also find humans "most distasteful" to be around. Having long ago evolved beyond their need for physical bodies and their related limiting qualities, the Organians do not like to be reminded of what they once were. Perhaps they also miss the pleasures they gave up along with their bodies. It is interesting that when the Organians restore themselves to their former appearances, most of the males elect to become middle-aged men, whereas the females materialize mainly as young women (in the scene in which Kirk and Spock first beam down near the main gate).

was a system of straps that kept the "suit" on straight, and a rolling platform not unlike a skateboard. A small patch of white and red area was fitted with a rubber bladder so that it could pulsate.

Prohaska also appeared in his "Mugato" suit in "A Private Little War." He was famous as the "dancing bear" on "The Andy Williams Show," and appeared in the "Lost in Space" episode "The Forbidden World." Prohaska's son was in training with his father, and appeared as the creature in "Pickman's Model" on "Night Gallery." Father and son devised the mask and costume effects for "The Primal Man," a TV miniseries on human evolution. The entire production crew flew out to a desert location and there was a plane crash. Among those killed were Janos Prohaska and his son.

There are at least two different versions of the optical painting that was created to represent the underground mining complex. The most effective is seen outside Vanderberg's office window. Despite the use of rocks and pipes to add depth to the paintings, these are the least convincing optical art to appear on "Trek." One of the paintings reappeared as the background of the Providers' complex in "Gamesters of Triskelion."

Most of the modernistic furniture in Vanderberg's office also appears in "The Menagerie."

The "caves" of Janus VI share a fault common to virtually all man-made movie caverns; despite many hanging rock formations and occasional boulders their floors are completely smooth.

One of Dr. McCoy's best lines appears in this episode: "I'm a doctor, not a bricklayer."

Take every prejudice man has ever had against his fellow man. Combine these with generous helpings of grease and grime, aggressive instincts, and general bestiality. Add completely negative emotions, a tight tribal culture, and the perpetual opinion that the entire universe stinks except for their little corner . . . and you have the Klingons. Every Klingon should be born with an implanted plaque that states, "With friends like me, you don't need enemies." There is not much that one can say in praise of a civilization with inspirational gems like, "Ten thousand throats can be slit in one night by a running man."

In the midst of these two opposing life forms, the presence of Captain Kirk and Mr. Spock is almost a trifle funny. Our people are there to serve as pawns. They are watched and secretly despised by the Organians. They are hounded by the Klingons. Throughout it all, Kirk and Spock manage to retain their best "Why me?" expressions. Kirk's courageous "commando raid" against the Klingon ammunition dump is an unnecessary act; the Organians are the real masters of the situation.

Coon's teleplay brings out the frightening power and black humor present in these circumstances. Kirk and Kor, and with them the entire Federation and Klingon Empire, are reduced to the demeaning rank of "children" being told to "Pay attention, kiddies, or we'll smack you where it hurts."

A large part of "Errand of Mercy's" underlying horror factor is brought out by the talented director John Newland, who is no stranger to the macabre things in life (and death). He created the TV series "ALCOA Presents," which is better known by its syndication title "One Step Beyond." His combined roles of creator/host/director in this series were as all-encompassing as Gene Roddenberry's roles in "Star Trek" and Rod Serling's contributions to "The Twilight Zone." Newland even appeared in an episode of "One Step Beyond," "The Sacred Mushroom." "One Step Beyond" is still one of the most horrifying series on TV, partially because of Newland's "gimmick" of basing his adventures upon documented supernatural experiences. In "Thriller," Newland starred in and directed the ghost story, "The Return of Andrew Bentley" (which also starred Reggie Nalder). Newland's underplaying techniques both as actor and director were also exercised in his new syndicated TV series "The Next Step Beyond."

John Abbott (Ayelborne) obtained his initial dramatic training at the Old Vic Theatre and has played a long succession of diversified character roles for years, dating back to *The Saint in London* (1939) and *The War in the Air* (1940). Among his feature films are *Deception, Madame Bovary, Anna and the King of Siam,* and *They Got Me Covered* (in which he played reporter Bob Hope's mysterious contact man "Fonescue"). On television he can also be seen in "Great Ghost Tales" ("Mr. Arcularis"); "Lost in Space" ("The Dream Monster"); and "The Man from U.N.C.L.E." ("The Birds & the Bees Affair").

Peter Brocco (2nd Organian) is a noted character actor remembered by fans of "The Adventures of Superman" for his appearances in "The Secret of Superman" (Dr. Ort, a deranged physician who suspected that Lois Lane was the secret identity of Superman), "The Clown Who Cried" (Crackers the crooked clown), and the leader of "The Phantom Ring." His other appearances include "Lost in Space" ("Deadly Games of Gamma Six"), "The Man from U.N.C.L.E." ("The Deadly Smorgasbord Affair"), and "The Twilight Zone" ("Hocus, Pocus & Frisby" and "The Four of Us Are Dying").

The performer who really walks away with this episode is John Colicos (Kor). Calculating his characterization to chill the blood and to provide the direct opposite of William Shatner's Captain Kirk, Colicos' every twisted expression is a scary delight to behold. Colicos is best remembered for his recurring role of Baltar, the villain of Universal's TV series "Battlestar Galactica."

The exterior of the Organian gateway is probably the same set created for the Rigel Fortress of "The Cage." Stock footage of an old Scottish fortress is briefly seen over Kirk and Spock's dialogue. The effectiveness of this shot makes one wonder why additional stock shots were not used in other episodes (especially those photographed completely on interior sets).

There is only one subtle clue to the true nature of the Organians, before the actual revelation. In their primitive culture, with a total absence of scientific instrumentation, the large doors to their council room open and close by themselves throughout the entire episode.

THE CITY ON THE EDGE OF FOREVER

Episode #28
Story Outline   5/13/66
Rewrite draft   1/27/67
Final draft script   2/1/67
Filmed in early February 1967

WRITER   Harlan Ellison
DIRECTOR   Joseph Pevney
COMPOSER   Alexander Courage
PHOTOGRAPHIC EFFECTS   Film Effects of Hollywood

While treating Sulu after an accident on the bridge, Dr. McCoy accidentally injects himself with an overdose of cordrazine, an experimental drug. In a delirious state, he transports down to the planet below to

A character study of Mr. Spock, trapped in "The City on the Edge of Forever" (Leonard Nimoy).

which the *Enterprise* has come to investigate strange "ripples in time." Beaming down with a landing party, Kirk and Spock confront a "living machine" known as the Guardian of Forever. When McCoy leaps through the machine's portal, he vanishes into Earth's past and, because of something he does there to change history, the *Enterprise* ceases to exist. The landing party, stranded, decides to try to undo what McCoy has done. Kirk and Spock leap through the device into the New York City of 1930. There, Kirk meets and falls for Edith Keeler, a forward-thinking social worker. Spock, who manages to use vintage 1930 equipment to construct a tricorder monitor device, discovers that Edith has two possible futures. She can either begin a pacifist movement that will enable Germany to win World War II, or she can die in a traffic accident. Kirk realizes that in order for history to restore itself and the *Enterprise,* Edith must die. He commits the most difficult act of his life when he prevents McCoy from saving Edith Keeler. Returning through space and time, Kirk leaves the Guardian's planet immediately before any other tragedies can occur. (The revised script, adapted for the series by Gene Roddenberry, won the 1968 International Hugo Award, for Science Fiction.

Harlan Ellison's original story outline and first draft script for this episode are almost completely different from the finished production. Ellison's script won the Writers' Guild of America Award (for the most outstanding dramatic episodic teleplay for 1967–68). The episode is structured around Edith Keeler and associated time displacements, and is filled with purposeful sensitivity. His complete first draft script, plus an introduction by Ellison, is available in the Pocket Books paperback *Six Science Fiction Plays,* published in New York in 1976.

The differences between Ellison's original script and the finished episode have been the subject of many debates and conversations in "Star Trek" fandom. The attention lavished on this episode centers on the fact that "The City on the Edge of Forever" is regarded by many Trek fans as the best episode of the series.

Kirk and company become anachronisms several times in Trek episodes including "Tomorrow Is Yesterday" and "Assignment: Earth," but in this segment their problems are infinitely greater than those faced in the other adventures. In "Mirror, Mirror," Kirk's entire universe turns upside down, but it is *Kirk* who is displaced, *not* the rest of the universe. Here, things are different. It is not just a matter of returning home but of restoring history's balance so that there *is* a home to return to. In the event of failure, Starfleet and the United Federation of Planets would cease to exist, while the landing party would be trapped in Earth's past; the past, in its distorted form, would be a nightmare.

In addition to these universal problems, Kirk and Spock must fight against nightmares of their own. Kirk, separated from his *Enterprise,* finds another lady to replace his ship. Like the *Enterprise,* Edith Keeler's graceful exterior contains a decidedly powerful, dynamic interior. It is no wonder that Kirk is drawn to her, but unfortunately the same qualities that provide the attraction are the threat to historical order.

No sacrifice is too great to ensure the safety of his ship in "The City on the Edge of Forever" (William Shatner).

Edith Keeler is an innocent focal point, unaware of the incredible forces at work around her. Kirk must try to comfort himself by realizing that all this has *already happened;* he is powerless to change Edith's fate. He knows that if Edith knew all the facts she would probably jump in front of the truck herself, to save all those who would otherwise have died. This probability does not make things any easier for Kirk. It is hard for him to think about conditional futures knowing that he has taken the initiative to cause the death of the woman he loves. In Ellison's first draft script, Kirk freezes at the crucial moment; it is Spock who prevents a third party from rescuing Edith. This ending, beautifully written by Ellison, would not have worked within "Star Trek's" continuity. Although the audience would have sympathized with Captain Kirk, it would never again have been able to accept him as the prime mover of the series' events. In the final version, Kirk *does* stop McCoy and thus fulfills his command responsibilities. In this moment he both sacrifices his world and regains it.

It is easy to imagine Mr. Spock taking the initiative in this dramatic instant, because the Vulcan has more to lose on a personal basis. Kirk could have married Edith and found happiness of a sort. Spock had no chance of survival (let alone happiness) in that era. He could have communicated with nobody but his captain, and he would have ceased to have thought of Kirk in that role had Kirk failed to act out of loyalty to the universe. Ellison's first draft includes a sequence that reminds us of the prejudices against "aliens" that were rampant in some circles in 1930. Spock could not even have explained his presence on the Earth of that era. He would undoubtedly have been hunted down and killed the instant he first removed his stocking cap.

Instead of accenting the tragedy of Mr. Spock's being reduced to an anonymous "stranger in a strange land," the filmed version of "City" emphasizes the ironic humor of his situation. The Vulcan, with all his technical knowledge, is forced to find employment as a janitor and handyman, while secretly constructing a superscientific" "mnemonic memory circuit" using primitive tools and materials that Spock describes as "stone knives and bearskins."

In one of the most enjoyable comedy sequences in "Star Trek," Kirk and Spock are confronted by a New York City patrolman who is concerned about the duo's criminal behavior. The cop sees nothing but their bundle of stolen clothes, but Kirk does not realize this. With all of "future history" in the balance, this is such a trivial predicament that Spock feels safe in enjoying it all. Kirk immediately puts his foot in his mouth, and the Vulcan helps him jam it in further. Finally, after having enjoyed the spectacle of his captain lying through his teeth while being scared out of his mind, Mr. Spock ends the entire confrontation by putting the bewildered policeman to sleep with the first Vulcan Nerve Pinch ever executed on Earth.

The hapless derelict "Rodent" seems to be a secondary focal point in time who crosses paths with Kirk, Spock, and McCoy before destroying himself with McCoy's phaser.

Joan Collins (Edith Keeler) made her film debut in Britain, in 1952. Coming to the United States she acted in such films as *The Land of the Pharaohs* and *The Girl in the Red Velvet Swing,* in addition to a large number of other feature films for 20th Century-Fox studios. Ms. Collins was the female lead in *Quest for Love,* a romantic science fiction film involving a love affair spanning two parallel universes. She also appeared in two horror films. *Tales from the Crypt* and

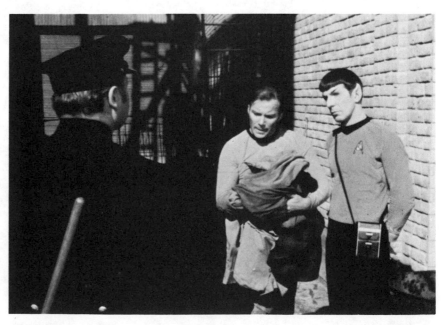

Kirk and Spock attempt to account for themselves to a circa 1930 New York City cop in "The City on the Edge of Forever" (William Shatner, Leonard Nimoy).

The Devil Within Her. On television, she can be seen in episodes of "The Man from U.N.C.L.E.' ("The Galatea Affair"), "Batman" (as "The Siren"), and "Space 1999." On one episode of "Mission: Impossible," she portrayed a young spy with whom Jim Phelps fell in love. When she died in the episode's finale, Phelps' fellow IMF agents helped him to recover. The story was similar to "The City . . ." in some respects.

The voice of the Guardian of Forever may sound familiar. It belongs to actor/announcer Bartell La-Rue, who delivered the "Good morning, Mr. Phelps" prologues of "Mission: Impossible." His voice also appears in the "Star Trek" episodes "The Gamesters of Triskelion," "Patterns of Force," "Bread and Circuses," "Assignment Earth," and "The Savage Curtain."

Hal Baylor (the policeman) also appeared as a huge robot in the film version of Harlan Ellison's story *A Boy and His Dog*.

John Harmon (Rodent) also appears in "A Piece of the Action."

Author Harlan Ellison is one of today's most prolific, honored, and controversial creators of speculative fiction. His credits are too many to be adequately discussed in this book. His television contributions include an adaptation of his study of teenage gangs, "Memo from Purgatory" for "Alfred Hitchcock Presents" (the episode featured actor Walter Koenig), and two of the most popular episodes of "The Outer Limits," "Demon with a Glass Hand" (directed by Byron Haskin) and "The Soldier" (with Michael Ansara).

Alexander Courage's use of "Goodnight, Sweetheart," a romantic song of the period, fits well in conjunction with stock footage of the Brooklyn Bridge to provide effective points of identification to the New York of 1930. Stock footage is also integral in the scenes involving the Guardian of Forever. The historical "playbacks" include scenes from many old motion pictures, probably including some of Cecil B. De-Mille's Paramount spectacles.

The Guardian itself is an effective piece of design and construction. The set, which makes good use of carefully placed and proportioned ruins, evokes the necessary feelings of isolation and alien civilizations. The design reputedly did not please everyone involved in the production; some "Trek" staffers reportedly referred to it as "the big donut." The large prop was equipped with nozzles that released vapor clouds on cue; stock footage could either be double-exposed or matted over the central circle of the device.

Jerry Finnerman's cinematography deserves applause. His photography is usually excellent in "Star Trek"; in this episode it is phenomenal. Highly specialized lighting and focal techniques give "City" an almost mystical visual quality.

At the end of the episode's "teaser," Kirk looks up into the sky on the Guardian's planet, and the camera follows his gaze into an optically achieved transition to a starry background that is very reminiscent of a "Twilight Zone" style fadeout.

The name "Keeler" is significant because Edith is stated as being a "focal point" in time, and the "keel" of a boat is defined as the chief structure extending the length of the vessel; the structure that either holds the ship together or causes its destruction.

OPERATION: ANNIHILATE

Episode # 29
First draft script   1/19/67
Final draft script   1/24/67
Revised final draft   2/3/67
Second Revised final   2/13/67
Original title   "Operation: Destroy"
Filmed in middle February 1967

WRITER   Stephen W. Carabatsos
DIRECTOR   Herschel Daugherty
COMPOSER   Alexander Courage
PHOTOGRAPHIC EFFECTS   Westheimer Company

The planet Deneva, current home of Captain Kirk's brother and his family, is in the path of an interplanetary epidemic of mass insanity. Approaching the planet, the *Enterprise* intercepts a radio message from a Denevan pilot who deliberately steers his ship into the sun in a successful attempt to escape an unknown danger. Beaming down with a landing party, Kirk discovers his brother (George Samuel Kirk) dead, his sister-in-law (Aurelan) dying, and his nephew (Peter Kirk) unconscious. Deneva has been invaded by batlike aliens that intertwine with human nervous systems, manipulating their victims with excruciating pain. McCoy, remembering the Denevan who flew into the sun, begins to theorize about the creatures. Spock, infected by the invaders, volunteers to be McCoy's guinea pig and is temporarily blinded by exposure to intense light. McCoy discovers the light intensity needed to kill the creatures, and a chain of trimagnesite satellites is orbited to free the Denevans from their nightmare.

The first draft script, titled "Operation: Destroy," lacked any reference to Captain Kirk's brother. In that version, Aurelan was in love with Kartan, the young Denevan who flew his ship into the sun to escape the creatures' control. Aurelan and her father, who were not infected, were brought aboard the *Enterprise,* and took part in the research that eventually destroyed the creatures.

The final episode is more meaningful than the first draft script, thanks to a consolidation of story elements and the addition of George Samuel Kirk.

James Kirk's brother is introduced to us in conversation in "What Are Little Girls Made Of?" There, it is established that George (only James Kirk calls him "Sam"), his wife, and three children saw the captain off on his five-year mission. By the time "Operation: Annihilate" takes place, Peter Kirk is the lone child in the family.

Jim Kirk, up until this time, was established as a loner with the exception of his warm personality toward his friends and female acquaintances. We know virtually nothing about Kirk the family man, except that some of his relatives were killed on Tarsus IV years before he signed on the *Enterprise*. Experiencing the loss of his brother with the captain makes us realize that Jim Kirk is as human as the rest of us, despite his carefully developed defense shields.

The demands upon James Kirk in this episode were brought beautifully to life by William Shatner's performance. Kirk knows that if he cannot kill the creatures, he will be forced to destroy the planet Deneva and all its infected inhabitants to stop the spreading of the "plague." Mr. Spock, also infected, is himself in danger. Add to these factors the personal loss of his brother, and Kirk's situation in this episode makes him a prime candidate for a vacation on Elba Two. Shatner's performance here is similar to his delivery in "The Enemy Within," emphasizing the stresses within him. In "The Enemy Within," though, Kirk had to appear as an incomplete individual. During this episode, Kirk's strengths are still apparent, even though he is being torn apart inside with the dual demands of personal grief and the responsibilities of command.

William Shatner's acting motivations in this situation were probably aided by what has got to be the most atypical bit of casting in "Star Trek." Despite the usual terrifying production deadlines, Shatner took time out to appear as the dead body of George Samuel Kirk. Equipped with grayed hair and a moustache, this novel portrayal marks the only time in the series that Shatner appears as anyone other than Captain Kirk (except for portrayals of duplicates of the captain or as James Kirk himself possessed by other entities). This unique role was probably taken by Shatner for professional reasons, rather than as an ironic joke.

In 1962, Shatner starred in "Without Stick or Sword" on "The Naked City" as a young Burmese fisherman. To make sure that he portrayed an individual instead of a racial caricature (as often happens when Caucasian actors portray Orientals), Shatner is reputed to have spent several days at a Burmese consulate, studying Burmese gestures, mannerisms, and speech patterns. If he could go through this detailed research for a TV guest role, he may have portrayed George Samuel Kirk to assure a feeling of genuine identification with an individual he had never met.

"Operation: Annihilate" was also a demanding episode for actor Leonard Nimoy. Mr. Spock began this adventure by functioning normally (a demanding role unto itself), and was then taken over by the creatures. Nimoy, throughout most of the story, portrayed Spock as subtly fighting back intense agonies. The actor's use of short, strangled movements, twitches, and special eye movements skilfully made the audience aware of what Spock was going through. Spock's apologetic and ironic approach to his predicament was created just as ably, along with the Vulcan's atypical wild and undisciplined attempt to take over the *Enterprise*.

Craig Hundley (Peter Kirk) also appears as Tommy Starnes in "And the Children Shall Lead."

Exterior Deneva locations were photographed at the California headquarters of the T.R.W. Corporation. A series of symmetrical buildings, landscapes, and decorative ornamental sculptures, this modernistic complex provided the ideal surroundings for a colony of the future. Motion picture serials (such as Mascot's 1935 *The Phantom Empire)* and TV series (including "Rocky Jones: Space Ranger") have long made use of interesting architectural shapes, a practice that is now being implemented regularly in budget-conscious TV production.

The parasitic aliens were marionettes constructed by Wah Chang. They were suspended from wires and swung back and forth across the set.

A surviving "blooper" features producer Roddenberry standing on a staircase used in this episode, while dubbed voices (from the soundtrack of "Patterns of Force") shout "Hail the fuehrer."

The glowing optical effect that was created to represent the Denevan sun in the episode's teaser is one of the most attractive effects sequences in the series. It appears to have utilized animation supplemented by reflecting bright lights into the *Enterprise* bridge as the ship pulled away from the sun.

Dr. McCoy's experimental chamber is seen in Paramount's 1976 comedy feature, *The Big Bus*. The chair in which Spock sits within this chamber is also seen in "Dagger of the Mind" and "Whom Gods Destroy." It may not have been constructed especially for "Star Trek," as a similar piece of furniture appears in the feature film *Planet of Blood* (American International Pictures–1966).

Second Season Production Credits

WRITERS   Various

DIRECTORS   Various

PRODUCED BY   Gene L. Coon, John Meredyth Lucas

EXECUTIVE PRODUCER   Gene Roddenberry

ASSOCIATE PRODUCER   Robert H. Justman

SCRIPT CONSULTANT   D. C. Fontana

ASSISTANT TO THE PRODUCER   Edward K. Milkis

THEME MUSIC BY   Alexander Courage

MUSIC COMPOSED AND CONDUCTED BY   Various

DIRECTOR OF PHOTOGRAPHY   Jerry Finnerman

ART DIRECTOR   Walter M. Jefferies

FILM EDITORS   Bruce Schoengarth, Donald R. Rode, Fabian Tjordmann, John W. Hanley

UNIT PRODUCTION MANAGER   Gregg Peters

ASSISTANT DIRECTORS   Elliot Schick, Rusty Meek, Phil Rawlins

SET DECORATORS   Joseph J. Stone, John M. Dwyer

COSTUMES CREATED BY   William Ware Theiss

PHOTOGRAPHIC EFFECTS   Various

SOUND EFFECTS EDITOR   Douglas H. Grindstaff

MUSIC EDITOR   Jim Henrickson

RE-RECORDING MIXERS   Elden E. Ruberg, CAS, Gordon L. Day, CKS

PRODUCTION MIXER   Carl W. Daniels

SCRIPT SUPERVISOR   George A. Rutter

CASTING   Joseph D'Agosta

SOUND   Glen Glenn Sound Co.

MAKEUP ARTIST   Fred B. Phillips, SMA

HAIRSTYLES   Pat Westmore

GAFFER   George H. Merhoff

HEAD GRIP   George Rader

PROPERTY MASTER   Irving A. Feinberg

SPECIAL EFFECTS   Jim Rugg

KEY COSTUMER   Ken Harvey

A Desilu (Paramount) Production in association with Norway Corp.

7 Second Season Episodes

CATSPAW

Episode #30
Filmed in early May 1967

WRITER Robert Bloch
DIRECTOR Joseph Pevney
COMPOSER Gerald Fried
PHOTOGRAPHIC EFFECTS Westheimer Company

On planet Pyris VII, Kirk, Spock, and McCoy encounter three witches, a castle, and crewmen Sulu and Scott who have been transformed into "zombies." Aliens Korob and Sylvia are responsible for the "trick or treat" trappings, using black cats, magic wands, and evil spells to terrify the *Enterprise* crewmen. Only Spock is unaffected by the scare tactics. The aliens are on a mission of conquest and have used a transmuter device to assume human form. Sylvia, affected by her new body, tries to ensnare Kirk into becoming her partner and lover. When Korob aids Kirk and company to escape, Sylvia changes into a gigantic black cat and crushes him. Kirk destroys the "magic wand" transmuter device, causing the castle to vanish and Korob and Sylvia to resume their actual, alien shapes. They are, in reality, fragile creatures and they soon die. Sulu and Scotty are restored to normal and "Halloween" is over.

This episode was conceived as "Star Trek's" Halloween segment for 1967, which is why "Catspaw" can be summed up by three words, "trick or treat." Everything in the story is designed by the aliens Korob and Sylvia to chill the blood of the humans who are unfortunately trapped within their custom-made haunted house. Fortunately for the *Enterprise* crew, the aliens underestimate our friends and cannot induce Kirk and company to think in terms of superstition rather than science.

Scaring Mr. Spock is a hopeless task. The Vulcan, who knows a good deal about Earth's history and customs, is completely in the dark about Terran superstitions. Perhaps he chose to ignore the more unscientific facets of his Terran education.

Ironically, the aliens employ shape-changing to enable themselves to survive in an Earth-type environment. This procedure is well known within the Terran world of superstition, where it is referred to as transvection and generally applies to humans who change themselves into animals for evil purposes. Sylvia's transformation into a gigantic black cat is a good example of this phenomenon.

Theo Marcuse (Korob) appeared in "Voyage to the Bottom of the Sea," "The Twilight Zone" ("To Serve Man" and "The Trade-Ins"), "The Time Tunnel" ("Devil's Island"), "The Invaders" ("The Leeches"), and "The Man From U.N.C.L.E." ("The Re-Collector's Affair," "The Minus X Affair," and "The Pieces of Eight Affair").

Antoinette Bower (Sylvia) can be seen in the "Thriller" episodes "Waxworks" and "The Return of Andrew Bentley" (as the co-star of actor-director John Newland).

The eerie music of composer Gerald Fried is reminiscent of his score for "Amok Time," which was written shortly after he wrote the music for this episode. The first glimpse of the aliens' castle, rising out of the fog, is extremely effective thanks to Fried's menacing melodies.

The cat used in this episode may also have been seen in "Assignment: Earth" as Isis the cat. In both episodes, the same device is used to inform the audience of the shape-changing activities involved. A piece of jewelry around the neck of the human counterpart is later seen around the neck of the cat after the transformation has been made.

The "giant cat" illusion is somewhat disappointing because although the miniature corridor looks impressive with the cat walking through it, no attempt is made to insert the live actors into the same shot via mattes or split-screen. In some scenes an offstage shadow, or an exaggerated meow, proves extremely inadequate to convince us that a giant cat is, in fact, stalking our friends. The castle's exterior is also seen in "The Squire of Gothos."

The beautifully fashioned silver *Enterprise* charm is currently stored in the Smithsonian Institution, and will hopefully be put on display there sometime in the near future.

The alien forms of Korob and Sylvia are partially disappointing and partially effective at the same time. They are marionettes composed of blue fluff, pipe cleaners, crab pincers, and whatever other odds and ends could be found economically when the "creatures" were being fashioned. They appear convincingly alien, but they were also operated with thick, black threads that are painfully obvious even after the puppets have stopped moving.

An extremely amusing moment occurs as Captain Kirk is chained to a wall near McCoy and Spock. The captain begins to refer to McCoy as "Bones," until he notices a skeleton also chained to the wall. For the rest of the episode he refers to McCoy as either "Doc" or "McCoy."

METAMORPHOSIS

Episode # 31
First draft script   4/19/67
Filmed in middle May 1967

WRITER   Gene L. Coon
DIRECTOR   Ralph Senensky
COMPOSER   George Duning
PHOTOGRAPHIC EFFECTS   Westheimer Company

The shuttlecraft *Galileo* is transporting the ailing Assistant Federation Commissioner Nancy Hedford back to the *Enterprise,* when it is suddenly drawn off course by a mysterious cloud creature. Depositing the shuttle on planet Gamma Canaris N, the creature vanishes just before Kirk, Spock, McCoy, Scotty, and Commissioner Hedford meet another castaway. The stranger seems honestly happy to see them, but Kirk and company are bothered by the feeling that they know this man. The stranger is revealed as Zephram Cochrane, a famed scientist from Alpha Centauri who discovered Space Warp Drive over 100 years ago. At the age of eighty-seven, Cochrane decided that he wanted to die in outer space, so he boarded a ship and headed away from Alpha Centauri, only to be waylaid by the cloud creature, which Cochrane calls the Companion. Kirk communicates with the Companion with a universal translator and learns that the creature is in love with Cochrane. At first, Cochrane is unable to accept this, especially since he is falling in love with Nancy Hedford. When Nancy's death is imminent, the Companion forsakes its immortal state to unite with the Earthwoman. Cochrane accepts the love of Companion/Nancy and stays on the planet with her.

The first draft script for this episode has one main difference from the final version. Scotty was included in the shuttle crew; the engineer would have enjoyed meeting Zephram Cochran and talking shop with so illustrious a scientist. It was Scotty who got "zapped" by the Companion and, together with Mr. Spock, constructed the device to short-circuit the entity.

"Metamorphosis" is one of the most sensitive episodes of "Star Trek" because of its romantic aspects and the diversified backgrounds of the tale's lovers. The relationship here is actually a complex triangle. Zephram Cochrane is a legendary scientist, a native of the Alpha Centauri region. The Companion is more outwardly alien to us by contemporary standards, although *both* she and Cochrane are not from Earth. Nancy Hedford *is* Terran, but in terms of her lack of familiarity with the concept of love she is perhaps the most alien of the trio.

Nancy has never had time for love, electing instead to devote herself to ending conflicts throughout the universe. She is apparently good at her job, but is also living proof of Dr. Elizabeth Dehner's observation that "women professionals do tend to overcompensate."

At first, Cochrane (who is himself an alien by our standards, hailing from Alpha Centauri) is overcome by prejudice when he discovers how the Companion regards him. In his era, other races had been discovered, most likely including those that bore little resemblance to those of Earth and Alpha Centauri. Cochrane's momentary lapse into a negative attitude of the past is understandable, especially when one considers how quickly he recovers. Part of his momentary attitude against the Companion may really have been anger at himself for never having stopped to consider what the Companion actually thought of him.

Like Gene Coon's "The Devil in the Dark," "Metamorphosis" is an eloquently expressed editorial against mankind's talent of making enemies of creatures who are physically different from humans. It is an application of the Vulcan principle of IDIC: Infinite Diversity in Infinite Combinations. In both adventures, Mr. Spock probably identifies the closest with the central figures of attention, because he owes his own existence to this same principle.

Glenn Corbett (Zephram Cochrane) handles his role with just the right amount of dramatic projection. At first he seems almost tired, portraying a man who is weakened as a result of his long period away from his fellow creatures. Later, his characterization becomes stronger, strengthened by companionship and his growing feelings of attraction for Nancy Hedford.

Corbett is best remembered for his recurring role as Linc Chase in "Route Sixty-Six" (1963–64). He was also a star of the series "The Road West" (1966–67), in which he portrayed Chance Reynolds (his sister in the series was played by Kathryn Hays). He also appears in episodes of "The Night Gallery" ("Brenda," co-starring Barbara Babcock), "Land of the Giants" ("The Weird World," in which he also plays a space traveler trapped away from his native world), and "The Man From U.N.C.L.E." ("The Hong Kong Shilling Affair").

Elinor Donahue's fever-ridden characterization of

Spock and Kirk find themselves face to face with a living legend in "Metamorphosis" (Leonard Nimoy, William Shatner).

Nancy Hedford suggests that in ordinary circumstances Nancy is a much nicer person to be around. Ms. Donahue is best remembered for her regular role as daughter Betty (Princess) Anderson in "Father Knows Best" (her mother in the series was Jane Wyatt; her brother was Billy Gray, who also appears in "The Day the Earth Stood Still"). In "The Odd Couple," she portrayed Miriam Welby from 1970 to 1975. Her most obscure recurring role was in the TV series "Many Happy Returns" (as Joan Randall) from 1964 to 1965.

"Metamorphosis" was the first "Star Trek" episode to be scored by composer George Duning. His subsequent Trek work (especially "The Empath") is every bit as sensitive as his contributions to this segment, in which his melodies went perfectly with author Coon's beautiful script. Duning is best known for his motion picture scores, including the adventuresome *"The Devil at Four O'Clock,"* the humorously occult *"Bell, Book and Candle,"* and the famous *"Picnic"* (for which he also wrote the song "Moonglow").

The Companion itself was a series of animated overlays and colored lighting effects skillfully combined into a soft-focus conglomeration of compelling colors. Because the Companion was always transparent, there was no need for mattes; the effect was double-exposed over the backgrounds.

The interior set for this episode featured "real" clouds, which were provided by clouds of smoke generated at the rear of the set, photographed in slow motion.

Mr. Spock's childlike curiosity gets the better of him again as he recklessly decides to touch the Companion.

In "Journey to Babel," Dr. McCoy hints that Kirk usually gets in the last word in situations. This allegation is borne out at the end of an act in this episode. As Kirk and Spock are being choked by the Companion, McCoy shouts for the creature to release them. After the camera fades to black, the last sounds we hear are a dramatic bit of music followed by Kirk's strangled exclamation of "Aarghh!"

FRIDAY'S CHILD

Episode # 32
Filmed in late May 1967

WRITER D. C. Fontana
DIRECTOR Joseph Pevney
COMPOSER Gerald Fried
PHOTOGRAPHIC EFFECTS Vanderveer Photo Effects

Kirk and company visit planet Capella IV to prevent the Klingons from forming an alliance with the Capellans, a warlike but honorable people. When Captain Kirk prevents the slaughter of Eleen, the wife of deposed High Teer Akaar, he violates Capellan tradition. Kras, a visiting Klingon, is quick to make use of the situation, and partially as a result of his interference our friends become hunted criminals. After McCoy delivers Eleen's baby, she attempts to surrender herself to save her child's life. The Klingon kills the current Teer. Eleen's newborn son, named "Leonard James Akaar," is named the new ruler. Kirk and company leave Capella having arranged diplomatic relations with the planet's government.

The first draft script of "Friday's Child" has Akaar's brother, Maab, scheming with henchman *Keel* to kill Akaar, on the planet referred to here as *Ceres VII*. Eleen hated her baby in this draft, and took it to Maab for him to kill in exchange for permitting her to live. McCoy, Kirk, and Spock, attempting to rescue the child, were captured. Status-seeking Eleen outfoxed herself; Maab had her executed for adultery. Eleen's father became the new Teer's regent, and Maab was executed by his people for attempting to plot with the Klingons. Kirk and company were pardoned and left as friends.

"Friday's Child," in its finished concept, deals realistically with the observation that as we venture out into space we are bound to experience cultures in which the customs are at least a bit odd to Terrans. As a change of pace, this episode begins with a briefing, at which Kirk and company become acquainted with the proper way to stay respected (and alive) on Capella IV.

After Kirk thoroughly botches things, the added complications of Klingons and Eleen's impending childbirth must be faced. Eleen has her child in a mountain cave, in the series' 1967 Christmas episode.

In the end everything works out smoothly, thanks to the Klingon urge for betrayal being far superior to anyone else's. Kras the Klingon has misjudged the Capellans; they may like to fight, but they hate deceit. Everyone is left happy and content with the exception of Mr. Spock, who is forced to undergo the terrible ordeal of holding a human baby.

Julie Newmar (Eleen) has appeared in motion pictures since the early 1950s, including *Seven Brides for Seven Brothers* and *The Marriage-Go-Round*. On television, she starred as an Indian Princess on "F Troop," as Catwoman on several episodes of "Batman," and in "The Twilight Zone" episode "Of Late I Think of Cliffordville." From 1964 to 1965 she starred as Rhoda the Robot on the CBS series, "My Living Doll."

Tige Andrews (Kras the Klingon) appeared regularly in three TV series. He was one of Sergeant Bilko's platoon in "You'll Never Get Rich" from 1955 to 1959.

Following his army career he became one of "Robert Taylor's Detectives" (Lieutenant Johnny Russo) and then founded "The Mod Squad" as Captain Adam Greer from 1968 to 1973.

The Klingon battle cruiser made its debut at the start of the third season in "Elaan of Troyius." In "Friday's Child," a "fill-in" Klingon vessel is used. In appearance, the ship resembles a "flatiron" shape with a rear fin. Glowing a bright orange, it shimmers on the *Enterprise*'s viewscreen for several seconds and then vanishes without ever becoming distinct.

The outdoor terrain in this episode also appears in "Shore Leave," "Arena," "The Alternative Factor," and in such films as *The Werewolf of London* (Universal–1935) and *Buck Rogers* (Universal–1939). On TV, it is visible in the opening credits for the "Broken Arrow" TV series.

Two amusing sequences occur as Kirk becomes familiar with the customs of Capella. First he gets helpful advice from McCoy like "Don't take the fruits." Then there is the old variation of "Me Tarzan, You Jane" in which McCoy urges Eleen to admit "The child is *mine.*" Of course, she repeats "The child is *yours,*" which causes Spock to await an explanation from his emotionally erratic friend the doctor.

WHO MOURNS FOR ADONAIS?

Episode # 33
Filmed in late May, early June 1967

WRITERS   Gilbert A. Ralston, Gene L. Coon (story by Gilbert A. Ralston)
DIRECTOR   Marc Daniels
COMPOSER   Fred Steiner
PHOTOGRAPHIC EFFECTS   Modern Film Effects

In the vicinity of planet Pollux IV, the *Enterprise* encounters a huge, green hand that materializes in space and holds the starship motionless. The "hand" is not flesh and blood, but a form of energy belonging to a humanoid figure who identifies himself as the god Apollo, the last survivor of the band of space travelers who visited old Earth and dwelt on Mount Olympus. Apollo wishes the *Enterprise* crew to stay on Pollux IV to worship him. When Mr. Scott objects to the attention Apollo shows to Lieutenant Carolyn Palamas, the engineer protests and is hurled through the air by a thunderbolt from Apollo's hand. The "god" also demonstrates other abilities, including the power to become giant-sized at will. Kirk enlists the aid of Lieutenant Palamas, who has fallen in love with Apollo. With her aid, Kirk fights the alien and destroys his temple, the source of the entity's abilities.

Seeing that he has lost both his cause and Carolyn, Apollo discontinues his physical existence and the *Enterprise* continues on its way.

The popular "ancient astronaut" theory postulates that space travelers visited Earth many centuries ago, and were accepted as gods by our ancestors. In the era of the United Federation of Planets, the alien, if his intentions were not hostile, would be greeted and encouraged to join the UFP. Unfortunately, Apollo chooses to antagonize the *Enterprise* personnel and jeopardize the starship's mission.

The United Federation of Planets governs itself with laws that owe much to the teachings that Apollo and his companions left on Earth (and probably on other planets as well). Mr. Spock would surely have realized this and attempted to communicate peacefully with Apollo, trying to form a symbiotic relationship with the alien instead of trying to destroy his power. But Apollo commits the one act that Spock cannot possibly forgive; he rejects the Vulcan outright, injuring his pride.

Meanwhile, Apollo is attempting to undermine Captain Kirk's power by attacking the *Enterprise,* the focal point of Kirk's existence. By making instant enemies of Kirk and Spock, Apollo sets the stage for his own defeat. Apollo destroys his physical self, Kirk is sorry, and Carolyn is in a state of shock; no one benefits from Kirk's "victory" over the immortal. The Federation loses a powerful potential ally, to say nothing of his unfulfilled potential as the greatest historian in the galaxy (with the possible exception of Flint from "Requiem for Methuselah").

Montgomery Scott's attachment for Carolyn Palamas is the engineer's first entanglement with a woman in "Star Trek." His later involvement with Mira Romaine (in "The Lights of Zetar") is one of the few other times we see Scotty devoting his attentions to ladies other than the *Enterprise.*

Michael Forest (Apollo) did a fine job with his role. Moments of rage, resignation, and sensitivity are all well acted. Throughout the entire episode, Forest uses just the right amount of egotism to convince his audience that they are experiencing an adventure with a character who is more than human.

Leslie Parrish (Carolyn Palamas) also runs the gamut of emotions, from cool professionalism to outright hero worship. Her conflicts are beautifully conveyed. Ms. Parrish has acted in situations with other legendary characters: she portrayed Daisy Mae Yokum in Paramount's 1958 film version of *L'il Abner.*

Fred Steiner's score for this episode is among the strongest in the entire series, and sections of it are present in many later episodes of "Star Trek." He would later set another immortal's adventure to music by writing the score for "Requiem for Methuselah."

"Who Mourns for Adonais" has some intricate photographic effects, which were accomplished in a number of ways. The episode utilizes traveling mattes (as Apollo becomes a giant); double exposures (Apollo's face and giant hand seen floating in outer space), and animation (Apollo's energy bolts and the *Enterprise*'s phasers).

Scotty's back flip after being hit by Apollo's energy bolt was actually executed by a stunt double, who probably wore a special concealed harness with which he could be pulled backward on cue to achieve the illusion of being repelled by Apollo. This dramatic effect was also employed in "The Changeling" and the "Outer Limits" episode "The Sixth Finger."

Apollo's temple was constructed on an indoor studio set, despite the presence of dubbed-in bird sounds, swaying trees (courtesy of hidden stagehands), and a well-placed stock shot of an actual outdoor lake.

William Theiss's Greek-style gown for Carolyn is a legend among "Star Trek" fans. Evidence suggests that the top was supported by actress Leslie Parrish's willpower and natural resources, but it seems likely that hidden threads helped to avoid a wardrobe accident that would never have been permitted on the air.

Speaking of censorship, it is amazing that the scene in which Carolyn is ravaged by wind, thunder, lightning (and presumably Apollo) was permitted to be shown on network television in 1967. There *was* a bit of censorship here, though. The first draft script for this episode ended with Dr. McCoy pronouncing Carolyn pregnant with Apollo's child.

AMOK TIME

Episode # 34

Final draft script   5/2/67
Second revised final draft   6/5/67
Filmed in early and middle June 1967

WRITER   Theodore Sturgeon
DIRECTOR   Joseph Pevney
COMPOSER   Gerald Fried
PHOTOGRAPHIC EFFECTS   Westheimer Company

When Mr. Spock starts behaving oddly, Captain Kirk asks Dr. McCoy to examine the Vulcan. McCoy reports that Spock is undergoing serious internal processes that will be fatal if they continue. Spock explains to Kirk, confidentially, that he has entered *pon far,* the Vulcan mating cycle. If Spock does not return to Vulcan immediately to fulfill rituals and obligations that will culminate in his taking a wife, he will die. The Captain disobeys other orders and takes Spock to Vulcan instead. Kirk and McCoy are invited to accompany Spock as he undergoes the ceremony of *koon-ut-kal-if-fee;* "marriage or challenge." Spock's aged relative, T'Pau, an esteemed political figure in Federation circles, conducts the ceremony which does not prove to be as simple as Captain Kirk expected it to be. T'Pring, Spock's betrothed bride, chooses ritual combat, demanding that Spock fight Kirk to the death. McCoy injects Kirk with a medication that makes it appear that Spock has killed his captain. After Spock returns to the *Enterprise* and learns that his captain is really alive and well, the Vulcan shows the first moment of emotion he has ever expressed of his own accord. Spock's feelings cancel out his mating urge, and Kirk's professional neck is saved as Starfleet Command approves T'Pau's request for the *Enterprise* to divert to Vulcan.

Author Theodore Sturgeon's script for "Amok Time" is filled with wondrous details about the Vulcans. Sturgeon became so involved in the ethics and life-styles of Spock's people that he even included suggestions for their wardrobe; the possible fabrics that would look best, and other specialized details. In the original script, Kirk did not have to depend upon T'Pau's influence to justify his diverting the *Enterprise* to Vulcan; he knew the Federation officials on the other planet where the ceremonies were to take place, and arranged to have the festivities postponed until after he got Spock back to Vulcan. (As a tribute to a key "Star Trek" staffer, Sturgeon called this other planet "Fontana IV.") There was an interesting touch during the combat sequences; when the "ahn-woon" was announced, Kirk was puzzled when he did not receive this new weapon. He had no idea that "ahn-woon" meant "unarmed combat."

As Mr. Spock's background evolved throughout the first season of "Star Trek," the series' fans began to develop an intense curiosity about his planet, Vulcan. If Spock, being only half-Vulcan, could do so many interesting things, what would full-blooded Vulcans be capable of? How would they live? How incredibly peaceful, logical, and fascinating would their planet be?

While the first season Trek episodes were being rerun on NBC, the first rumors of "Amok Time" leaked out to fandom. During the coming season there would be an episode that would actually take place on Vulcan. It seemed too good to be true. Then came the 1967 World Science Fiction Convention; NYCON.

NYCON was held in New York City over the Labor Day weekend. For "Star Trek" fans, the highpoints of the gathering were the screenings of the Trek "blooper reel" and "Amok Time," both provided by Gene Roddenberry, who personally introduced them. DeForest Kelley's opening credit and Mr. Spock's initial behavior drew applause, as did Spock's happy exclamation upon seeing his friend Jim alive after the scenes on Vulcan. The episode was very well received, although many of the fans wanted to see other parts of Vulcan and, of course, Spock's parents.

Dr. McCoy saves the lives of both Kirk and Spock with a single injection in "Amok Time" (William Shatner, DeForest Kelley, Leonard Nimoy).

For some, the first reaction was surprise seeing the episode begin in space rather than on Vulcan. After witnessing Spock's initial temper tantrums, most speculation was dropped until the episode was over. Some expected to see Vulcans by the dozens, preferably in a city environment with plenty of new sets and opticals. Others speculated upon what changes would be introduced in Spock, now that his heritage was no longer a secret.

Working only with the fact that Mr. Spock comes from Vulcan, a planet of logical individuals who shun emotions, Theodore Sturgeon produced an intriguingly imaginative, highly original representation of the most important Vulcan ritual. If the *koon-ut-kal-if-fee* was only a shadow of the planet's former savagery, just what was ancient Vulcan like? This question did not need answering in "Amok Time"; the trappings of the episode speak for themselves. The rituals, weapons, clothing, and environment are beautifully alien.

Thanks to Jerry Finnerman's cinematography, especially his occasional hand-held camera shots to indicate Spock's frenzied point of view, the confined indoor sets of "Vulcan" seem almost acceptable on occasion.

The visual portion of the episode suffers from the

indoor sets depicting the planet Vulcan. Other means could have been used to achieve the look of another planet. In 1964, Paramount had released *Robinson Crusoe on Mars,* a quality science fiction adventure film in which an American astronaut was marooned alone on the Red Planet. Matte paintings of the planet's red sky were created for that project. These could probably have been integrated into the episode, as well as the Mars landscape created by Chesley Bonestell for Paramount's 1953 *The War of the Worlds.* Exotic landscape stock footage could also have been tinted red to suggest the sky and higher temperature of Vulcan.

Location photography in Death Valley or Monument Valley would have been very effective, if photographed through red or yellow filters, especially if combined with available matte paintings. The outdoor enclosure used in *Arena* could also have been redressed and utilized. Unfortunately, location shooting is very costly, and although other second-season Trek episodes were photographed outdoors, "Amok Time" was not.

Celia Lovsky (T'Pau) was extremely effective largely because of her accent, her inherent dignity, and her facial similarity to Leonard Nimoy. Her use of the word "human" as if it was a curse word was a good touch. Ms. Lovsky was married to Peter Lorre, and came to this country with him in 1935 (for his appearances in the films *Mad Love* and *Crime and Punishment).* She appears in many motion pictures, including *The Power* (Metro Goldwyn-Mayer–1968), and television roles including *One Step Beyond* ("Message from Clara") and *The Twilight Zone* ("Queen of the Nile").

Arlene Martel (T'Pring) created a highly sensuous Vulcan, leading one to believe that there is occasionally more to Vulcan life than logic and *pon far.* Like Celia Lovsky, Ms. Martel looks extremely natural in Vulcan makeup and dress. She has visited some "Star Trek" conventions, including one memorable appearance dressed as T'Pring, and can be seen in "The King of Knaves Affair" on "The Man from U.N.C.L.E.," and in the classic "Outer Limits" episode, "The Demon with a Glass Hand" (written by Harlan Ellison). In the "Twilight Zone" episode "Twenty Two," she was billed as Arline Sax.

Lawrence Montaigne (Stonn) also appears in "Balance of Terror," and can be seen in "The Invaders" ("Ransom," with Alfred Ryder) and "The Time Tunnel" ("Massacre" and "Idol of Death").

Byron Morrow (Admiral Komack) appeared regularly as Captain Keith Gregory in "The New Breed" from 1961 to 1962 (co-starred with Leslie Neilsen); Commander Adams in "Forbidden Planet," and is featured in "Twilight Zone's" "People Are Alike All Over."

Composer Gerald Fried's marvelous score for this episode apparently established him as the Vulcan musical expert for Trek; he also scored "Journey to Babel." His lonely string melody for Mr. Spock became the Vulcan's musical trademark and is heard in many other episodes. His brass and percussion "fight" music is more than sufficiently alien and violent (and bears a resemblance to the music he later wrote for *Roots,* in the initial episode where the slavers arrive). The "marriage party approaches" cue is filled with great power and emotion.

The wardrobe for "Amok Time" is also extremely effective. William Theiss outdid himself here, and made good use of the "Balance of Terror" Romulan helmets painted silver instead of gold.

THE DOOMSDAY MACHINE

Episode # 35
First draft script   5/10/67
Filmed in late June 1967

WRITER   Norman Spinrad
DIRECTOR   Marc Daniels
COMPOSER   Sol Kaplan
PHOTOGRAPHIC EFFECTS   Cinema Research Corp.

Investigating the destruction of several planetary systems, the *Enterprise* discovers the crippled starship U.S.S. *Constellation.* Commodore Matthew Decker, the *Constellation*'s captain, is discovered in a state of shock, the only person left aboard the ship. With his ship severely damaged, Decker had transported his entire crew down to a planet that has since been destroyed by the giant destructive agent, a "berserker" planet killing weapon constructed by a long dead alien race. While Kirk and a party stay aboard to repair the *Constellation*'s engines and weapons system, Decker is beamed back to the *Enterprise* with McCoy. The guilt-ridden Decker takes command of the *Enterprise,* and attempts to use the starship to confront and destroy the planet killer. Kirk contacts the *Enterprise* and enables Spock to take command away from Decker, whereupon the commodore steals a shuttlecraft and launches himself into the planet killer. Decker dies, but his strategy inspires Kirk to rig a self-destruct switch on the *Constellation* and send the damaged ship into the huge alien device. A transporter malfunction almost prevents Kirk from escaping the *Constellation* in time, just before the ship's exploding engines destroy the doomsday machine's destructive power forever.

"The Doomsday Machine" combines elements of horror, obsession, guilt, and suspense to produce an episode that is extremely well done and never slows down.

Commodore Matthew Decker is presumably a man very similar to Captain James Kirk, but he has made a terrible error. In choosing to beam his crewmen down to a planet, instead of insisting that his entire crew stick with their ship, Decker must live with the terrible guilt of having unknowingly caused the deaths of his people. In holding himself answerable to this responsibility, Decker acquires a death wish so strong that he doesn't even suspect that he's trying to repeat the pattern with the *Enterprise* and Kirk's crew.

The Matt Decker we see during this episode is not the same man who existed before the disaster that drove him into deep shock. As Kirk plays back Decker's starship log, we hear the calm and authoritative voice of a strong leader, and we therefore appreciate the complete horror that is evident on Kirk's face as he first sees his old friend sitting amid the ruins of his starship.

Decker's death wish culminates in his stealing a shuttlecraft and heading straight into the Planet Killer. We see the commodore fighting not to turn his craft around, while being simultaneously fascinated, petrified, and relieved that death is about to reunite him with his crew. His terror is made even more tragic by Kirk's attempts to save him. If Decker had heard Kirk's last plea, ". . . We're stronger *with* you than *without* you," the commodore might have tried to save himself.

Apparently, discovering Decker, Dr. McCoy enters into a sympathetic stupor that prevents him from seeing the obvious. As McCoy searches for a valid reason to declare Decker unfit to assume command of the *Enterprise,* he completely forgets that he found Decker in a state of deep shock; hardly the ideal condition for a starship captain.

The tension of Kirk's escaping from the *Constellation* is enormous, probably the closest moment to a classic "cliffhanger" in the entire series.

William Windom's portrayal of Commodore Decker is extremely powerful, and surely one of the greatest characterizations in "Star Trek." Windom ably conveys a sympathetic individual who has lost everything he ever deemed important. But, as a result of the carefully conveyed aggression of the individual, we still share Dr. McCoy's urge to push Decker's face in when he almost destroys the *Enterprise*. To aid his portrayal of an obviously neurotic officer, Windom uses a variety of mannerisms, including his constant fiddling with the tape cartridges in the same manner with which the insane Captain Queeg of *The Caine Mutiny* (portrayed in a less subtle manner by Humphrey Bogart) played with his exercise ball.

To degrade Spock, Decker permits the Vulcan to speak to Kirk at the command chair intercom, beckoning him down to the center of the bridge as though Spock was some sort of household pet.

Windom's performance manages to do wonders with a potential cliché. When reminded by William Shat-

ner that the third planet (onto which Decker had beamed his crew) has ceased to exist, Mr. Windom delivers an emotional "Don't you think I know that?"

William Windom had recurring starring roles in three TV series. He is best remembered as Glen Morley in "The Farmer's Daughter" (1963–66), and also starred as John Monroe in "My World and Welcome to It" (1972) and as Stewart Klein in "The Girl with Something Extra" (1973–74). He can also be seen featured in segments of "The Twilight Zone" ("Miniature"), "Night Gallery" ("They're Tearing Down Tim Riley's Bar"), "The Invaders" ("Doomsday Minus One" and "Summit Meeting"), and "Thriller" ("Man of Mystery").

Author Norman Spinrad's first science fiction novel, *The Solarians,* was published in 1966, and his writing career goes back to the early 1960s. His best known novel is *Bug Jack Barron,* published in 1969.

Composer Sol Kaplan's music for "The Doomsday Machine" is one of the most dramatic and successful scores created for a "Star Trek" episode. With the use of brass, strings, and percussion (piano), Kaplan's melodies are almost Wagnerian in their ability to express grandeur and tragedy.

The Planet Killer miniature is a rough cone; the menacing, energized interior of the device was animated and matted into the center of the model. The design of the Doomsday Machine is apparently different from author Spinrad's description of it. He reportedly intended the device to be covered with visible, glistening alien weapons.

A bit of artistic license is seen as the shuttlecraft enters the maw of the Planet Killer. If this sequence was done true to proportion, the shuttle could not have been clearly seen; it would have been too small. So it appears to be just a little smaller than a starship for this one scene.

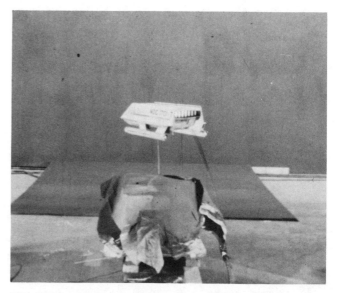

The miniature shuttlecraft, supported from beneath for a distance shot in "The Galileo Seven."

In some scenes, the *Constellation* miniature is a customized, assembled AMT plastic model kit. As the damaged starship is entering the machine, its aft view lacks much of the detail visible on the series' actual miniatures.

A rear projection effect allows Kirk and Spock to walk in front of the *Enterprise* view screen during the last scene of the episode.

The "auxiliary control room" on the *Constellation* appears to be a redress of the *Enterprise* briefing room; there are no other new sets in this segment.

The "pretzel-shaped" insignia worn by Commodore Decker was not worn by Commodores Stone and Mendez.

The hand prop identified in *The Making of Star Trek* as a "ray generator and energy neutralizer" is used by Scotty on the *Constellation,* whereas the small "offensive-defensive ray gun" is used as a soldering iron by Kirk (and also appears as the laser beacon in "The Squire of Gothos").

A trivial observation is the fact that the black trimming is missing from the "V" neck on Kirk's fatigue tunic during this episode.

Also lost, in one brief line of dialogue (". . . 30 seconds later . . . poof!") is Scotty's Scottish brogue.

WOLF IN THE FOLD

Episode # 36
Revised Final draft script   6/21/67
Filmed in late June, early July 1967

WRITER   Robert Bloch
DIRECTOR   Joseph Pevney
COMPOSER   Gerald Fried
PHOTOGRAPHIC EFFECTS   Vanderveer Photo Effects

Kirk and McCoy have taken Scotty to planet Argelius Two for a therapeutic leave. Scotty has recently suffered an accidental head injury, caused by a female crew member. A series of brutal murders of young women give the appearance that Mr. Scott may be the killer. The real murderer is exposed as a previously unknown, ancient life form that first appeared on Earth as Jack the Ripper. The entity, in its current incarnation of Chief City Administrator Hengist, is trapped and transported into outer space.

Gene Roddenberry maintained "Star Trek's" high quality by never forgetting that writing science fiction is no different from writing any other type of story. Any script must have a premise, a purpose, and believable individuals. Any references to gadgetry and special effects are inserted as afterthoughts to enhance the story. If these rules are followed, a good story can

Horror meshes with science fiction as Mr. Scott is suspected of being a latter-day Jack the Ripper in "Wolf in the Fold" (James Doohan).

easily be transformed into good science fiction. So can a good mystery or horror story.

Author Robert Bloch combined mystery and horror to make "Wolf in the Fold" one of the most interesting, terrifying, and unique Trek episodes.

In 1961, Bloch wrote an episode of Universal's TV series "Thriller" (hosted by Boris Karloff), called "Yours Truly, Jack the Ripper." Adapted from Bloch's short story of the same title, "The Ripper" was discovered operating in an American city during the 1960s. The theory was advanced that the Ripper was actually a life form with an extremely long life span. It was ultimately discovered in possession of a Scotland Yard inspector.

If anything, "Wolf in the Fold" is more successful than its earlier first cousin. One of the most horrifying moments in "Trek" comes as Kirk casually observes that, when mankind ventured in space, this thing came with him to terrorize other worlds. Equally as chilling is Scotty's description of the creature; "Cold it was, like a stinking draft out of a slaughterhouse."

The suspense and impact are greatly increased by having Scotty suspected of being the murderer. Is Mr. Scott actually capable of committing murder even after a serious head injury? The possibility would have been increased in a scene that was deleted from the final script. When Lieutenant Tracy beamed down to administer the "psycho tricorder" test, Scotty was initially to have remarked "A Woman!," as if protesting against being tested by a female. Jaris was then supposed to inquire about this remark; doesn't Mr. Scott like women, he wondered. Kirk would then have replied that Scott wasn't well because of a recent head injury.

Robert Bloch is best known as the author of *Psycho,* a 1959 novel filmed a year later by Paramount Pictures as a classic horror film directed by Alfred Hitchcock. For "Star Trek," Bloch also wrote "What Are Little Girls Made Of?," and would later write "Catspaw."

John Fiedler (Hengist) is a skilled actor who forces his presence to be as grating as his carefully controlled voice. For the more enthusiastic devotees of character actors, Fiedler is known as the smaller version of actor Percy Helton (a performer who specialized in the same types of roles).

Fiedler appeared regularly as Alfie Higgins, the comedy relief character of "Tom Corbett: Space Cadet (1950–56)." He appeared in "Micky and the Contessa," an unsold TV pilot produced in 1966, and in two episodes of "The Twilight Zone" ("Cavender Is Coming" and ("The Night of the Meek"). In "The Night Stalker," he was mortician Gordon Spangler, affectionately dubbed "Gordy the Ghoul" by Karl Kolchack.

Charles Dierkop (Morla) appeared in "Voyage to the Bottom of the Sea" ("The Left-Handed Man"), "The Man from U.N.C.L.E." ("The Off-Broadway Affair"), and in the recurring role of Sergeant Pete Royster in "Police Woman."

Pilar Seurat (Sybo) was also in "Voyage to the Bottom of the Sea" ("The Silent Saboteurs," which co-starred George Takei) and U.N.C.L.E. ("The Abominable Snowman Affair").

Charles Macauley (Prefect Jaris) also appears as "Landru" in "The Return of the Archons."

William Theiss enhanced the characters of Hengist and Jaris by providing Fiedler with an unsympathetic solid black costume (reminiscent of the garment he designed for the equally hated Nilz Barris in "Tribbles") and Macauley with a long, flowing costume.

Gerald Fried composed the scores for "Wolf in the Fold" and "Catspaw." Because both episodes are similar in content, the "Catspaw" score is used heavily in this episode. Kara dances to the same music to which Vina danced in "The Cage," and additional "Cage" music is used to score Sybo's empathic trance.

During the trance scene, Jerry Finnerman positioned his camera high above the soundstage floor, and shot straight down onto the set. This camera angle, together with the music and editing, makes this an extremely effective moment.

Earlier Trek costumes and sets are in evidence here. Finnegan's shirt from "Shore Leave" shows up outside the Argelian café, the exterior of which is probably left over from "Errand of Mercy." Jaris' living room includes the wall designed for opticals in "The Menagerie" and "A Taste of Armageddon." The prefect's basement is a redress of the cell in "Catspaw" and "Return of the Archons."

The entity's possession of the *Enterprise* computer is shown with inset mattes of swirling red-brown paints and double-exposed brown smoke (similar to the opening credits of the old "Checkmate" TV series).

The only negative feature of this episode is the lack of resemblance between John Fiedler and his stunt-double when Hengist tries to flee from the *Enterprise* briefing room.

THE CHANGELING

Episode #37
First draft script 5/1/67
Filmed in early and middle July 1967

WRITER   John Meredyth Lucas
DIRECTOR   Marc Daniels
COMPOSER   Fred Steiner
PHOTOGRAPHIC EFFECTS   Westheimer Company

The *Enterprise* investigates the destruction of the Malurian System's four billion inhabitants and locates the unexpected source, a portable computer/ space probe of great power called Nomad. When the device threatens the *Enterprise,* Kirk has no choice but to beam it aboard. Kirk and company are temporarily saved when Nomad mistakes Captain James Kirk for its creator, Terran scientist Jackson Roykirk. Nomad, a space probe launched in 2020 to seek out alien life in the galaxy, had been damaged by a meteor that had confused its programming and cut it off from Earth. It had then encountered an alien probe, Tan-Ru, which had been launched to secure sterilized soil samples. The resulting hybrid mechanism believes that its mission is to destroy imperfect life forms; its altered programming and offensive/defensive weapons made "the changeling" capable of fulfilling its new mission. Kirk uses the machine's confused image of him as a basis for its destruction. He convinces Nomad that it is imperfect, and the device is transported out into space just before it self-destructs.

The first draft script of "The Changeling" began dramatically with the probe, called *Altair* in this version, absorbing the power of four photon torpedoes fired from the *Enterprise.* To contact Altair, Kirk jettisoned a huge cloud of ionized particles and beamed a huge "television" image of himself into space. The probe did not board the *Enterprise* until the start of Act Two, at which point the starship personnel showed a great deal of curiosity about its capacities and mode of power. Scotty got "zapped" while attempting to examine it; in this version his brain was crushed, but Altair had no difficulty putting the engineer together again in prime working order. Mr. Spock seemed almost obsessed with the idea of salvaging the probe's knowledge banks before destroying it, and even pointed out that "killing" Altair would technically be an act of murder. In the end of the first draft script, Kirk used Altair's perfectly logical trend of thought to destroy the probe. The captain ordered all the literary works in the starship's computer banks flash fed into Altair. Unable to absorb this resulting torrential flow of illogic, Altair went into his self-destruct phase.

"The Changeling" is a good argument against humanity's egotistical opinions concerning its superiority. Nomad, created in an accident, is far more powerful than anything mankind has ever managed to create. This brings up the question of how all this power was able to evolve out of two probes, neither of which was originally programmed to do anything that required nearly that much energy. If we presume that the changed machine(s) completely reworked their internal capacities, we arrive at some interesting conclusions. For instance, how were both damaged machines able to synthesize the parts they needed to repair themselves, and merge into one unit? Second, where did the superior science come from? If the originators of Tan-Ru possessed such a superior science, why would they need space probes? With such power at their disposal, they could have visited the stars themselves. Apparently we are expected to take the presence of the superior science completely on faith. The episode is sufficiently intriguing that we *can* just take this point for granted and enjoy the adventure.

Part of the episode's attraction probably results from the sequence wherein Nomad repairs the "unit Scott." The shock of seeing our friendly engineer hurled through the air is surpassed as we learn he is dead. Nomad's casual offer to restore "the unit" to working order is completely unexpected, and Scotty's complete ignorance of what has happened to him makes the entire situation even stranger. One wonders whether anyone ever bothered to sit Scott down and explain what really occurred. It is fortunate that this adventure occurred after "Wolf in the Fold," or the mental fitness of Mr. Scott would have been in even more doubt than it was in that segment.

Lieutenant Uhura's experience of having her brain drained adds more strangeness to this episode. In tampering with Scotty and Uhura, the mechanical and human extensions of the very fabric of the *Enterprise,* Nomad cancels out any sympathy the audience may have had for it. There is a flaw in the Uhura sequence, though. Unless we presume that her amnesia was partial, there is no way she could have retained her original personal memories while losing all her factual knowledge.

The most unusual sequence in the adventure is Mr. Spock's Mind Meld with Nomad. While in contact with the probe, the Vulcan seems simultaneously more human and more alien than usual.

Actor Vic Perrin, who supplied the voice for Nomad, was heard in other Trek episodes for shorter periods. His delivery of Nomad's dialogue, with just enough inflection to remain automated without being boring, adds much to the episode.

The visual star, Nomad itself, was a beautifully conceived hunk of metal, lights, and other materials. Designed and assembled by "Star Trek's" special effects department, headed by James Rugg, Nomad presented problems because of its ability to levitate. During various sequences, depending upon the required camera angles, Nomad was either suspended from wires attached to an overhead track or mounted on a special, concealed wheeled cart pushed by an off-camera technician.

Parts of Nomad were later "cannibalized" and incorporated into the Romulan Cloaking Device (in "The Enterprise Incident") and Flint's M-4 robot (in "Requiem for Methuselah").

THE APPLE

Episode # 38
Second revised final draft   7/12/67
Filmed in middle and late July 1967

WRITERS   Max Ehrlich, Gene L. Coon
   (Story by Max Ehrlich)
DIRECTOR   Joseph Pevney

On Gamma Trianguli VI, Kirk and company are forced to ignore the beautiful landscape when they encounter poisonous plants, exploding rocks, and extremely dangerous weather conditions. In contrast, the planet's humanoids are a gentle, childlike people who call themselves The Feeders of Vaal. Vaal is a computer, constructed many years before in "the dim time," which survives by "metabolizing" the natives' offerings into energy. The landing party must defeat Vaal and his people (led by the high priest Akuta) before the machine can destroy the *Enterprise* by decaying its orbit. After a major battle with the villagers, and Spock's being hit by a lightning bolt (just a flesh wound), the starship's phasers destroy Vaal.

Of all the "Star Trek" episodes involving the destruction of a computer, this one is the weakest. For centuries, Vaal has been "babysitting," keeping its subjects in ignorance of sociological and technological progress. Despite their cultural atrophy, the people are happy; there is no sickness and no jealousy, only complete harmony. Into this environment beam Kirk and company, bringing "the apple" into the planetwide "Garden of Eden." The analogy is complete: Vaal the computer appears to be a large serpent head carved in rock. Our people's "fruits of knowledge" are their phasers, tricorders, communicators, and philosophy. In these circumstances the "serpent" is actually Kirk for wanting to introduce new ways to the Feeders of Vaal.

Captain Kirk is not likely to believe that "ignorance is bliss," especially when it is a machine causing the situation. Kirk does not see himself as a destructive influence, but as an authority figure releasing the inhabitants to evolve their own productive culture and become their own providers. But does Kirk have the right to assume this role? He is probably in violation of the Prime Directive, for even if Vaal is a machine, we must presume that it was programmed by individuals who once ruled this planet.

Kirk takes it upon himself to give these people the right to run their own lives, without giving them the chance to decide what they actually want. He imprisons them when they try to feed Vaal, and the natives are helpless as the *Enterprise*'s guns blast the computer. Things might have turned out differently if Vaal was capable of speech, or if Spock had entered into a Vulcan Mind Meld with Akuta to "converse" with the machine.

As the Feeders of Vaal stand deprived of their deity and stripped of the immortality that Vaal had been providing for them, they laugh at their newfound freedom to enjoy sexual intercourse. The Federation will undoubtedly be providing aid for these people, and it is going to be a difficult transition for them. It would have been interesting to return to this world and see how the Feeders of Vaal learned to feed themselves.

Keith Andes (Akuta) probably found it difficult to portray a simpering computer link. In 1959 he starred as Police Lieutenant Frank Dawson in his syndicated TV series, "This Man Dawson." He appeared regularly from 1963 to 1965 as Keith Granville in "Glynis," and from 1965 to 1966 as Jeff Morgan in "Paradise Bay." He co-starred with James Doohan and Skip (G. V.) Homeier in the "Outer Limits" episode "The Expanding Human."

You will have to look closely at Vaal follower Makora to recognize him as actor David Soul. Soul appeared regularly as Joshua Bolt on "Here Come the Brides" (co-starring with Mark Lenard and Robert Brown from 1968 to 1970), and as Ted Warrick on "Owen Marshall: Counselor at Law" from 1971 to 1974, before achieving stardom as Ken "Hutch" Hutchinson on "Starsky and Hutch" (1975–1979).

Most of the budget for "The Apple" probably went to rent the tremendous number of "greens" necessary to convert a studio soundstage into a jungle. "Vaal" itself did not cost too much to construct; it appears to consist of heavy crinkled paper, sprayed chemical foam, plastic eyeballs, and fangs. Chemical smoke provided an added illusion of "life."

An array of animated effects was double-exposed over Vaal to produce the starship phaser barrage that "killed" the computer. The effect would have been improved if the entire structure shimmered and disappeared like Apollo's temple in "Who Mourns for Adonais."

When Spock is hit by lightning, the effects consist of (1) an animated bolt, (2) a stunt double's somersault, (3) a dramatic view of Leonard Nimoy clad in a shirt

The painting of Talos IV, before it was matted onto the *Enterprise* viewscreen in "The Cage."

with a smoking slit cut into its back, and (4) a thunderous sound effect.

The purposely damaged Spock shirt was later auctioned off at the 1967 World Science Fiction Convention (NYCON), and is presently in the hands of a collector.

MIRROR, MIRROR

Episode #39
Outline 3/2/67
Filmed in late July, early August 1967

WRITER Jerome Bixby
DIRECTOR Marc Daniels
COMPOSER Fred Steiner
PHOTOGRAPHIC EFFECTS Vanderveer Photo Effects

Kirk, McCoy, Scotty, and Uhura transport back to the *Enterprise* after initiating diplomatic relations with the peaceful Halkan Council. As a result of turbulent atmospheric conditions, the transporter malfunctions, depositing our people on a parallel *Enterprise* in another universe where the Federation has developed along Klingon principles. In return, the parallel universe's Kirk, McCoy, Scotty, and Uhura are deposited on our *Enterprise,* where they are immediately locked up by Spock. For our people, transplanted into a hostile environment, the situation makes it difficult to remain alive until they return; if they *can* return. Kirk discovers his counterpart's attractive Captain's Woman, and the Tantalus Field, a stolen alien invention that instantly does away with parallel-Kirk's enemies. Foiling parallel-Sulu's Gestapo-like security people, and an aborted attempt by parallel-Chekov to take over command, our people find an ally in parallel-Spock, who assists in their return trip. *Our* Mr. Spock returns the parallel crew members simultaneously, and everything is back to normal.

Jerome Bixby's story outline for "Mirror, Mirror" had Kirk beaming into the parallel universe alone, finding a parallel Federation where phasers were as yet unknown. The parallel Federation was *not* evil; just a bit backward, and had just lost a war to the *Tharn* Empire (the name was retained for the Halkan leader in the final draft). Kirk used electronic parts from the ship's systems to build a phaser weapon and conquer the Tharn.

In the outline, Kirk was subject to fainting spells; the entire parallel universe was also suffering structurally and was treating Kirk like an invading germ, gradually poisoning him. The parallel-Kirk was *married.* The parallel-*Enterprise* crew worked closely with Kirk to defeat the Tharn.

In the outline, parallel-Spock was more Vulcan than human, and more savage in temperament. *McCoy* was the one with the beard, a fact that initially made Kirk recoil from him in shock. (Fortunately, Kirk reacted better to this in *Star Trek—The Motion Picture.)* The parallel-McCoy was injured in the final confrontation with the Tharn; our McCoy had also been injured back at home. Upon returning, Kirk met the nurse who had treated McCoy in our universe; our counterpart of the parallel-Kirk's wife.

There's an old saying that "opposites attract"; this is certainly one reason why "Mirror, Mirror" is so popular. This episode provides the unique opportunity to encounter an *Enterprise* run by unscrupulous counterparts of our friends.

The act of coming face to face with your hidden, inner drives is something that many people pay vast sums of money to arrange via psychoanalysis. (Just ask Jim Kirk about it; he was through it all before in "The Enemy Within.") For any of us it probably would have been completely disastrous. But for our well-adjusted starship friends it is just another mission.

The differences between the two universes are expressed in obvious terms. The parallel Federation becomes the equivalent of our Klingons, Romulans, and ancient brigands all rolled into one slimy package. It would have been interesting to have seen the parallel-Kor as the equal of our Kirk. It would have been logical for our people to seek out a parallel-Klingon ship and ask for their aid, but it also would have added needless plot complications and taken up too much time. The focal points of both universes are the Halkans, who seem to be the same in both "worlds."

A more subtle point of consistency is Mr. Spock (or, rather, *both* of him). The parallel-Spock is a warrior advancing along with the conquests of the Federation Empire. Although careful to conduct his life like a logical chess game, parallel-Spock still emerges as a man to be liked and trusted. In the final analysis, Kirk realizes that the matrix holding both universes together is the inexorable flow of logic. Things are evolving differently in the parallel environment, but the state of both universes can eventually be the same. As Landru would say: "The good is all."

Kirk proves this to parallel-Spock with a logical demonstration. His premises read like a geometrical theorem: Things equal to the same thing are equal to each other. Given: the premise that waste of life and the infliction of misery are both present and desirable. Conclusion: the Federation Empire is both present . . . and undesirable. Therefore, any attempts by qualified personnel to bring about the eventual end of the Empire could only be in the best interest of the universe. Kirk points to parallel-Spock as the most qualified person around; one can almost see the logical wheels turning in parallel-Spock's head. With the Tantalus

Field placed at his disposal, parallel-Spock is left with the knowledge the change is needed, the conviction to carry it through . . . and the power to safeguard himself from the illogical Empire.

To reenforce the alien background of the parallel environment, many changes were created throughout the *Enterprise*. The most apparent of these is parallel-Spock's beard, which adds a quality of forceful conviction to the Vulcan.

Costumes were altered to resemble the warlike garishness of Klingon clothes. Insignias are attached to the opposite locations they usually occupy on the shirts. Because of their specialized natures, these variations in wardrobe were never seen again in "Star Trek."

A significant alien impression is conveyed by parallel-Sulu. The capable, exuberant, and most definitely likable Sulu of our world is transformed into a scarred, furtive, and lustful red-shirted figure. The forceful benevolence of McCoy is brilliantly conveyed here, and serves to reenforce the Doctor's likable qualities along with those of parallel-Spock (once again proving how similar these friendly enemies actually are). DeForest Kelley's ever-sensitive portrayal also makes it painfully clear that McCoy, the one person almost left behind, is also the one man who could never have survived in the hostile environment. In a rare moment, Scotty's concern for his captain becomes evident as he grasps Kirk's arm, calls him "Jim," and wordlessly wishes him luck.

Nichelle Nichols should have been given many other chances to show Uhura functioning under pressure away from her switchboard. Uhura emerges in "Mirror, Mirror" as decidedly more forceful, adaptable, human, and gorgeous than usual.

Barbara Luna is extremely beautiful in her dual role of Captain's Woman/Lieutenant Marlena Moreau. Ms. Luna has portrayed exotic women in many feature films, including *The Devil at Four O'Clock* and Irwin Allen's *Five Weeks in a Balloon*. She also appears in a "Man from U.N.C.L.E." episode, "The Man from Thrush Affair."

Vic Perrin (Tharn) appears in the pilot film of *Dragnet: 1967*. He is also seen in "The Adventures of Superman" segment "The Golden Vulture," and "Twilight Zone" episodes "People Are Alike All Over" and "Ring-a-Ding Girl." Perrin's *voice* is well known to science fiction fans as the "Control Voice" of "The Outer Limits." On "Star Trek," his talented voice is featured in "The Corbomite Maneuver," "Arena," and possibly as the redubbed Keeper of "The Menagerie."

In addition to the more blatant physical changes, such as the Empire's symbol of a planet bisected with a sword, there are more subliminal differences. Kirk's command chair is given a higher back (which is later seen on Commodore Wesley's chair in "The Ultimate Computer"). Objects commonly seen in other episodes are inverted. Personal knives are in evidence. To evoke

a further feeling of personal paranoia, communicators are sometimes used instead of wall-mounted intercoms. The engineering set is shown from a different angle by means of an elevated control room, which is also seen in "I Mudd."

A different optical is used for the parallel-transporter effect. It is similar to the shimmer later created for the Klingon transporter effect, and is accompanied by a stronger sound effect than that usually employed.

"Mirror, Mirror" was written by science fiction and fantasy author Jerome Bixby, who edited *Planet Stories* magazine for a short time and contributed to other science fiction magazines as well. His first science fiction tale was "Tubemonkey," published in 1949. For "Star Trek," he also wrote "Day of the Dove" and "Requiem for Methuselah." "Twilight Zone" adapted his story "It's a Wonderful Life," which tells of a boy who can work miracles and illustrates horrors not unlike those that "Charlie X" would have unleashed if given the chance. (Billy Mumy, who later starred in "Lost in Space," played the little boy.) Bixby also wrote the science fiction film *It: The Terror from Beyond Space* (United Artists–1958), which some critics agree was a basis for the film *Alien*.

"Mirror, Mirror" was nominated for science fiction fandom's Hugo Award. It is generally regarded by fans as one of the most well-written, -produced, -directed, -acted, and -enjoyed episodes of "Star Trek." When New York City's Museum of Modern Art showed a series of science fiction films a few years ago, the episode they chose to represent "Star Trek" was "Mirror, Mirror."

THE DEADLY YEARS

Episode # 40
Produced in early August 1967

WRITER   David P. Harmon
DIRECTOR   Joseph Pevney
COMPOSERS   Fred Steiner, Sol Kaplan
PHOTOGRAPHIC EFFECTS   Westheimer Company

While visiting planet Gamma Hydra IV on a routine mission, an *Enterprise* landing party including Kirk, Spock, Dr. McCoy, Scotty, Chekov, and Lieutenant Arlene Galway are exposed to a strange disease. The illness, a radiation poisoning spread by a comet, causes greatly accelerated aging; Robert Johnson (age twenty-nine) and his wife Elaine (age twenty-seven) have been transformed almost overnight into aged individuals whom McCoy is powerless to save. Kirk and the rest of the landing party, with the exception of Chekov, begin to age rapidly as McCoy desperately seeks an antidote. Dr. Janet Wallace, an old friend

The Romulan "bird of prey" ship designed and constructed for "Balance of Terror."

of Kirk's, aids the researchers. Commodore George Stocker, aboard the starship enroute to his new command at Starbase Ten, admires Kirk but nevertheless convenes an extraordinary competency hearing after which Stocker assumes command and heads the *Enterprise* to his starbase. Unfortunately, the shortcut he follows leads through the Romulan Neutral Zone. McCoy discovers the antidote just in time to cure himself and his patients and to enable the restored Kirk to save the *Enterprise* by using the tried-and-true "corbomite" bluff.

Old age is now thought to be more of a "disease" than a natural process; an unpleasant part of life that will be made much easier by new discoveries that will enable us to enjoy many more years of active life. Science has already enabled us to extend our lifetimes, and by the time of "Star Trek's" future the age of retirement will probably be closer to 100 than to 65. In any case, we grow old gradually while enjoying our lives, and in the era of the starship *Enterprise* the process should be less rapid than it is today. Unfortunately, this is not the case in "The Deadly Years."

Kirk and company had faced identity crises before in "The Naked Time," "Mirror, Mirror," and other adventures, but the threat of old age depriving them of all the essential characteristics necessary for the performance of their starship duties is an especially insidious prospect.

Captain Kirk, to whom virility is especially important, does not age as quickly as the others because of his intense determination to hang onto his youth. Mr. Spock, because of his Vulcan heritage and life span, also ages comparatively slowly. Dr. McCoy, shouldering the responsibility to cure his friends, ages very quickly. Scotty, with his life-loving metabolism, iron-

ically ages the quickest. As Dr. McCoy observes in this episode, different individuals age at different rates. Within this tale, each person's rate of aging is probably determined by the individual's ability to contribute drama to the tale despite his progressive deterioration.

People adopt certain mannerisms as they grow older, all of which result from the body's degeneration. The posture becomes stooped, the voice quavers, and the eyes squint. To convey these mannerisms, the stage techniques of actors William Shatner, DeForest Kelley, Leonard Nimoy, and James Doohan were used very effectively. To supplement their talents, special makeups were created so that Kirk, McCoy, Spock, and Scotty could age before our eyes.

Makeup artist Fred Phillips and his staff worked wonders within a short span of time. Earlier stages of transformation were accomplished with makeup pencils and wigs.

For the more drastic transformations, other makeup appliances were created to change the shapes of each actor's features. DeForest Kelley was the greatest problem, because his makeups involved depicting the "old country doctor" aging in great detail. In his "last phase" makeup, actor Kelley wore rubber appliances glued over his cheeks, chin, and neck, and beneath his eyes. The rubber was carefully attached to his face, and his entire face was coated with pale makeup. Shadows, creases, age spots, and other touches were applied last of all.

William Shatner's makeup included a small strip of rubber inserted under his lower lip. This made his mouth appear to acquire, exaggerated, additional wrinkles.

Both Kelley and Doohan were also fitted with gray eyebrows. Kelley and Shatner had their hands covered with thin, crumpled rubber to produce wrinkles; age spots were added over these. Padding appears to have been used to stoop Doohan's back, and all three wore shirts that were too large for them to make them appear less muscular.

The actors aided in making their makeup effective. DeForest Kelley manipulated his rubberized lips to make it appear that he had lost his teeth. Shatner spoke with a slight lisp and moved his hands to suggest that he was feeling the arthritis pains the script indicated. Nimoy, wearing gray sideburns and heavy eye makeup, squinted his eyes and rasped his voice. James Doohan merely stopped functioning at all, assuming a sad-eyed expression that was extremely painful to see.

Sarah Marshall (Dr. Janet Wallace) had performed with William Shatner before, in an episode of "The Nurses" coincidentally entitled "A Difference of Years," and appears in segments of "Thriller" ("The Poisoner" and "God Grant That She Lye Still") and "The Twilight Zone" ("Little Girl Lost"). In the "Daniel Boone" episode "Hero's Welcome," she co-starred with actor Charles Drake.

Charles Drake (Commodore Stocker) made a fine "chair-bound paper pusher," managing to create a sympathetic character with little to work with. His acting career includes appearances in such vintage films as *Now Voyager* and *A Night in Casablanca,* and science fiction titles *It Came from Outer Space* (Universal–1953) and *Tobor the Great* (Republic–1954). He hosted the syndicated TV series "Rendezvous" in 1958, and starred in "The Man from U.N.C.L.E." segment "The Thrush Roulette Affair."

Beverly Washburn (Lieutenant Arlene Galway) also had to endure special aging makeup, which seemed especially peculiar on her considering the fact that her career began as a child actress appearing in movies including *Superman and the Mole-Men* (Lippert–1951) and *Hans Christian Andersen* (Metro-Goldwyn-Mayer–1952). She appeared regularly as young Kit Wilson in the TV series "Professional Father" in 1955, as daughter Vickie in "The Loretta Young Show" (1962–63), in episodes of "One Step Beyond" ("Premonition") and "Thriller" ("Parasite Mansion"), and in "Science Fiction Theatre."

Laura Wood (Laura Johnson) also appears in "Charlie X."

Felix Locker (Dr. Robert Johnson) appeared as an aging scientist in *Frankenstein's Daughter* (Astor Pictures–1958).

The repeated views of young Uhura and Sulu reinforced the images of Kirk and company becoming old before our eyes. For an aged Uhura, see "And the Children Shall Lead." Actor George Takei aged very effectively in the feature film *Ice Palace* (Warner Brothers–1959).

The aging has another strange effect on Dr. McCoy, restoring his Southern accent and "old country doctor" mannerisms to their fullest.

Commodore Stocker manages to catch Mr. Spock off guard on the matter of the Vulcan's being more qualified for command than the aged Captain Kirk. Had Spock been his normal self, Stocker could never have tricked him by using logic. Spock is not spared from being picked on by Dr. McCoy, either. Having established that taking the antidote is anything but pleasant, McCoy gleefully informs the Vulcan that he has removed all the breakables from sick bay in preparation for his visit.

It was originally planned to have Kirk take the antidote and, accompanied by the still aged Spock, return to normal slowly while en route from sick bay to the bridge. For unknown reasons, this sequence was eliminated and replaced with another showing Kirk returning to normal on the sick bay bed. (Dr. Wallace announced that the antidote was working, as the camera zoomed in for a close-up of Kirk's crotch, signifying that his youth was being restored.)

In a marvelous bit of respect to the series' continuity, Mr. Chekov turns and smiles at Mr. Sulu as Kirk mentions "corbomite." Chekov was not around for "The Corbomite Maneuver," but apparently Sulu had filled him in about it at sometime in the past.

I MUDD

Episode # 41
First draft script   5/23/67
Filmed in middle August 1967

WRITERS   Stephen Kandel, David Gerrold
DIRECTOR   Marc Daniels
COMPOSER   Samuel Matlovsky
PHOTOGRAPHIC EFFECTS   Vanderveer Photo Effects

An extraordinary *Enterprise* crewman, Norman, reveals himself as an android after locking the starship on a course toward a specific planet. The unknown world is populated by a race of extremely sophisticated androids who have outlived their human creators. The androids desire only to serve mankind and wish to spread throughout the galaxy, eliminating problems caused by human frailties. To do this, they must first rule the galaxy; the seizure of the *Enterprise* is their first step toward this goal. Arriving on their planet, Kirk and company learn that the androids have a guest; Harry Mudd, who crashed on their world after escaping from the scene of his most current crime. Mudd has proclaimed himself the emperor of their planet, but the androids, recognizing Harry as a severely flawed example of humanity, plan to strand him with the *Enterprise* people after they leave in the starship. Mudd aids Kirk, Spock, McCoy, Uhura, Scotty, and Chekov in defeating the androids, using illogical behavior that gives the mobile mechanisms electronic nervous breakdowns.

The first draft script for "I Mudd" dwelt much longer on Norman's diverting the *Enterprise* to Mudd's planet. After he revealed that he was an android, Norman was examined and Scotty mentioned that he wished to take Norman apart, quickly adding that it was "nothing personal." Norman understood.

In "I Mudd," the most likable arch-villain of the universe stages a nontriumphal return, this time attempting to enlist a planetful of advanced androids to aid him in running rampant through the galaxy.

Fortunately, the androids are perceptive devices. After permitting Harry to run rampant on their world, creating any number of attractive female (?) androids and synthesizing other goodies for himself, the marvelous machines understand that Harcourt Fenton Mudd is an extremely misguided soul. From Harry, the androids learn all about human greed, lust, gluttony, and deceit. It is no wonder that, when attempting to find a purpose for themselves, the androids conclude that humankind needs their specialized talents in order to survive. All this eventually leads to the funniest "pull out the plug" story ever presented on "Star Trek."

Even Mr. Spock seems to enjoy himself as the drama of the occasion justifies his behaving in a decidedly non-Vulcan manner. He lies, he partakes in pantomime, and seems to take great delight in his capacity for behaving foolishly when the situation calls for it.

If Mr. Spock is actually enjoying himself, the same definitely cannot be said about Harry Mudd toward the end of this adventure. Unfortunately for Harry, he has elected to gloat about having left his wife, Stella Mudd, deserted back on Earth. Stella, who resembles a cross between the Bride of Frankenstein and the Wicked Witch of the West, gave Harry the courage to begin his wanderings through outer space. Harry, more dangerous than a Doomsday Machine when he's in good form, has created an android duplicate of his wife that he can command to "shut up" at will. Kirk's sense of humor, which is every bit as perverse as Mudd's, induces the androids to mass produce the "Stella" model android to serve as Harry's "probation officers" during his stay on the planet.

William Shatner and Nichelle Nichols, as Kirk and Uhura, provide a moment of true drama in the midst of the bizarre goings on. Uhura, seemingly hoping that the androids will grant her "immortality" by transferring her mind into an android body, appears to betray her captain's escape plan to the androids. As Kirk approaches her afterward, we do not know what to expect until he embraces her; her behavior has been part of the *real* escape plan.

Richard Tatro (Norman) deserves a special award for never cracking a smile throughout the entire episode. His carefully measured "mechanical" voice pattern and his precise movements created an ideal image of an android.

Rhae and Alyce Andrece (The "Alice" Series) appeared in the "Batman" episode "Nora Clavicle and the Ladies' Crime Club."

This was composer Samuel Matlovsky's only "Star Trek" assignment. His pleasant melodies captured the humor of the situation without losing sight of the drama behind Captain Kirk's program of calculated mayhem.

The idea of casting identical twins as the android "series" enabled the impossible to be accomplished within the episode's budget. Through the use of split screens, as many as six of one model were shown at once.

Two of the female "series" were clothed in the costumes created by William Theiss for actresses Karen Steele and Maggie Thrett in "Mudd's Women." (Duplicates of important costumes are usually produced when the episode budget allows; in case of damage to a garment, this saves costly production delays.)

"I Mudd" does have one unanswered riddle. Dr. Leonard McCoy is the greatest physician in all of Starfleet. He is an expert in life forms throughout the galaxy, and is certainly a conscientious and perceptive individual. How, then, does McCoy manage to give Norman a physical examination without seeing the little metal door hinged into where Norman's navel should be?

THE TROUBLE WITH TRIBBLES

Episode #42
First draft script   7/21/67
Revised final draft   8/1/67
Filmed in late August 1967

WRITER   David Gerrold
DIRECTOR   Joseph Pevney
COMPOSER   Jerry Fielding

The *Enterprise* is diverted to Space Station K-7 to protect an important shipment of quadrotriticale, a specialized grain. Captain Kirk finds his responsibilities and his patience severely taxed by Federation Undersecretary of Agricultural Affairs Nilz Barris and his pesty assistant, Arne Darvin. The arrival of a Klingon ship, commanded by the arrogant Captain Koloth, does not make matters easier for Kirk. He must grant the Klingons permission for rest and recreation on K-7 under the terms of the Organian Peace Treaty, while protecting the glorified wheat. Kirk's real problem turns out to be space trader Cyrano Jones, a dealer in rare commodities including tribbles. Tribbles, living fluffballs that do nothing but coo, eat, and multiply, soon threaten to overwhelm the *Enterprise* and space station. The tribbles get into the grain bins and devour the wheat (correction: quadrotriticale). Widespread tribble casualties reveal that the grain was poisoned by Arne Darvin, whom the Klingon-hating tribbles expose as a Klingon. A disaster is prevented and a Klingon agent is exposed, thanks to the tribbles, which Kirk compels Cyrano Jones to remove from the space station. Scotty beams the *Enterprise*'s crop of tribbles to the Klingon battle cruiser as a parting gift.

The evolution of this episode is examined in detail by the leading expert on tribbles, author David Gerrold, in his 1973 Ballantine paperback book aptly titled *The Trouble with Tribbles*. Gerrold's book includes his story outline and revised final draft script, along with a wealth of information about the episode's serious and humorous aspects. "Tribbles" is the only "Star Trek" episode thus far to have been the subject of an entire book devoted to its creation and production.

"Tribbles" is loaded with dangerous situations for Kirk and company, including the introduction of a parasitic life form that could conceivably overrun the entire galaxy. Klingons are present in force; a veritable swarm of them, including a Klingon spy planted within the ranks of the Federation. The entire population of a planet comes close to being poisoned. Despite these serious occurrences, "The Trouble with Tribbles" usually prompts fans to giggle, laugh, or at least smile at the thought of other dangers, such as Kirk's treatment of Nilz Barris, Scotty's fight with the Klingons, the antics of Cyrano Jones, and Kirk's close encounter under a grain bin filled with tribbles.

The real secret of the episode's appeal lies in the successful efforts of author Gerrold to inject personal humor into the lives of Kirk, Spock, and our other *Enterprise* friends.

Kirk juggles the Klingon Captain Koloth, Cyrano Jones, Barris, and Darvin, and thousands of tribbles without dropping any of his problems before solving them. McCoy attempts to solve the tribble-overpopulation problem without ever discussing reproductive biology out loud in any detail. Mr. Scott has a knockdown, drag-out fight with the Klingons not after his captain is insulted but after his beloved *Enterprise* is ridiculed. Uhura shows her charms and Chekov has his first taste of Scotch. Even Mr. Spock gets into the act with his exclamation of ". . . He heard you; he simply could not believe his ears" (probably inspired by *Mad* magazine's "Star Trek" satire in which this gag also appeared).

Chief Engineer Montgomery Scott, who is sometimes neglected in the midst of "Star Trek" adventures, figures prominently in the action of this episode. For the first time, we learn that Scotty's passion for studying technical journals sometimes outweighs his desire for shore leave. The final punch line is also Scotty's; his solution of transporting the tribbles into the Klingons' ship is said by Mr. Scott to cause ". . . no tribble at all."

This is also one of the more prophetic "Star Trek" episodes. It forecast the presence of wildly multiplying creatures called "tribbles," and within the world of "Star Trek" fans, it was quite correct. Tribbles became an overnight sensation, and many individuals (including the episode's writer, Gerrold) began to create them. They were (and still are) sold at Trek conventions. A major toy company once advertised a line of Tribbles, and more limited quantities of the colorful furballs materialized on keychains, stickpins, bracelets, and shirts.

The cast of "Tribbles" included some veteran character actors.

Whit Bissell (Mr. Lurry) is a highly respected member of the Hollywood community. His association with the Screen Actors Guild, and his participation in endeavors to safeguard the rights of performing artists, were among the topics discussed during his first appearance at a science fiction convention several years ago. Among his many roles in motion pictures, Bissell has appeared in *The Invasion of the Body Snatchers* (Allied Artists–1956), *I Was a Teenage Frankenstein* (AIP–1957), *The Time Machine* (Metro-Goldwyn-Mayer–1960), and *The Creature from the Black Lagoon* (Universal–1953). On television, he appeared regularly as General Heywood Kirk in "The Time Tunnel" (1966–67), and he is seen in episodes of "One Step Beyond" ("Brainwave"), "The Invaders" ("Dark Outpost"), "Voyage to the Bottom of the Sea" ("The Peacemaker"), "Land of the Giants" ("Secret City of Limbo"), and "The Man from U.N.C.L.E." ("The Batcave Affair").

William Schallert (Nilz Baris) expertly created one of the most irritating Federation citizens ever encountered on "Star Trek." Schallert has been seen in dozens of motion pictures, including *The Man from Planet X* (United Artists–1951) and *The Incredible Shrinking Man* (Universal–1956). He appeared regularly on television as an aide to "Commando Cody: Sky Marshall of the Universe," and as Martin and Kenneth Lane; the fathers of *both* Patty Duke's incarnations on "The Patty Duke Show" (1963–66). He also taught school as Mr. Pomfritt on "The Many Loves of Dobie Gillis" (1959–63), and portrayed former "Control" chief Admiral Harold Harmon Hargrade on "Get Smart," in addition to guesting in segments of "One Step Beyond" ("Epilogue") and "Land of the Giants" ("The Clones").

Stanley Adams (Cyrano Jones) also wrote for "Star Trek" (he co-wrote "The Mark of Gideon"), and appeared in segments of "The Twilight Zone" ("Once Upon a Time" and "Mr. Garrity and the Graves") and "Lost in Space" ("The Great Vegetable Rebellion"). He co-starred as Jed Timmins in "Pistols and Petticoats" (1966–67). In a 1966 episode of "The John Forsythe Show," Mr. Adams appeared in an episode entitled "Funny, You Don't Look Like a Spy," along with a character named "Miss Tribble."

William Campbell (Captain Koloth) also played Trelane in "The Squire of Gothos."

Michael Pataki (Korax the Klingon) appeared regularly in the TV series "Get Christie Love," "Friends and Lovers," and "Spiderman," and co-starred with Leonard Nimoy on the "Twilight Zone" episode "A Quality of Mercy."

Space Station K-7 was an unorthodox representation of a space station, not at all resembling the more graceful wheel shapes seen in films such as "The Conquest of Space" and "2001: A Space Odyssey," and the TV series "Rocky Jones, Space Ranger."

From outside the space station, the *Enterprise* was seen orbiting K-7. From within Lurry's office, however, the *Enterprise* and the starscape could be seen remaining stationary. The starship, as seen through the station office's window, is a custom-assembled plastic model kit.

Mr. Lurry's suit appears to be left over from the wardrobe of "The Devil in the Dark."

BREAD AND CIRCUSES

Episode # 43
First draft script   5/2/67
Third revised final draft   9/12/67
Filmed in middle September 1967

WRITERS   Gene L. Coon, Gene Roddenberry (Story by John Kneubuhl)
DIRECTOR   Ralph Senensky
MUSIC EDITOR   Jim Henrickson
PHOTOGRAPHIC EFFECTS   Vanderveer Photo Effects

Captain Kirk, Mr. Spock, and Dr. McCoy visit planet 892-IV, after they discover the wreckage of the S.S. *Beagle,* a Federation vessel. On the surface they meet a band of primitive-looking people, and are then captured by a group of well-armed individuals. Kirk and company learn that the planet is technologically on a par with twentieth-century earth. The world's civilization, though, closely resembles that of ancient Rome. Kirk meets Captain Merik, the former commander of the *Beagle,* and discovers that Merik betrayed his own crew, instructing them to beam down so that they could die in the arena. The *Beagle*'s captain is now known as First Citizen Merikus, and the Empire's proconsul, Claudius Marcus, is using him to convince Kirk to beam down the *Enterprise* crew. McCoy and Spock are sentenced to die in the arena, and Kirk's execution seems imminent. Scotty, sensing that something is wrong, cuts off the planet's electrical power enabling Kirk to free Spock and McCoy. Merik saves the trio, slipping them a stolen communicator before the proconsul stabs him. Back on the *Enterprise,* Kirk realizes that the persecuted Children of the Son are actually the counterpart of the early Christians.

This episode's script went through several drafts, most of which were very different from the final episode. In one version, Spock had to be returned to the *Enterprise* so that he could be treated for the Vulcan equivalent of appendicitis. In a later (revised final) draft, Kirk violated the Prime Directive by revealing his mission to Septimus, the leader of the Children of the Son, whereupon Spock and McCoy argued over whether the directive had actually been disobeyed. As an interesting touch, the Empire's doctors studied

A rare glimpse of Dr. McCoy functioning as a scientist, not a doctor, in "A Private Little War" (DeForest Kelley).

anatomy by examining the losers in the arena events, and were anxious to learn the inside story of Mr. Spock.

This episode is a prime example of Gene Roddenberry's parallel world theory being put into practice. Paramount Pictures had contemporary studio settings that are seen here, as well as in "Miri," "A Piece of the Action," and other segments of Trek. The studio was also the point of origin for the historical epics of Cecil B. DeMille, including *The Sign of the Cross* (1932), *Cleopatra* (1934), and *The Crusades* (1936). Doubtless bits of all these wardrobes are seen in "Bread and Circuses." A few location shots completed the settings for this adventure, which could probably also have been shot in the middle of Los Angeles and at the nearest vacant baseball stadium.

There is more in this episode than just leftover costumes from older epics of early Christianity. Throughout the tale, Kirk and company presume Septimus' people to be sun worshippers, when in actuality they are *Son* worshippers. The powerful but inherently peaceful Flavius is extremely suggestive of earlier counterparts in religious epics, but the script does not push this to the point of being overly obvious to the viewer.

This is one of the few times we are treated to a serious confrontation between Spock and McCoy. The two friendly enemies are locked together in a cell and, considering their imminent death, they dwell upon the motivations for their traditional feud. Mr. Spock confides proudly that he is not afraid to die, and that he is in fact prepared for it. Dr. McCoy theorizes that Spock is not afraid of death because he has always been more fearful of living. The short conversation ends in both friends uniting in their worry over what has become of Captain Kirk. The sequence, which should have been longer, is sometimes edited entirely from the episode in syndication.

In the hands of "Star Trek's" dominant Genes (Roddenberry and Coon), this episode also becomes a marvelous satire of survival within the television industry. Proconsul Maximus presumes that because Kirk and company are so advanced on a technological level, they have never heard of the entertainment medium called television. When Kirk is told that television entails constant (literal) battles to remain in the public eye, Kirk seems to be familiar with the problem. One of the guards also taunts a gladiator with a threat that says it all: "You bring this station's ratings down, and we'll do a special on you."

Rhodes Reason (Flavius) is the brother of actor Rex Reason, seen in many science fiction and horror films, including *This Island Earth* (Universal–1955). Rhodes is featured in segments of "Time Tunnel" ("The Walls of Jericho") and "Thriller" ("Girl with a Secret").

Ian Wolfe (Septimus) has an acting career that goes back to 1935, when he appeared in *The Raven* (at Universal with Boris Karloff and Bela Lugosi), and *Mad Love* (at Metro-Goldwyn-Mayer with Peter Lorre and Colin Clive). His other feature film appearances include *On Borrowed Time* (Metro-Goldwyn-Mayer–1939) and the Sherlock Holmes film *The Scarlet Claw* (Universal–1944). On television, he can be seen in "Father Image" on "One Step Beyond," and also in "Star Trek" as Mr. Atoz in "All Our Yesterdays."

William Smithers (Merik/Merikus) is featured in "The Plant Man" on "Voyage to the Bottom of the Sea" and "The Possessed" in "The Invaders."

Watch the announcer for a glimpse of actor/vocal artist Bartell LaRue, whose voice appears in several other Trek segments.

John Kneubuhl, who wrote this episode's story, penned the "Invaders" segment "Storm." Kneubuhl also scripted some of the best episodes of "Thriller," including "Pigeons from Hell" and "Papa Benjamin."

Naming Captain Merik's ship the S.S. *Beagle* may be more than a tribute to scientist Charles Darwin's vessel. Author A. E. Van Vogt's chronicle of starship life, *The Voyage of the Space Beagle,* is a popular science fiction novel that contains many things in common with "Star Trek." This may have been a tribute to the book by authors Coon and Roddenberry. (The stories that comprise *The Voyage of the Space Beagle* originally appeared in *Astounding Science Fiction* magazine from 1939 to 1943.)

JOURNEY TO BABEL

Episode #44
First draft script   8/22/67
Second revised final script   9/19/67
Filmed in late September 1967

WRITER   D. C. Fontana
DIRECTOR   Joseph Pevney
COMPOSER   Gerald Fried
PHOTOGRAPHIC EFFECTS   Westheimer Company

The *Enterprise* is en route to an important Federation conference on a planet code-named Babel. Traveling aboard the starship are delegates from many worlds, including Vulcan's Ambassador Sarek and his Terran wife, Amanda, Mr. Spock's parents. Spock and his father have not gotten along for almost twenty years, a fact that causes embarrassment for Kirk but not for Spock. The journey is also complicated by an unidentified vessel that is following the *Enterprise,* and by tensions between various delegates, especially between Sarek and Tellerite Ambassador Gav. When Gav is murdered, Sarek is the prime suspect. The Vulcan is also suffering from a heart condition and needs an immediate operation to save his life. Spock must act as the blood donor, but when Captain Kirk is attacked and stabbed by Thelev, a member of the Andorian party, Spock assumes command of the *Enterprise* and refuses to step down until the unidentified ship following the *Enterprise* is stopped. Spock's mother is unsuccessful in her appeals to her son to permit the operation to be performed. Kirk fakes a return to the bridge to trick Spock into reporting to sick bay. The unidentified (Orion) vessel attacks and is destroyed. Thelev, who is actually a surgically altered Orion masquerading as a Tellerite, commits suicide. The operation on Sarek is successful and, cleared of the murder charge, Sarek resumes diplomatic relations with his son.

D. C. Fontana's first draft script for "Journey to Babel" tells the same story seen in the final episode with minor differences, and contains some interesting touches not found in the final version. Sarek, Amanda, and their party are *transported* aboard the *Enterprise.* (In the rewrite it was probably decided that the shuttlecraft would provide a more dramatic entrance and, if only the full-scale mock-up was used in conjunction with stock footage of the miniature, the more exciting sequence would cost less than creating a special photographic effect involving the transporter.) Amanda engaged in a short debate with her son, unsuccessfully attempting to restore father-and-son conversation between Sarek and Spock. The most important ambassadors (including Sarek and Amanda, Shras the Andorian, and Gav the Tellerite) were shown at a formal dinner, which featured dialogue that was transferred to the later buffet scene when the dinner sequence was edited out. In supplementary dialogue that did not survive into the final version, we learned that Sarek and Amanda had been married for thirty-eight (Vulcan?) years, that Sarek had been an astrophysicist before he became an ambassador, and that Sarek's father was Ambassador Shariel, a famous Vulcan.

"Journey to Babel" is one of the most popular "Star Trek" episodes, because of the introduction of Mr. Spock's parents, the profusion of colorful alien types, and the story's constant flow of action.

Mr. Spock's parents were spoken about in the earliest Trek episodes produced, but always in the past tense. In this episode we learn that Sarek does *not* resemble the hideous Balok face in "The Corbomite Maneuver," and that Spock probably *did* tell his mother he loved her during his childhood (despite his laments to the contrary in "The Naked Time").

Trek fans first learned about this segment at the same science fiction convention that premiered "Amok Time." Rumors ran rampant at that gathering; no details of the script were known, and most fans speculated that the tale would unfold at Spock's fam-

ily residence on Vulcan. But, as Sarek would say, "No matter." The finished result would be interesting and welcome regardless of its locale. D. C. Fontana, exercising her customary attention to characterization, sensitivity, and continuity, created a masterpiece of a Trek adventure in "Journey to Babel."

Throughout the story, Mr. Spock appears to feel very uncomfortable having his childhood (in the person of his mother) following him around the *Enterprise.* To conceal his anxiety from the starship crew, and from Dr. McCoy in particular, Spock attempts to act more unemotional than usual. Even though his sanity is probably at stake along with his father's life, he gives a flawless performance that fools everyone except Amanda, Kirk, and McCoy. Captain Kirk finally saves the day by indulging in a specialty of his; deception. Kirk puts on a flawless performance himself, limping back up to the bridge and concealing his true condition from his Vulcan friend so that Spock can run to sick bay and get on with the transfusion.

In the midst of the serious occurrences, there are also some very enjoyable moments, such as Amanda's revelation about Spock's pet "teddy bear" (a living Sehlat with six-inch fangs). The relationship between Sarek and Amanda is enigmatic. He is a Vulcan, and yet he indulges in an occasional hint of a smile and other expressions of love, including the finger-touching gesture.

Mark Lenard (Sarek) won the hearts of "Star Trek" fans everywhere, for his wonderful characterization of Spock's father, a role that permitted the performer to emote (outwardly) only a little. Mr. Lenard also appeared in "Balance of Terror."

Jane Wyatt (Amanda) is certainly one of the most prominent performers to appear on "Star Trek." Her stage career began in the 1930s. In 1935 she appeared in the stage version of *Lost Horizon,* and two years later she co-starred with Ronald Colman in the filmed version (directed by Frank Capra and released by Columbia Pictures). Ms. Wyatt is best remembered by TV watchers as Margaret Anderson in "Father Knows Best."

Reggie Nalder (Shras) appeared in two frightening episodes of "Thriller" ("The Return of Andrew Bentley" and "Terror in Teakwood"), and in other striking television roles including "The Dead Don't Die" (1974) and "Salem's Lot" (1979).

William O'Connell (Thelev) also appeared as an alien in "The Outer Limits" episode "The Chameleon."

Actor Billy Curtis makes a brief, no-dialogue appearance at the buffet as one of the two little, copper-colored ambassadors. Curtis also appeared in *Superman and the Mole-Men* (Lippert–1951) and portrayed a Martian in the "Superman" TV episode "Mr. Zero."

Composer Gerald Fried wrote the score for "Amok Time," and in "Journey to Babel" we also hear his melodies introducing Vulcans and violence. His sensitive "Spock theme" introduced in "Amok Time" is also featured here, and would later be used in "The Paradise Syndrome."

The only distinctive special effect seen in this segment (along with shuttlecraft stock footage and phaser effects) is the Orion starship, a star-shaped animation that is never clearly seen.

Costumes from other episodes are seen in this one, including Lazarus' suit from "The Alternative Factor" and an Organian robe from "Errand of Mercy" (both worn by ambassadors).

Two other interesting items appear in Dr. McCoy's office; the couch from Kirk's starbase quarters in "Court-Martial," and the Tantalus Field device from "Mirror, Mirror."

A PRIVATE LITTLE WAR

Episode # 45
First draft script   8/30/67
Filmed in late September, early October 1967

WRITER   Gene Roddenberry (Story by Judd Crucis)
DIRECTOR   Marc Daniels
MUSIC EDITOR   Jim Henrickson
PHOTOGRAPHIC EFFECTS   Vanderveer Photo Effects

The *Enterprise* journeys to the planet Neural, which Kirk had visited thirteen years before. Klingons are attempting to take over the planet using their customary tactic of arming a segment of the population (the Hill People) while the Klingons themselves stay hidden in the background. Spock, wounded in an ambush, is removed back to the *Enterprise* while Kirk and McCoy search for Tyree, the tribal leader whom Kirk had befriended in his youth. Kirk, bitten by a deadly Mugatu, is cured by Tyree's mystic witch-wife, Nona. While Kirk tries to convince Tyree to fight with the weapons the Federation will provide, Nona indulges in intrigues of her own. She steals Kirk's phaser, but the Hill People murder her before she can demonstrate its power. Her death turns Tyree into a fighting man. Kirk and McCoy leave the planet, deeply saddened that they could do nothing to end the hostilities and, in fact, have compounded the conflict by providing a balance of power.

Don Ingalls wrote the first draft script of "A Private Little War." This earliest version contains more specific references to the Vietnam conflict; the Neural tribesmen dress in Mongolian-type clothes, and Apella (the puppet of the Klingons) was described as a "Ho Chi Minh" type. A security man was shot during the initial attack, and Spock stayed with the landing party.

Kirk's first visit to the planet had taken place shortly before this encounter; the friendship between Kirk and Tyree developed entirely during the second visit. When the *Gumato* attacked Kirk, Spock killed it with a spear rather than use a phaser near the tribesmen. In this draft, the Klingon ship was smuggling rifles to the Hill People. There was also a personal conflict between Kirk and Krell; the Klingon had met the captain at the Organian Peace Treaty Conference and had disliked him on sight.

The story told in "A Private Little War" was patterned after the Vietnam conflict that was still raging when this episode was produced. Kirk himself cites the parallel in the situation, and mentions that a balance of power must be employed on Neural exactly as it was

Kirk and "Bones" help the wounded Mr. Spock in "A Private Little War" (William Shatner, Leonard Nimoy, DeForest Kelley).

Captain Kirk and Lieutenant Uhura, two dynamic personalities, functioning side-by-side in a tense situation (William Shatner, Nichelle Nichols).

(the Neuralese equivalent of a Terran Gypsy), manipulates her own brand of medicine combined with local folklore; an effective mixture that even astounds Dr. McCoy. Because of her "cure," we are unaware for a short while if Captain Kirk is functioning on his own, or if he is being influenced by Nona.

Nancy Kovack (Nona) created a character in this episode that is reminiscent of her role as Medea in *Jason and the Argonauts* (Columbia–1963). In that role she also danced sensuously for the hero and had occasion to rub Jason's arm with a magical leaf, just as she rubbed Tyree's arm with a narcotic plant. Ms. Kovack also appeared in episodes of television's "The Invaders" ("Task Force") and "The Man from U.N.C.L.E." ("The King of Diamonds Affair," with Ricardo Montalban).

Michael Witney (Tyree) successfully tackled a difficult role, simultaneously projecting auras of innocence and strength.

The Neuralese patrol leader was portrayed by Paul Baxley, one of "Star Trek's" regularly featured stuntmen.

The Mugato was portrayed by Janos Prohaska, whose specialized artistry also provided us with the Horta in "The Devil in the Dark" and Yarnek, the rock creature of "The Savage Curtain."

implemented in twentieth-century conflicts on Old Earth.

Kirk is operating at a disadvantage here as a result of several factors. Mr. Spock, who usually advises him on delicate matters such as these, is fighting for his life on the *Enterprise.* Dr. McCoy, who is with Kirk on Neural, is opposed to his captain's strategy. Kirk is also saddened by his part in ending a "paradise" type of existence, something he has done on other occasions. Kirk is also being affected by the calculating charms of Nona, the wife of his friend Tyree.

Tyree understands very little of what is happening to his way of life. He sees Jim Kirk as his friend "from another place," a very special person who can presumably find the means to end the nightmare initiated by the Klingon-backed Hill People.

The story's conflicts are made even more dramatic by intercutting from the planet to the *Enterprise,* to check up on Mr. Spock's condition. Spock, tended to by Dr. M'Benga (Booker Marshall), an able young physician who interned in a Vulcan ward, undoubtedly recommended M'Benga's second appearance, in "That Which Survives."

In contrast to the treatment administered by Dr. M'Benga and Nurse Chapel is the mystical cure that cures Kirk of his Mugato poisoning. Nona, a Kanutu

THE GAMESTERS OF TRISKELION

Episode # 46
First draft script 8/1/67
Original title "The Gamesters of Pentathlan"
Filmed in late October 1967

WRITER Margaret Armen
DIRECTOR Gene Nelson
MUSIC EDITOR Jim Henrickson
PHOTOGRAPHIC EFFECTS Cinema Research Corp.

As Captain Kirk, Lieutenant Uhura, and Mr. Chekov are about to beam down on a routine survey mission, they are abducted by means of a powerful transporter beam. They arrive on the planet Triskelion in the trinary star system M-24 Alpha. Kirk and company learn that they are to be used as gladiators, to fight in games staged for the amusement of the Providers, the rulers of the planet. While Mr. Spock attempts to determine where his captain has been spirited away to, Kirk and his companions experience various ordeals, including excruciating pain inflicted by Galt, the Master Thrall. When the *Enterprise* arrives and orbits Triskelion, the Providers capture the starship. To save all aboard, Kirk proposes a wager with the Providers, who are actually aged and bored beings resembling disembodied brains. Kirk is pitted against Shahna, whom he has attempted to teach about love and loyalty. He wins the contest. The Providers pay the price and free the *Enterprise* crew, as well as every Thrall on the planet.

The first draft script for "Triskelion," called "The Gamesters of Pentathlan," featured Mr. Sulu instead of Mr. Chekov. As the second season began production, actor George Takei (Sulu) was on location for a feature film role in *The Green Berets,* and was unable to appear in any Trek episodes for a few weeks. The script was changed to feature Chekov instead, and served as an excellent vehicle for actor Walter Koenig and his alter-ego, Mr. Chekov.

Most of the technologically developed aliens in "Star Trek" who outclass the Federation's sophistication usually seem to be out for other peoples' good. In "The Gamesters of Triskelion" we meet the Providers, who are certainly advanced in terms of their machines if they can abduct Kirk and company to a planet eleven light years out of their way, and threaten the *Enterprise.* The Providers, though, are not out for the good of the galaxy; they are bored, brainy types out for their own amusement.

In convincing the Providers to let their slaves go, Captain Kirk exercises a variation of his time-honored ability for outwitting machines. Perhaps the disembodied brains, after depending for centuries upon their life-support machines, have become part machines themselves, and are therefore easy prey for Kirk's talent of outthinking sophisticated mechanisms.

Whereas Mr. Chekov is assigned Tamoon, who is unattractive to say the least from the Ensign's viewpoint, Captain Kirk gets Shahna, who looks like a fugitive from a futuristic "spacemate of the month" foldout. Kirk proceeds to enlighten her in reference to various Terran customs such as kissing, hugging, and discussing freedom.

After an initial dramatic outburst, Kirk seems to forget about Lieutenant Uhura, locked away with Lars the Drill Thrall, who thinks of her as extremely attractive. Lars is a perceptive individual, for a Drill Thrall.

With all this happening, there is also some pretty heavy stuff going on within this episode. Other "Star Trek" episodes get their messages of freedom's values across while still emerging as nice, enjoyable episodes that preserve the values inherent in "Star Trek." If we look at "The Gamesters of Triskelion" seriously, there are features that are not only unnecessary but disturbing to see in Trek.

Our people are being mistreated, intentionally hurt and forced to live as slaves, in addition to being initially kidnapped. Lieutenant Uhura is left in the hands of someone who has anything but aesthetic designs on her. The question is: Is it worth all this unpleasantness to get the point of the episode across? The answer is debatable.

Angelique Pettyjohn (Shahna) appeared in the feature film *The Mad Doctor of Blood Island* (Hemisphere–1959), and was reportedly screen-tested for a role in *Planet of the Apes* (20th Century-Fox–1968). She has appeared at recent "Star Trek" conventions with an entertaining show in which she appears as Shahna as well as her real self.

Jane Ross (Tamoon) steals the show during her scenes with Chekov. Her size, together with a solid yellow complexion and bright green lipstick, clearly drove Chekov crazy with desire . . . the desire to get away from her. Although her scenes are brief, Ms. Ross shows a flair for comedy that makes her characterization one of the more pleasant features of this episode.

Dick Crockett (the Andorian Thrall) coordinated the stunts for this episode and appeared in many other Trek segments, including the well-remembered fight sequence in "The Trouble with Tribbles."

The business of a Terran spaceman teaching a cute young space lady about kissing was also seen in "Forbidden Planet," as well as in other science fiction feature films such as *Queen of Outer Space, Catwomen of the Moon,* and *Abbott and Costello Go to Mars.*

The Providers are flexible rubber creations that were lit from within and constructed with the ability to pulsate. They are extremely similar to the "space brains" that appeared in the science fiction feature, *Space Children* (Paramount–1958).

OBSESSION

Episode # 47
Filmed in early and middle October 1967

WRITER   Art Wallace
DIRECTOR   Ralph Senensky
COMPOSER   Sol Kaplan
PHOTOGRAPHIC EFFECTS   Westheimer Company

While Kirk was a young lieutenant, serving on the U.S.S. *Farragut,* a cloudlike creature attacked the ship, killing half the crew including Captain Garrovick. Eleven years later, Ensign Garrovick, the son of the late captain, is stationed on the *Enterprise.* On the surface of planet Argus X, a landing party including the ensign encounters the same gaseous creature. Kirk chases it through space, and suddenly the creature turns to fight. It enters the *Enterprise* and begins to emerge from the ventilation shaft in Ensign Garrovick's quarters. Spock is visiting the ensign at the time, and the Vulcan is the first person the creature encounters; tasting Spock's copper-based blood, it flees back toward its native planet, Tycho IV. Kirk and

Captain Kirk wearing his second season wraparound tunic in "The Immunity Syndrome" (William Shatner).

Garrovick prepare a trap, baited with a large jar of blood attached to a matter/antimatter bomb. The creature is destroyed, freeing both Kirk and young Garrovick from their guilt.

When a man thinks of only one thing to the exclusion of all else, he is obsessed. The most well-known literary study in obsession is Herman Melville's brilliant novel, *Moby Dick.* Fortunately for the *Enterprise,* Captain Kirk's motivation in this instance is *not* obsession. If it were, Kirk would have been just as unbalanced as Commodore Decker was in "The Doomsday Machine." Spock would have been correct in worrying about his captain's mental health, and Kirk might very well have destroyed his career, if not the *Enterprise.*

Kirk's reason for declaring war against the creature is based upon facts. An entity that feeds upon humanoid blood (although it does not seem too hungry for Mr. Spock's), can become either solid or immaterial at will, can propel itself through space at enormous speeds, and is *intelligent* would be most dangerous to any settlement within the galaxy, especially if it is just

about to reproduce. Spock and McCoy, not knowing all the facts initially, worry about the motivations of their captain and friend just as they do in "The Conscience of the King."

Mr. Spock betrays an emotional concern for the well-being of Ensign Garrovick. Garrovick may merit this attention solely because he is the son of one of Captain Kirk's heroes. It is also possible that Spock identifies with young Garrovick because he knows what it is like to be measured by some in the light of a famous father.

In soothing Garrovick, Spock leaves himself vulnerable. He is useless as a psychiatrist because he cannot admit to having feelings. Garrovick feels that the discussion between them is pointless, and Spock feels inadequate because of this. In the midst of both their bad feelings, the creature makes an unscheduled appearance because the ensign has accidentally left his cabin ventilation system open. While Garrovick leaves, Spock stays behind and performs one of the most illogical acts of desperation we witness in "Star Trek."

In the privacy of the closed cabin, the Vulcan technological wizard deliberately places his hands against the grid through which the creature is coming, and attempts to stop the gaseous entity while being fully aware that his strategy may cause his death. The fact that his impulsive action *does* work is strictly incidental.

Stephen Brooks (Ensign Garrovick) co-starred regularly on three past TV series; "Mr. Novack" (as Mr. Peeples, 1963–65), "The Doctors and the Nurses" (as Dr. Lowery, 1965), and "The F.B.I." (as agent Jim Rhodes, 1965–74).

The gas creature represented another challenge that was successfully met by "Star Trek's" ingenious special effects staff. In the outer space sequences, the entity was sometimes represented by colored smoke that was photographed in slow motion and double-exposed over a starry background (like the Murasaki Effect in "The Galileo Seven"). On the planet, it was either a cloud of thick smoke blown out of hidden pipes or a series of animated overlays similar to the effect used to generate the Companion in "Metamorphosis."

THE IMMUNITY SYNDROME

Episode #48
Story outline   8/14/67
Final draft script   10/17/67
Filmed in late October, early November 1967

WRITER   Robert Sabaroff
DIRECTOR   Joseph Pevney

COMPOSERS Sol Kaplan, Fred Steiner
PHOTOGRAPHIC EFFECTS Vanderveer Photo Effects

In deep space, the U.S.S. *Enterprise* encounters a huge living creature that appears to be a gigantic one-celled life form. The entity is cutting a destructive swath through the universe. Kirk realizes that his starship must stop the creature. The *Enterprise* assumes the role of "antibody" and presses forward to the attack. The entire crew feels the effects of the giant intruder; fatigue and depression set in. Mr. Spock pilots the *Enterprise*'s shuttlecraft into the "heart" of the creature, where he determines that it is getting ready to divide into two. Just before the multiplication can take place, Spock fires a charge into the creature's nucleus, killing it. Spock succeeds in returning to the *Enterprise* as his life-support systems are about to expire.

Robert Sabaroff's outline for "The Immunity Syndrome" described the creature as a living, giant virus living in a "cell" that consists of our universe. Three unmanned probes were dispatched to study the phenomenon. The weakness, depression, and fear aspects were accentuated; at one point McCoy nearly died.

McCoy and Spock were united in the enthusiasm over the chance to study the gigantic virus. The *Enterprise*'s polarity, and that of everything on board, has been reversed, which accounted for the illness of the crew. When Spock and two crewmen left the ship in a shuttle-laboratory to study the virus, their reports were radioed back to the *Enterprise* while the organism tried to digest the shuttle. Finally, the theory of the universe within a universe, within a universe, and so on was discussed, and the conclusion was reached that man's purpose may be to function as antibodies for the universe.

Costs were held down for "The Immunity Syndrome" by eliminating any guest stars for the segment. The only "guest" in this episode is the one-celled creature itself, specifically created for use in this segment of "Trek," through the wizardry of the Vanderveer Photo Effects people. The creature was probably manufactured by photographing swirling red, blue, and yellow paints, and matting them into an amoeba-shaped framework. This was combined with an outer-space background, and the little lost *Enterprise* was inserted over it all.

The scenes of the *Enterprise* entering the organism are among the best effects generated for the series, as were the scenes involving the *Galileo II*.

(An imaginative teacher of biology at a Boston area university who was a "Star Trek" fan snuck in a shot of the *Enterprise* in the amoeba on a final in microbiology. Some of her students actually identified the image as a legitimate microscopic structure.)

In "The Immunity Syndrome," we also see more of the continuing feud between Spock and McCoy. Both are science specialists, and each would like to think of himself as Kirk's closest friend. When Spock and McCoy both volunteer for this mission, their feud becomes clear to the audience, but not to Kirk who is too busy worrying about which of his friends he will "condemn" by assigning him the mission.

Despite their "jealousy," Spock and McCoy actually think the world of each other. The mission must be fulfilled by someone, and McCoy feels intense guilt that it will not be *him* going out to die. Of course, it would never occur to McCoy to be honest with Spock

Mr. Spock, in the isolation of the shuttlecraft, prepares for the worst in "The Immunity Syndrome" (Leonard Nimoy).

and tell him this. He instead expresses his guilt in sarcasm directed at Spock. Perhaps it is better this way, for Spock knows that "Bones" would only admit his liking for him if death were a certainty.

Dr. McCoy does not even wish Spock success for this reason, although he almost silently mouths a prayerful plea for his friend to come back safe and sound. Later, to keep up the pretense of this mutual feud, Spock twists the knife by commenting: "Tell McCoy he should have wished me luck."

No new footage was taken of the shuttle miniature for this episode. All the views we see are old shots, matted against new backgrounds. The interior of the shuttlecraft was altered considerably. Seats were removed and replaced with computer banks and colorful gauges. Much of this equipment appears to be left over from "The Menagerie."

But what does it all *really* mean? "The Immunity Syndrome" was produced close to the end of "Star Trek's" second season, shortly before the regular year-end battle to keep the series from being cancelled. It is therefore possible that the giant, one-celled creature is really a symbol, representing the hostile forces in broadcasting, such as rating services, sponsors, and network executives.

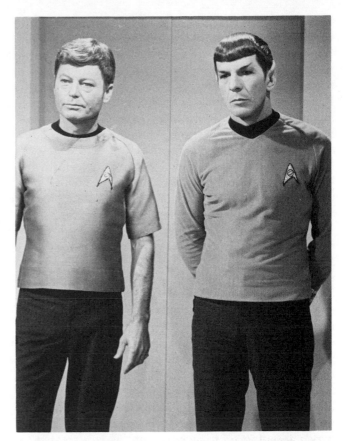

Occasionally, Dr. McCoy and Mr. Spock have been known to appear together without their customary barrage of mutually hurled insults (DeForest Kelley, Leonard Nimoy).

A PIECE OF THE ACTION

Episode # 49
First draft script   9/28/67
Final draft script   10/30/67
Original title   "Mission into Chaos"
Filmed in early November 1967

WRITERS   David P. Harmon, Gene L. Coon (Story by David P. Harmon)
DIRECTOR   James Komack
MUSIC EDITOR   Jim Henrickson
PHOTOGRAPHIC EFFECTS   Westheimer Company

One hundred years before the start of the *Enterprise*'s five-year mission, the Federation vessel U.S.S. *Horizon* visited the isolated planet Iotia. The Iotians, being an imitative people, modeled their planet's culture on a book that had been left behind by one of the *Horizon*'s crew. The book, *Chicago Mobs of the Twenties,* published in New York City in 1992, inspired the Iotians to create a flawless planetwide imitation of a fragmented and violent old-time Chicago, ruled by a handful of rival gangs. It is to this weird civilization that the *Enterprise* comes. At first the landing party, consisting of Kirk, Spock, and Dr. McCoy, have difficulty handling their situation until Kirk begins to speak in the idiom of the planet. Bela Oxmyx, a key gang leader who first makes contact with our people

and wants to use the *Enterprise*'s weapons to take over Iotia, is astounded by the change in "the Feds," as is rival gangster Jojo Krako, who has the same idea. By playing according to Iotia's unique rules, Kirk succeeds in uniting the planet's most influential gangsters and sets up a world government under Bela Oxmyx. Kirk leaves behind the illusion that the Federation will expect a "piece of the action" from Iotia's new government. McCoy accidentally leaves behind his communicator, which may lead Iotia to become a supertechnological giant by the time of their next visit from the Federation.

The first draft script for this episode was entitled "Mission into Chaos," and was more complex than the finished episode. The mission was to negotiate a friendship and alliance treaty with planet Dana Iotia Two, on the border of the Romulan Neutral Zone. Romulans had approached boss Oxmyx to make a similar deal, leading Oxmyx to defy both the Romulans and the Federation. When the Romulans learned that Kirk was talking to Oxmyx, they sent two emissaries (Rorek and Ramo) to the headquarters of boss Krako, and provided two Romulan weapons (called Morkons) so that Krako could hit Bela. Meanwhile, Kirk and company had escaped using the card game *farfel* (in which the losing hand was known as *drek*), and gained possession of the Morkons. This infuriated the Romulans, who beamed down a squad that was, in turn, surrounded by an *Enterprise* security squad. A treaty was negotiated with Kirk because of fear of the Romulans. The bosses, in trying to elect an ambassador to the Federation, each voted for themselves resulting in all twelve being beamed up to the *Enterprise* to take a trip and appear before the Federation council. The first draft ended with Kirk gleefully anticipating what would happen when the council met the Iotians.

Although "Star Trek" has its share of comedies, it is actually a serious TV series, concerned with the welfare of the universe. "A Piece of the Action" is an extremely strange "Trek" episode, because it is the only comedy segment structured around the contamination of a planetary culture by the crew of a Federation starship.

Kirk accepts the bizarre state of affairs on the planet and proceeds to play along with it to achieve a relationship between the UFP and Iotia. (A short time before, Kirk and company had experienced a more literal version of the old proverb When in Rome, Do as the Romans Do, in "Bread and Circuses.") Thanks to Kirk's acceptance of the situation, we are treated to this delightful exercise in burlesque in which Kirk and Spock become Abbott and Costello (or, if you count McCoy, more like the Three Stooges), in an adventure that could easily have been called "The Untouchables Syndrome."

There are definitely priceless moments in this episode, such as the game of Fizzbin, Kirk's attempt to drive a vintage car, the captain's impression of a "Godfather" type, and the great moment when even Mr. Spock gives in to the logic of the situation and brandishes his "heater" while showing off his zoot suit. Additional funny moments, such as Mr. Scott's attempts to master twentieth-century slang, and Mr. Krako's abbreviated visit to the *Enterprise,* are well worth waiting for.

Anthony Caruso (Bela Oxmyx) has appeared as gangsters on many TV series, most notably in "The Adventures of Superman" ("Tsar of the Underworld").

Victor Tayback (Jojo Krako) turned in an excellent performance as a Damon Runyon-type, leading to the speculation of what would happen to the galaxy if Boss Krako ever went into partnership with Harry Mudd. Tayback appeared regularly on three TV series; as Officer Haseejian in "The Streets of San Francisco" (1972), as bar owner Pizuti in "The Super" (1972), and as police captain Barney Marcus in "Griff" (1973–74). He is most famous for his recurring role as Mel, the diner owner in "Alice."

John Harmon (Tepo), also seen in "The City on the Edge of Forever," was featured in episodes of "The Twilight Zone" ("The Dummy") and "The Adventures of Superman" ("The Runaway Robot," "Superman in Exile," and "The Magic Necklace").

"A Piece of the Action" is a good example of an economical "Star Trek" episode. The vintage wardrobe and props featured in the tale would ordinarily be expensive to rent or buy, but Trek was photographed at the Desilu/Paramount studios where the television series "The Untouchables" was also produced. The trappings of that famous TV series were taken out of mothballs for this segment. The classic cars used in the episode probably also came from this same store of specialized props.

The somewhat unsuccessful attempt of Kirk to drive "the flivver" (which was probably recorded into the captain's log with the greatest of reluctance) is significant as well as humorous; it is the only time in any "Star Trek" episode that we see Kirk (or any other *Enterprise* crew member) use a surface vehicle for transportation.

BY ANY OTHER NAME

Episode #50
Revised final draft script   11/7/67
Filmed in middle November 1967

WRITERS   D. C. Fontana, Jerome Bixby (story by Jerome Bixby)
DIRECTOR   Marc Daniels

Rojan and his fellow Kelvans journey to our galaxy from their native planet Kelva, in the Andromeda Galaxy. The Kelvans, who were originally bulky, tentacled creatures, have assumed human form while determining whether planets in our galaxy would be suitable for colonization by the Kelvan Empire. Rojan and his followers, ready to return home with their report, lure the *Enterprise* to them and succeed in taking over the starship, with the intention of using the *Enterprise* to take them back to Andromeda. Preparing for the 300-year journey, Rojan, Kelinda, Hanar, Tomar, and the other Kelvans transform most of the *Enterprise* crew into small tetrahedronal blocks. Kirk, Spock, McCoy, Scotty, and others are spared from this conversion process and plot to win back control to their starship. To do this, our people take advantage of the aliens' newly acquired human emotions. With the aid of carefully cultivated jealousy, plus a little food, alcohol, and drugs, the Kelvans soon find themselves at each others' throats, enabling Kirk and company to retake the *Enterprise* and restore the crew to normal. The Kelvans realize that they cannot return to Andromeda; they are too human to survive there and they agree to permit the Federation to locate a world for them to settle down on.

The situation in this episode is very serious. An *Enterprise* crewman is murdered, the starship itself is commandeered, and the Federation vessel is forced to leave our galaxy on a journey that will take over three centuries to complete. Despite the circumstances, "By Any Other Name" manages not to take itself too seriously and emerges as an enjoyable adventure.

One of the most charming points about "Star Trek" is its ability to fill us with confidence about the future of mankind, without ignoring human weaknesses. This segment is filled with reminders that humans are not perfect creatures, and that sometimes our "imperfections" may also serve as our greatest security.

Beginning with the discovery that Kelvans in their human state are capable of delighting in their new physical capabilities, Captain Kirk and his friends launch an attack in which the "superior" aliens are helplessly outclassed.

In one unforgettable sequence, Mr. Scott goes to work on the alien Tomar, determined to put him out of action by getting him dead drunk. Scotty's entire stock of drinkables is exhausted in his valiant attempt, right down to a final bottle of alien liquor which even Mr. Scott knows nothing about, except that "It's green!" Scotty almost walks away from the successful attempt, leaving the alien unconscious. At the last minute, just as Scott is about to leave his cabin to report complete success, the engineer joins the alien in a state of total, temporary oblivion.

As usual, in the midst of the crisis, Captain Kirk finds a reason to go woman-hunting. The attractive female alien Kelinda is effectively seduced by the captain, firing the romantic instincts of the alien leader Rojan. Pleased with his victory, Kirk would later use almost identical tactics in "The Wink of an Eye."

As a result of Kirk's strategy, the Kelvans discover that they are no longer alien to this galaxy. They have adapted too well, and are finally part of the erratic humanoid population of the Milky Way.

Warren Stevens (Rojan) is no stranger to filmed science fiction, having served early in his acting career as Doctor Ostrow, crewman on Cruiser C-57D in "Forbidden Planet." Stevens starred regularly in three television series; as Lieutenant Storm in "The 77th Bengal Lancers" (1956–57), as one of the repertory company of talented performers in "The Richard Boone Show" (1963–64), as Eliot Carson in "Return to Peyton Place" (1972–74); he was also the voice of film production tycoon John Bracken in the first season of "Bracken's World." (During this series' second season, the role of Bracken was played by Leslie Neilsen, who had portrayed Stevens' Commander Adams in "Forbidden Planet.") Mr. Stevens also stars in many TV series segments, including episodes of "The Outer Lim-

its" ("Keeper of the Purple Twilight"), "The Twilight Zone" ("Dead Man's Shoes"), "One Step Beyond" ("The Riddle"), "Land of the Giants" ("Brainwash" and "A Place Called Earth"), "The Time Tunnel" ("One Way to the Moon"), "Voyage to the Bottom of the Sea" ("The Saboteur," "Deadly Invasion," and "Cave of the Dead"), "The Man from U.N.C.L.E." ("The Children's Day Affair") and "Science Fiction Theatre" ("Time Is Just a Place").

Robert Fortier (Tomar) gave a great straight-faced performance as Scotty's hangover-fated drinking partner.

The purple galactic barrier reappears in this episode, utilizing the same views seen in "Where No Man Has Gone Before," this time superimposed onto the *Enterprise*'s regular view screen.

The costume created for Barbara Bouchet (Kelinda) features a William Theiss trademark, the flair for exposing otherwise ignored parts of the human anatomy to create extremely sensuous effects. The midsection of Ms. Bouchet's costume tapers along with her streamlined figure.

To obtain *his* costume, Rojan undoubtedly raided the uniform stores of Space Station K-7, or the pergium mines of Janus VI; his suit is identical to those seen in "The Trouble with Tribbles" and "The Devil in the Dark."

RETURN TO TOMORROW

Episode # 51
Story outline   5/9/67
Second revised final draft script   11/22/67
Filmed in late November, 1967

WRITER   Gene Roddenberry
   (Story by John T. Dugan)
DIRECTOR   Ralph Senensky
COMPOSER   George Duning
PHOTOGRAPHIC EFFECTS   Vanderveer Photo Effects

Answering a mysterious S.O.S. from a dead planet, Kirk, McCoy, and Dr. Anne Mulhall are transported underground to confront the three survivors of that planet's civilization. Sargon, Thalassa, and Henoch have preserved their conscious minds within circular containers and have remained in this state for centuries. They now wish to "borrow" the bodies of Kirk, Spock, and Dr. Mulhall so that they can construct android bodies to house their minds permanently. Sargon assures Kirk that his people will be safe, their minds encased for a short time within the same containers his people now occupy. McCoy is concerned because of the high metabolic rate necessary for "possession." The real danger, however, is Henoch, who appropriates Spock's body without any intention of giving it back. Henoch telepathically forces Nurse Chapel to poison Sargon (in Kirk's body), and then destroys the globe that houses Spock's mind. Fortunately, Spock's consciousness had already left the globe, hidden within the mind of Nurse Chapel. Henoch is tricked into leaving Spock's body. Sargon and Thalassa vacate the bodies of Kirk and Dr. Mulhall voluntarily, announcing (after one last kiss) that they will be happy to roam the universe together in their noncorporeal state.

"Return to Tomorrow" explores the plight of the highly advanced aliens who miss their human condition. Their predicament, and the individuals themselves, are treated with dignity in a fine script that is well directed and supplemented with a sensitive musical score.

Kirk is immediately responsive to Sargon's request to borrow his body and two others of his crew. Dr. McCoy is against the project, because of the physical dangers involved. When Kirk sees that McCoy's mind is not thinking beyond the issue of personal risk, Kirk indulges in another of his series of pep talks in favor of exploration, education, and the establishment of relations with alien life forms, despite personal risk.

What Kirk has not taken into account is that, although Sargon seems to be as idealistic as himself, the others in the situation (Henoch and Thalassa) are very much subject to human failings. Henoch has been trying to interest Thalassa in becoming a participant in the universe's oldest romantic triangle and he has been repeatedly spurned. Now that he has a body once again, Henoch renews his romantic campaign with the greatest of vigor. This makes things extremely awkward. Sargon, in Kirk's body, is completely absorbed in his newfound host and is supposedly off somewhere flexing Kirk's muscles.

Fortunately, Sargon is not as guillible as he seems. He is really off assuring the safety of Spock's mind (which is much more worthwhile than "Spock's Brain") by spiriting the Vulcan's consciousness into the body of Nurse Christine Chapel.

Christine Chapel had first declared her love for Mr. Spock in "The Naked Time." Spock apologized to her then, and later repeated that it would not be possible for him to acknowledge his feelings for Christine. But Spock was now more humanized. It would have been interesting to learn who was really responsible for picking Chapel's body for Spock. It is doubtful that the nurse had the initial idea, although she couldn't have objected too loudly to the notion. (It *was* a matter of life and death!) Although it is stated that Chapel was picked because her choice would have seemed unlikely to Henoch, it might also have been Spock's consciousness who suggested the strategy to Sargon.

This episode marks yet another challenge for the acting talents of Leonard Nimoy. In "Return to To-morrow" he portrays not only the stoic Vulcan but the evil and calculating Henoch as well. The actor completely changed his facial expressions and other mannerisms to make his transition. In earlier episodes, Nimoy had proven his ability for humorous roles; in this episode, he also proved what a good "heavy" he could make as well.

William Shatner's trancelike mannerisms in the underground cavern where he is first "possessed" by Sargon add greatly to the episode. Shatner amplified the mystical nature of the exchange by imitating the behavior of a medium being manipulated by his "control."

"Return to Tomorrow" was the "Star Trek" debut of actress Diana Muldaur (Dr. Anne Mulhall/Thalassa), who returned as Dr. Miranda Jones in "Is There in Truth No Beauty." Ms. Muldaur has been a regular cast member of three TV series. In the CBS soap opera "The Secret Storm" she portrayed Ann Wicker, in the short-lived ABC series "The Survivors" (1969–70) she was Belle, and in "McCloud" she appeared as Chris Coughlin, star Dennis Weaver's romantic interest. Diana Muldaur also appears in the horrifying feature film *The Other,* and co-starred in Gene Roddenberry's TV pilot/TV movie *Planet Earth.*

Composer George Duning once again proved himself the best choice to compose the most sensitive scores required for "Star Trek." His melodies for Sargon and Thalassa suggest ancient power coupled with love and desperation.

The impression of shifting consciousnesses was reinforced by the use of an echo effect on the voices of the possessed Kirk, Dr. Mulhall, and Mr. Spock.

The android body was portrayed by an unidentified actor whose upper body and head were completely encased with sprayed-on latex. In the famous "Star Trek Blooper Reel" we see him removing his makeup while someone tells him "You wanted show business? Well, you *got* it." In the same reel we see William Shatner clowning around by grasping Sargon's globe and announcing "Have no fear: Sargon is here!"

PATTERNS OF FORCE

Episode # 52
Filmed in early December 1967

WRITER   John Meredyth Lucas
DIRECTOR   Vincent McEveety
COMPOSER   George Duning
PHOTOGRAPHIC EFFECTS   Westheimer Company

Historian John Gill, stationed on the planet Ekos as a Federation cultural observer, has violated the Prime

Directive. Arriving at Ekos, the U.S.S. *Enterprise* is fired upon by atomic missiles, although records indicate that the planet does not possess nuclear technology. Kirk, who was taught history by Gill at Starfleet Academy, beams down with Spock to investigate. In an effort to centralize Ekos' political structure, Gill has re-created a frightening imitation of Nazi Germany. Intending only to re-create the efficient and united aspects of the Nazi bureaucracy, Gill has been subjugated by his aide, Melakon, who runs Ekos as a police state, using the drugged Terran as a figurehead. Kirk works with the underground of Zeon, a nearby planet whose inhabitants have become Melakon's targets for persecution. Infiltrating Melakon's headquarters as Gill is about to deliver a rigged speech on television, Kirk and McCoy revive the historian. Gill denounces the regime before Melakon kills him. The Ekotians turn on Melakon, and Gill's misguided experiment comes to an end.

It seems that whenever we meet people from Kirk's Academy days, or anybody who is respected within the Federation, they are revealed as geniuses who are really tragedies waiting to happen. Some, like Dr. Roger Korby, do not have any control over their impending tragedies; others, like Dr. Tristan Adams, appear to court disaster willingly. John Gill appears to be the only one of the crowd to achieve his own downfall out of sheer idiocy.

It was unfortunate that John Gill was apparently scatterbrained enough to forget the original Nazi regime's negative factors, and it was even more unfortunate that the ambitious and deranged Melakon was there to capitalize on Gill's mistakes.

Just as historian Gill overreacted in his attempts to aid Ekos, it appears that this episode's script was overdone as well. The trappings of the Nazi regime were re-created by using Hollywood's store of props and uniforms that were left over from World War II-type movies. But "Patterns of Force" also sought to re-create the horror of Nazi Germany by creating a caricature that included corruptions of the names of original Nazi victims. The victimized planet is Zeon (for "Zion"), and principal Zeon character names include Isak (an altered form of "Isaac"), Devod (for "David"), and Abram (Abraham).

There was even a "Sara." The young heroine's name is Daras, spell it backward and discard the "d," and if this seems farfetched try taking the name of the episode's party chairman, Eneg, and spell it backward. It's a wonder that there also weren't characters named Llib and Dranoel.

Although the episode's subject matter is certainly no laughing matter, "Patterns of Force" also features a very funny scene. Kirk, who has recently been soundly flogged, bends over to furnish Spock with a human platform so that the Vulcan can facilitate their escape. As Kirk suffers in silence, the Vulcan

steps all over his highly sore back and seems to drag out the proceedings as long as possible. The prisoner in the next cell wonders if the two are committing suicide; Kirk wonders if their neighbor is right, after Spock has been on his back for awhile.

After the prison breakout, things become even more serious, with a graphic description of a young girl's terrible death and the information that many other Zeons are being slaughtered. And still we have more humor, this time provided by Dr. McCoy, who has beamed down with uniform boots that are too tight.

David Brian (John Gill) is a respected performer, who should have been featured in this episode instead of being seen only as a living corpse for a few seconds. Brian is best remembered as the star of the TV series "Mr. District Attorney."

Skip Homeier (Melakon) would later appear as Dr. Sevrin in "The Way to Eden." A former child actor, Homeier starred in his own TV series as detective Lieutenant "Dan Raven" (1960–61). He also appears in episodes of "Voyage to the Bottom of the Sea" ("The Day the World Ended," "The Amphibians," and "Attack"), "Science Fiction Theatre" ("The Dark Side"), "One Step Beyond" ("The Bride Possessed"), and "The Outer Limits" ("Expanding Human," with Jimmy Doohan and Keith Andes).

Valora Noland (Daras) is featured in "The Man from U.N.C.L.E." segment "The Round Table Affair."

Three important "Star Trek" personnel also appear in this episode; Paul Baxley (first Nazi trooper), Bart La Rue (the announcer), and Ed McCready (a guard).

THE ULTIMATE COMPUTER

Episode # 53
Filmed in middle December 1967

WRITER   D. C. Fontana (Story by Laurence N. Wolfe)
DIRECTOR   John Meredyth Lucas
COMPOSERS   Fred Steiner, Sol Kaplan
PHOTOGRAPHIC EFFECTS   Howard A. Anderson Company

Dr. Richard Daystrom, who developed the Duotronic Breakthrough in computer technology twenty-five years ago, fears that he is regarded as a prodigy who has lost his touch. Obsessed with proving himself, Daystrom devises a method to use his own mental patterns to program his new M-5 computer and convinces Starfleet Command to test the M-5 by installing it on the U.S.S. *Enterprise*. Although Captain Kirk expresses reservations about the machine's presence, and the consequential reduction in the starship's crew, the tests appear successful at first. But when Commodore Robert Wesley leads a squad of four starships in practice maneuvers against the *Enterprise,* the M-5 takes over complete control of the starship and responds as though the attack is real, destroying the crew of the starship *Excalibur.* Dr. Daystrom suffers a nervous breakdown. Kirk, treating the M-5 like an errant child, forces the machine to realize what it has done. This enables Scotty and Spock to "pull out the plug" of the machine, restoring the *Enterprise* to Captain Kirk's control.

As man's machines become more complex, the relationship between human beings and their manufactured servants becomes more complex as well. In "Star Trek's" era, mankind has reached a point at which his machines are incredibly complex by our century's standards. Captain Kirk occupies a central position in man's future dealings with machines.

Kirk has been known to destroy machines that dominate humans, as the populations of Beta III ("The Return of the Archons"), Eminiar VII ("A Taste of Armageddon"), and Gamma Trianguli VI ("The Apple") could testify. He cares deeply about the rights of man versus the power of the machine, especially since Samuel T. Cogley prevented the captain's career from being destroyed by a computer's "testimony" in "Court-Martial." Kirk seems to have a good understanding of when an individual's life is being overly influenced by a machine; but does this understanding extend to *his own* life as well? This is a matter open to debate, when one considers that Kirk appears completely committed to a relationship not with a woman but with the starship *Enterprise.*

In "The Ultimate Computer," Captain Kirk finds his command of the *Enterprise* being threatened by the M-5 computer. This discovery leads Kirk, McCoy, and the audience to speculate whether the captain's reservations against the machine are inspired by sincere doubts about the M-5, or by a professional (and possibly *personal)* jealousy of encountering a machine that is better qualified than himself to command the *Enterprise.*

Dr. McCoy's diagnosis of the situation is difficult to reach because the doctor shares the captain's suspicion of machines, as well as a great concern for his friend's future, but must reach conclusions based upon facts, not emotions. McCoy aids Kirk by reminding him of his human identity. Mr. Spock sympathizes more with Kirk than with the machine. Spock's devotion to "that man on the bridge" is expressed eloquently in this episode.

Fortunately for Kirk and company, the situation is completely and finally resolved as the M-5 (and Dr. Daystrom as well) reveals itself to be incompetent to command the *Enterprise.* Unfortunately, wresting command from the machine cannot be achieved by convening an extraordinary competency hearing (like the one Commodore Stocker called against Kirk in "The Deadly Years"). Before control of the *Enterprise*

is regained, an engineering staffer is dead, an ore freighter is destroyed, the crew of a starship is destroyed, and the *Enterprise* is almost decimated as well.

In the final analysis, "The Ultimate Computer" serves as a powerful reminder that if man patterns his machines after himself, the machines bear his weaknesses as well as his strengths.

Actor William Marshall (Dr. Richard Daystrom) turns in a beautiful performance as a man as closely committed to his machine as Kirk is devoted to the *Enterprise.* Marshall's imposing physical stature combines perfectly with his vocal and emotional projection. His Daystrom is intended to be an exceptional human being and emerges as one of the most magnetic individuals who ever beamed aboard the *Enterprise.* In feature films, Marshall appeared as a genie in *Sabu and the Magic Ring,* and is best known as *Blackula,* the screen's first black vampire. On television, he has appeared in episodes of "The Man from U.N.C.L.E." ("The Vulcan Affair" and "The Maze Affair" with Barbara Luna) and "Secret Agent" ("The Galloping Major").

The ore freighter destroyed by the M-5 was stock footage of the Sleeper Ship created for "Space Seed." The majority of the other optical effects in "The Ultimate Computer" were also stock footage, including the battle between the *Enterprise* and the other starships. One brief scene of four starships heading toward the *Enterprise* was accomplished by taking one view of the starship miniature and printing it four times, in two different sizes, matted into the *Enterprise*'s main viewing screen.

Animation was used to create a colorful power beam that stretched between the M-5 and the *Enterprise* engines. The small M-5 control box on Kirk's command chair was a good constant reminder to Kirk (and the audience) that Daystrom's computer was intruding upon the captain's command of the *Enterprise* throughout much of this episode.

THE OMEGA GLORY

Episode # 54
First draft script   6/7/65
Filmed in middle and late December 1967

WRITER   Gene Roddenberry
DIRECTOR   Vincent McEveety

The *Enterprise* discovers the starship *Exeter* in orbit around planet Omega IV, its crew reduced to crystallized powder by a deadly virus. Kirk, Spock, and McCoy, who are exposed to the disease, beam down to the planet and meet *Exeter* Captain Ronald

Tracey. Tracey believes that something in Omega's atmosphere can induce immortality in humans, as it apparently has in the planet's Oriental rulers, the Kohms. To assure a place for himself on this planet, Tracey has violated the Prime Directive, using phaser power against the Kohms' enemies, the Yangs. When the Yangs capture Tracey's village, Kirk discovers that Omega is the scene of a parallel evolution resembling war-ravaged counterparts of Yankees (Yangs) and Communists (Kohms). Tracey attempts to denounce Kirk and Spock by inferring that Spock is a representative of Satan. Kirk, however, gains the confidence of the Yangs by reciting their "worship words," which are actually a distorted version of the Preamble to the United States Constitution. Prolonged exposure to Omega's atmosphere has cured our people of the virus and, with Tracey under arrest, Kirk and company leave Omega IV.

Because the first draft script of "The Omega Glory" was originally written early in "Star Trek's" evolution as a possible second pilot, the earliest "Omega" script is markedly different from the finished episode. Some of these differences have already been mentioned in Chapter 3. In addition, the *Enterprise*'s instrumentation was closer to the technology of "The Cage," with more devices recognizable by today's technical standards.

The ship's computer with the female personality seen in "Tomorrow Is Yesterday" was also presented in this draft; Spock berated Kirk for having the computer overhauled on a female-dominated planet.

The U.S.S. *Argentina*'s chief medical officer was shown dissolving on camera.

On Omega, Kirk discovered an apparently rejuvenated Captain Tracey. Tracey's transformation was finally explained as psychosomatic facial and emotional improvement caused by his respite from starship command decisions.

The most interesting differences between the first draft and the completed episode concern Mr. Spock. In the script, Spock uses his allure to obtain information from a young Omegan female. Later, the Vulcan touches the top of another woman's head and she becomes docile, sinking to the floor where she sits in a dazed condition. (This may have been the initial inspiration for what later developed into the Vulcan Nerve Pinch.) Spock brought the girl out of her trance by closing her eyes and slapping her face. This "hypnosis," witnessed by another Omegan, led to Spock's being declared a servant of the devil.

The first draft climaxed in a western-style gunfight between Kirk and Tracey, during which Tracey shot Spock twice, once at point-blank range with an old-fashioned rifle. Spock survived because his heart was located in his stomach area instead of in his chest.

"The Omega Glory" is an exciting action episode,. similar to "A Private Little War" because both take place in outdoor settings and involve frontier-type cultures. In this episode, we have the added threat of a misguided starship captain who has broken the Prime Directive. The Yangs and Kohms are both intriguing cultures. Kirk's experience at initially attempting to befriend the Yang captives is highly dramatic, and Spock's helpless position as he attempts to communicate with Kirk, who has been knocked cold by the huge Yang, is well played.

A good deal of drama is provided by Captain Tracey, a strong figure even in the throes of his obsession with immortality. His fights with Kirk, and even the stares exchanged by the two conflicting figures, are genuinely dynamic.

The device of having Mr. Spock denounced as "a devil" adds another touch of novel excitement to this episode.

With all this drama and novelty, "The Omega Glory" is usually remembered by "Star Trek" fans because of guest appearances by the American flag and the United States Constitution. The parallel affects Kirk profoundly, causing his impassioned reading of the Constitution's preamble. As Kirk reads it he is reminded that, just as the United States was composed of colonies banded together under one banner, the United Federation of Planets is similarly structured. At one point, the episode's musical score includes a few bars of the "Star Spangled Banner."

The close-ups of Mr. Spock's eyes, as he is willing the Omegan woman to bring the communicator to him, are very effective. The same scene also furnishes a good look at the "working" communicator (which we also glimpse in "Friday's Child").

ASSIGNMENT: EARTH

Episode # 55
First draft pilot script   11/14/66
First draft series script   12/20/67
Filmed in early January, late February 1968

WRITERS   Gene Roddenberry, Art Wallace (Story by
  Gene Roddenberry)
DIRECTOR   Marc Daniels
MUSIC EDITOR   Jim Henrickson
PHOTOGRAPHIC EFFECTS   Vanderveer Photo Effects

The *Enterprise*, having traveled backward in time to the Earth of 1968, intercepts an incredibly powerful transporter beam. A humanoid named Gary Seven materializes aboard the starship claiming to be an Earthman who had been raised on another planet unknown to the Federation. After a battle in which he proves immune to a Vulcan Nerve Pinch, Mr. Seven escapes to Earth. Kirk and Spock follow to learn the truth about him, and to make sure that he does nothing to jeopardize Earth. Seven has been dispatched to our planet to prevent the launching of a series of orbital bombs. With the aid of the bewildered and reluctant Roberta Lincoln, a young secretary, Seven eludes Kirk and transports himself to Cape Kennedy to sabotage the controls of a rocket. Scotty attempts to beam Seven aboard before his mission is completed but Roberta accidentally activates controls that divert Seven to his New York City headquarters. Kirk and Spock race to stop Seven from doing anything more to the rocket, but at the last instant he convinces Kirk of his sincerity. Kirk permits Seven to detonate the rocket, saving history from being altered. As the *Enterprise* returns to its own time, Gary Seven and Roberta ready themselves for other missions.

"Assignment: Earth" first appeared as a half-hour series pilot script, dated November 14, 1966 (while the first season of "Star Trek" was still in production). In the original concept, Gary Seven was an Earthman from the future who had been sent back to our era to combat the Omegans, an evil alien race that had mastered time travel. Working as a private investigator in a large, unspecified city, Mr. Seven was assisted by the bewildered young Roberta Hornblower in his fight against the shape-changing Omegan agents, Harth and Isis. The Omegans, who could mentally enslave Earthmen into being their servants, strove to change history to their advantage by corrupting various Terran individuals. Gary Seven's amazing scientific devices included a computer that could alter the recent past, canceling out damage that had been done by the Omegans. No one from the *Enterprise* appears in this pilot version of the script; there is not even any mention of "Star Trek."

When "Assignment: Earth" apparently did not sell as a separate TV series, the concept was rewritten into the "Star Trek" format. The series-oriented first draft script (dated December 20, 1967) established the *Enterprise*'s presence in our era by having the bridge crew watch an episode of NBC's TV series "Bonanza" on the view screen. Gary Seven's transporter beam came from *very* far across space. After Seven was confined in the *Enterprise* brig, he confided his mission to Dr. McCoy, turning the tables on Bones by asking him to think like "a Doctor, not a mechanic." Young Roberta *London,* recruited by Mr. Seven, was beamed up to the *Enterprise* for interrogation. The frightened Roberta was soothed by Uhura who reassured her that she was still among Earth people.

In "Tomorrow Is Yesterday" it was established that, with proper safeguards and precise calculations, the U.S.S. *Enterprise* could navigate back and forth in time, as well as space. With a variety of story possibilities that were not dependent upon time travel, "Star Trek" producers Gene Roddenberry and Gene L. Coon did not utilize this ability until this episode.

Throughout the episode, we are not told everything about Gary Seven. In fact, we know that he first attempts to lie to Roberta, telling her that he's from the CIA. How do we know he is telling the truth when he tells Captain Kirk that he's an Earthman raised on another planet? During a fight, we see that Mr. Seven is immune to Mr. Spock's Vulcan Nerve Pinch. Although this could be the result of some form of martial arts training, it may also be the result of Mr. Seven's not really being human at all. Gary is also familiar with Mr. Spock's people, the Vulcans; he knows that the *Enterprise* is from the future because the ship's human crew is working side by side with a Vulcan. Have Seven's people influenced the history of Vulcan as well as of Earth?

There are other unanswered questions about Gary Seven's people. How many worlds have they aided, and how many years has their work been going on? Could Seven's people be unknown even to the powerful Organians of "Star Trek's" era? It is even possible that Gary's mentors are the legendary race known as the Preservers. Presuming that Gary's people are not humanoid, or are no longer dependent upon physical bodies, it is even possible that *they* are Organians, operating from an unknown planet other than Organia.

Gary Seven may not even be as humanoid as he appears. His co-worker, Isis, is an established shapechanger. The audience has no idea whether Isis is a cat who can appear as a woman, a woman who can appear as a cat, or a third variety of creature who can assume both appearances at will. The same possibilities can apply to Gary as well.

These unknown quantities and possibilities are balanced by the presence of Roberta Lincoln, a unique young lady who passes the ultimate sanity test; experiencing an impromptu "close encounter" with Mr. Spock in twentieth-century New York City.

Robert Lansing (Gary Seven) is an extremely popular performer who has starred in many motion pictures, including *The 4-D Man* (Universal–1959, with Lee Meriwether) and *Empire of the Ants* (American International Pictures–1978, with Joan Collins). His television series starring roles include "The Man Who Never Was" (as Peter Murphy and Mark Wainwright in 1966), "Eighty-Seventh Precinct" (as police Detective Steve Carella, in this beautifully produced 1961–62 adaptation of Ed McBain's mystery series of police adventure), and "Twelve O'Clock High" (as Brigadier General Frank Savage, 1964–66). Lansing also guest-starred in episodes of "Thriller" ("The Fatal Impulse," with Elisha Cook, Jr.), "One Step Beyond" ("The Voice"), and "The Twilight Zone" ("The Long Morrow," with Mariette Hartley).

Teri Garr (Roberta Lincoln) first attracted attention on "The Sonny and Cher Show," followed up by appearances on "The Sonny Comedy Revue." Her usual, *Close Encounters of the Third Kind* (Columbia–1978) and *Oh God* (Warner Brothers.–1978). The beautiful Ms. Garr's characterization of Roberta is best described by a comment little Bobby Benson directed at Klaatu in "The Day the Earth Stood Still:" "I like you, . . . you're a real screwball."

Other performers in this episode include Bruce Mars (Finnegan in "Shore Leave") as a policeman, Bartell La Rue (whose vocal talents are featured in "The City on the Edge of Forever" and other Trek episodes) as the voice of mission control, Paul Baxley (stunt double and actor in other Trek segments) as the Cape Kennedy security chief, and James (Scotty) Doohan as a Cape Kennedy radio voice.

"Assignment Earth" makes extremely effective use of NASA footage. Views of Cape Kennedy and selected rocket launches are expertly edited into the episode's action. The "Star Trek" cameras never actually visited the Cape; imaginative use of split-screen photographic techniques created a composite of a Paramount studio soundstage and a rocket awaiting launch. For the close-ups of Gary Seven crawling along the rocket's gantry crane, rear-projected views of the Cape were integrated with footage of actor Lansing crawling along a small mock-up set constructed in the studio.

Music editor Jim Henrickson did a great job adapting preexisting "Star Trek" music to produce an entertaining and effective score for this episode.

The Beta-Five computer console was later slightly modified to appear as the Atavachron in "All Our Yesterdays."

The last scene, in which Kirk and Spock stand talking with Gary and Roberta, and Kirk comments that "I'm sure you two will have many interesting adventures together," establishes that "Assignment Earth" was intended as a pilot film for a series chronicling the exploits of Gary Seven and Roberta.

Third Season Production Credits

WRITERS Various
DIRECTORS Various
PRODUCER Fred Freiberger
CO-PRODUCER Robert H. Justman
EXECUTIVE PRODUCER Gene Roddenberry
ASSOCIATE PRODUCERS Edward K. Milkis, Gregg Peters
STORY CONSULTANT Arthur H. Singer
THEME MUSIC Alexander Courage
ADDITIONAL MUSIC Various
ART DIRECTOR Walter M. Jefferies
DIRECTORS OF PHOTOGRAPHY Jerry Finnerman, Al
   Francis
FILM EDITORS Bill Brame, Donald R. Rode
UNIT PRODUCTION MANAGER Gregg Peters
ASSISTANT DIRECTORS Gil Kissel, Claude Binyon, Jr.,
   Gene DeRuelle
SET DECORATOR John M. Dwyer
COSTUMES CREATED BY William Ware Theiss

PHOTOGRAPHIC EFFECTS Various
SOUND EFFECTS EDITOR Douglas H. Grindstaff
MUSIC EDITOR Richard Lapham
RE-RECORDING MIXER Gordon L. Day, CAS
PRODUCTION MIXER Carl W. Daniels
SCRIPT SUPERVISOR George A. Rutter
RECORDED BY Glen Glenn Sound Co.
CASTING Joseph D'Agosta, William J. Kenney
MAKEUP ARTIST Fred B. Phillips, SMA
HAIR STYLIST Pat Westmore
GAFFER George H. Merhoff
HEAD GRIP George Rader
PROPERTY MASTER Irving A. Feinberg
SPECIAL EFFECTS Jim Rugg
*A Paramount Production in association with Norway
   Corp.*
*Douglas S. Cramer; Executive vice president in charge of
   production*

SPECTRE OF THE GUN

Episode # 56

Story outline   4/19/68
Revised final draft script   5/14/68
Original title   "The Last Gunfight"
Filmed in late May 1968

WRITER   Lee Cronin (Lee Cronin—pseudonym for Gene L. Coon)
DIRECTOR   Vincent McEveety
COMPOSER   Jerry Fielding
PHOTOGRAPHIC EFFECTS   Westheimer Company

The *Enterprise* encounters a "warning buoy" marking the territorial boundary of Melkotian space. Kirk ignores the message to turn back, and, in return, the telepathic Melkots transport Kirk, Spock, McCoy, Scotty, and Chekov to a surrealistic re-creation of a Wild West town. Our people are to reenact the famous gunfight at the OK Corral, cast in the losing roles. When Mr. Chekov is "killed" before the gunfight, Spock detects an inconsistency with the actual historical gunfight. Using this, plus a trio of Vulcan Mind Melds, Spock enables his friends to accept the gunfight as an illusion. When the "Earps" shoot, their bullets pass harmlessly through Kirk and company. Kirk refuses to murder the "Earps" and "Doc Holliday" although he knows that they are insubstantial Melkotian manifestations. The Melkots become convinced of Kirk's peaceful intentions and invite our people to stay and establish diplomatic relations.

The story outline for this episode (entitled "The Last Gunfight") omitted reference to Mr. Chekov. A security officer appeared in Chekov's place and was killed, but he did not return unharmed as Chekov did in the final version. The sequence with the warning buoy was not included, and the aliens were called "The Shawnian."

Throughout the outline, Kirk and company experienced extremely frustrating occurrences. The "townspeople" could come and go as they pleased; the *Enterprise* people were stopped by force fields geared to their individual body readings. When Kirk visited the "Earps" office to convince him that he was *not* who they thought he was, he pointed to Spock's pointed ears. "Wyatt" responded that "Frank McClowery" was, in fact, pointy-eared.

In a good bit of characterization, the outline had McCoy react with fascination at "Doc Holliday's" tuberculosis symptoms; he then offered to cure Holliday, but the illusion declined treatment.

The outline climaxed when Kirk and company ambushed the pseudo-Earps. The "Earps" began commenting on "the code of the West" being violated, and the illusion abruptly vanished. The Shawnians had decided that the humans were insane because the "code" was in Kirk's memories, but he did adhere to it. The aliens did not believe in punishing irrational creatures, and the starship was freed.

In the final episode, it would have been more effective to show Chekov being killed while defending Kirk or Spock and not while romancing an "illusion woman." The Federation beliefs reflected in "Spectre of the Gun" were not introduced in this episode: Kirk's reluctance to kill also saved the day in "Arena."

Depicting the voice of the "warning buoy" as a telepathic message perceived by every *Enterprise* crewmember in his or her native language is a plot device that fits neatly into "Trek's" previous episodes. Spock points out that telepaths can be dangerous enemies; he is undoubtedly remembering what happened on

Captain Kirk readies himself for the Vulcan Mind Meld in "Spectre of the Gun" (William Shatner, Leonard Nimoy).

For one of several moments from the series, two minds from two different worlds are merged in "Spectre of the Gun" (William Shatner, Leonard Nimoy).

Talos IV with the Talosians in "The Cage." The need to ignore illusions and to concentrate on realistic solutions is also present in "The Squire of Gothos," "Shore Leave," and "Catspaw."

Kirk's decision to continue onward in the face of unknown perils originates in "Where No Man Has Gone Before." "Spectre of the Gun" is a worthwhile episode if only because it combines these bits of Federation (and Kirk's) philosophy for the first time, supplemented with Spock's recollections of the first pilot's adventure, and the episode's surrealism.

The settings for "Spectre of the Gun" are only partially completed because they are based upon Kirk's fragmented and idealized memories of this place and time. In the exterior views of buildings we see only random walls and rooftops. In the saloon, pictures apparently hang in midair. The corral itself consists only of a front fence and a swinging sign.

The combination of spotlights and odd camera angles on the "Earps" in the climactic sequences make them appear as soulless phantoms. To emphasize the artificial appearance of this place and its people, no attempt is made to hide the shadows of windblown trees on the red sky backdrop.

The final execution and editing of the Mind Melds and gunfight is flawless. The aforementioned touches, supplemented with views of our people standing fearlessly and almost unblinking as the bullets rip harmlessly through them into the fence, are definitely successful in achieving their desired impact.

Jimmy Doohan's talented voice is once again heard as the vocalization of the "warning buoy." The Melkotian itself is voiced by the talented character actor Abraham Sofaer, the Thasian of "Charlie X."

William Zuckert (the sheriff) was regularly seen as the police chief in "Captain Nice."

Ron Soble (Wyatt Earp) was featured as Jim the Indian on ABC's 1966–67 TV series "The Monroes" (which also co-starred Liam Sullivan of "Plato's Stepchildren").

The town barber is Ed McCready, who also appears in "Dagger of the Mind" and "Miri."

The Melkotian buoy resembles an hourglass, a symbol of suspense and danger (as in "The Wizard of Oz").

The Melkot itself was constructed by artist Mike Minor, who did extensive work on "The Tholian Web," designed much of the film *Flesh Gordon,* and worked on *Star Trek—The Motion Picture.*

The Melkot was cast in rubber. The eyes were translucent plastic, through which bright lights were reflected. In addition, strong colored lights were shown onto the front of the creature. Swirling smoke on the miniature set completed the eerie illusion of the "floating" head. An unlikely (but possible) story indicates that the uneven bottom of the creature was composed of strands of spaghetti taken from the studio restaurant.

ELAAN OF TROYIUS

Episode # 57
First draft script   5/16/68
Filmed in late May, early June 1968

WRITER   John Meredyth Lucas
DIRECTOR   John Meredyth Lucas
COMPOSER   Fred Steiner
PHOTOGRAPHIC EFFECTS   Howard A. Anderson Company

The Tellun star system has two planets, Elas and Troyius, which have been at war with each other for centuries. It is imperative that the two worlds make peace with each other because although the system is part of the Federation, the Klingons have their eyes on it. To assure peace, Elaan, the Dohlman of Elas, beams aboard the *Enterprise* for her voyage to Troyius and her marriage to that planet's leader. Elaan is arrogant and seems to be ignorant of the importance of her coming marriage. Petri, the Troyian ambassador, attempts to teach Elaan enough manners to adjust to life on Troyius. Elaan stabs him for his trouble. The future of the marriage, the alliance, and the fate of this system now become the responsibility of Captain Kirk, who begins to educate Elaan. Kirk's task is complicated not only by the Dohlman's reluctance but by her body chemistry; when she cries, her tears cause the captain to fall in love with her. A Klingon vessel, threatening the *Enterprise,* is aided by Kryton, a member of Elaan's party who sabotages the starship's power. Elaan's jewelry proves to be composed of dilithium crystals, which enable the *Enterprise* to defeat the Klingon ship. Kirk frees himself from Elaan's spell by remembering that his first love is the *Enterprise*. Charmed by Kirk, Elaan determines to succeed in her mission to unite Elas and Troyius.

With a name derived from Helen of Troy, and plot elements from *The Taming of the Shrew*, "Elaan of Troyius" is an enjoyable "Star Trek" episode with a lot of action, suspense, and intrigue.

In "Journey to Babel" we see that the *Enterprise* has facilities for transporting a large number of passengers. In this episode, however, Elaan is quartered in Lieutenant Uhura's cabin. The unselfish lieutenant has volunteered her quarters for the Dohlman's use, but the reasons for this necessity are unknown. Perhaps Kirk and Uhura feel that Elaan would feel more at home in a custom-decorated cabin than in a bland, undecorated room.

In being permitted to see Uhura's quarters (which are also seen in "The Tholian Web"), we learn even more about the popular communications officer. Relics of animal life (including a zebra skin bedspread, which probably means that the zebra will not be an endangered species in "Star Trek's" era), sculptures, masks, and decorated wall panels reveal Uhura's individuality and artistic taste.

Kirk's efforts at "taming" Elaan, and the Dohlman's attempts to avoid the captain's teachings, are balanced by the diplomatic efforts of Petri, the Troyian ambassador whose mission in this episode is probably the most difficult he has ever been assigned in his entire professional life.

France Nuyen (Elaan) had previously worked with William Shatner during the Broadway run of *The World of Suzie Wong*. Her most famous role in motion pictures is probably as the young daughter of "Bloody Mary" in *South Pacific* (20th Century-Fox-1956). Ms. Nuyen also appeared opposite Jeffrey Hunter in the 1966 science fiction/espionage film *Dimension Five,* and is featured in "The Man from U.N.C.L.E." episode "The Cherry Blossom Affair."

Jay Robinson (Lord Petri) is best known as the mad emperor Caligula in the feature film epics *The Robe* (20th Century-Fox-1953) and *Demetrius and the Gladiators* (20th Century-Fox-1954). On television, he has appeared regularly as the star of the Saturday morning series "Dr. Shrink," and is featured in "The Night of the Living House," a segment of "The Wild, Wild West." In "Elaan of Troyius" he accomplished the difficult task of bringing Petri to life as an irritating yet likable character.

The Klingon ship, which appears for the first time in "Star Trek" in this episode (unless one counts the different design used briefly in "Friday's Child"), is a wooden miniature that included no interior lights. The model is eighteen inches long, carved from wood, and painted gray and green. It is currently housed in the National Air and Space Museum in Washington, D.C., and was recently loaned back to Paramount Pictures' Magicam installation for reference use during the making of *Star Trek—The Motion Picture*.

William Ware Theiss created an impressive assortment of costumes for this episode. Elaan, who beamed aboard in a provocative ceremonial costume, was also seen in a leisure dress, an ornate silver suit, and an orange gown. All of these creations bore the Theiss trademark of exposing various portions of the limbs and torso to produce an extremely sensuous effect, complementing the natural contours of the woman in the costume.

Additional costume challenges were met by dressing Elaan's male entourage in costumes that are reminiscent of ancient Japanese ceremonial costumes producing a result not unlike the wardrobe designed by John Armstrong and Rene Hubert for the futuristic sequences in *Things to Come* (United Artists/London Films-1936).

A scene in the *Enterprise*'s recreation room, showing Kirk, McCoy, and Uhura watching Spock play his Vulcan harp, was apparently edited from this episode before it was first televised.

THE PARADISE SYNDROME

Episode #58
Story Outline   3/22/68
First draft script   5/29/68
Final draft script   6/3/68
Original title   "The Paleface"
Filmed in middle June 1968

WRITER   Margaret Armen
DIRECTOR   Jud Taylor
COMPOSER   Gerald Fried
PHOTOGRAPHIC EFFECTS   Vanderveer Photo Effects

On a beautiful Earthlike planet, which is threatened by a collision with a huge asteroid, Kirk and company discover peaceful tribesmen greatly akin to American Indians. Near the village is a huge obelisk, covered with incomprehensible writing. As Kirk explores this structure he falls through a trapdoor and is exposed to a strange ray that renders him unconscious. McCoy and Spock fail to find him, and are forced to leave him on the planet while the *Enterprise* attempts to destroy the asteroid. Kirk revives afflicted with partial amnesia and is accepted by the Indians, who revere him as a god. The *Enterprise,* attempting to fracture the asteroid with high-power phaser beams, damages its engines and is forced to precede the asteroid back to the planet traveling at sublight speed. The journey takes several months, during which Kirk has fallen in love with, and married, the beautiful priestess, Miramanee. Meanwhile, Spock deciphers the writings on the obelisk, which his tricorder had recorded, and learns that an ancient race called the Preservers had "seeded" the planet with its population and provided an asteroid deflector, which is housed within the obelisk. Kirk, who is now known as Medicine Chief Kirok, has no idea how to activate the obelisk. Spock and McCoy beam down just as Kirk and Miramanee are being stoned by the frightened tribesmen. The asteroid is deflected and Kirk's memory is restored, but the pregnant Miramanee dies along with Kirk's unborn child.

The story outline of this episode, called "The Paleface," indicated that this planet was located in a meteor and asteroid belt and was the only world in the region that contained life. The asteroid deflector was originally represented as a totem pole covered with hieroglyphics. Kirk's amnesia was brought about by a head wound, which led to the captain's confused mental state. Spock, unable to destroy the asteroid, beamed down to evacuate the Indians. Kirk (Kirok) perceived the landing party as enemies; Spock stunned his captain and returned him to the *Enterprise,* transporting him up along with the Indian population. The Indians had to be sedated aboard the ship; it was the first time they were ever in such confined areas. Kirk's memory was restored when he realized that he was fighting his friend, Spock, The deflector mechanism was hidden in a vast, underground area in a cavern the Indians said was inhabited by a spirit. The Indians, including Miramanee who *survived* pregnant with Kirk's child, were returned to their planet.

"The Paradise Syndrome" is an atypical "Star Trek" episode in several respects. Although the story centers around Kirk, we see the captain functioning not in his traditional capacities but as the leader of a tribe of primitives on a planet far from the location and life-style of the *Enterprise.* When Captain Kirk is transformed into Medicine Chief Kirok, his role does not really change too much.

Kirok is still a leader of men, whose abilities are recognized as very special and whose experience is needed in order to enable his village to survive. Kirk's old-West roots are brought to life here, as he tackles the elements of the planet. Memories of Federation technology enable the Indians to enjoy the benefits of irrigation, food preservation, and the use of lamps for the first time. His attraction to the opposite sex is still very evident, with the most beautiful woman in the tribe returning the attraction.

Even in this situation, when Kirk has escaped from the technology and the protocol of the *Enterprise,* he is still haunted by visions of her; dreams of "the strange lodge that moves through the sky." His obligations in the capacity of medicine chief, however, fail to

William Shatner's intense and magnetic portrayal of Captain Kirk gives "Star Trek" an appeal that ranges beyond its format and scripts.

negate the familiar situation of Kirk's having "no beach to walk on" for a limited time.

The exotic aspects of this episode were aided greatly by the location photography that is evident throughout much of the segment. The initial view of the lake and the Indian village far away evokes an extremely peaceful image. When seen together with Kirk, Spock, and McCoy, the guiding forces behind the command of the *Enterprise,* the village represents the return to the simpler past that McCoy refers to as "the Tahiti syndrome."

Dr. McCoy's wish to beam down to a planet and be received as a godlike figure is realized by Kirk in this episode, although the captain does not recall the wish at the time. As McCoy beams down with Spock after Miramanee has been fatally injured, the good doctor is also finally received as a representative of "The Great Spirit," fulfilling his year-long ambition.

The imposing appearance of the obelisk also aids the visual success of this episode. The size and shape of the obelisk provide an effective contrast to the Indian culture; it produces an impact somewhat akin to that produced by the rectangular alien object of *2001: A Space Odyssey*.

Sabrina Scharf (Miramanee) had portrayed a native American before, in the "Daniel Boone" episode "Requiem for Craw Green," which featured Jeffrey Hunter and Pamelyn Ferdin. Ms. Scharf also appeared in "The Man from U.N.C.L.E." sgement "The Pop Art Affair."

Rudy Solari (Salish) had recurring roles in four television series; as Frank in "Redigo" (1963), Nagurski in "The Wackiest Ship in the Army" (1965–66), Casino in "Garrison's Gorillas" (1967–68), and as the attorney in "Return to Peyton Place" (1972–74). He is also seen in segments of "The Outer Limits" ("The Invisible Enemy") and "Voyage to the Bottom of the Sea" ("The Last Battle").

Richard Hale (Goro) appeared in the "Thriller" episode "Remarkable Dr. Markesan."

Director Jud Taylor began his Hollywood career as an actor, appearing in "The Fugitive" ("Glass Tightrope"), and as Dr. Thomas Gerson, a recurring role on "Dr. Kildare" (a series Taylor also produced). His television directorial credits include horror, fantasy, and space-oriented TV movies, such as *Weekend of Terror, Search for the Gods, The Disappearance of Flight 412, Future Cop* (a 1976 effort concerning a robot policeman), and *Return to Earth* (a 1976 drama depicting the emotional state of astronaut Buzz Aldrin after his return from the moon).

Composer Gerald Fried contributed much beautiful music to "Star Trek" episodes, and other TV series (including the offbeat "Mr. Terrific" and "It's About Time"). In "The Paradise Syndrome," we hear sensitive melodies that suggest the alien yet familiar nature of the extraterrestrial Indian community seen in this episode, and the love affair between Kirk (Kirok) and Miramanee. His battle sequence melodies are reminiscent of his score for "Amok Time," whereas his traditional Indian-type music was the precursor to some of Fried's brilliant score for *Roots*.

The views of the *Enterprise* traveling backward in front of the asteroid are extremely effective, as are the phaser beam and deflector beam sequences involving the purple heavenly body (which would later be featured in "For the World Is Hollow and I Have Touched the Sky").

The purple memory beam that gives Kirk his amnesia, and the orange-yellow deflector beam both add to the visual quality of this episode.

The most intriguing scene in "The Paradise Syndrome" occurs as Kirk revives the partially drowned Indian boy, using artificial respiration. The boy had been thought dead by the tribesmen; Kirk's "miraculous" deed assures his acceptance as a visiting deity, just as actor Walter Huston's similar deed led to his being treated as a god in *The Treasure of the Sierra Madre* (Warner Brothers–1948).

THE ENTERPRISE INCIDENT

Episode #59
First draft script   6/7/68
Final draft script   6/13/68
Filmed in late June 1968

WRITER   D. C. Fontana
DIRECTOR   John Meredyth Lucas
COMPOSER   Sol Kaplan
PHOTOGRAPHIC EFFECTS   Howard A. Anderson Company

Captain Kirk, while apparently in an overworked and confused state, takes the *Enterprise* into Romulan space. The Federation starship is immediately surrounded by three Romulan ships which demand Kirk's surrender. Kirk and Spock beam aboard the Romulan flagship, where Kirk is denounced by Mr. Spock, who confesses that his captain has been under severe stress and has acted without orders to enter Romulan territory. The female Romulan commander is highly interested in Mr. Spock and attempts to induce him to defect to the Romulans. Spock seems to be interested in her offer. McCoy is beamed aboard the Romulan vessel and, as he examines Kirk, the captain turns and attacks Spock. Spock uses a Vulcan form of self-defense, apparently killing Kirk, and the captain's body is returned to the *Enterprise*. The entire affair has been a hoax to gain possession of the Romulan Cloaking Device. Kirk, surgically altered to resemble a Romulan, is beamed back aboard the flagship and steals the device. After the theft, Spock is declared a traitor and, as he awaits execution, he is located and beamed back to the *Enterprise* by Scotty, along with the Romulan commander. The *Enterprise* escapes when the Cloaking Device is hurriedly put into operation by Scotty. Kirk is left with the unexpected bonus of the capture of the Romulan commander. And Spock is left to contemplate the deceit he has practiced on the Romulan commander.

The first draft script of "The Enterprise Incident" had the Vulcan Death Grip applied at the back of the neck, rather than directly over the face. The Cloaking Device was a prismatic type of mechanism, situated in a laboratory, a spare constructed for another ship, rather than an already operational model. Both Kirk and McCoy were surgically altered to appear Romulan, and they both accompanied Spock back to the Romulan vessel to steal the Cloaking Device. When Spock was discovered in the forbidden corridor, McCoy had to talk Kirk out of attempting to rescue him. Spock, in turn, lied and gave the impression that he had been alone and had destroyed the device.

In "Balance of Terror" we meet the Romulans whom we discover to be a mysterious and honorable people. In "The Enterprise Incident," when we learn of an alliance between the Romulans and the Klingons, we presume that the sole motivation for the alliance is a mutual wish between the two empires to defeat the United Federation of Planets. The situation is comparable to the alliance between the Japanese and the Nazis during World War II.

Like "Balance of Terror," this episode is a study in comparative values. Vulcans do not lie, so the Romulan commander believes Mr. Spock's statements regarding his captain. Spock probably justifies his actions in the Terran half of his mind. He has not lied, he has merely conducted a charade to preserve the sense of values to which he has pledged his loyalty. Neither the Romulan Commander nor Spock bears the other any grudge, and whereas there can be no further relationship between them, it is understood that each was merely seeking to fulfill his duty.

Kirk's "nervous breakdown" is masterfully played. He appears to be unsure of his priorities and distrustful of everyone. His apparent attempt to kill Spock is disturbingly convincing, and for a while we are not sure of what is really happening.

Part of this doubt comes from William Shatner's effective repertoire of mannerisms during his "mad" scenes. He lets his arms hang loosely at his side, and permits his mouth to hang open at times. The desperation he conveys in "The Enemy Within" is effectively transformed into a skillfully conveyed image of disorientation, distrust, and fear.

The issue of invisibility is not new to science fiction literature. Many individuals have practiced this art in films; in Trek, Bele flew an invisible ship in "Let This Be Your Last Battlefield."

Joanne Linville (the Romulan commander) has appeared in other science fiction, fantasy, and horror-oriented TV series episodes, including segments of "The Invaders" ("Moon Shot," "The Pit"), "The Twilight Zone" ("The Passerby"), "One Step Beyond" ("The Dead Part of the House," "Moment of Hate"), and "Great Ghost Stories" ("William Wilson").

John Meredyth Lucas also directed segments of "The Night Gallery," including "The Housekeeper," "The Hands of Borgus Weems," and "The Different Ones."

The *Enterprise* corridors, painted and lit differently than usual, were decorated with alien devices and doubled for the Romulan ship's corridors. Costumes and helmets from "Balance of Terror" were reused in this episode, too, as were portions of "Nomad" from "The Changeling" and a fiberglass globe from "Return to Tomorrow," which were combined to produce the cloaking device.

Photographic effects abound in this episode; special mattes were generated of the Klingon ship, and skillfully combined with views of the *Enterprise* to provide effective visual drama.

The ear tips on the Romulans were not as graceful as those used for Vulcans. This may have interfered with their logical development as compared to Vulcans, which may explain why Romulans drink from square drinking glasses.

Mr. Spock's unique characteristics make him the best first officer in Starfleet (Leonard Nimoy).

Lieutenant Uhura, the beautiful communications officer of the U.S.S. *Enterprise* (Nichelle Nichols).

AND THE CHILDREN SHALL LEAD

Episode # 60

Story outline   3/22/68
First draft script   6/18/68
Filmed in late June and early July 1968

WRITER   Edward J. Lakso
DIRECTOR   Marvin Chomsky
COMPOSER   George Duning
PHOTOGRAPHIC EFFECTS   Vanderveer Photo Effects

Arriving at the planet Triacus, the *Enterprise* finds that the scientists in the Starnes scientific expedition have all committed suicide to escape an unknown, evil presence. The scientists' children are unharmed and seem strangely oblivious to their parents' deaths. Beamed aboard the starship, the children are cared for while Kirk and company attempt to learn the full truth. The evil presence is an entity named Gorgan who has sneaked aboard the *Enterprise* with the intention of siphoning off his power through the children and using the starship to take him to planets where he can lure other innocents into following him. To prevent the *Enterprise* crew from fighting him, Gorgan renders Kirk incapable of giving orders, frightens the ship's officers with illusions, and influences Spock's mind into believing that there is nothing wrong. Kirk's distress shocks Spock back to normal. The children are shown tricorder tapes of their parents and their graves, and suddenly see Gorgan not as "the friendly angel" but for what he actually is; an ugly, evil force rendered harmless by the loss of its followers. The entity fades away and all is well.

The depiction of children in the grip of evil forces usually produces an effective mood of horror, as it did in films such as *The Space Children* (Paramount–1958) and *Invaders from Mars* (20th Century-Fox–1953). This episode examines not only the effects of the evil Gorgan on the children but the nature of the evil as well. It introduces the living embodiment of negative values and studies how it attacks those in proximity to it, concentrating upon the children as they are the most easily deceived potential victims around, especially after experiencing the loss of their parents.

Captain Kirk treats Gorgan much like he would treat any entity (or machine) that prevented humanity from attaining its maximum of happiness, fulfillment, and freedom of choice. After initially encountering Gorgan in a cave on Triacus, Kirk proceeds to drag the evil influence out of the darkness, into the open. On the bridge of the *Enterprise,* Kirk exorcizes the evil Gorgan from his starship.

The sequences in which the *Enterprise* crew are affected by Gorgan's illusions are effective, although they are extremely reminiscent of events that occur in "Charlie X." Kirk's fear of losing command only serves to give him the strength he needs to defeat Gorgan. Mr. Sulu, who is prone to fantasizing about being a swashbuckler, fancies that he sees an endless tunnel of approaching swords. Uhura's innermost fear of being old and disease-ridden is made apparent here for the first time.

Noted attorney Melvin Belli's portrayal of Gorgan appears stilted, possibly because of the static positions Mr. Belli had to maintain as a result of the photographic effects involved. Belli's delivery is nonemotional, not the sort of impassioned presentation one would expect from a top defense attorney. "Star Trek" fans prefer the more eccentric concept of the evil entity Redjac, as conveyed by actor John Fiedler in "Wolf in the Fold."

Pamelyn Ferdin (Mary Janowski) appeared regularly in "Lassie" (as Lucy Baker in 1972), "The Paul Lynde Show" (as Sally Simms, 1972–73), and "The Odd Couple" (as Felix's daughter, Edna Unger, 1970–

75) before landing her recurring role in the successful Saturday morning science fiction TV series, "Space Academy."

Craig Hundley (Tommy Starnes) also appeared as the captain's nephew, Peter Kirk, in "Operation: Annihilate."

The "flybys" of the starship *Enterprise* are very well done in this episode, utilizing some novel and dramatic angles of the well-lit miniature starship.

The old age makeup employed on Nichelle Nichols in this episode is very effective. Thin latex appliances, like those created for William Shatner, DeForest Kelley, and James Doohan in "The Deadly Years," were applied to Nichelle's cheeks, lips, eyes, neck, and hands to create the impression of sagging skin. Even though the makeup is well designed and nicely applied, Ms. Nichols is too beautiful to allow the illusion to work for more than an instant.

As in the case of "Miri," when director Vincent McEveety's son Steven appeared in the cast (reportedly along with William Shatner's daughters), the role of young Steve O'Connel in this episode is portrayed by Caesar Belli.

SPOCK'S BRAIN

Episode #61
Story Outline   4/22/68
Filmed in middle July 1968

WRITER   Lee Cronin (pseudonym for Gene L. Coon)
DIRECTOR   Marc Daniels
COMPOSER   Fred Steiner
PHOTOGRAPHIC EFFECTS   Westheimer Company

While the starship *Enterprise* is on a routine mission in deep space, a young woman materializes on the bridge, touches a button on her wristlet, and everyone aboard the starship is rendered unconscious. When Kirk and company awaken, they are alarmed by Spock's absence, which is horribly explained when McCoy summons them to sick bay and they see Spock lying motionless on a diagnostic bed. The young woman has stolen Spock's brain! Kirk follows the alien's trail to the sixth planet in the Sigma Draconis system. McCoy rigs up a device to remotely control Spock's brainless body and they, joined by Kirk and Scotty, beam down. On the planet's surface they discover a primitive tribe, but underground they find a race of beautiful women living in a scientifically advanced environment. Kirk and his people match wits with the females, who are using Spock's brain to run their planet's power. The women are led by Kara, the brain thief. After some difficulty, Kirk locates Spock's brain and, using a wondrous device called "The Teacher," McCoy gains enough temporary knowledge to reverse Kara's damage and restore Mr. Spock to normal.

Lee Cronin's story outline for "Spock's Brain" featured the Vulcan's disembodied mind using Vulcan disciplines to avoid insanity. When Kirk discovered Mr. Spock's voice coming over his communicator, Spock asked him to disconnect his brain from the machines that were keeping it alive; a reaction caused by the Vulcan's belief that his new existence was nonproductive. Later, when Spock became aware that his brain was coordinating the vital functions of an entire planet, Spock had to be ordered to stop his control over the machines so that his brain could be restored to his body. There was no mention of a "teacher machine," and in the first draft Dr. McCoy received no instantaneous transfusion of "the old knowledge." The operation to restore Mr. Spock's brain was performed after McCoy studied the planet's advanced surgical techniques, combining them with his previous medical experience. Working with alien doctors, McCoy did most of the actual work. As Spock began to recover, he announced that the Doctor had not done enough studying; some of the Vulcan's ganglia had been jangled, but with the aid of mental disciplines he was already beginning to regain physical control over himself.

The concept behind this episode is an interesting one. It has long been known that the human brain is "the controller" of the body's functions, and as such it is the most efficient mechanism of this type known. It is not inconceivable that another planet's scientific developments would revolve around coordinating the machinery of its world with a humanoid brain; provided, of course, that the techniques existed for securing the brain unharmed, and hooking it up to the required machines with its power sufficiently amplified to run everything required of it.

The problems with this episode lie in the manner in which Spock's brain is taken and restored, as well as the manner in which Spock's disembodied intelligence communicates during his ordeal.

The introductory scenes of Kara beaming aboard the *Enterprise,* putting the entire ship to sleep, and stealing Mr. Spock's brain are effectively weird, as is the first view we see of Spock's body lying in sick bay. In "The Menagerie," Dr. McCoy confirms that medical science, in "Star Trek's" era, has learned to tie into all bodily organs *except* the brain. It therefore seems highly unlikely that, while McCoy could sustain life within Spock's brainless body in sick bay, he could cause the body to walk and still keep it "alive" despite the lack of machines (except for a hatlike device) while the landing party is planetside.

IS THERE IN TRUTH NO BEAUTY?

Episode #62
Story outline   5/24/68
First draft script   7/5/68
Filmed in late July 1968

WRITER   Jean Lisette Aroeste
DIRECTOR   Ralph Senensky
COMPOSER   George Duning
PHOTOGRAPHIC EFFECTS   Cinema Research

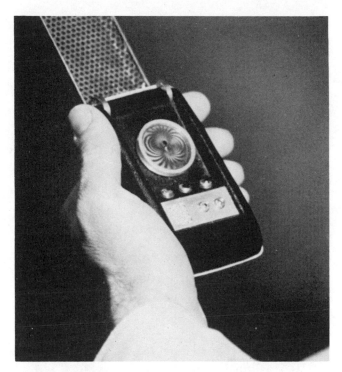

The "working" communicator includes a rotating central disk and blinking lights.

When Mr. Spock's voice is heard over Kirk's communicator, it is not explained how the Vulcan's brain manages to speak in Spock's customary voice, even though his body is separated from his mind. Although it was established in "The Menagerie" that Spock could electronically recreate any voice with the aid of computers, it is difficult to accept the Vulcan applying his knowledge under such adverse circumstances. It would have been much more effective to have Scotty rig the universal translator to receive Spock's brain's telepathic emanations.

The sequence involving "The Teacher" machine and its transformation of Dr. McCoy is very well done. DeForest Kelley's performance, together with the machine's design and the cinematography, are effective, culminating in McCoy's observation that, with the knowledge of the Teacher, ". . . A child could do it" (restore Spock's brain back to its rightful place).

The operation itself is difficult to accept, as Spock advises the doctor how to proceed when the knowledge of the Teacher begins to wear off. To believe that the complex procedures could be carried out while the patient converses with the operating physician taxes one's imagination to the limit.

It almost would have been preferable to have Scotty put Spock's brain and body through the transporter, materializing everything where it belonged. This procedure would also have explained how Mr. Spock goes through this entire episode and never loses his well-trained head of hair.

The Medusans are a race with wonderful mental abilities, including navigational capabilities exceeding those of humanoids. Physically, the Medusans appear as energy patterns arranged in frequencies and colors that are too dazzling for humanoid eyes to behold. In a pioneering experiment, the lovely Dr. Miranda Jones beams aboard the *Enterprise* with Kolos, a Medusan encased within a protective container. Traveling with them is Larry Marvick, one of the men who designed the *Enterprise*'s engines. Marvick, rendered slightly irrational by his love for Miranda, is to aid in an exchange of technical information with the Medusan, "translated" by the telepathic Dr. Jones. Marvick, however, attempts to kill the Medusan. The sight of the alien, without its protective box, renders Marvick insane, and in the throes of his madness he visits the engineering section and plunges the *Enterprise* into another dimension. Mr. Spock dons a protective visor and melds minds with the Medusan to guide the *Enterprise* back home. But Spock forgets his visor when he separates from Kolos. The Vulcan's life and sanity are in danger until Dr. Jones puts aside her jealousy of Spock's superior telepathic abilities and cures the Vulcan by entering his temporarily disordered mind. Finally, Miranda's ability to look upon the Medusan without harm is explained; she is completely blind, her dress being a complex sensor web that gives her the ability to "see" obstacles and judge distances.

The story outline of "Is There in Truth No Beauty?" featured Dr. Miranda Jones, described as a professional telepath taking part in the first collaboration between humans and Medusans, a project codenamed *Ariel.* Larry Marvick was honest in expressing his dislike of the Medusan; he conveyed his sentiments directly to Miranda. After Marvick's exposure to the Medusan, he invaded *the bridge,* killed two crewmen, wrecked the communications console, and accelerated the *Enterprise* out of our universe and into the void. Dr. Jones and the Medusan had previously "discussed" the theoretics of navigating in interdimensional voids, which led Mr. Spock to mind-meld with the Medusan. The meld took hours to complete;

Spock's complex entanglement with the alien was cancelled out by Miranda's guiding the Vulcan through a mental re-creation of his fight with Captain Kirk seen in "Amok Time."

"Is There in Truth No Beauty?" is one of the most successful "Star Trek" episodes in terms of its faithfulness to the series' regular characters and the tale's constant surprises.

The story has sensitivity, mystery, action, and more than the hint of romance between Miranda and the Medusan. As a result of Larry Marvick's nature, jealousy also enters into the picture, and because of Marvick's plunging the *Enterprise* into the interdimensional void, suspense and adventure are also present.

The focal point of the tale is Dr. Miranda Jones, a beautiful young scientist who inspires love from Marvick, evokes elements of envy from Mr. Spock, brings the gentleman to the surface of Dr. McCoy, and attracts the interest of Captain Kirk. Miranda wants nothing to do with these men; her sole concern is developing her telepathic rapport with Kodos, the Medusan.

We have witnessed a Terran and an alien romantically involved in other Trek segments. The Companion was ultimately united with Zephram Cochrane in "Metamorphosis," but only after she merged with Terran Nancy Hedford. Amanda Grayson married Sarek of Vulcan and managed to produce an offspring who is the best science officer in the fleet. Carolyn Palamas was attracted to Apollo in "Who Mourns for Adonais," but circumstances did not permit their relationship to flourish. This time around, Miranda presumably achieves her relationship with Kolos.

The mystery involved with this unusual relationship, in which two entities are attracted to each other's minds regardless of physical differences (Kolos may even lack *any* physical form at all), is that although the sight of Medusans drives Terrans insane, Miranda can look upon Kolos without harm. Throughout most of the episode we have no idea of whether Dr. Jones is *already* insane, or if there is some other explanation. The scene at dinner, as Miranda perceives that someone (Marvick) is contemplating murder, is very well played.

Scotty almost signs the death warrant for the *Enterprise*. Knowing that Marvick is one of the ship's engines' designers, he cannot resist inviting the engineer to come and try out the controls of the starship. Unfortunately, Marvick takes Scotty up on his invitation while he is insane (resulting in near disaster for the ship, but some of the best photographic effects in the series: beautiful animated purplish effects like those in "Where No Man Has Gone Before").

The device of having Mr. Spock join his mind with that of Kolos is a beautiful idea, which is very well handled. Leonard Nimoy is given a rare chance to emote as Mr. Spock, as the Vulcan/Medusan enjoys his newfound ability to smile and spouts poetry to Lieutenant Uhura. But this good-natured conduct is a prelude to Spock (or Kolos?) forgetting his visor while the two separate. The final crisis, where Miranda recognizes and triumphs over her jealousy of the Vulcan's total merging with Kolos, rounds out the episode.

Diana Muldaur (Dr. Miranda Jones) also appears in "Star Trek" as Dr. Ann Mulhall in "Return to Tomorrow." She appears in two episodes of "The Invaders" ("Seekers," and "The Life").

"Miranda Jones" was the name of a character in a previous Roddenberry television effort, in "The Lieutenant" episode entitled "The Proud and the Angry."

THE EMPATH

Episode # 63
Revised final draft   7/23/68
Filmed in late July, early August 1968

WRITER   Joyce Muskat
DIRECTOR   John Erman
COMPOSER   George Duning
PHOTOGRAPHIC EFFECTS   Westheimer Company

On a remote planet, the U.S.S. *Enterprise* seeks to explain the disappearance of Federation researchers Dr. Linke and Dr. Ozaba. Kirk, Spock, and McCoy discover record tapes that show the missing doctors literally disappearing into thin air. While they are trying to analyze what occurred, the three are also seized and materialize in the presence of the "kidnappers," aliens Lal and Thann. Kirk and company discover that Drs. Linke and Ozaba are dead, their bodies preserved in huge specimen jars. The only other living being present is Gem, a beautiful young woman who lacks the power of speech. Kirk and McCoy are taken one at a time and experimented upon by Lal and Thann, resulting in terrible injuries that are cured when Gem, an empath, absorbs their injuries and pain into her own body. When McCoy is gravely injured by the aliens, Kirk is prevented from aiding him or inducing Gem to cure him. On her own, Gem begins to cure McCoy, although she knows that his injuries and pain may kill her. The entire, apparently senseless series of brutalities has been a test to determine if Gem's race is worthy enough to be saved from a disaster that will destroy her planet's solar system, which unfortunately also contains another populated planet. This was the only means that Lal and Thann could devise to determine which planet would be saved; they do not possess the means of saving both populations. Kirk and his friends return to the *Enterprise*.

The teaser for "The Empath," in which we see the disappearances of Dr. Linke and Dr. Ozaba, promises to signal the start of an interesting mystery, but the remainder of the episode develops into something very different.

Aliens Lal and Thann are faced with a problem; they have two planets full of humanoids that are going to be destroyed, and the time and technology to save only one of the populations. They apparently care a great deal about making the right choice in the matter. This evidently means that they have compassion, but if this is so, why should they go to the lengths they resort to, causing misery to innocent people and indulging in the cruelest of behavior? Of course, these are aliens, who may have different types of customs, but there are some unanswered questions. For instance, why didn't the aliens ask the Federation for assistance, instead of making mincemeat out of two doctors and attempting to do the same to Kirk and company?

The most interesting facet of this episode is Gem, the empath. Kathryn Hayes (who plays Gem) deserves a great deal of the credit for the success of the episode. She is an excellent mime, and although Gem never utters a single word throughout the story, Ms. Hayes' gestures and facial expressions add life and beauty to her character. When she appeared at a "Star Trek" convention, the fans were delighted to learn that her sensitivity in "The Empath" is present in the actress as well as in her characterization. Ms. Hayes, who appeared regularly on the afternoon "soap opera" "The Guiding Light," formerly had a recurring role as Elizabeth Reynolds in "The Road West," from 1966–67 (portraying the sister of the series' hero, played by Glenn Corbett). She has also acted in segments of "The Man from U.N.C.L.E." ("The See Paris and Die Affair," with Alfred Ryder) and "The Night Gallery" ("She'll Be Company for You," with Leonard Nimoy).

Composer George Duning, a native of Indiana who attended the Cincinnati Conservatory at the University of Cincinnati, Ohio, began his career in the 1940s, when he arranged music for radio orchestra leader/comedian Kay Kyser. For eighteen years, he directed Kyser's series "The College of Musical Knowledge," before going on to create many successful songs, including "Strangers When We Meet," "The 3:10 to Yuma," "Why Cry Baby," and the themes to the films *Picnic* and *Houseboat.* Duning's many movie scores include "From Here to Eternity," "Picnic," "Houseboat," "The World of Suzie Wong," "The Devil at 4 O'Clock," "Toys in the Attic," and the occult comedy "Bell, Book and Candle" (Columbia–1958). On television, his theme and episode scores for the highly acclaimed series "The Naked City" are well remembered. For "Star Trek," Mr. Duning created some of the series' most sensitive music, including his scores for "Metamorphosis" and "The Empath." His theme for Gem is reminiscent of the music he created to

describe a young blind girl (Barbara Luna) in "The Devil at Four O'Clock" (Columbia–1961).

"Nightmare," an episode of "The Outer Limits," also featured a series of ordeals inflicted upon Earthmen by humanoid aliens. In "Nightmare," the suffering was a war game, rather than an all-important experiment.

THE THOLIAN WEB

Episode # 64
Story outline   5/1/68
Final draft script   7/30/68
Original title   "In Essence Nothing"
Filmed in early and middle August 1968

WRITERS   Judy A. Burns, Chet L. Richards
DIRECTOR   Ralph Senensky
COMPOSER   Fred Steiner
PHOTOGRAPHIC EFFECTS   Vanderveer Photo Effects

The U.S.S. *Enterprise* discovers another Federation starship, the U.S.S. *Defiant,* adrift in an unexplored quadrant of space. Beaming aboard in space suits, Kirk, Spock, McCoy, and Chekov discover that the *Defiant*'s crew is dead. Before their deaths, the crew had mutinied and apparently engaged in other forms of violence among themselves. The *Defiant* is discovered to be drifting into another dimension; its substance is becoming nonexistent. The landing party is safely transferred back to the *Enterprise*, except for Kirk, who is still stranded aboard the *Defiant* when it vanishes from sight. Mr. Spock calculates when the ghost ship will rematerialize. At that time the *Enterprise* will theoretically be able to rescue Captain Kirk, provided that his oxygen has not yet run out. The wait proves extremely hazardous. This segment of space, because of its peculiar situation, renders the crew hostile to each other. When Kirk is presumed dead after the initial "interphase" fails to rematerialize the *Defiant,* the crew's morale sinks to a point at which several crewmembers (and finally the entire bridge crew) seem to see Kirk's ghostly figure. The captain is actually alive, and Spock realizes that there is still a chance to retrieve him. The Tholians, a hitherto unknown alien race, enter the scene and accuse the *Enterprise* of trespassing into their space. They weave an energized "web" around the starship. Spock manages to flee the web barely in time, while also managing to take Kirk's ghostly form with the *Enterprise.* Kirk is beamed aboard after he materializes, his space suit's oxygen supply almost completely gone.

The story outline for this episode, entitled "In Essence—Nothing," began as the *Enterprise* found the lost starship *Scimitar,* and beamed a landing party

Nurse Chapel and Dr. McCoy attempting to discover an antidote in "The Tholian Web" (Majel Barrett, DeForest Kelley).

aboard to investigate, clad in *life support shields* (personal force fields), not space suits. Kirk was immediately presumed dead, with no interphase retrieval procedures initially attempted. Uhura left the memorial service for Kirk early, profoundly affected. At first, McCoy did not believe that Uhura actually saw Kirk; after a physical examination, however, McCoy believed her but Spock did not. Dr. McCoy berated Spock for being too logical and for refusing to allow for the presence of hope that Kirk was still alive. At Chekov's suggestion, Spock decided to take the *Enterprise* into the other dimension to escape the Tholians' web. The web was shattered by the power generated by the starship, and the *Enterprise* crossed over. In the other dimensional plane the starship had the upper hand, leading the Tholians to accept the overtures of peace initiated by the retrieved Captain Kirk.

"The Tholian Web" is definitely an adventure story, in which Captain Kirk literally ventures into "Where No Man Has Gone Before," and comes back to tell about it. Because of Kirk's absence from the *Enterprise* throughout most of the story, we see how much the starship depends upon him for its operations, and how much the *Enterprise* crew depends upon his stabilizing influence.

In "The Paradise Syndrome," Kirk is isolated from the *Enterprise,* but he is presumed missing, not dead. With the captain's dynamism *completely* out of the picture in "The Tholian Web," things begin to fall apart. The symptoms generated by the "hostile" segment of space have something to do with the problem, but in the case of the conflict between Dr. McCoy and

Mr. Spock, the differences in opinion come mostly from within themselves. Apparently, the two can accept themselves as each other's friends only if Captain Kirk fits somewhere into the relationship.

The viewing of Kirk's last will and testament is a great touch; it clarifies much about the relationship between Kirk, Spock, and McCoy, and it aids in resolving the conflicts generated in this adventure. The culminating moment, when Spock actually calls McCoy "Bones," is a tearjerker and quite a pleasant surprise. It also brings up an interesting question: did McCoy faint from his illness or because of the shock caused by Spock's long-awaited attempt at familiarity?

The ironic timing of other outbursts, such as the crewman who goes berserk during Kirk's memorial service and Mr. Chekov's temporary flight into insanity, adds a peculiar form of humor to this episode that is topped by Uhura, in sick bay, asking McCoy "Doctor . . . will I become like Chekov?" One almost expects McCoy to look into the camera and say something like "Now *that* I've got to *see!*"

The fact that Uhura is the first to see the captain's spectral figure is very interesting, especially when one recalls that Kirk and Uhura are paired together in "Plato's Stepchildren." Although nothing was really made of it in the series, there might easily have been a relationship between Kirk and Uhura, even though a semiprofessional relationship between Uhura and Spock also seems likely (he even lent her his prized Vulcan harp to play in "The Conscience of the King").

Co-author Judy Burns later became a story editor on the hit TV series "Vegas."

Director Ralph Senensky does a wonderful job of

balancing all the elements in this episode (as he also does in "Is There in Truth No Beauty?"). His directing credits conform to Gene Roddenberry's practice of working with people who are familiar with westerns (which are more easily recognized as period pieces than is science fiction). Senensky's western experiences include directing episodes of "The Big Valley," "The High Chaparral," and "The Wild, Wild West." His other science fiction-fantasy experience includes segments of "The Twilight Zone" ("Printer's Devil") and "The Night Gallery" ("The Ghost of Sorworth Place").

Visually, "The Tholian Web" is a special photographic effects fan's dream with great miniature photography, animation effects, and even an alien composed of nonliving materials, creative lighting, and opticals. "Star Trek" won a well-deserved Emmy Award for this episode, for which some of the work was contributed by artist Mike Minor (who went on to work on *Star Trek—The Motion Picture*).

The most controversial part of this episode seems to be the space suits, which various fans either like or dislike. The suits have since been seen on segments of "The Lucy Show" and "Mork and Mindy."

FOR THE WORLD IS HOLLOW AND I HAVE TOUCHED THE SKY

Episode #65
Story outline   5/21/68
Final draft script   8/7/68
Revised final draft   8/8/68
Filmed in middle and late August 1968

WRITER   Rick Vollaerts
DIRECTOR   Tony Leader
COMPOSER   George Duning
PHOTOGRAPHIC EFFECTS   Howard A. Anderson Company

The planet Yonada, unknown to its inhabitants, is a huge, spherical spaceship. Its population lives within it, governed by a sophisticated computer called The Oracle, which has been programmed to conceal the nature of Yonada from its people until the unique ship reaches its journey's end. When the *Enterprise* discovers Yonada, the planet-ship is on a collision course with a huge asteroid. Dr. McCoy, who has just discovered that he is ill with a fatal disease, insists on joining the landing party going to Yonada. There, McCoy falls in love with Natira, The Oracle's beautiful high priestess. The feeling is mutual; Natira wishes to marry McCoy, but only if he will stay on Yonada with her while obeying the will of The Oracle. After great

difficulties, Captain Kirk succeeds in gaining access to The Oracle and, with the aid of Spock, penetrates its defenses and reprograms it to bypass the asteroid. Yonada, built centuries before by the Fabrini civilization, includes a huge computer bank with the superior technologies and sciences of the Fabrini, including a cure for Dr. McCoy's ailment. Natira realizes that McCoy's place is with his own people; he must leave her although she will always love him. Kirk promises McCoy that the *Enterprise* will be on hand to greet Natira and her people when their ship arrives at its destination (a habitable world) within a year.

In the story outline for this episode, Mr. Scott was ill with an irreversible blood condition; his red cells were crystallizing as a result of a rare condition brought about by radiation exposure. The incurable disease gave him three years to live. When the asteroid was discovered, only Kirk and Scotty beamed down into the "ship," and were accepted by the people whose religion spoke well of visitors who came from places other than Yonada. Space regulations permitted Scotty to retire to any place of his choosing. Kirk attempted to talk his friend out of staying; Yonada was on a collision course toward *a highly populated planet*. Scotty was so anxious to stay, he struck Kirk and challenged him to a fight. When the walls of The

Dr. McCoy, who has saved so many lives, is helpless to save himself in "For the World Is Hollow and I Have Touched the Sky" (DeForest Kelley).

Oracle room began to close in toward them, Kirk phasered through the wall into the engine room. The Oracle finally apologized, and exchanged its knowledge banks with the starship's computer, making Scotty's cure possible.

"For the World Is Hollow and I Have Touched the Sky" is another of "Star Trek's" successful love stories, and because of the subject of the romance it emerges as one of the most memorable segments of the entire series.

The *Star Trek Writers' Guide* mentioned that Dr. McCoy had been married before he had joined Starfleet. This marriage ended in divorce and, because of the unknown but painful facts behind the divorce, Dr. McCoy chose to leave Earth, leaving behind his daughter, Joanna, who was studying to be a nurse. We never learned anything about McCoy's unhappy marriage in the series, and unfortunately we never met his daughter, either. From time to time, McCoy's Southern gentlemanly charm was directed toward various guests aboard the *Enterprise,* and in "Man Trap" we actually met a representation of Nancy Crater, a former close female friend of McCoy's.

In this sensitive story, Dr. McCoy's love-at-first-sight affair with the beautiful and duty-minded Natira is well handled. Just as Natira senses McCoy's warm interior personality despite his usually flawless, gruff exterior (to which Natira was fortunately not subjected), actor DeForest Kelley again makes the Trek audience aware that McCoy is much more complex than he is sometimes depicted.

For a man who admittedly does not enjoy "making house calls," McCoy's visit with Natira appears as though it might be permanent until McCoy's Starfleet loyalties and the necessity of the situation get the better of him. This is one of the times during "Star Trek" that many fans wished for a two-part episode, so they could see how this relationship resolved itself.

Katherine Woodville (Natira), the real-life wife of "The Avengers" co-star Patrick Macnee, also appears in episodes of "The Night Stalker" ("Primal Scream"), and "Secret Agent" ("Colony Three").

John Lormer (Old Man) also appears in the "Star Trek" segments "The Cage" and "The Return of the Archons." He can also be seen in "The Invaders" ("Valley of the Shadow").

Director Tony Leader has had extensive credits in TV western series, including such old standbys as "Sugarfoot," "Rawhide," and "Lawman." He won the 1965 Western Heritage Award for his direction of "The Virginian" episode, "The Horse Fighter." In the science fiction department, Leader directed segments of "The Twilight Zone" ("Long Live Walter Jameson" and "The Midnight Sun"), and "Lost in Space" ("Island in the Sky," and the series' premiere episode, "The Reluctant Stowaway").

Visually, this episode is extremely attractive, with the asteroid from "Paradise Syndrome" pressed back into service, some colorful costumes created by William Theiss for Natira and other Yonadans, and the marble-type look of The Oracle chamber.

The sacred *Book of the People* bears a striking resemblance to another honored volume, *Chicago Mobs of the Twenties* from "A Piece of the Action."

THE DAY OF THE DOVE

Episode # 66
Story outline   6/3/68
First draft script   8/9/68
Revised final draft   8/19/68
Filmed in late August 1968

WRITER   Jerome Bixby
DIRECTOR   Marvin Chomsky
COMPOSER   Fred Steiner
PHOTOGRAPHIC EFFECTS   Westheimer Company

The U.S.S. *Enterprise* and a Klingon battle cruiser commanded by Kang the Klingon cross paths orbiting planet Beta XII-A. Kirk and company are convinced that the Klingons have murdered the Federation colonists on the planet and Kang is convinced that the *Enterprise* has damaged his ship. In reality, the damages have been manufactured by a malevolent energy-being that feeds off the insecurities and aggressive instincts of humanoids. Chekov, convinced that his brother Piotr was killed by Klingons, is especially aggressive against Kang and his people. The Klingons attempt to conquer the *Enterprise,* but are instead captured. The entity turns the *Enterprise* into a battleground. Phasers are transformed into swords, so that the crew members cannot vaporize each other and wounds are inflicted and heal so that mortally injured individuals recover to fight again and again. Chekov goes completely berserk and attempts to rape Kang's wife, science officer Mara. Finally, Kirk convinces Kang that they are all being manipulated by the hostile entity. The two commanders call a truce and join in a back-slapping session of mutual laughter. The creature is driven off the *Enterprise* by the resultant good feelings and the Klingons are safely dropped off at the nearest outpost.

"The Day of the Dove" is a very well-conceived tale, making effective use of the Klingons, an intriguing and potent enemy.

In respect to the alien entity that feeds off peoples' aggressions, the story is similar to "Wolf in the Fold," in which Redjac also feeds off peoples' negative emotional emanations. The balance of hatred that was present between the Klingons and the Federation in "Errand of Mercy" is back in full force here. Kirk's recognition of this hostility, which he hates to see within himself, provides him with the inner strength to determine that there is an unknown factor responsible for the *Enterprise*'s predicament.

The entity itself is more powerful than Redjac and furthers hostilities by manufacturing false recollections of atrocities, epitomized by Mr. Chekov's rage at the death of his brother, Piotr. Sulu sets the record straight, recalling that Chekov *never had* a brother.

The final scene in which Kirk and Kang stand together and laugh to get the entity to leave is an indication that the Organians are right; one day Klingons and humans will work together in friendship. The fact that Kang almost breaks Kirk's back with his good-natured slap is purely incidental.

Michael Ansara (Kang) is perfectly cast, and plays his part with all the expertise gathered from his years of portraying exotic heroes and villains in feature films including *Voyage to the Bottom of the Sea* (20th Century-Fox–1960). On television, Ansara is famous for portraying Cochise in the series "Broken Arrow" (1956–60), and he also had a recurring role as the Blue Djin in "I Dream of Genie" (which starred his wife, Barbara Eden). Among his many TV guest appearances are other roles in science fiction, fantasy, and horror series, including "The Outer Limits" ("The Soldier," written by Harlan Ellison), "Voyage to the Bottom of the Sea" ("Hot Line," and "The Hunters"), "The Time Tunnel" ("Secret Weapon," "The Kidnappers"), "Lost in Space" ("The Challenge"), "Land of the Giants" ("On a Clear Night You Can See Earth"), and "The Man from U.N.C.L.E." ("The Arabian Affair").

Director Marvin Chomsky's other credits include episodes of "The Wild, Wild West" ("The Night of the Iron Fist" and "Night of the Undead") and "Hawaii 5-0" ("Three Dead Cows at Makapu"), the pilot for "The Magician," and the 1970 TV movie *Assault on the Wayne* (starring Leonard Nimoy). He is best known for his direction of parts 3, 4, and 6 of the epic TV movie special, *Roots*.

Hostilities were accented in this episode with the use of "hot" red and brown lights focused on the Klingons, both planetside and in the *Enterprise*'s engineering section. The optical effect designed for the Klingon transporter was harsher than the Federation's transporter effect.

This is the only Trek segment in which we see a female Klingon (Mara, portrayed by actress Susan Johnson), for whom William Theiss designed an effective feminine variation of the standard Klingon uniform. Fred Phillips' makeup aided the portrayal, which was exotic, credible, and visually attractive.

One of the quickest of Trek's photographic effects is also present in this episode; the sequence of the *Enterprise*'s phasers destroying the damaged Klingon ship.

PLATO'S STEPCHILDREN

Episode #67

Story outline   6/13/68
Original title   "The Sons of Socrates"
Filmed in early and middle September 1968

WRITER   Meyer Dolinsky
DIRECTOR   David Alexander
COMPOSER   Alexander Courage
PHOTOGRAPHIC EFFECTS   Vanderveer Photo Effects

A distress call from the planet Platonius results in Dr. McCoy's beaming down with Kirk and Spock to aid the stricken Platonian leader, Parmen. Although Parmen and his people have no resistance to physical disease, they are powerful telekinetics who immediately attempt to enslave Kirk and company. The Platonians' dwarfed jester, Alexander, befriends Kirk and his people and attempts to help; but he is powerless to interfere because of his lack of telekinetic powers. Parmen and his people force Kirk, Spock, and McCoy to undergo humiliating experiences, some of which drive Mr. Spock to his psychological breaking point. Crew members Uhura and Chapel are also beamed down and forced to undergo bizarre charades with Kirk and Spock to amuse the Platonians; Mr. Spock is forced to sing a ballad. Dr. McCoy determines that the chemical substance kironide is responsible for the powers of Parmen and his followers and mixes a concentrated batch of the stuff. Alexander does not accept the injection, because he does not want to be like Parmen. Kirk and Spock take the dosage and develop the Power, canceling out the effectiveness of Parmen's deadly pranks. Our people leave Platonius, taking Alexander who will be dropped off at a nearby Federation planet to begin a new life.

The story outline for this segment, entitled "The Sons of Socrates," had the *Enterprise* being tossed about in space by the power of Parmen's delirium. In the scenes involving the degradation of Kirk and company, Kirk was paired with a young yeoman who admired him greatly, whereas Uhura was paired with Dr. McCoy. Uhura sang the song. Spock was forced to hit McCoy and McCoy was compelled to butt the Vulcan in the stomach as Christine and the female yeoman were forced to fight. No mention was made of Kirk and company's losing their powers after they had left the planet.

In terms of the events that take place on Platonius, "Plato's Stepchildren" is similar to "The Gamesters of Triskelion" and "The Empath," involving Kirk and company in demeaning, bizarre activities. Just as "The Empath" has Gem to provide sensitivity, this segment features the tragic individual, Alexander.

In other episodes, the men of the *Enterprise* find themselves pitted against some extremely dangerous foes, including telepaths such as the Talosians in "The Cage" and the Melkotians in "Spectre of the Gun," but the telekinetic Parmen and his Platonians are the most dangerous, resembling a community of people like Gary Mitchell ("Where No Man Has Gone Before") and Charles Evans ("Charlie X").

The cruel antics of Parmen and his people are offset by the presence of Alexander, who lacks the Power and has therefore never lost sight of his human condition. Throughout the episode, Alexander provides our people with encouragement to minimize the damages done by Parmen.

In the performances induced by Parmen, both Kirk and Spock have highly unpleasant experiences. Spock performs his song, "Maiden Wine"; Captain Kirk is forced to slap his own face over and over.

Liam Sullivan (Parmen) was regularly featured as Major Mapoy in the western-adventure series, "The Monroes" (in which Ron Soble portrayed a likable Indian), and is also visible in segments of "The Twilight Zone" ("The Silence"), "Lost in Space" ("His Majesty Smith"), and in episodes of the soap opera "The Secret Storm" (in the recurring role of Alan Dunbar).

Michael Dunn (Alexander) is best remembered by television viewers for his charmingly villainous recurring role of Dr. Miguelito Lovelace in "The Wild, Wild West" (1965–69), and was also featured in episodes of "Night Gallery" ("The Sins of the Fathers") and "Voyage to the Bottom of the Sea" ("The Wax Men"). His most famous feature film appearance was in the 1965 movie "Ship of Fools."

Writer Meyer Dolinsky also scripted episodes of "The Outer Limits" ("Zzzzz," "Obit," and "Architects of Fear").

"Plato's Stepchildren's" main distinction is the inclusion of the kiss between Captain Kirk and Lieutenant Uhura, the first interracial kiss featured on network television.

WINK OF AN EYE

Episode # 68

Story outline 3/22/68

Filmed in middle and late September 1968

WRITER Arthur Heinemann
(Story by Lee Cronin) (Lee Cronin—pseudonym of Gene L. Coon)
DIRECTOR Jud Taylor
COMPOSER Alexander Courage
PHOTOGRAPHIC EFFECTS Cinema Research Corp.

Responding to a distress call from the planet Scalos, the *Enterprise* discovers a beautiful city with no signs of life except mysterious insectlike buzzing sounds. The sounds are the result of Scalosian attempts to communicate; the inhabitants of the planet have been poisoned by radiations from the core of Scalos, resulting in incredibly accelerated metabolism in males and females and male sterility. On the *Enterprise,* Kirk is administered a dose of Scalosian water, which accelerates him to the level of the beautiful Deela, Queen of Scalos, who needs his help to repopulate her planet. Kirk records a tape informing Mr. Spock of the situation. To Spock and the entire *Enterprise* crew, Kirk has ceased to exist; they cannot perceive accelerated individuals except as "insect sounds." McCoy finds an antidote to the Scalosian water, and then Spock drinks the water and accelerates himself. Locating Kirk, Spock administers the antidote to the captain, staying behind in his accelerated state to undo the Scalosians' damage to the *Enterprise.* The defeated aliens are returned to their world.

Captain Kirk's metabolism accelerated greatly in "Return to Tomorrow," while his body was being "possessed" by the energy-being Sargon. During that adventure, Dr. McCoy mentioned that Kirk's body could only stand short bursts of such activity before serious damage resulted and, during his metamorphosis, the captain showed signs of being weakened by the ordeal. The Scalosian water accelerates Kirk to an incredible degree in comparison to his earlier experience, and yet he shows no such signs of weakness.

Ignoring the questions and puzzles that may arise from this episode's science, we are left free to appreciate the tale's aspects of mystery, suspense, and humor. From these aspects "Wink of an Eye" is an enjoyable episode, particularly when one considers the human aspects of Captain Kirk and his enjoyment of the notion that Deela has selected him to aid in the repopulation of her planet. From the moment when Kirk first feels her split-second kiss, Kirk the man and Kirk the captain both consider the issues at stake here.

Topping the list in the "moments the network censors did not notice but should have" department is the highly enjoyable sequence in which Kirk and Deela adjourn to the captain's cabin to discuss the business at hand. There is a cut to another scene just as we are led to believe that Deela has Kirk right where she wants him, and that he is not objecting too strenuously. When the scene cuts back to Kirk and Deela, she is standing before his mirror, combing her hair, and he is putting his boots on.

Two additional sequences add elements of eeriness to the episode. Crewman Compton's death again accents Captain Kirk's anguish at losing a crewman. In a more upbeat sequence, Mr. Spock's superspeed tour of the *Enterprise,* in which he invisibly repairs hundreds of systems and circuits before returning to his normal state of metabolism, enables him to act out his symbolic role as the starship's scientific guardian *angel* (although Dr. McCoy would probably rather view the Vulcan as a devilish figure).

Kathie Brown (Deela, Queen of Scalos) appeared regularly as Angie Daw in the 1967 TV series, "Hondo," and can also be seen in a segment of "Kolchak," "The Night Stalker" ("The Sentry"), in which she costarred with her husband, actor Darren McGavin.

Writer Arthur Heinemann's TV work dates back to the days of live television, when he adapted two segments of the "United States Steel Hour," "Midsummer" and "The Lost Autumn."

The Scalosian city, seen in the background of Deela's taped plea for help, is a reused optical painting, which was originally created for "A Taste of Armageddon."

THAT WHICH SURVIVES

Episode # 69

Story outline   8/8/68
Final draft script   9/16/68
Original title   "Survival"
Filmed in late September, early October 1968

WRITER   John Meredyth Lucas
(Story by Michael Richards—
pseudonym of D. C. Fontana)
DIRECTOR   Herb Wallerstein
COMPOSER   Fred Steiner
PHOTOGRAPHIC EFFECTS   Howard A. Anderson Company

Preparing to beam down and investigate puzzling geological conditions on an unexplored Class M planet, Kirk, McCoy, Mr. Sulu, and geologist Lieutenant D'Amato witness a beautiful woman appear in the *Enterprise* transporter room. She attacks an ensign as Kirk and company are dematerializing, helpless to assist. When our people materialize they are unable to contact the *Enterprise,* which has been hurled many light years away. The woman, Losira, is a holographic projection materialized by a computer left behind by the Kalandans, an extinct alien race who had used the planet as a scientific outpost. Losira's image keeps materializing aboard the *Enterprise* and on the planet; whenever it appears, people die. A young engineering officer is killed aboard the *Enterprise,* and Lieutenant D'Amato is killed on the planet's surface. Mr. Sulu narrowly escapes death. Just as Kirk and company are about to be destroyed by the projection, Spock beams down and destroys the ancient computer, canceling out the holograms of Losira that were designed to repel everyone except Kalandans from the planet.

In the story outline for this episode, entitled "Survival," the image of Losira was more brutal than in the final version and also manufactured illusions that caused the *Enterprise* people to fight among themselves. Chekov perceived McCoy as a monster, whereas Sulu saw a fellow crewman as a monster and Uhura thought she saw Sulu attack another crewman. Kirk was almost induced to stab himself while in his quarters.

"That Which Survives" is an imaginative episode of "Star Trek," despite the presence of similarities to other Trek segments. It is also a sensitive episode, although the story contains action, sudden death, mystery, and suspense.

The device of a computer materializing the image of a humanoid is present in "The Return of the Archons." In that episode, however, the image of Landru is spectral rather than solid in appearance. Losira makes her entrances by materializing as a thin, vertical line that expands horizontally into the figure of a beautiful woman. (This effect can be compared to the way in which a televised image first appears on the picture tube when a set is turned on, but despite this similarity it is not certain at first whether Losira is a living being or a holographic projection.)

A typical moment on the bridge of the *Enterprise* (William Shatner, Leonard Nimoy, George Takei).

While the image of Losira kills several people, the hologram's behavior seems to indicate that the *real* Losira, who apparently programmed the computer, transferred some of her respect for life into the device. There is no feeling of malevolence in the hologram's actions; it appears to be doing its duty with reluctance.

The funeral of Lieutenant D'Amato provides a sensitive moment, as the body of the geologist is ceremonially covered with the same varieties of alien rocks that had intrigued him just a short time before.

Lee Meriwether (Losira)'s television career includes recurring roles in four TV series: as Ann Reynolds in "The Young Marrieds" (1964–66), as Ann the technician in "The Time Tunnel" (1966–67), as the wife in "The New Andy Griffith Show" (1972), and as the daughter-in-law-co-worker of "Barnaby Jones." Ms. Meriwether, a former Miss America, also appeared in segments of "Land of the Giants" ("Rescue") and "The Man from U.N.C.L.E." ("The Mad, Mad Tea-party Affair"). Her feature-film roles include parts in *The 4-D Man* (Universal–1959; as the love interest for the star, Robert Lansing) and *Batman* (20th Century-Fox–1966; as Catwoman, a role played on television by Julie Newmar).

Two colorful varieties of animation effects are present in "That Which Survives"; the method by which "Losira" materializes and the spectacular view of Mr. Sulu's phaser beam bouncing harmlessly off the beautiful holographic projection.

LET THIS BE YOUR LAST BATTLEFIELD

Episode # 70
Filmed in early October 1968

WRITER   Oliver Crawford (Story by Lee Cronin—
    pseudonym of Gene L. Coon)
DIRECTOR   Jud Taylor
COMPOSER   Fred Steiner
PHOTOGRAPHIC EFFECTS   Westheimer Company

The *Enterprise* intercepts a stolen Federation shuttlecraft and rescues the thief, a humanoid named Lokai who asks for diplomatic asylum. Lokai, a native of the planet Cheron, is part white and part black. Soon after Lokai's arrival, another native of Cheron (similarly colored) appears on the *Enterprise*. Bele, who says he is Cheron's chief officer attached to the commission of political traitors, denounces Lokai and attempts to take him back to Cheron. Kirk resists Bele's undiplomatic extradition attempts, which culminate in the near destruction of the *Enterprise*. The starship ultimately arrives at Cheron, and during the long voyage Bele and Lokai are literally at each other's throats. Orbiting Cheron, Spock discovers that it is a dead world; the inhabitants have killed each other with their insistent hatreds. Bele and Lokai chase each other around the *Enterprise*, and then beam down to their dead planet where they will continue their fight.

Many "Star Trek" episodes are concerned with the problem of prejudice; the Vulcan concept of appreciating the existence of Infinite Diversity in Infinite Combinations is an eloquent statement on the issue. The events that unfold in "Is There in Truth No Beauty?" are sensitive and subtle in exploring the differences between life forms, and how these differences can be resolved for the benefit of all concerned. "Let This Be Your Last Battlefield" examines prejudice without any concern for subtlety, literally tackling the problem in "black and white."

The story seems solely concerned with bringing Bele and Lokai together aboard the *Enterprise* to compare their left and right sides and decide which is their "better half." In confining itself to this fundamental study, the episode suffers in terms of its logical realities.

Even if we accept that the Federation has never heard of the existence of Cheron's two-toned humanoids, we must still wonder how two entities as conspicuous as Bele and Lokai have crossed into Federation territory and remained unnoticed. Lokai, who "hitchhiked" at least part of the way, would most certainly have been seen, especially on Starbase Four, where he stole a shuttlecraft. To evade notice in such an isolated environment, Lokai would have had to keep a low profile.

Bele and Lokai possess superhuman powers, but these abilities seem more pronounced in Bele (Lokai does not stop Bele from directing the starship toward Cheron), although the two seem equally matched when they engage in hand-to-hand combat on the bridge.

Kirk's threat to activate the self-destruct mechanism of the *Enterprise* furnishes a suspenseful scene that is well directed and well played, utilizing effective close-ups of Kirk, Spock, Scotty, and the two aliens.

Frank Gorshin (Bele), one of the most famous impressionists in the world, is best known for his imitations of celebrities, such as James Cagney, Kirk Douglas, and Richard Widmark. One of his first acting roles was in *The Invasion of the Saucer Men* (American International Pictures–1957), a humorous tale of Earth being menaced by little men from outer space. Television audiences recall his wonderfully insane renditions of the Riddler in the "Batman" TV series (including that series' pilot episode, "Hey, Diddle, Diddle, Smack in the Middle").

Lou Antonio (Lokai) is an accomplished director as well as a highly skilled actor. He has directed segments of the TV adaptation "Rich Man, Poor Man" (and has in turn been directed by Leonard Nimoy in the "Night Gallery" episode "Death on a Barge"). Mr. Antonio appeared regularly as Barney in the 1974 series "The Snoop Sisters." His most unique role besides Lokai was probably as a chimp transformed into a man on an episode of "Bewitched."

Al Francis' cinematography for this episode includes the extremely effective coverage of a transporter sequence in which the camera is on the transporter platform, rather than by the control console. This single experiment is the closest thing to a subjective (first person) camera transporter shot to appear on "Star Trek."

Budgetary considerations probably accounted for some of the episode's shortcomings. For instance, we hear about concerned personnel on Ariannus and Starbase Four, but we never see (or hear) them. Stock footage, including views of destruction on Cheron and the more specialized Trek inventory of the shuttlecraft and *Enterprise* miniatures, abounds in this segment. The real budget saver here is Bele's spaceship; very fast and streamlined, and conveniently invisible.

Frank Gorshin apparently had a good time appearing in "Star Trek"; the third season Trek blooper film shows the performer poised on the transporter platform, suddenly transforming himself into James Cagney. Another blooper sequence has Gorshin and Lou Antonio running down the *Enterprise* corridor eluding each other until they meet and collide with great impact.

Part of Mr. Gorshin's amusement may have resulted from the design of Bele's costume, which is similar to the skintight, turtlenecked costume he wore as the Riddler.

WHOM GODS DESTROY

Episode #71
Story outline   7/26/68
First draft script   9/5/68
Produced in middle October 1968

WRITER   Lee Erwin (story by Jerry Sohl, Lee Erwin)
DIRECTOR   Herb Wallerstein
COMPOSER   Fred Steiner
PHOTOGRAPHIC EFFECTS   Howard A. Anderson Company

Captain Kirk takes the *Enterprise* to Elba II, a planet that houses an asylum for the care of the galaxy's last group of insane humanoids. Kirk brings with him a new wonder drug that, when used in conjunction with other treatments, can cure these individuals. Beaming down, Kirk and Spock are met by an individ-

ual who appears to be the colony's governor, Donald Cory. In reality, however, their host is Garth of Izar, a brilliant former starship captain. Garth was an inmate of Elba II until he used a mysterious shape-changing power to assume the appearance of Cory and trick the guards into releasing him from his cell. Imprisoning the real guards and Governor Cory, Garth freed the inmates and took over Elba II. Garth uses a variety of tactics to attempt to gain possession of the *Enterprise*. His attempts, involving the aid of the beautiful Orion inmate Marta, are unsuccessful. In a rage, Garth has Marta executed, dragged into the poisonous atmosphere beyond the asylum dome, and destroyed with a powerful explosive he has invented. The *Enterprise* crew, commanded by Mr. Scott, is powerless to penetrate the asylum's force field and cannot transport security people down to aid Kirk. When Garth transforms himself into Kirk's double, Mr. Spock deduces which is the imposter and stuns Garth. After control of the asylum is restored to Cory, we see that Garth, with the aid of a rehabilitation chair (which he had altered and used to torture Kirk and Cory), is on his way to recovery.

In the first draft script of "Whom Gods Destroy," Garth of *Titan* was more brutal, having thrown the asylum guards out of the dome and watched, laughing, as they suffocated. The atmosphere within the asylum was more graphic. Inmates were shown exhibiting symptoms of various mental illnesses. Garth tortured Governor Cory in a cage of the inmate's design that created an electronic simulation of hell.

Three plot devices are evident in "Whom Gods Destroy," two of which are present in several "Star Trek" episodes: (1) An important person within the Federation is introduced and is discovered to be mentally unbalanced (if the Federation has a health plan for its Starfleet people, it probably costs them a lot to maintain); (2) a humanoid gains superhuman abilities as a result of the intervention of an alien influence; and finally, (3) an insane asylum taken over by its inmates is a cinematic device that was first made famous in the classic horror film *The Cabinet of Dr. Caligari* (UFA– 1919).

"Dagger of the Mind" takes us into a Federation institution similar to the asylum located on Elba II in this episode. Despite the horrible "curative" measures employed by Dr. Adams in "Dagger of the Mind," the Elba II installation, as mismanaged by Garth, emerges as the more blatant "chamber of horrors" of the two.

William Shatner and Leonard Nimoy made some subtle changes in their characterizations of Kirk and Spock to enable them to function within the exaggerated framework of Garth's insanity. In this segment, Kirk appears more vocal than usual, whereas Mr. Spock seems more sedate.

Actor Nimoy makes it apparent that Mr. Spock regards the behavioral aberrations of Garth and his friends with revulsion and pity.

In an extremely subtle hint, director Herb Wallerstein and Nimoy inform the audience that "Spock" is actually now Garth in disguise by having "the Vulcan" speaking with Kirk and casually holding his phaser aimed directly at the captain, something the real Spock would never do.

Steve Ihnat (Garth), an extremely gifted actor who was equally able to portray heroes or villains, deserves much of the credit for making this episode as interesting as it is. Ihnat presented Garth as a madman, logical and gentle one instant and suddenly violent and discordant a moment later.

Ihnat's villainous feature film roles include his appearances in the 1965 movie *The Chase* and the 1966 film *In Like Flint*. On television, Ihnat was featured in the 1971 pilot film for *The Sixth Sense* ("Sweet Sweet Rachael"), and appeared in episodes of "The Outer Limits" ("The Inheritors"; the series' only two-part segment) and "Voyage to the Bottom of the Sea" ("The Price of Doom," with Jill Ireland and David Opatoshu). In a 1966 episode of "Honey West" ("A Million Bucks in Anybody's Language"), Ihnat portrayed a villain named "Garth."

Yvonne Craig (Marta) also appeared in "In Like Flint," as well as other feature films. The former ballerina is best known for her recurring role as Batgirl in the "Batman" TV series, and is also featured in episodes of "Voyage to the Bottom of the Sea" ("Turn Back the Clock"), "Land of the Giants" ("Wild Journey"), and "The Man from U.N.C.L.E." ("The Brain Killer Affair," with Nancy Kovack and Abraham Sofaer).

Keye Luke (Governor Cory) appeared in feature films in the 1930s, including the classic *The Good Earth* (Metro-Goldwyn-Mayer–1937) and as "Number One Son" opposite Warner Oland in the earliest "Charlie Chan" films. He is best known to television viewers as Master Po, the blind but all-seeing teacher of Caine in "Kung Fu."

Story co-writer Jerry Sohl also co-wrote "The Invaders" segment "The Watchers," and wrote that series' "Dark Outpost" episode.

The Tellarite makeup introduced by Fred Phillips for "Journey to Babel" appears in this episode in a slightly simplified version and would later appear in "The Lights of Zetar" modified in the same manner; the original appliance was cut to omit the deep-set eyes seen in "Babel."

When the *Enterprise* phasers are attempting to penetrate the asylum's force field, they are aimed at a fixed position although the planet is seen to revolve.

Marta's costume is a very simplified version of the Orion slave girl's outfit in "The Cage." The space suits from "The Tholian Web" are also seen in "Whom Gods Destroy," together with Dr. Adams' robe from "Dagger of the Mind" (and Dr. Adams' "neural neutralizer" chair from the same episode).

THE MARK OF GIDEON

Episode # 72
Story Outline 7/12/68
Filmed in late October 1968

WRITERS George F. Slavin, Stanley Adams
DIRECTOR Jud Taylor
COMPOSER Fred Steiner
PHOTOGRAPHIC EFFECTS Westheimer Company

Captain Kirk beams down to Gideon, a disease-free planet that the United Federation of Planets is attempting to recruit as a member. Something apparently goes wrong with the transporter, and Kirk never arrives in the Gideon council chambers. A frustrated Mr. Spock attempts to secure permission from Starfleet to beam down and search for Kirk. Kirk has, as Spock suspects, actually been kidnapped by the Gideons, who have transported him down in the middle of an exact duplicate of the U.S.S. *Enterprise,* which is empty except for himself and a beautiful young woman, Odona. Gideon is actually a terribly overpopulated planet, whose people hold life sacred. Because of the extreme overcrowding of the planet Gideon councilman Hodin has lured Kirk into the starship mockup so that he can infect his daughter with Vegan choriomeningitis, a virulent disease he has survived but still carries in his blood. Odona will die, but she will also infect others on Gideon with the disease, finally paving the way for that world's reduction in population. Mr. Spock finally locates the captain, and then brings Kirk and Odona back to the *Enterprise.* Odona, now cured, also carries the virus. She happily returns to Gideon to infect other citizens of that world with the potentially fatal disease.

The story outline for "The Mark of Gideon" is very different from the filmed episode. The Gideons were virtually immortal, because of their ability to instantly regenerate damaged cells within their body. A party of Gideons, beamed aboard the *Enterprise,* took over the transporter room and forced Kirk, Spock, and other key personnel to beam down, so they could function as living blood banks for antibodies that would cancel out the immortality of everyone on the planet (except for the ruling council). Using these antibodies, the Gideons unsuccessfully attempted to use Odona and two others to produce deadly germs.

"The Mark of Gideon" is essentially a mystery story. Captain Kirk disappears, and from the *Enter-*

prise crew's point of view it is not certain what has become of him, although Spock and company are suspicious of the Gideon council. From Captain Kirk's point of view, the mystery is greater. Kirk believes that he has never left the *Enterprise,* but that everyone else aboard her has vanished. To supplement the mystery, the beautiful Odona appears on the empty *"Enterprise"* with Kirk, but provides no helpful information to aid Kirk in discovering what is really happening. The audience knows only that Kirk is *not* aboard the *Enterprise* and that Odona is part of some unknown plan.

The biggest mystery about this entire episode is how the Gideons could create a duplicate of the starship *Enterprise* that is so perfect it fools Captain Kirk so completely. Kirk knows his ship inside-out and (as he observes) is even familiar with its functional *sounds.* To Spock, Scotty, and a few others within the Federation and Starfleet, the *Enterprise* is certainly no mystery in terms of its fabrication and capabilities, but to the universe at large (and especially to those *outside* of the Federation), the starship is an awesome, secret vehicle.

The sudden appearance of the bogus starship could have been more believable if it was mentioned that Captain Kirk had been drugged by the Gideons to dull his perceptions and to induce him to accept whatever mock-up they had the technology to create. Unfortunately, this possibility is negated by Mr. Spock, who also refers to the mock-up as an exact duplicate of the *Enterprise.*

Another great mystery in this episode is why Kirk, who thinks that his entire crew has somehow vanished without a trace, treats Odona as he does. Kirk does not interrogate her with any severity, and instead seems to take her at her word, although she supplies him with no helpful information and claims to have amnesia.

Despite these riddles, there are some excellent touches in this episode. We experience a look at the bureaucracy of Starfleet. We have previously seen indications of the ponderous and stubborn hierarchy of the Starfleet, notably in "Amok Time," but in this episode we see that even Mr. Spock has a boiling point when it comes to dealing with the Earthside "chairbound paper pushers" who make the decisions regarding starship priorities.

Spock is not the only one whose patience wears thin during the captain's disappearance. If Scotty had heard Hodin describe him as a ". . . very excitable repairman," he probably would have beamed down and punched the Gideon councilman in the nose.

The split-second glimpses of demoralized, hooded crowds pressed together outside the mock-up starship's "windows" are effective in making the viewer wonder what is really happening on Gideon. When the truth is made known, Odona's description of the overcrowded conditions on her planet seems like a recollection of some of the larger "Star Trek" conventions.

Two unusual camera angles are seen in this episode. When Krodak transports down to the *Enterprise,* we see him vanish on the starship's viewing screen. When Kirk is seated in the Gideon council room, the camera shoots up at Kirk and Hodin through a transparent tabletop.

The sound of an amplified human heartbeat is used in this episode to create tension. This technique is present in many films, including *Dr. Jekyll and Mr. Hyde* (Paramount–1931) and *Hamlet* (Rank–1948).

One final mystery remains about this tale. The Gideons were obviously prepared to take extremely bizarre measures to solve their overpopulation problem. But if their planet was really so incredibly crowded so that people were willing to kill to enjoy a moment's privacy, where did Hodin and his council find the space to construct the duplicate of such a large vehicle as the U.S.S. *Enterprise?*

THE LIGHTS OF ZETAR

Episode #73
Story outline   9/12/68
Final draft script   10/28/68
Filmed in early November 1968

WRITERS   Jeremy Tarcher, Shari Lewis
DIRECTOR   Herb Kenwith
COMPOSER   Alexander Courage
PHOTOGRAPHIC EFFECTS   Vanderveer Photo Effects

Lieutenant Mira Romaine is aboard the starship *Enterprise* to supervise the transfer of new equipment to planetoid Memory Alpha, the central library facility of the United Federation of Planets. Mr. Scott is romantically attracted to Mira, and the attraction is mutual. When an energy storm of unknown nature destroys all the scholars on Memory Alpha, Lieutenant Romaine exhibits an ability to predict where the "storm" will strike next. The energy enters the *Enterprise* and possesses the mind and body of Mira. The storm is actually a collective mentality, the surviving life force of the last natives of Zetar, a dead planet. Mira's psychological attributes make her an ideal host for the "Lights," who communicate through her as though they were spirits speaking through a medium. The Zetars refuse to leave Mira's person, insisting that they have a right to live, even at the expense of her own individual life. The "Lights" are finally extinguished by placing Mira in a pressure chamber and subjecting the Zetars to conditions to which they cannot adapt. Mira, recovered, accomplishes her mission on Memory Alpha, which has been heavily damaged by the invading Lights.

In the story outline for "The Lights of Zetar," Mira Romaine was Scotty's new engineering assistant and shared his fascination for machinery. After the Lights attacked *Memory Seven,* they penetrated the *Enterprise* and affected the bridge crew as though they had been subjected to electrical shocks. Mira, as she was "possessed," was encased in glowing light. Mira had always regarded herself as a trifle strange, because of her experiences with visions and other similar phenomena. Scotty was extremely defensive about Mira's problems; when Mr. Spock questioned Mira at one point, Scotty *hit* the Vulcan. In an attempt to "short circuit" the Lights, which could cancel out gravity and sound, the *Galileo* was steered into the storm. Mira was placed into a cryogenic chamber instead of a decompression chamber to drive the Lights out of her.

The essential element of "The Lights of Zetar" is the possession and exorcism of Lieutenant Mira Romaine. The episode is an indication of how "Star Trek" sometimes explored topics that would become very popular a short time later, in this case after the release of the movie *The Exorcist.* The intriguing device of Mira's revealing the comings and goings of the Lights dates back to Bram Stoker's novel, *Dracula,* in which Mina Harker, possessed by the malevolent Count, was able to "see" his movements from afar. In addition to these elements combining science and the supernatural, there is also an emphasis on the romantic relationship between Scotty and Mira.

Mr. Scott was extremely affected by the sight of "Mudd's Women," but it was in "Who Mourns for Adonais" that we saw him actively pursuing a specific female, the lovely young Lieutenant Carolyn Palamas. His short-lived fascination with the beautiful dancer, Kara, in "Wolf in the Fold" was not really a romance, but a shore leave diversion. In "The Lights of Zetar," Scott's attraction to Lieutenant Romaine is partially based upon a common bond that should have detracted from the relationship rather than adding to it.

Mira's father, Jacques Romaine, had been a chief engineer for Starfleet. This would account for her attraction toward Scotty. Mr. Scott, an ageless individual who thought nothing of falling for the younger Lieutenant Palamas, would probably have stayed away from a woman who identified him with her father. Scotty, however, apparently does not see this, or does not care.

It is possible that Mira was the only woman who had shown any attention to Mr. Scott. Perhaps Scott's intense attachment to his engines reminded Mira of her father and provided her with an initial reason for seeking a relationship with Scotty, whereas any other woman would probably have been scared away from Scott because of his dedication to his machinery.

This episode's musical score, composed by Alex-

The captain may command the five-year mission, but Mr. Scott alone can get the *Enterprise* there (James Doohan).

ander Courage, was largely music from "Where No Man Has Gone Before." Because of similarities in plot and pacing (both episodes deal with the possession of *Enterprise* crew members by alien energy forces), the music fits very well. The scenes in which the *Enterprise* first encounters the Lights, and Mira is initially possessed by them, utilize the same music that accompanied the *Enterprise*'s entry into the galactic barrier and the "possession" of Dr. Dehner.

The Lights were produced by the skillful use of animation combined with preexisting footage of the *Enterprise* miniature.

One flaw is present as we see Mira floating weightless in the atmosphere chamber. Although actress Jan Shutan (Mira) appears to be floating leisurely in midair (probably thanks to a hidden board supporting her from beneath), her hair falls downward when it should "float" (as it would have with the use of wires).

THE CLOUDMINDERS

Episode # 74
Story Outline   8/14/68
Original title   "Revolt"
Filmed in middle November 1968

WRITER   Margaret Armen (Story by David Gerrold,
Oliver Crawford)
DIRECTOR   Jud Taylor
COMPOSER   Fred Steiner
PHOTOGRAPHIC EFFECTS   Cinema Research Corp.

In quest of the crucial and rare element zienite, which is needed to stop a plague on planet Merak II, the *Enterprise* journeys to the world of Ardana, a planet rich in zienite. The substance is excavated by miners known as Troglytes, who are forced to live on the harsh surface of Ardana, whereas the planet's ruling class resides in the luxurious city of Stratos, which floats high above the surface. When the Troglytes refuse to turn over the zienite, Captain Kirk is drawn into their struggle for equality. Plasus, the High Advisor of Ardana's ruling council, maintains that the Troglytes are naturally inferior beings. While Mr. Spock is involved in a relationship with Droxine, the daughter of Plasus, Kirk befriends Vanna, a Troglyte leader. Kirk, Plasus, Vanna, and other Troglytes enter a zienite mine, where Kirk causes a cave-in that isolates them. Without protective gas masks, they all become prone to violent, unreasoning behavior. Plasus, now aware of the reason for the Troglytes' mental state, reflects upon his planet's social structure as the Troglytes gather the zienite needed by Captain Kirk.

The classic science fiction film *Metropolis* (UFA–1926) situated its workers in an underground factory/city environment, whereas the idle rich lived in a luxurious, art deco city filled with skyscrapers, landscaped gardens, multileveled highways, and numerous land and air vehicles.

The 1936 film *Things to Come* situated its futuristic city *underground,* utilizing artificial sunlight. The serial *Flash Gordon* (Universal–1936) featured a floating city, which was kept aloft by slave workers tending an "atom furnace." The cloud city of Stratos is supported by unknown methods, hopefully not involving the use of Troglyte slaves.

It is no surprise that Captain Kirk becomes involved in the Troglytes' fight to obtain rights equal to those of the Stratos-dwellers. Kirk has always championed the downtrodden, and his attraction to the beautiful Troglyte Vanna probably intensifies his interest in the only group of people who are capable of providing the zienite that Kirk must obtain.

While Captain Kirk is becoming more deeply involved with Vanna and her cause, Mr. Spock is extremely attracted to Plasus' daughter, Droxine. This relationship *is* a surprise, especially considering some of the conversation between Spock and Droxine.

The year before, Dr. Spock had found it necessary to discuss the Vulcan mating cycle with his captain. Although Kirk is the Vulcan's closest friend, it was difficult for Spock to speak of the *pon far* and other related topics. T'Pau had indicated in no uncertain terms that these subjects were not to be discussed in the presence of "outworlders." In "Cloudminders," though, Mr. Spock not only mentions his mating cycle but indicates that he is sorry that he has met Droxine between *pon fars*. Although it is logical for Spock to notice and appreciate Droxine's intelligence and beauty, Spock's perception of her does not account for his discussion of topics other than "the parabolic intersection of dimension with dimension."

Jeff Corey (Plasus) is not only an actor but a director and an acting teacher as well. Corey was one of Leonard Nimoy's acting instructors and, like Nimoy, Corey also directed segments of "The Night Gallery" (including "Quoth the Raven," "Certain Shadows on the Wall," "Fright Night," "Tell David," and "The Academy"). In addition to other directing assignments, Corey directed the "Sixth Sense" episode "Eye of the Haunted." Corey, whose acting career began in 1941 (when he appeared in the classic fantasy film *All That Money Can Buy,* also released as *The Devil and Daniel Webster*), has played a long succession of generally villainous roles (such as in *The Killers, Seconds,* and *True Grit*). Television audiences can see him in segments of "The Outer Limits" ("O.B.I.T."), "The Night Gallery" ("The Dead Man"), and "The Adventures of Superman" ("Unknown People," the two-part episode originally released theatrically in 1951 as "Superman and the Mole-Men," with Beverly Washburn and Billy Curtis also in the cast).

Fred Williamson (Anka) achieved fame on the football field, where he was known as "The Hammer," before entering the acting field.

THE WAY TO EDEN

Episode #75
Story outline   8/27/68
Original title   "Joanna"
Filmed in late November 1968

WRITER   Arthur Heinemann (Story by Michael Richards,
pseudonym for D. C. Fontana, and Arthur
Heinemann)
DIRECTOR   David Alexander

When Captain Kirk sights a stolen spaceship, the *Aurora,* the *Enterprise* gives chase and beams the *Aurora*'s passengers aboard just before the cruiser's engines overheat and explode. The *Enterprise*'s new guests are a group of oddly dressed young idealists who are looking for a new life on the supposedly mythical planet Eden. Their leader, a brilliant engineer named Dr. Sevrin is a carrier of sythococcus novae, a disease deadly to those not immunized against it. He is also insane and implements plans to gain control of the *Enterprise* and to escape to Eden. One of Sevrin's followers is Irini Galliulin, a beautiful young woman who was once romantically involved with Mr. Chekov. Another follower is the son of the Catullan ambassador to the Federation, which results in Kirk's receiving instructions to handle the group gently and to allow them the freedom of the *Enterprise*. Sevrin employs his engineering knowledge to rig up an ultrasonic device that almost kills Kirk and company. Stealing a shuttlecraft, the young people flee to the planet Eden, which Spock has discovered for them. Kirk and a landing party follow them down, only to discover that Eden's soil and vegetation are highly poisonous. One youngster, a likable man named Adam, is dead. The others are rescued, except for Dr. Sevrin, who kills himself by tasting a highly toxic fruit.

The story outline for this episode, entitled "Joanna," featured Dr. McCoy's daughter, Joanna, instead of Irini Galliulin. Joanna, who was McCoy's only child, was included in the later editions of the *Star Trek Writers' and Directors' Guide,* along with other biographical information on the doctor. Joanna was said to be a nursing student back on Earth, with only an occasional letter from her father to remind her of his existence. The appearance of Joanna would have provided additional insight into the character of Dr. Leonard "Bones" McCoy, but for unknown reasons she was written out of the episode's final script.

In recent years, nostalgia-minded individuals have reached back into history to influence contemporary tastes in fashion and music, recalling elements of "simpler" times and transplanting these elements into today's more complex way of life. In "Star Trek's" era, the urge to return to more tranquil surroundings is definitely present (as specifically voiced by Kirk and McCoy in "The Paradise Syndrome"). It is therefore easy to imagine why Dr. Sevrin's desire to "go back to nature" would be so popular with the young people who joined him in becoming "space hippies."

Spock, of all people, is the logical choice to show sympathy for Sevrin and his people because they are seeking the same thing *he* wants; a place in which to feel at home. This common bond, plus the fact that Spock finds relaxation in expressing himself with music, accounts for the Vulcan's participation in a "jam session" with Adam and his hippie friends. Mr. Spock is so involved with the young people's dream that he applies his scientific skills to locate the "mythical" planet Eden.

Although the planet Eden actually exists, it does not prove to be the object of the young people's desires. Its very ground is hostile, its vegetation is deadly, and its apparent beauty is not meant for those who seek it.

The planet has a lot in common with Dr. Sevrin who, because of his affliction, can also cause death to those around him. Sevrin's disease can be cured only in highly technological surroundings; his madness causes him to flee from this fact. Even if the planet Eden would have proven hospitable, Sevrin's presence would eventually have killed his companions.

Dr. Sevrin's expertise in ultrasonics almost causes the destruction of the *Enterprise*. He lies to his followers, telling them that the starship's crew will be rendered unconscious by the sounds, which are actually deadly. It is Mr. Spock who first reacts to the ultrasonic sounds, because of his superior pair of ears.

Mr. Spock is not the only individual on this voyage with an unusual pair of ears. Dr. Sevrin's ears are puzzling, since the man appears to be Terran (although he *is* said to have worked on the planet Tiburon). It is possible that Sevrin's ears are (1) in their natural state, or (2) the result of an operation (possibly an extreme variation of having one's ears pierced).

Irini (Mary-Linda Rapelye) is apparently included in this adventure to provide a substitution for Joanna McCoy. The relationship between Irini and Pavel Chekov could have provided more insight into the young Russian navigator than it actually contributes, but it is still effective in adding to Chekov's substance.

Actor Skip Homeier (Dr. Sevrin) also appears as Melakon in "Patterns of Force."

Phyllis Douglas (Girl Number Two) also appears as Yeoman Mears in "The Galileo Seven."

The space cruiser *Aurora,* which is seen in the episode's teaser, was produced by taking the miniature alien ship from "The Tholian Web" and treating it to a new paint job plus a new pair of nacelles (which appear to make use of parts from *Enterprise* and Klingon ship plastic model kits).

REQUIEM FOR METHUSELAH

Episode # 76

Story outline   10/2/68
First draft script   11/19/68
Filmed in early December 1968

WRITER   Jerome Bixby
DIRECTOR   Murray Golden
COMPOSER   Fred Steiner (Brahms paraphrase by Ivan Ditmars)
PHOTOGRAPHIC EFFECTS   Westheimer Company

When an outbreak of deadly Rigellian fever strikes aboard the *Enterprise,* the starship journeys to planet Holberg 917-G in search of ryetalyn, the fever's antidote. Kirk, Spock, and McCoy beam down to the palatial residence of the mysterious Mr. Flint and his beautiful young ward, Reena Kapec. Kirk falls in love with Reena while Flint's servant robot gathers the crucial ryetalyn. Kirk and company notice that Flint's home is filled with rare art treasures created by some of the most talented and noted individuals in Earth's history. Flint is actually an immortal who has wandered the Earth for centuries, existing as Leonardo da Vinci, Johannes Brahms, and many other important individuals. After settling on Holberg, Flint ended his loneliness by building a succession of "Reena" androids, the last of which is the Reena whom Kirk loves. Kirk and Flint fight over Reena, but the sensitive android witnesses the conflict, suffers a breakdown, and "dies." McCoy discovers that Flint, too, will soon die; in leaving Earth's atmosphere Flint unwittingly cancelled out his immortality. Mr. Spock uses a Vulcan Mind Touch to erase the painful memory of Reena from Jim Kirk's mind.

The story outline for this episode contained some touches that are reminiscent of the classic science fiction film *Forbidden Planet* (Metro-Goldwyn-Mayer– 1956). For instance, Flint's home was of futuristic design, guarded by Flint's all-purpose robot. In one scene, Kirk and McCoy attempted to sneak into Flint's home to look around: when Flint's robot discovered them, Reena stopped it from attacking them. As Kirk embraced Reena, Dr. McCoy guarded the doorway. Finally, Kirk fought a monster that was actually an illusion thrown around Flint's robot. Other portions of the outline had Kirk and his companions discovering an undried Michelangelo painting in Flint's studio. The *8,000* year old man was also *Beethoven* (Spock's favorite composer because of his music's logical, mathematical construction). Mr. Spock enabled Kirk to forget Reena by using mental suggestion from a distance, while Kirk was in his cabin and the Vulcan was on the bridge.

"Requiem for Methuselah" tells the story of Flint, who is truly a timeless individual. His incredibly long lifetime (6,000 years in the final episode) has enabled him to gather experience and knowledge from the finest minds of history. Flint's enormous quantity of spare time has made it possible for him to read every available book, study every art and science in existence, and transform himself into a unique genius. Flint's longevity, however, has also given him the same loneliness known by other long-lifed individuals within the "Star Trek" universe (including Apollo and Zefrem Cochrane).

After acquiring the knowledge to build a "daughter" who would never age and die, Flint used the alias of "Mr. Brack" to purchase his small planet, build his huge residence and begin a long series of experiments that would culminate in the creation of Reena. (An alien named "Brack" had appeared in the film *This Island Earth*).

Captain Kirk, arriving on Flint's world, has something in common with the scientist: he has also relied upon a machine to supply him with a sense of companionship and purpose. It is no surprise that Kirk, like Flint, should become attracted to the symmetrical beauty of the machine-woman, Reena.

Other fine touches in this episode include Reena's inexplicable attraction to the laboratory (the place of her "birth"), Mr. Spock's Chopin rendition, and the Vulcan's gift of forgetfulness to his captain. Despite its many resemblances to other works of science fiction and fantasy, "Requiem" is one of the most interesting and beautiful "Star Trek" segments.

Lost Horizon (Columbia–1937) featured a scene (deleted before the film was released) in which an explorer performed an unknown Chopin piece that had been taught to him by an incredibly old pupil of the composer. The scientist on *The Island of Lost Souls* (Paramount–1932) sent a visiting man to his creation, a panther transformed into a woman, to see if she was capable of falling in love. An episode of "The Twilight Zone" ("The Lateness of the Hour") featured a lonely old scientist who constructed an android "daughter" who was programmed to think that she was human. In mythology, Pygmalion sculpted a woman who was given life by the gods. In this episode, Reena's surname of "Kapec" is derived from the Czechoslovakian writer Karel Capek, who invented the word "robot" for his 1921 play, *R.U.R. (Rossum's Universal Robots)*.

The late James Daly (Flint) was a popular television actor since the 1950s; after starring in the "Hallmark Hall of Fame" segment "Give Us Barabbas," he went on to star as adventurer Michael Powers in the series "Foreign Intrigue" (1953–54). His most remembered recurring role is that of Dr. Paul Lochner on "Medical Center" (which premiered in 1969). Daly can also be seen in episodes of "The Twilight Zone" ("Next Stop Willoughby") and "The Invaders" ("Beachhead" and "The Peacemaker"). Mr. Daly portrayed Flint as a brooding, secretive man with equal helpings of menace and tragedy, a well executed, difficult sketch.

Louise Sorel (Reena), who also created a mysterious and tragic character (with just the hint of a seventeen-jewel movement) can also be seen in "The Night Gallery" episodes "Pickman's Model" and "The Dead Man" (with Jeff Corey).

Murray Golden also directed the "Invaders" segment "Labyrinth" (by Art Wallace).

James Daly's characterization was aided by his makeup (a set of expressive eyebrows not unlike those of Dr. McCoy), his hairstyle (resembling that of a Michelangelo statue), and his costume (an excellent William Theiss design combining elements of futuristic style and a suit that might have been worn by Prince Hamlet).

Flint's residence was the same optical painting used as the Rigel Fortress in "The Cage." Also in the interests of economy, Flint's (M-4) robot incorporated parts of the Nomad probe created for "The Changeling."

The ending of this episode, in which Spock erases the memory of Reena from Kirk's mind, is short and precisely presented, and is also one of the most sensitive moments in "Star Trek."

THE SAVAGE CURTAIN

Episode # 77

Final draft script 12/6/68
Filmed in middle December 1968

WRITERS Gene Roddenberry, Arthur Heinemann
(Story by Gene Roddenberry)
DIRECTOR Herschel Daugherty
COMPOSER Fred Steiner
PHOTOGRAPHIC EFFECTS Vanderveer Photo Effects

While surveying the planet Excalbia, a world that apparently consists of nothing but a lavalike surface, the U.S.S. *Enterprise* is scanned by a powerful energy source on the planet below. Soon afterward, an entity who resembles Abraham Lincoln and who claims to be the famous man, materializes in space near the *Enterprise* and requests to be beamed aboard. Against the recommendations of Dr. McCoy, Kirk and Spock decide to accept Lincoln's invitation to visit the surface of Excalbia. There, a rock creature named Yarnek announces that the *Enterprise* men will participate in a battle between good and evil, so that Excalbians can learn about these humanoid philosophies. On the "good" side are Kirk, Spock, Lincoln, and the legendary Vulcan peacemaker, Surak. Representing the "bad" side are Kahless the Klingon, Zora (a merciless criminal scientist), Genghis Khan, and Colonel Green (an unprincipled, aggressive Terran killer). After only Kirk and Spock, Genghis Khan and Zora are left alive, Yarnek returns our people to the *Enterprise.*

Evidently, the concepts of good and evil are not known throughout "Star Trek's" universe. To acquaint themselves with the ideals of these concepts, Yarnek forces Kirk and Spock into a combat contest not unlike those faced by *Enterprise* personnel in "The Gamesters of Triskelion," "Bread and Circuses," and "Arena" (although the Metrons' purpose in "Arena" is to *stop* conflict, whereas the Excalbians wish to *create* it).

Because of the philosophy discussed in its script, "The Savage Curtain" is more of a morality play than an action episode. The script is important to "Star Trek" largely because it introduces two individuals who are analogous to Kirk and Spock respectively, Lincoln and Surak.

Abraham Lincoln is a person who epitomizes concepts that are deeply appreciated by creator Roddenberry and his creation Kirk. Lincoln's presence on the *Enterprise,* and throughout most of the episode's action, enables the audience to observe Kirk behaving more like a human being than a starship captain. The figure of Lincoln is also compatible with the Vulcan, Surak.

The Vulcans are widely regarded as the most impressive and interesting race introduced in "Star Trek." Their intriguing nature is largely based on our lack of acquaintance with their capabilities and customs. What little we know of Vulcans is conveyed to us by Mr. Spock, who is hardly typical of his people. It was possible that, because of the Vulcans' numerous differences from Terrans, we would not have been able to identify with pure-blooded Vulcans existing without Terran influences. The only other Vulcan we know is Sarek, whose prime influence is Amanda. In "The Savage Curtain" we meet Surak, who enables us to understand the Vulcan credo. Quiet and compassionate, Surak has rejected the expression of his emotions to enable his people to unify themselves and, like Lincoln, he is killed for his efforts.

Actor Barry Atwater deserves the major share of credit for the successful presentation of Surak. His Vulcan is filled with subdued dignity and completely likable qualities; that is particularly astounding considering that Mr. Atwater is also remembered for his horrifyingly undead performance of vampire Janos Sgorzny in the 1972 TV movie (pilot) *The Night Stalker* (written by Richard Matheson). The versatile Mr. Atwater can also be seen in episodes of "The Outer Limits" ("Corpus Earthling"), "The Twilight Zone" ("The Monsters Are Due on Maple Street"), "The Night Gallery" ("The Doll of Death"), "Voyage to the Bottom of the Sea" ("The Buccaneer" and "No Way Back"), "The Man from U.N.C.L.E." ("The Do It Yourself Dreadful Affair"), and "One Step Beyond" ("The Day the World Wept," in which Atwater portrayed Abraham Lincoln).

Lee Bergere (Lincoln) can also be seen in segments of "One Step Beyond" ("The Storm") and "The Man from U.N.C.L.E." ("The Tigers Are Coming Affair," with Jill Ireland). He appeared regularly as George in the comedy series "Hot L Baltimore." In this episode, he injected a warm and intimate quality into his portrayal of Lincoln; at times, he conveyed the impression that Lincoln regarded Kirk almost as a son.

Phillip Pine (Colonel Green) is one of those ageless actors who still looks largely the same as he did in the 1950s. His long and varied television career has featured appearances in "The Adventures of Superman" ("The Talkative Dummy," "The Broken Statues"),

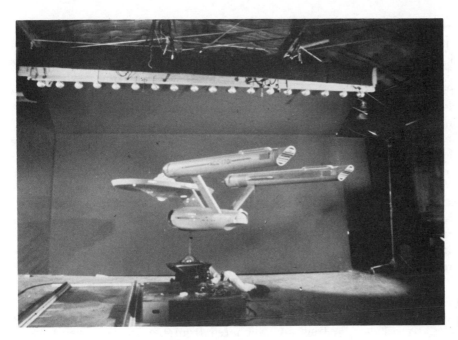

The fourteen-foot long *Enterprise* miniature ready to be photographed.

"The Outer Limits" ("Hundred Days of the Dragon"), "Twilight Zone" ("The Four of Us Are Dying," with Peter Brocco), "One Step Beyond" ("Where Are They"), and "Voyage to the Bottom of the Sea" ("And Five of Us Are Left"). Pine appeared regularly as good guy Sergeant Newman on "The Blue Knight."

Robert Herron (Kahless the Klingon) was also actor Jeffrey Hunter's stunt double in "The Cage."

Janos Prohaska (Yarnek), who appeared as alien creatures in "The Devil in the Dark" and "A Private Little War," was similarly featured in episodes of "The Outer Limits" ("The Sixth Finger" and "The Probe") and "Land of the Giants" ("Comeback").

Director Herschel Daugherty's television career dates back to the 1950s, and includes segments of "The Time Tunnel" ("Kill Two By Two" and "The Town of Terror"), "The Six Million Dollar Man" ("The Peeping Blonde"), "Circle of Fear" ("Dark Vengeance"), and "Thriller" (including "The Weird Tailor," "Parasite Mansion," and "Dialogues with Death"). Previous to "Star Trek," Daugherty directed William Shatner in segments of "Thriller" ("The Grim Reaper") and "For the People" ("With Intent to Interference").

ALL OUR YESTERDAYS

Episode # 78
Story outline   9/23/68
Final draft script   12/12/68
Revised final draft   12/17/68
Original title   "A Handful of Dust"
Filmed in late December 1968

WRITER   Jean Lisette Aroeste
DIRECTOR   Marvin Chomsky

On the planet Sarpeidon, which is about to be engulfed in the explosion of its sun, Kirk, Spock, and McCoy discover a huge library. The aged librarian, Mr. Atoz, has supervised the transferral of his planet's people into past eras by the use of a machine called the *atavachron*. When Kirk hears a woman's scream while he is examining a past era, he leaps through the atavachron's portal to help. Spock and McCoy, attempting to locate Kirk, unintentionally enter Sarpeidon's ice age, where they meet the beautiful exile, Zarabeth. With the aid of another traveler in time, Kirk returns to the library. Meanwhile, in the past, Spock has fallen in love with Zarabeth and his human half begins to dominate him. Zarabeth tells Spock and McCoy that they cannot return to the present without dying, but she has erroneously assumed that they were "prepared" (as she was) to live only in the past. Returning to the place where they entered the ice age, Spock and McCoy locate the time portal and, guided by Kirk's voice, return to the present. Zarabeth remains isolated in the past. Atoz enters the past to join his family and the *Enterprise* leaves as Sarpeidon is destroyed.

The story outline for this segment, entitled "A Handful of Dust," bore little resemblance to the completed episode: the most outstanding difference was the complete *absence of Zarabeth*. Kirk, Spock, and McCoy went to Sarpeidon and found the planet in ruins, except for the undamaged library containing the unnamed time-portal machine. Kirk unwittingly entered the past into a locale resembling San Francisco's Barbary Coast, but escaped back to the library with the aid of another time traveler. Spock and McCoy, attempting to follow Kirk, found themselves in a desert wasteland. Spock coped with the climate, but McCoy was dying from the heat when the duo was captured by mutant humanoids. While Kirk battled Mr. Atoz, his fellow time traveler aided Spock and McCoy to return to the library. Their return was almost disastrous when McCoy became "stuck" in the portal, his arm in the library and the rest of him in the desert. Finally, Kirk's time traveling benefactor destroyed the time machine to prevent further interruptions of the planet's past, resulting in the library collapsing in ruins behind our fleeing friends.

The strange events that befall Captain Kirk, Mr. Spock, and Dr. McCoy in "All Our Yesterdays" are brought about by our friends themselves. Kirk succumbs to his usual weakness for the opposite sex by leaping before he looks. Arriving in a Sarpeidon locale resembling seventeenth century England, the captain finds himself jailed on a charge of witchcraft (merely because he materializes out of thin air and converses with a disembodied spirit voice called "Bones").

Spock and McCoy, understandably concerned about their friend the captain, attempt to follow him and instead propel themselves into the cold, lonely hell of an alien ice age.

The real problems this time around are the predicaments of Spock and McCoy. The Vulcan is able to adapt to the icy climate despite his native world's hot, thin atmosphere. Dr. McCoy, however, possesses none of Spock's remarkable adaptive features and comes close to freezing to death. At this point the beautiful and tragic Zarabeth enters the tale and creates more complications for the duo.

In "The Immunity Syndrome" it is established that Spock is able to receive telepathic impressions from a doomed starship's Vulcan crew. Apparently, Spock's receiving abilities are greater than we imagined because once Spock is exposed to anxiety regarding his attraction to Zarabeth, and his worry over Kirk's and McCoy's survival, he turns away from Vulcan logic and begins to act more and more human. We are led to believe that his sudden conversion into an emotional "cave man" type is the result of his being stranded in the past, in an era when the distant Vulcans were illogical savages, fighting among themselves. The only conclusion is that at least part of Spock's ability to maintain his Vulcan decorum results from his constant telepathic attachment to his father's race.

Do the Vulcans constantly reach out their minds to all their people on Vulcan and beyond, to produce a complex communal impulse to exclude emotional responses from their lives? Unfortunately, we never learn more about this intriguing possibility.

Spock's conversion into an emotional, woman-seeking, meat-eating primitive human also provides problems for McCoy; the doctor finds himself acting as the psychoanalyst for his transformed friend, whose superior strength could crush the life out of the Terran physician at any moment.

Zarabeth, the sole witness to the drama being played between Spock and McCoy, had almost adapted to the idea of spending the rest of her life utterly alone in her exile; it is no wonder that she wants Spock to stay with her. Mr. Spock's farewell to her is as emotional for the television audience as it is to Spock, Zarabeth, and McCoy themselves.

Mariette Hartley (Zarabeth), a recurring player in "The Hero" (as Ruth Garrett, 1966–67) and "Peyton Place" (as Clair, 1964–69), co-starred in Gene Roddenberry's 1973 TV pilot film *Genesis II* (with Percy Rodrigues). In "The Twilight Zone" episode "The Long Morrow," she played a young woman who was tragically alienated from her space traveler fiancé (portrayed by Robert Lansing). More recently, Ms. Hartley has been noted for her appearances in a series of enjoyably humorous commercials for Polaroid with actor James Garner and her temporary assignment as co-host on NBC's "Today" show.

Ian Wolfe (Mr. Atoz) also appears as Septimus in "Bread and Circuses."

The atavachron's monitor screen and control console were fashioned from pieces of Gary Seven's Beta Five computer constructed for "Assignment Earth."

The view of Kirk vanishing into the (time portal) brick wall was accomplished with an imaginative use of the "split screen" process in which two separate photographic images are combined on one piece of film. Kirk "vanished" by stepping into the seam between the two images (1) the empty side of the wall and (2) his side of the wall.

Mr. Atoz is certainly the best name for a librarian, considering the name is spelled "A" TO "Z."

TURNABOUT INTRUDER

Episode # 79

Story outline   5/8/68

First draft script   12/1/68

Final draft script   12/20/68

Revised final draft   12/30/68

Filmed in late December 1968, early January 1969

WRITER   Arthur H. Singer (Story by Gene Roddenberry)
DIRECTOR   Herb Wallerstein
MUSIC DIRECTOR   Richard Lapham
PHOTOGRAPHIC EFFECTS   Westheimer Company

Dr. Janice Lester, who was once romantically involved with James Kirk, hates the captain because of his rise in rank and his choice to pursue the *Enterprise* instead of her. She lures Kirk to planet Camus II, where she has discovered an alien mechanism capable of transferring two minds into each other's bodies. Using the device, Dr. Lester transfers her consciousness into Captain Kirk's body and his mind is trapped in Janice's body. Dr. Coleman, Janice's current lover and partner, sees that Kirk's mind is kept sedated. Mr. Spock becomes suspicious, and by a Vulcan Mind Meld he determines that Captain Kirk's mind *is* trapped in Dr. Lester's body. Janice's mind, functioning in Kirk's body, initiates court-martial proceedings against Spock and all who believe that the captain's mind is not where it belongs. But she is unable to control her emotions and during the proceedings she loses her temper, arousing the suspicions of the other crew members. When "Kirk" charges McCoy and Scotty with mutiny and imposes the death penalty, the entire crew knows that something is seriously wrong. Fortunately, Kirk, with the assistance of the telepathic Mr. Spock, fights the effects of the mind transfer and, through concentration, the transfer wears off.

Captain Kirk has survived crises that have confined and frustrated him physically and emotionally. He has experienced his mind and body being separated into two halves (in "The Enemy Within"), but his experiences in "Turnabout Intruder" provide Kirk with his most pressing and intimate problems, separating him from his friends, his command, and his own physical body.

Captain Kirk and his crew have been exposed to many scientific realities that previously would have seemed impossible. The scientific studies written by Mr. Spock and Dr. McCoy regarding such entities and phenomena as Thasians, Organians, the Guardian of Forever, and the existence of other dimensions have probably been received with initial disbelief from many Federation personnel. Scientific discoveries that alter individual's ideas about the nature of their universe and their own identities are especially difficult to accept. Perhaps this is why, even among his friends on his starship, Kirk (in Janice's body) has a difficult time proving his case.

Logically, Captain Kirk knows Spock, McCoy, Chapel, Scotty, and the other officers in his crew so intimately that he could probably cite dozens of facts that would convince these people of his identity, no matter *what* body his mind was in at the time. Unfortunately, the shock of transition, the drugs administered to Janice's body, and the incredible nature of his predicament, combine to make things extremely difficult for Kirk (and very suspenseful for "Star Trek" fans).

Spock's realization of Kirk's situation affects the Vulcan so that he is unable to suggest methods that would quickly bring out the truth. At the trial, for example, Spock could have asked "Kirk" and "Janice" to recite any information that only the captain would know; the self-destruct sequence of the *Enterprise,* information regarding a recent mission, or details about Captain Kirk's life and family. But even if Spock had thought of this approach, would the *Enterprise* personnel have believed what was happening, especially amid the denials of "Captain Kirk"?

In a 1963 episode of "The Outer Limits" ("The Human Factor"), actor Gary Merrill starred as a research scientist at an isolated military installation whose brain was transferred into the body of a deranged individual (and vice versa). When the scientist attempted to convince his colleagues of what had happened accidentally, he was promptly thrown into a straitjacket. Only his close personal relationship with a co-worker (portrayed by Sally Kellerman) saved the hero of that episode, just as Kirk's close friendship with Spock serves a similar function in "Turnabout Intruder."

Actress Sandra Smith (Dr. Janice Lester) gives an extremely dedicated and effective performance in this episode. This was the only occasion in "Star Trek" that a performer other than William Shatner portrayed Captain James T. Kirk, and Ms. Smith rose to the challenge of this unique and strenuous assignment. Sandra Smith subsequently appeared regularly as Dr. Lydia Thorpe on the television series "The Interns," from 1970 to 1971.

Dr. McCoy has been known to question the captain's commands on the bridge of the *Enterprise* (William Shatner, Nichelle Nichols, DeForest Kelley).

Barbara Baldavin (Communications Officer Angela) also appeared in "Balance of Terror" and "Shore Leave."

"Turnabout Intruder" was inspired by *Turnabout,* a novel written in 1931 by Thorne Smith (who is best remembered for his "Topper" books). The book concerned a husband and wife whose intellects are transferred into each other's bodies by magical means. The tale was filmed as *Turnabout* (United Artists–1940) and was the subject and title of a short-lived television series.

10 Star Trek—The Motion Picture

The Long Road Back to the *Enterprise*

By the start of 1972, "Star Trek" was being syndicated in over 170 worldwide television markets.[1] Trek-oriented books continued to be produced, and fanzine publication continued to flourish. A group of "Star Trek" fans, "The Committee," had planned the first Trek convention and were nervously awaiting the weekend of January 21–23, when their gathering would be held at New York City's Statler-Hilton Hotel.

Between 300 and 400 people were originally expected to attend this first Committee convention, but the convention's advance registration soon reached over *700*, with a projected figure of 1,500 attendees.[2] The final attending registration was approximately *3,000* and assured Trek's fans that their favorite series was still enjoying a large and active following.

Future conventions would break this attendance record at least several times over, but this first large-scale experiment was very important to the future of "Star Trek." In addition to the convention's "trading post" (dealers' room) area, other prime attractions were a specially provided NASA exhibit (indicating the beginnings of the agency's interactions with Trek fans) and a talk given by Dr. Isaac Asimov (who would later serve as the special science consultant for *Star Trek—The Motion Picture*).

At one point during the convention, some of the organizers huddled around a television set to watch the debut of *The People,* a television movie that featured William Shatner. The movie was well received. Shatner's role in this science fiction vehicle, which had nothing to do with "Star Trek," started a discussion group debating whether Trek could return to television as a new production featuring the series' original cast. It was just a dream, all hope and no substance, until the rumors started.

By the last day of the convention, rumors of a "Star Trek" revival were running rampant. In its coverage of the convention, *TV Guide* acknowledged these rumors, attributing them to someone from Paramount's television division; there was, it seemed, a possibility that "Star Trek" could indeed be brought back as an all-new television series.[3] From that time, until the appearance of *Star Trek—The Motion Picture,* Trek fans never stopped hoping for the return of their favorite escapist vehicle, the starship *Enterprise.*

For almost a decade the dream persisted, discouraged by numerous changes in plans, but *encouraged* with announcements of production preparations that resulted in the production and release of "Star Trek's" multi-million dollar return.[4] During those ten years, science fiction became accepted by motion picture audiences all over the world. The big-budgeted science fiction and fantasy epics, which began with *Star Wars'* wonderfully successful reception, firmly established themselves in favor of yesterday's high-budgeted musicals, espionage tales, and western epics. Circumstances had evolved to encourage the conversion of a dream into a reality. *Star Trek—The Motion Picture* would reunite the series' full, original cast on an *Enterprise* that was no longer limited by television deadlines and budgets and which utilized cinematic techniques that had not existed when the original "Star Trek" series was produced.

"Star Trek" the television series, which had produced its quality visualizations of the future by taxing the ingenuity and dedication of its artists to their limits, would remain as a monument to imagination, art, and optimism, which is still loved by "Star Trek" fans everywhere. Fanzines would still be written, and books (like this one) would still be published about the series. In addition, Trek fans would find their horizons expanded by the visual and philosophical wonders of *Star Trek—The Motion Picture.*

"Star Trek" on the Big Screen

"Star Trek" is successful for many reasons, especially because of its concern with conveying the spirit of human adventure. In the future, Trek tells us, mankind will use the tools of science to explore beyond our world. We shall see undreamed-of wonders and discover countless new friends and concepts. Our horizons will be expanded beyond one planet, and we will eventually visit other galaxies and universes. But wherever we go, we shall still retain our human natures and it will be as men that we react to the riddles, discoveries, and dangers that we will encounter in outer space.

Star Trek—The Motion Picture concerns itself with these unknowns, with the vastness of outer space, and

Dr. McCoy is still concerned about the captain's motivations (DeForest Kelley, William Shatner).

with the need that all men have to discover ourselves in the face of our universe. Man's questing nature comes from his search for his own identity. We each have our own individual ideas of happiness; everyone of us wishes to *attain something,* to acquire knowledge, position, companionship, or a combination of these goals. This *attainment,* as it applies to human, Vulcan, Deltan, or machine, is the central theme of *Star Trek—The Motion Picture.*

The Story

The years between the *Enterprise*'s original five-year mission, and the events represented in *Star Trek—The Motion Picture* have not changed James T. Kirk's nature at all. Upon returning from his tour of duty on the *Enterprise,* Kirk found himself revered as a hero by his Earthbound colleagues. He was given a desk job by his superiors, and he probably took the job because for a time he believed that now was the time for him to find that "beach to walk on" that had so far eluded him.[5] After a time, however, Kirk discovered that his personal paradise was really the command chair of the *Enterprise,* and that he had no urge to be ". . . a chair-bound paper-pusher."[6]

The presence of V'ger furnishes Kirk with a return ticket to his starship captain's rank, and also provides him with a challenge that is more crucial than most of his past missions put together. His solution of the V'ger problem would not have been possible, though, without the heroism of Willard Decker.

Captain Willard Decker is no stranger to the obligations, challenges, and lures of command, or to the necessity for making correct decisions regardless of personal safety. His father, Commodore Matthew Decker, had been familiar with all these aspects of command.[7] Will Decker had been recommended for special starship commanding officer training by Admiral Kirk, who probably saw that the two Deckers had a lot in common. Kirk identifies with Will's urge to command a starship, and in turn Will probably regards Kirk with as much respect as he accords his late father.

Kirk and Decker have much in common, especially their obsession that personal entanglements should not come between them and their careers. Just as the young Jim Kirk had relationships with women that somehow managed to end before lasting commitments could be made, young Will Decker had been involved with Ilia while he was stationed on her homeworld Delta.[8]

We do not know why James Kirk drives himself to command, or why he feels simultaneously drawn to, and trapped by, the *Enterprise*.[9] But we do know that Kirk will never leave the *Enterprise* as long as it is the vehicle that enables him to give security to others and to enjoy it himself as well. Decker, on the other hand, has learned to love command; probably because of the teachings of his father and the respect he has learned to lavish on both the memory of the man and his command. Apparently, Decker's motivations for commanding the *Enterprise* are different from Kirk's; it is doubtful that Kirk would have been able to stand another commander taking his ship out from under him.[10] We also know that, given the choice of a woman's love or his ship, Kirk would always choose to be captain.[11] At the end of his human existence, Will Decker chooses to join with V'ger; or, more exactly, he apparently chooses to consummate his relationship with Ilia, whose mind is now a part of V'ger. Decker attains his union while following the necessary course of his duty as he saves the *Enterprise,* the life of all aboard her (including his mentor and friend, Kirk), and the totality of the planet and the system on which he has been raised.

Kirk's happiness at Decker's exit from the scene is accounted for by several facts. Decker had fulfilled his duty and accomplished it in such a way that Kirk was once again free to command the *Enterprise,* probably on a permanent basis. Most importantly, Kirk (who had witnessed the death of Will's father, also while in the performance of his duty) knew that he had witnessed Decker's rebirth instead of his death. Willard Decker had succeeded in finding his own identity, attaining happiness at last.

Mr. Spock, a product of two different systems working toward the same peaceful end, has been attempting to discover his identity all his life. Because of his Vulcan upbringing, Spock has usually been inclined to disavow his human half. Spock's years of attendance at Earth's Starfleet Academy, and his tours of duty aboard the *Enterprise* under Captains Pike and Kirk, had provided him with much insight into himself.

Early in his starfleet career, while he was surrounded by Terrans, Spock had permitted his long-buried human emotions to surface occasionally.[12] In deference to his mother, Amanda, Spock functioned openly as a human. Away from the prohibitive teachings of the Vulcan way, human emotions were not features to be concealed. But the teachings of his Vulcan father, Sarek, were probably enough to cause guilt within Spock whenever he allowed himself the luxury of being human.[13] This guilt, plus his awkwardness concerning his emotions, probably accounted for Spock's decision to serve as a *Vulcan* under Captain James T. Kirk. These and other motivations, known only to Spock himself, apparently accounted for his decision to return to Vulcan to achieve total logic and to attain his place as the son of Sarek.[14]

Spock's wish to shed his emotions by attaining *Kolinahr* is negated by a combination of factors. No matter which half of himself he chooses to live by, Mr. Spock will still experience alienation and guilt. These feelings of insecurity, plus his recollections of his emotional entanglements with Chris Pike, Jim Kirk, Christine Chapel, and Leila Kalomi, probably serve to inspire an emotional reaction as Spock senses V'ger's presence. The female Vulcan master, in touch with Spock's mind, informs him of what he will later accept as his truth; that *Kolinahr,* and the Vulcan way of life, are not for him.[15] At first, Spock feels drawn to V'ger and wishes to meld with this concentration of pure logic. However, upon experiencing V'ger's essence, Mr. Spock realizes that knowledge itself cannot bring him what he seeks. In that moment Spock admits to him-

The *Enterprise* travels on (Leonard Nimoy, Marcy Lafferty, William Shatner, Stephen Collins, George Takei).

self that what he is seeking is . . . happiness.[16] In facing this conclusion, Mr. Spock chooses to cease being addressed as "the Vulcan," and begins a new mission on the *Enterprise,* a two-way relationship with Kirk and McCoy and a new life as a human with Vulcan features.

Spock's heart is still where his liver should be, and his ears are still pointed, but one cannot help but speculate what the new relationship will be between McCoy and Spock and whether Spock will discover genuinely friendly feelings toward Mr. Scott, because of their mutual love of machinery and the *Enterprise.* The relationship between Kirk and Spock will probably remain relatively unchanged, for there has always been an intense friendship even though Kirk was usually the only one who verbalized it. Mr. Spock has now attained a sort of "anti-*Kolinahr,*" casting out his denial of his human traits.

For Ilia, there is no such conflict, no question of choice. Just as the Vulcans learned to unite by suppressing their emotions and therefore repressing themselves, the Deltans relish their constructive emotional characteristics. The Deltans, in this respect, are the opposites of the Vulcans. Mr. Spock regarded the human behavior of Kirk and company as terribly excessive; Ilia probably regards it as highly introverted, compared to the Deltan life-style to which she is accustomed. Ilia states that she has signed an oath of celibacy; this is probably a regulation that must be followed before a Deltan is allowed to serve in a starship crew (unless it's an all-Deltan starship).

Ilia, who had experienced a relationship with Will Decker, still likes him a great deal. Her initial expression of support for Decker upon learning that Kirk has relieved him of command indicates that she may be *in love with* Decker, while being bound by her oath of celibacy *not* to encourage their relationship. In this respect, Ilia is as repressed as Mr. Spock when it comes to concealing her emotions. Even so, it appears that Ilia and Decker may be on the way toward acknowledging their attachment for each other . . . until Ilia is "abducted" by V'ger. At least part of her look of desperation at the instant of her disappearance may be the result of her regret that she has left so much unsaid between herself and Will Decker.

The Ilia-probe's characteristics are derived from those of the real Ilia and are perfectly reproduced within the mechanism. Even though what remains of Ilia herself is now contained with V'ger, the Ilia-probe's personality includes Ilia's love for Decker. As a result of the Ilia-probe's confusion at these emotional sensations, Kirk and Decker are able to reach her enough so that she can aid them in fighting V'ger. V'ger is also confused by these emotional reactions of its probe and attempts to cast them out, just as Spock has disavowed *his* emotions for so long.

The strength of their love causes both Decker *and* the Ilia-probe to show their intense happiness as they merge with V'ger and also attain a union with each other. Fortunately for Earth, this merging apparently produces an understanding of, and a respect for, humanoid life within V'ger.

V'ger, whose attainment of intelligence was a cosmic accident, has retained its original programmed desire to serve its creators. Combined with its vast storehouse of knowledge and its urge to acquire all the additional enlightenment it can find, V'ger's knowledge of Earth leads to the supermachine concluding that its point of origin is the only place its quest for knowledge can end.

V'ger is also aware that when it has gathered the last scraps of knowledge, its purpose for existence will vanish. Its manufactured personality is so complex that V'ger has learned to *fear* the concepts of obsolescence and death. To prevent its own destruction, V'ger prevents itself from passing along its knowledge to "the creator." For awhile, V'ger is an intensely unhappy machine. It has self-awareness, it has conflicts, but it has *nothing* because of its inability to locate and understand its creator. V'ger then assures its humanity by reaching out for help and absorbing the entities Decker and Ilia into itself.

Before Decker merged with V'ger, V'ger had gained possession of Ilia but had only *used* her mind's knowledge instead of absorbing it and learning from it. Now, with the addition of these two human identities, V'ger knows the concepts of happiness and love. V'ger, at long last, has attained fulfillment by realizing that knowledge does not necessarily represent security. Identity and joy, the new V'ger knows, results partially from acknowledging the beauty of the universe and one's place within it.

V'ger, free to appreciate its newfound emotions and to resume its explorations of the universe, leaves Earth. At the same time Spock, relishing his new lifestyle, is aware that Kirk is as happy as he can possibly be, back in command of the U.S.S. *Enterprise.* Human, alien, and machine elements have been drawn together, interacted, learned from their experience, and formed new associations in their explorations of the universe. And Trek fans have experienced *Star Trek—The Motion Picture.*

In this particular science fiction film cycle, most of the offerings are extravaganzas involving constant spaceship battles, hideous monsters, and generally violent vibrations. They are action films set in outer space or on other planets, and they usually have only a minimal concern with projecting a constructive future for mankind. In the midst of these latter-day shoot-em-ups and monster-killers, *Star Trek—The Motion Picture* is a welcome change of pace. It presents the starship *Enterprise* as it has never been seen before, filled with visual and philosophical beauty. It is proof that (to paraphrase Commodore Stocker in "The Deadly Years") there is no limit of direction for a motion picture if it has the right men at the helm.

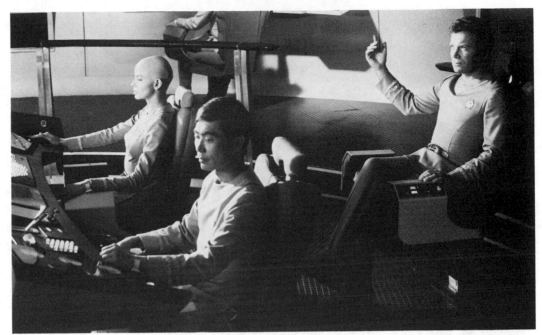

For the first time in a long while, Kirk once again commands the U.S.S. *Enterprise* in *Star Trek—The Motion Picture* (Persis Khambatta, George Takei, William Shatner).

The Director

Gene Roddenberry, the producer of *Star Trek—The Motion Picture,* is the present-day equivalent of the film's Admiral Nogura, overseeing all functions of starfleet. Robert Wise, as the director of *Star Trek—The Motion Picture,* can be looked upon as the modern-day equivalent of Captain Kirk. A motion picture, like a starship, is a vehicle with a crew and a mission. The director, like a captain, must have a deep commitment to his work and must tackle his task while utilizing all his capabilities and keeping the respect of his crew. Robert Wise was the perfect choice to direct *Star Trek—The Motion Picture* because of his previous cinematic experiences, his respect for, and understanding of, science fiction, and the tremendous respect he in turn enjoys within the motion picture industry.

Robert Wise began his motion picture career at RKO studios, and first distinguished himself as a film editor, starting with the features *Bachelor Mother* (1939) and *My Favorite Wife* (1940) and progressing to such difficult and classic projects as *Citizen Kane* (1941) and *The Magnificent Ambersons* (1942). RKO producer Val Lewton was a major influence on Wise during this period. Lewton, who is known for creating some highly effective horror films, gave Wise his first directing assignment; to complete *The Curse of the Cat People.*

The Curse of the Cat People (RKO–1944) concerned a young girl and her experiences involving an imaginary playmate. The only "monsters" in the film are produced by the girl's own mind, which is helped along by hearing a well-told ghost story. The film featured characters from the earlier Val Lewton film *The Cat People* (RKO–1942), but has much more sensitivity than the original. The film taught Wise about the most effective methods of generating fear, a skill at which he would later become brilliant.

Wise's next project, which had much to do with horror, was *The Body Snatchers* (RKO–1945), in which the main horror was that once upon a time, medical researchers could find human bodies to experiment on only by dealing with the vilest of people: grave robbers. One scene, in which a corpse (Boris Karloff) appears to be returning to life on a speeding coach in a dead-of-night lightning storm, is extremely effective although no supernatural forces are actually brought into play.

Game of Death (RKO–1945), a remake of an earlier RKO classic, *The Most Dangerous Game* (1932), was directed by Wise, without the benefit of the optical paintings that were utilized so effectively in the original. He still gave the remake a directorial atmosphere similar to the original.

The Day the Earth Stood Still (20th Century-Fox–1951) is the most important of Robert Wise's science fiction/horror efforts because of its subject matter (still as relevant today as it was over twenty-five years ago), its wonderful directorial and photographic beauty, and Michael Rennie's superb characterization of Klaatu, a Spock-like alien.

Original plans for *The Day the Earth Stood Still* called for star Claude Rains to play Klaatu. Instead,

William Shatner and Robert Wise relax for a moment during the production of *Star Trek—The Motion Picture.*

the night, when ghostly sounds and sights terrify her, Ms. Harris reaches over and grasps the hand of her bedmate. When the manifestations are over, she sees the other young woman returning from another room; she had been absent during the goings-on. In one of the most chilling moments ever filmed, Ms. Harris, horrified, asks "Whose hand was I holding?"

The Andromeda Strain (Universal–1971) derived its horror from an alien germ that killed but could not *be* killed until a talented group of medical researchers risked their own lives to kill the tiny monster before it wiped out mankind. Filmed in a coldly scientific style, in sterile surroundings (a secret underground government laboratory), *The Andromeda Strain* is a long but successful film, using the revelations and reactions of the scientists to convey the terror of the situation to the audience. Wise both produced and directed *The Andromeda Strain,* a film that acquainted him with the problems of shooting within highly reflective and specialized sets and dealing with complex scientific terminologies.

Audrey Rose (United Artists–1977) utilized the talents of Robert Wise as both executive producer and director. The film, a well-presented tale of a reincarnated little girl and the problems faced by the girl and her parents, builds steadily toward a powerful climax and an unexpected ending. Wise's ability to delve into the motivations and fears of individuals and to enable his audiences to become involved within the story and its individuals, comes powerfully across in *Audrey Rose,* a film that is very spellbinding, thought-provoking, and enjoyable.

Star Trek—The Motion Picture contains elements that Robert Wise had encountered before in various forms, including space travelers and their motivations and technology (*The Day the Earth Stood Still*), rebirth (*Audrey Rose*), and scientific environments (*The Andromeda Strain*). In addition, Wise's other films, including *Helen of Troy* (Warner Brothers–1956), *West Side Story* (United Artists–1961), *The Sound of Music* (20th Century-Fox–1964), and *The Sand Pebbles* (20th Century Fox–1966), had exposed him to vastness and conflict. *Run Silent, Run Deep* (United Artists–1958), a film concerning submarines, introduced Wise to the routine and alarms of shipboard life. His high regard for science fiction and his personal conviction that science still has a lot to learn about the limitations of man and the universe explain why Robert Wise was the natural choice to direct *Star Trek—The Motion Picture.*

Transition

The additional budget and time available for *Star Trek—The Motion Picture* meant that Gene Roddenberry and his staff were free to exercise their creative talents more than they had ever done before, to create

the imposing, dignified figure of Michael Rennie came to the attention of the film's creators. Rennie (as Klaatu), George Reeves (as Superman), and Leonard Nimoy (as Spock) are actors most usually identified because of their roles as individuals from other planets. The film's screenplay (written by Edmund H. North), high production values (including the construction of a Washington, D.C.-type of neighborhood on the Fox studio backlot), effective supporting roles (by actors Patricia Neal, Hugh Marlowe, Sam Jaffe, and Billy Gray), a great robot (Gort), well-integrated photographic effects (coordinated by Fred Serson), and the brilliant musical score by Bernard Herrmann, combine to make *The Day the Earth Stood Still* a complete and permanent success.

The Haunting (Metro-Goldwyn-Mayer–1964) again gave Wise the chance to frighten his audience, and he came through admirably, creating one of the best ghost stories ever put on film (on a par with the extremely effective *The Uninvited,* a Paramount film of 1944). Actress Julie Harris portrayed an introverted and unhappy psychic who works with a psychic investigator and is killed by an evil, haunted house. At the end of the film we hear her voice acknowledging that she is now a part of the house, along with the other victims the house has claimed over the years. During one scene in the film, Ms. Harris's character is asleep with another young woman because of both their wishes not to be alone in the house. In the middle of new images that had only been glimpsed or implied in the television series. Designs that had been created for the TV series could also be modified, within certain limitations.

The producer's primary worry apparently was to avoid changing established designs *too* much, so that the series' fans could enjoy the alterations and still feel familiar with the updated version.

In some cases, science had caught up with science fiction. Complex control surfaces could be more effectively lit using fiber optics and other techniques that were not available in 1964, when the television *Enterprise* was designed. Special photographic effects had progressed remarkably since the *Enterprise* passed through the galactic barrier in 1965 in "Where No Man Has Gone Before." Computer science had also flourished allowing the miniaturization of equipment and the development of new concepts in several fields (including the art/science of generating photographic effects).

Not all the changes were based upon freedom; some were necessitated by *limitations* caused by the difference between the television and motion picture formats. The television screen *reduces* people and their surroundings, whereas the motion picture screen *expands* people until they are larger than life. The pastel colors seen on the television series would seem too exaggerated on the big screen. Props and miniatures constructed for the original episodes would have to be redesigned to allow for the extreme close-ups necessary in a wide-screen motion picture. Even the starship *Enterprise* would have to be modified.

Approaching the New Starship *Enterprise*

"Star Trek's" audience had witnessed subtle changes in the interior and exterior designs of the starship *Enterprise* during the course of the television series. The motion picture version of the vehicle is based upon the old, familiar ship, but there are many differences, resulting in a sleeker, more impressive design.

The original *Enterprise* miniature used during television production is fourteen feet long. When work began on the feature film, a new *Enterprise* model was commissioned. This first modified version measured six feet in length. Constructed from heavy fiberglass and sheet aluminum, this version was discarded before its completion when it was decided to create another miniature using different techniques and a slightly larger size.

The miniature *Enterprise* that was ultimately seen in *Star Trek—The Motion Picture* is eight feet long and four feet wide. Constructed around an aluminum skeleton, which allows the ship to be supported from

five different points,[17] the movie's *Enterprise* can be photographed from every conceivable angle. The model, which weighs seventy pounds, is so detailed that each individual metal plate on the ship's exterior can apparently be seen. The interior is filled with miniature lights that enable the starship to provide its own illumination as it is seen hurtling through outer space.

If we board a travel pod and travel toward the ship, just as Kirk and Scotty do early in *Star Trek—The Motion Picture,* we can examine the new *Enterprise* section by section.

The *saucer* section's many lit portions enable it to be seen in great detail. The back of the saucer contains two illuminated portions and eight observation windows. The saucer's underside includes three lit structures radiating from its center, and the inscriptions "NCC-1701" (toward the front) and "Enterprise" (to the rear). The saucer's top includes the outside dome structure that houses the starship's bridge; it seems to reach upward in a cone-shaped projection rising from the surrounding section. The rear of the dome contains an access hatch (where the Vulcan shuttle bearing Mr. Spock docks during the film).

The elongated *engineering* section begins with a glowing blue, segmented sensor/deflector dish in place of the old, metallic one. The new dish is recessed into the front of the engineering section, and is ringed with whitish-blue lights. Atop the section is a sleek, new extension joining this portion of the ship to the pylon connected to the saucer. The front of this extension features a horizontal, black area containing two red, rectangular portions that almost resemble giant "eyes." There are six windowlike vents on the bottom of the section, near the front of the ship. Above these, on both sides of the vessel, is the *Enterprise* insignia; a blank, silver rendition within a solid red circle, followed by the inscription "Starship USS Enterprise United Federation of Planets." The rear entrance to the cargo (hangar) deck is now a cone-shaped, segmented door topped with red lights. The name "Enterprise" is inscribed below.

The *pylons* joining the engineering section to the starship's nacelles are now graceful "V" shapes, growing in width as they reach the nacelles.

The huge matter/antimatter engine *nacelles* are long, rectangular shapes sitting atop the tapered, winglike pylons. Toward the rear, on both the inner and outer sides, appears the lettering "NCC-1701 United Federation of Planets." Near the front of the nacelles, bright lights point the way to indentations lined with purple and blue stripes; their iridescent nature reflects the spectacular potential of the new starship *Enterprise.*

Entering the New Bridge

The new command bridge is built from twelve separate sections, each of which can be removed as needed, to allow camera access. The circular area is built on

The impressive entrance
of Mr. Spock onto the bridge
(Leonard Nimoy, Walter Koenig).

four levels, each a short step away from the next. The outer periphery, containing the operations stations, is the highest. One step down is the command chair, another step down is the navigation console, and below that is the lowest level, containing only floor space and separated from the outer (uppermost) area by a series of four curved segments of handrails, which form a circle.

The bridge now has a ceiling, with metallic ridges radiating outward from a transparent central hemisphere filled with security equipment and other newly designed devices.

The outermost part of the bridge is a solid circle of vital machinery that constantly controls and monitors the starship's operations. Directly behind the command chair we find the *science officer's station*. The old viewing scope is gone, replaced with a double row of display screens. The new instrument panels are larger and more complex than ever, and are framed by two circuit-filled rectangular extensions, that surround this station.

Two turbo lifts (one on each side of the science station) lead to and from the bridge. The new lifts are topped with circular lighting panels. Decorative, padded wall panels surround brightly lit schematic diagrams of the *Enterprise*'s interior, which indicate the turbos' positions within the ship.

Opposite the science officer's station, across the bridge, is the *main viewing screen,* a new, wide-screen monitor set within a curved, metal frame.

To the left of the viewing screen is the *security station,* a new addition recessed into the wall of the bridge. A small electronic map of the *Enterprise* pinpoints trouble areas during alert conditions.

Each seat is a graceful, strong, and complex device supported from beneath by a single metal column. The decorative upholstery and its inner mechanisms are shaped to fit the human spinal column, to provide comfort and protection. During alert conditions, the short, padded headrests rise automatically and the fabric-lined arms close swiftly over the crew members' laps to act as safety belts.

The new *command seat* is more compact than the original version. The old, boxed-in design has become a streamlined form almost identical to the bridge's other seats. The captain's headrest is larger, his seat is darker, and the safety-belt arms contain control and communications devices.

In front of the command seat is the *navigation console,* which is more fluidly and delicately shaped than the older version, and features a colorful array of colored lights, gauges, and other indicators, plus a sliding control with which the helmsman accelerates or decelerates the ship.

A Tour Through the New *Enterprise*

When Captain Kirk first familiarized himself with the *Enterprise* of *Star Trek—The Motion Picture,* he was undoubtedly very happy to be back, and probably walked through the starship's most important locales filled with a combination of elation and awe. Kirk discovered that all the old, familiar areas of his ship were now larger and more complex, reflecting the new advances in the technology of the United Federation of Planets.

The *engineering* area is multileveled, featuring a central vertical core two-and-a-half stories high. Looking down from the upper level, this core is seen to extend downward for another six levels, filled with swirling patterns of energy. Descending to the main engineering deck, one story down, we ride on a small lift platform in a circular, transparent tube. The engineering control panel features indicators to show the status of the engines, and if something goes wrong it is immediately seen on the diagram of the emergency alarm system. Looking from the panel to the engine core, we see a horizontal, reenforced tube that contains the vast power of the matter/antimatter reaction and seems to extend into infinity.

The new *sick bay* complex reflects a white, antiseptic look. Each bed is supported on a central column; at first glance the beds appear to be floating in midair. The adjoining examination room features an examination table lying atop a cantilevered support. The transparent tabletop conforms to the shape of the patient's body, while surrounding him or her with unseen sensors that reflect the readings onto a large viewing screen, providing the doctor with visual images enhanced with medical computer evaluations.

The *transporter* is much larger than its older version; the entire room *is* the machine. Its six transporting platforms are separated from the machine's operator by a protective, transparent screen. The area is kept darker than it used to be, which seems to indicate that updated transporter procedures require that surrounding power fields be held to a minimum. The transporter's walls are heavy and insulated.

The new *recreation deck* is three stories tall, and is situated in the rear of the saucer section. Huge walls slope gracefully upward to form a high, curved roof. At the entrance to the room is a series of five illuminated illustrations of famous vehicles called "Enterprise," including a sailing ship, an aircraft carrier, the prototype of the NASA space shuttle, and the original

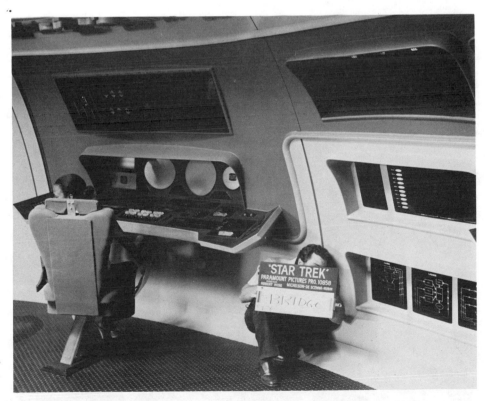

The U.S.S. *Enterprise* bridge, ready for the lights, cameras, and action.

starship *Enterprise*. Above this display is a large, four-sided curved enclosure bearing the seal of the United Federation of Planets, which also serves as the room's main viewing screen. Decorative furniture and a large assortment of electronic games can be removed when the area is needed as a briefing room.

The *captain's quarters* have been enlarged into a two-room suite incorporating living space and an office, the two areas being separated by a thin, sliding screen.

The *officers' quarters,* located on deck four, are also larger than their previous counterparts and are now known to include *sonic showers*. The shower stalls are also equipped with devices that clothe the officers in custom-fitted uniforms produced by the units.

The *officers' lounge* replaces the old briefing room at times, such as during the briefing between Kirk, Spock, and McCoy. One wall of the furnished room includes portholes where the officers can appreciate the beauties of outer space directly, without the aid of electronic viewscreens.

Even the ship's *corridors* have been modified. Possibly to compensate for the space taken up by the larger rooms within the *Enterprise,* the corridors are now lower and narrower than their older versions. Each bulkhead is composed of three sloping sections, which include slender support columns and padded surfaces to protect the crew in the event of sudden lurches or abnormal gravity conditions.

The new *Enterprise* also includes various entrances and exits that were never seen before. The standard *airlock* room consists of a control panel that is proba-

bly guarded constantly. Thruster suits, which permit the wearer to steer himself through space, are stored within the airlock area. The starship also contains specialized entrance points, such as the lift that exits somewhere near the outer periphery of the saucer section. In addition, each inhabited section of the *Enterprise* includes docking ports, such as the ones used by Kirk, Scotty, and Mr. Spock to enter the ship.

New Clothes for the Crew

In addition to the many specialized uniforms and working clothes created for *Star Trek—The Motion Picture,* the *Enterprise* crew has been issued new duty uniforms. A variety of styles has been introduced to fit all occasions and to permit individual crew members to change into whatever uniforms they wish to wear at various times.

The standard duty uniform consists of a tunic topped by a rounded collar including a lower, pointed decorative extension and trousers that incorporate the uniform's footgear. Insignia, stripes (if any) and belt buckles (which are reportedly life-function monitors tied into the ship's medical computer) are attached to the tunics. These uniforms come in two main colors; light golden-brown, and grayish-blue.

The more informal one-piece fatigues are suited for both work and leisure wear. The form-fitting garments lack the pointed collar extensions of the duty uniforms, but include the specialized belt buckles and the footwear joined to the suit. Rank stripes are worn on

Scotty in command of his brand new engines (James Doohan).

the shoulders and utility pouches are attached to the trousers. The long-sleeved tunic of the standard duty uniform can be substituted with a short-sleeved shirt with a V-shaped, open collar.

When we first see Admiral Kirk, he is wearing a uniform that appears to follow the same lines of the standard duty suit, except for a rounded turtleneck, and a two-tone color design. The trousers, and the majority of the jacket are dark green; the front and back of the jacket (conforming to the seam pattern on the duty uniforms) are white.

Outer jackets, containing pockets and apparently intended for planetside and other off-ship activities, are heavy green garments. Stripes along the upper sleeves reveal the wearer's rank and function. These jackets are probably always worn over the one-piece fatigue suits.

The Music of *Star Trek—The Motion Picture*

The return of symphonic motion picture scores was no surprise to the discerning ears of most "Star Trek" fans; the seventy-nine episodes of the television series contain dramatic music that complements each adventure and adds to the humanity and individuality of each main character. The television episodes' scores were produced under the restrictive limitations of deadline and budget that seem to influence all television production, but composers such as Alexander Courage, Fred Steiner, Sol Kaplan, Gerald Fried, and George Duning consistently produced extremely fine music that is an integral part of "Star Trek," the television series.

For *Star Trek—The Motion Picture,* composer Jerry Goldsmith was selected to create a score that could do justice to the *Enterprise,* its crew, and the vastness of its mission. Goldsmith composed and conducted music that accomplishes all this and more. His melodies, artfully conceived and combined, reflect the main theme of *Star Trek—The Motion Picture;* the idea of attainment applied to various individuals (and mechanisms) on many levels. Goldsmith's expansive score shows us Kirk's reattainment of the *Enterprise,* Spock's attempts to achieve fulfillment, Decker's and Ilia's wish to attain happiness together at last, the Ilia-probe's attempts to understand its human memories, and V'ger's epic attempt to attain the ability to perceive and appreciate its identity.

Jerry Goldsmith, a native of Los Angeles, California, has had a diversified musical education that includes majoring in music at the University of Southern California and studying under music masters such as Jakob Gimpel (piano), Mario Castelnuovo-Tedesco

(composition), and Miklos Rozsa (composition for motion pictures). In 1950, Goldsmith joined CBS and wrote music for that network's radio productions. Television work followed, and Goldsmith also began composing for feature films in 1957.

Goldsmith's television assignments included creating main title themes and individual episode scores for series such as "The Twilight Zone" (including the segments "Back There" and "The Invaders"), "Thriller" (some of their scariest studies in horror; his work on this series led to an Emmy Award nomination), and "The Man from U.N.C.L.E." (another Emmy nomination). His music is also heard in segments of "The Waltons" (another Emmy nomination), and in TV specials including "Babe" (for which he won an Emmy), "QB VII" (another Emmy), and in the "Bell System Family Theatre" episode "The Red Pony" (another Emmy Award-winning score). Perhaps his best known TV music is the theme for "Dr. Kildare"; and other main title series themes he wrote include "Black Saddle" and "The Lineup."

Goldsmith's distinguished list of feature film credits include productions dealing with elements of horror (*Magic, The Omen, The Mephisto Waltz, Shock Treatment, Coma, Seconds,* and *The Swarm*), and science fiction (*Planet of the Apes, Escape from the Planet of the Apes, The Illustrated Man, The Satan Bug,* and *Alien*). Some of his scores deal with highly unusual studies in mystery (*The List of Adrian Messenger*), suspense (*Capricorn One, The Boys from Brazil*), and other topics (*Freud, Our Man Flint, In Like Flint*).

Composer Goldsmith's score for *Star Trek—The Motion Picture* is a spectacular one consisting of highly unique musical themes, but in two cases the artist's previous work features parallels to this epic assignment. For his score of *The Blue Max* (20th Century-Fox–1966), a film concerning a young pilot's love of flying, Goldsmith composed melodies (specifically the film's main title theme and a selection entitled "First Flight") that capture the essence of escaping into the air. The weightless, soaring, ecstatic feelings of flight are akin to the exhilaration experienced by Captain Kirk on the *Enterprise.* For the exotic adventure film *The Wind and the Lion* (Metro-Goldwyn-Mayer–1975), Goldsmith created sounds indicative of an adventuresome culture. His musical descriptions of the film's central figure, a tribal leader ("The Raisuli" and "Raisuli Attacks"), and his surroundings ("Lord of the Riff," "The Palace," "The Legend," and "Something of Value") accomplish the same purpose as the music written to describe the Klingons in the *Star Trek* feature. If you like the score for *Star Trek—The Motion Picture,* you will probably also like the scores for *The Blue Max, The Wind and the Lion,* and other soundtracks by Jerry Goldsmith.

The Magic of Star Trek

Star Trek—The Motion Picture enables people who are "Star Trek" fans to continue to experience the spectacular satisfaction of voyaging among the stars aboard the starship *Enterprise*. Many thousands of people all over the world who are not familiar with "Star Trek" have probably also enjoyed the film's beauty enough to become interested in "Star Trek" the television series, and science fiction in general. Some of these individuals work within the field of motion pictures; many of the technicians who contributed their efforts to *Star Trek—The Motion Picture* are devotees of the original series. The actors themselves have been exposed to science fiction in various forms as a result of their portrayals. Some have written their own science fiction stories, others have become associated with present-day efforts to explore outer space.

One Paramount executive who has been involved with *Star Trek—The Motion Picture* since its earliest production stages, had no previous involvement with "Star Trek" or science fiction, except that he enjoys science fiction films (especially *The Day the Earth Stood Still)*. His acquaintances with people involved with *Star Trek—The Motion Picture* has led to new friendships with Gene Roddenberry, Robert Wise, and others. His experiences with "Star Trek's" fans (including fan club organizers, convention personnel, and writers of fan fiction) have made him aware of the enormous creativity inspired by "Star Trek." He is now on the subscription lists of various science fiction and media oriented magazines, and he is one of many individuals all over the world, in every conceivable profession, who have gotten caught up in the magic of "Star Trek."

What about tomorrow? Will other new "Star Trek" productions continue to appear on theatrical and television screens throughout the world? Probably so, because the public now accepts science fiction as something to feel comfortable with, rather than as something strange, and "Star Trek" represents science fiction in its fullest possible range of accomplishment, optimism, and discovery.

For all the people in the world whose lives have been enriched by "Star Trek," Trek will *always* be thought of in the future sense.

NOTES

1. "Star Trek Conclave in NY Looms as Mix of Campy Set," *Variety,* 19 January, 1972.
2. Ibid.
3. "Grokking Mr. Spock," *TV Guide,* 25 March, 1972. The rumor of "Star Trek's" revival as an all-new television series was mentioned in conjunction with Shirley Gerstel of Paramount Television.
4. During this period, there were countless rumors about Trek's return. Whether it would come back as a TV series or motion picture never seemed clear because of the impossibility of sorting the rumors from the facts. For an accurate account of the history behind "Star Trek's" return, read Chapter Two in *The Making of Star Trek—The Motion Picture* by Susan Sackett and Gene Roddenberry, published by Simon & Schuster in 1980.
5. In the TV episode "The Naked Time," by John D. F. Black, Captain Kirk verbalized his wish for a respite from the lonely pressures of command: "Flesh woman . . . to touch . . . to hold . . . a beach to walk on . . . a few days, no braid on my shoulder." Later in the episode, Kirk regarded Yeoman Rand and muttered "No beach to walk on . . ."
6. This was Captain Kirk's description of Commodore Stocker in "The Deadly Years," written by David P. Harmon.
7. The tragic closing chapter in the life of Will Decker's father is told in "The Doomsday Machine."
8. In "Shore Leave," we met Ruth, a woman with whom Kirk had a relationship in his youth. Other old friends of Kirk we meet in "Star Trek" episodes include attorney Areel Shaw ("Court-Martial"), endocrinologist Dr. Janet Wallace ("The Deadly Years"), and scientist Dr. Janice Lester ("Turnabout Intruder").
9. We *do* know that Kirk's love for adventure is at least partially derived from his pioneer ancestors (as revealed in "Spectre of the Gun").
10. In "Court-Martial," it is indicated that Kirk's professional life as Captain of the *Enterprise* matters more to him than his personal existence. He also reacts quite badly to the idea of an automated starship commander in "The Ultimate Computer," and in "Turnabout Intruder," Kirk (in Janice Lester's body) reflects more of a concern over the loss of his command than for his personal horror at being separated from his physical body.
11. The ultimate test of this choice is chronicled in "The City on the Edge of Forever." In the filmed version of the script, Kirk prevents Dr. McCoy from saving the life of Edith Keeler, choosing the starship (and all that it represents) over the woman he loves.
12. As an example, in "The Cage" (and in part one of "The Menagerie") we see Spock grinning and laughing over the appearance of a beautiful alien plant.
13. This guilt may have been at least partially responsible for the rift that developed between Spock and Sarek, as detailed in "Journey to Babel." Early in the series ("The Naked Time)" Spock admits to Kirk that he feels guilt about never being able to tell his mother he loves her.
14. At the end of "Journey to Babel," Spock and Sarek are on speaking terms again for the first time since Spock left Vulcan to join Starfleet.
15. One cannot help but conjecture that this female Vulcan Master may have been warned about Spock's powerful human half by T'Pau, the important Vulcan matriarch we met in "Amok Time."
16. Mr. Spock's admission was probably trying to force its way to his surface ever since, after his relationship with Leila Kalomi, he indicates that he will miss his brief life-style of romance. He reflects on his human, happy experience at the end of "This Side of Paradise."
17. The *Enterprise* built for the film can be supported from (1) the rear, through the hangar doors, (2) the front, behind the deflector, (3) and (4) through port and starboard side apertures, and (5) through the bottom, through the engineering section. This, and other information (as well as many photos) can be found in the February 1980 issue of *American Cinematographer* magazine, the issue devoted to *Star Trek—The Motion Picture.*

Bibliography

Bazelon, Irwin. *Knowing the Score: Notes on Film Music.* New York: Van Nostrand Reinhold Co., 1975.

Elwood, Roger, ed. *Six Science Fiction Plays.* New York: Pocket Books, 1976.

Gaster, Adrian, ed. *International Who's Who in Music and Musician's Directory.* 8th ed. Cambridge: Melrose Press, Ltd., 1977.

Gerrold, David. *The World of Star Trek.* New York: Ballantine Books, Co., 1973.

————. *The Trouble with Tribbles.* New York: Ballantine Books, Co., 1976.

Gianakos, Larry James. *Television Drama Series Programming: A Comprehensive Chronicle, 1959-75.* Metuchen: The Scarecrow Press, Inc., 1978.

Herbert, Ian, ed. *Who's Who in the Theatre, 1977.* 16th ed. Detroit: Gale Research Co., 1977.

Koenig, Walter. *Chekov's Enterprise.* New York: Pocket Books, 1976.

Nicholls, Peter, ed. *The Science Fiction Encyclopedia.* Garden City: Doubleday and Co., Inc., 1979.

Sackett, Susan, with Gene Roddenberry. *The Making of "Star Trek"—The Motion Picture.* New York: Pocket Books, 1980.

Terrace, Vincent. *The Complete Encyclopedia of Television Programs,* 1947-76. Cranbury: A. S. Barnes and Co., Inc., 1976.

Thomas, Tony. *Music for the Movies.* Cranbury: A. S. Barnes and Co., Inc., 1973.

Trimble, Bjo. *Star Trek Concordance.* New York: Ballantine Books, Co., 1976.

Weaver, John T. *Forty Years of Screen Credits, 1929-69.* Metuchen: The Scarecrow Press, Inc., 1970.

Whitfield, Stephen E., and Roddenberry, Gene. *The Making of "Star Trek."* New York: Ballantine Books, Inc., 1968.

Wicking, Christopher, and Vahimagi, Tise. *The American Vein: Directors and Directions in Television.* New York: E. P. Dutton, 1979.